# America at Work

# America at Work

## Choices and Challenges

Edited by
**Edward E. Lawler III**
**and**
**James O'Toole**

First published in 2006 by
PALGRAVE MACMILLAN™
175 Fifth Avenue, New York, N.Y. 10010 and
Houndmills, Basingstoke, Hampshire, England RG21 6XS
Companies and representatives throughout the world.

PALGRAVE MACMILLAN is the global academic imprint of the Palgrave Macmillan division of St. Martin's Press, LLC and of Palgrave Macmillan Ltd. Macmillan® is a registered trademark in the United States, United Kingdom and other countries. Palgrave is a registered trademark in the European Union and other countries.

The research for this book was supported by a grant from the Society for Human Resource Management.

The Society for Human Resource Management (SHRM) is the world's largest association devoted to human resource management. Representing more than 200,000 individual members, the Society's mission is to serve the needs of HR professionals by providing the most essential and comprehensive resources available. As an influential voice, the Society's mission is also to advance the human resource profession to ensure that HR is recognized as an essential partner in developing and executing organizational strategy. Founded in 1948, SHRM currently has more than 550 affiliated chapters and members in more than 100 countries. Visit SHRM Online at www.shrm.org.

ISBN-13: 978–1–4039–7297–2
ISBN-10: 1–4039–7297–4

Library of Congress Cataloging-in-Publication Data
    America at work : choices and challenges / edited by James O'Toole and Edward Lawler.
        p. cm.
    Includes bibliographical references and index.
        ISBN 1–4039–7297–4
    1. Quality of work life—United States. 2. Work—Social aspects—United States. 3. Career changes—United States. I. O'Toole, James. II. Lawler, Edward E.
HD6957.U5A485 2006
334.0973—dc22                                                    2006041612

A catalogue record for this book is available from the British Library.

Design by Newgen Imaging Systems (P) Ltd., Chennai, India.

First edition: August 2006

10 9 8 7 6 5 4 3 2

Printed in the United States of America.

# Contents

**Part 3    Organizational Effectiveness**

# List of Tables

# List of Figures

# Foreword

The chapters in this book were commissioned as resource papers for the 2006 New American Workplace project, an analysis of how jobs and careers in the United States have changed since the publication of the benchmark *Work in America* report in 1973. These chapters were written by outstanding scholars who have prepared overviews of the research in their diverse fields of expertise. The individual chapters stand as authoritative summaries of what is known about organizations, work, and workers and, as a collection, constitute a comprehensive look at how the workplace has evolved over three decades of incredible turbulence and change.[1]

When we commissioned these papers, we hoped simply that they would provide us with the factual background we needed to write our companion book, *The New American Workplace* (Palgrave Macmillan, 2006) We are extremely pleased that the papers have exceeded our expectations. They not only proved to be of invaluable use to us, and in their own right, they make important contributions to research, theory, and practice. Without reservation, we commend them to the attention of business mangers, human resource professionals, government policymakers, scholars, and students. In fact, they are a must read for every American who employs workers, is a worker, plans to work, or is concerned about the future of work in America.

Support for the writing of these papers was provided by the Society for Human Resource Management (SHRM), which gave the authors complete freedom to pursue their research interests and to state their opinions. Thus, the views in this volume do not necessarily represent the views of SHRM. The corporate sponsors of the Center for Effective Organizations also provided financial resources, and their continuing support makes it possible for the center's professional staff to do research and writing that influences both organizational theory and practice.

We owe special thanks to the advisory panel that helped us to select the topics and authors of these papers: John Boudreau, Debra Cohen, Susan Cohen, Jay Conger, David Finegold, Alec Levenson, and Susan Mohrman. And we wish to acknowledge members of our Center's staff who made great contributions to manuscript preparation: Dan Canning, Arienne McCracken, and Anjelica Wright.

Finally, we wish to acknowledge the expert copy editing of Catherine Dain, the noted author of mystery novels, who once again has proved that she is a Renaissance woman.

Edward E. Lawler III
James O'Toole
Los Angeles, California
May 2006

Part 1

# Quality of Worklife of Americans

# Working Alone: Whatever Happened to the Idea of Organizations as Communities?

*Jeffrey Pfeffer*

Remember when everyone was talking about organizational culture and the idea of building strong cultures to achieve competitive advantage (e.g., Kotter and Heskett 1992; O'Reilly 1989; Tushman and O'Reilly 1997, chapter 5)? Remember *Theory Z* and Ouchi's (1981) argument that Williamson's (1975) description of possible organizing arrangements was incomplete? Ouchi maintained that in addition to achieving coordination and control through market-like mechanisms such as prices and contracts on the one hand, and hierarchies or bureaucracies on the other, there was yet another way of organizing and managing employees, and that was through clan-like relationships among people (e.g., Ouchi and Jaeger 1978), characterized by high levels of trust and stability. More recently, Gittell's (2003) description of Southwest Airlines is consistent with the idea of achieving coordination through interpersonal trust and mutual adjustment of behavior (Thompson 1967). Gittell argued that Southwest's extraordinary level of productivity and performance has come through high levels of coordination and control achieved through interpersonal relationships rather than simply through relying on either formal mechanisms or incentives.

Remember Japanese management, with its emphasis on the total inclusion of people in the company and long-term, even lifetime, employment, and the corollary idea that employees were important stakeholders in enterprises with claims equivalent in their importance to those of shareholders (e.g., Aoki 1988)? Or to go even farther back, remember the welfare capitalism practiced by some large employers in the first three decades of the twentieth century? Many employers believed then that companies should take care of their employees and therefore offered benefits including company housing, paid vacations, health care, pensions, and, as in the case of Ford Motor Company, help from a "sociological department" in setting up a household, saving and investing money, and keeping employees away from alcohol and hustlers (Lacey 1986, 131–134). Employers provided assistance to their workforce both out of a sense of civic duty and moral obligation—Henry Ford, for instance, claimed to be interested in building men, not just cars—and also as a way of potentially avoiding unionization efforts and more intrusive government intervention in the employment relationship (e.g., Jacoby 1997).

Whatever the motivations, there were deeper connections between companies and their workers and more of a sense of communal responsibility than exists today. These ideas and the management practices associated with their implementation seem to have fallen by the wayside, at least in most organizations, and at least in the United States. As Cappelli (1999) has nicely shown, instead of building closer, more communal-like relationships with their workforce, over the past couple of decades most organizations in the United States have moved systematically to more market-like, distant, and transactional relationships with their people. Instead of taking care of and being responsible for their employees, companies have cut medical benefits for full-time employees and cut them even more aggressively for their retirees (Geisel 2002; Hofmann 2003). Meanwhile companies in large numbers have either changed defined-benefit pension plans to defined-contribution plans in which employees are more responsible for their own future economic security (Feinberg 2004) or have abandoned offering pension benefits altogether.

This trend toward more market-like and distant connections has spread throughout the world as other companies in other countries such as Japan and Western Europe seek to emulate U.S. practices in managing the employment relation. The idea that shareholders are preeminent has also taken hold more strongly in other countries, even as some in the United States question the long-term consequences of adopting this shareholder-first perspective (Jacobs 1991).

There are, of course, always important and noteworthy exceptions to these trends among both companies and countries, but the absence of much sense of community in most organizations is quite real and quite important for understanding the evolution of work in America, the relationship between organizations and their people, and the attitudes and beliefs of the workforce.

One consequence of the trend away from communal and caring relationships toward more arms-length, market-like transactions between organizations and their employees has been less trust and psychological attachment between employees and their employers. The evidence of job dissatisfaction, distrust, and disengagement is pervasive, as many surveys and studies from a number of industrialized countries tell the same tale: job satisfaction, employee engagement, and trust in management are all low and declining.

One survey by The Discovery Group reported that 52 percent of employees do not believe the information they receive from senior management (Katcher 2004). A survey of the U.S. workforce found that one in six workers say they have withheld a suggestion for improving work efficiency, and fewer than 40 percent trust their company to keep its promises (Princeton Survey Research Associates 1994). A 2003 survey by Korn Ferry found that 62 percent of global executives are unhappy with their current position of employment (Korn Ferry 2003). A Conference Board survey of 5,000 U.S. households conducted in August 2004 found that 67 percent of workers do not identify with or feel motivated to drive their employer's business goals, one quarter are just showing up to collect a paycheck, and almost half feel disconnected from their employers (Conference Board 2005). That study concluded that "Americans are growing increasingly unhappy with their jobs, with the decrease in job satisfaction pervasive across all age groups and income levels" (Conference Board 2005). Cappelli (1999, 122–123) summarized numerous surveys of employee attitudes and commitment, noting that since the 1980s the measures were "in a virtual free fall." Nor is this phenomenon confined to the United States. For instance, the Gallup organization "found that 80 percent of British workers lack commitment to their job, with a quarter of those being 'actively disengaged' " (Deloitte Research 2004, 4).

The logic linking the less communal aspect of companies and the rise of distrust, disengagement, and diminished satisfaction, although not extensively empirically demonstrated, seems clear. Trust is enhanced through longer-term interactions and by believing that the other party is taking your interests into account. Both longer-term employment and time horizons and the belief that senior leadership is concerned about employee welfare characterize more community-like companies. Because people value workplace friendships and working with people they like and respect and are more willing to expend extra effort when they feel psychologically connected to their organizations—again the link between the extent to which companies are more community-like and outcomes such as job attitudes and willingness to invest more effort at work seems clear.

Another consequence of the diminished sense of community inside organizations has been more incivility, defined as displaying a lack of regard for others in violation of norms of mutual respect (Pearson and Porath 2005, 8), and an increase in bullying in workplaces in which social ties and communal obligations are weaker. A study of 800 employees in the United States found that 10 percent reported witnessing incivility *daily* in their workplaces and one-fifth reported being the target of incivility at work at least once a week (Pearon and Porath 2005, 7). Furthermore, one-fourth of respondents who felt they were treated uncivilly intentionally cut back their work efforts, and one in eight left their job to escape the situation (Pearson and Porath 2005, 9–10).

The connection between community and workplace bullying and incivility seems evident. A sense of community and shared, mutual obligations and closer social ties among people would act to inhibit rude or nasty behavior. These inhibitions disappear in places characterized by more market-like and distant relationships among people and between people and their employers. Ironically and unfortunately, all of these changes in employee attitudes and behavior are occurring at the very moment when people's skills and discretionary effort are more important than ever for organizational success.

In this chapter, we briefly describe the evolution away from the conception of organizations as communities, what may have produced this change, as well as the opportunity provided to organizations that take a different approach and take the idea of the workplace as community more seriously. Putnam's (2000) description of the decline in many aspects of community in U.S. society more generally has been mirrored in work organizations, and few companies now embrace Theory Z or the many other books that recommend more inclusion of people in organizations and the creation of stronger social ties. We are not only "bowling alone," we are increasingly "working alone," even though there is important research that shows the importance of social capital for organizational success as well as individual success inside work organizations (e.g., Leana and Rousseau 2000; Coff and Rousseau 2000).

More communal relations among people and between organizations and their employees does seem to provide an advantage, but that many organizations nevertheless do not make decisions about managing their people consistent with this fact belies the common assumption that organizational leaders are rational, profit-maximizing decision-makers always choosing the best course of action. Instead, this discussion of the communal aspect of work in America makes clear, once again, the importance of values and beliefs in decisions that concern the relationships between companies and their employees. The importance of values has, in turn, implications for the education of managers both in school and inside companies as well as for the role of public policy in helping to shape the covenant between employers and their employees.

## The Choices Companies Make

Organizations and their leaders make two fundamental and important decisions about their workforce, from which many other decisions and management practices naturally follow. The first basic decision is where to draw the organization's boundaries—which activities and people to include in an employment relationship and which activities and people to leave outside the company, to treat in more market-like and impersonal ways (e.g., Williamson 1975). At the limit, of course, are virtual or almost-virtual companies with few or no actual employees. Thus, evidence suggests that more "externalized" work such as part-time employment and temporary and contract work is growing in importance and prevalence (e.g., Belous 1989; Segal and Sullivan 1997).

The second crucial decision, given that a company is going to have any employees at all, is what sort of relationship to forge with those employees, the people living inside the organization's boundaries, and, as a consequence, what kind of organizational culture to create. There are a number of interrelated dimensions that could be productively used to characterize this relationship between organizations and their people, including: (1) the expected duration of the relationship; (2) the degree of legalism and formalism that characterizes the employment relation; (3) related to the first and second dimensions, the extent to which the employment relation inside the firm is characterized by a market-like character (Cappelli 1999) in which outcomes from the external labor market such as wage rates and benefit arrangements are directly imported into the company; and (4) related to the preceding three dimensions, how organizations treat the degree of inclusion of people in the company. Do organizations adopt a more community-like role, being concerned with nonwork aspects of people's lives, or do they adopt a more transactional and limited approach, essentially buying labor for money in an exchange that can be terminated by either side for any, or no, reason?

### Forces Affecting the Community-Like Nature of Organizations

A number of explanations have been offered to account for the variation in the communal nature of companies both over time and across cultures, but none seems to be completely adequate or convincing, leaving an important topic for further research. The first and most obvious explanation for the decline in the degree and forms of attachment between companies and their employees is the greater competition and/or increased financial stringency faced by organizations. So, for instance, Jacoby (1997) argued that welfare capitalism was a casualty of the Great Depression, Cappelli (1999) maintained that the more market-like interactions between companies and their employees were a natural and logical response to increased competitive pressure and the consequent requirement for lower costs, including labor costs; explanations for changes in Japanese and European organizations toward a more American-like model often point to increasing global competition and economic integration as a cause.

But the data are not completely consistent with an explanation stressing more competition as a cause of declining community-like ties in work organizations, nor does this account make logical sense. Barley and Kunda's (1992) study of the rise and fall of regimes of normative and rational control in organizations provides some relevant evidence, if we assume that normative control is related to more communal relationships inside companies. Their study found that variations in economic conditions explained variation in control regimes over time. But as Barley and Kunda noted, neither the extent of competition nor the munificence or scarcity of the environment did or could explain the rise or fall of normative control. That's because both normative and rational control approaches promise enhanced efficiency and effectiveness. In other words, since communal-like relations presumably *increase* employee motivation and organizational performance, there is no logic to arguing that such organizing principles should decline in use just because companies face more competition.

Furthermore, welfare capitalism emerged in the late 1800s and early 1900s when economic competition was, if anything, fiercer than at any other time including the present. Griffin, Wallace, and Rubin (1986, 149) noted that the average business failure rate during the period 1890–1928 was more than twice that of the post–World War II average. And so-called Japanese management practices such as single company unions and long-term employment relations actually emerged in full flower after World War II, when Japan was facing unprecedented levels of economic hardship.

Finally, many of the companies most noted for their communal nature (e.g., Southwest Airlines and the Men's Wearhouse) operate in industries (airlines and retailing) that are beset with competition and financial stringency. To the extent that stronger attachments and a less transactional relationship promote discretionary effort, reduced turnover, and, as a consequence, higher levels of productivity, it is far from logically clear why increased competitive pressure should not *increase* rather than decrease the communal nature of companies.

A second explanation for variation is national culture. Ouchi (1981), for instance, emphasized the difference between American agriculture with its dispersed (and presumably larger) farms and Japanese rice growing, where the farmers lived in closer proximity to each other. While not denying that there are important differences across countries, particularly in the extent to which nations seem to embrace individualistic competition or more collective and communal ways of interrelating (e.g., Hofstede 1980), this explanation also has some problems. In the first place, there is a great deal of variation in management practices across organizations situated in similar industries within the same country. And even in single countries, such as Japan, and even in the same company, organizations often treat their women and part-time employees quite differently from the portion of the labor force that is considered to be core.

It is not clear whether national cultural values about how people ought to be treated and the communal nature of companies can readily account for this differential treatment of people inside the same organization. Moreover, the relatively rapid change in management practices experienced, for instance, in the United States, which went from the organization man of the 1950s to the free agents of the 1980s and 1990s, makes lodging an explanation in something as stable as national values and culture problematic.

A third explanation is institutionalization and imitation. There is no doubt that companies play "follow-the-leader," and consulting organizations and benchmarking practices are among the forces that encourage imitation and the spread of management ideas. Even a study of downsizing, which one might think is one of the most economically driven decisions, found strong evidence of mimicry (Budros 1997). There is also no doubt that management approaches such as welfare capitalism and more inclusion or more market-like relationships with employees come into and go out of fashion, and that management practices are at least to an extent driven by fads and fashions (Abrahamson 1996). The difficulty with this explanation is that not only does it leave much contemporaneous variation across companies unexplained, but it also leaves largely unexplored the causes or sources that determine what comes into fashion and what goes out, and which ideas are in vogue.

Yet another explanation lodges the source of variation in the values and experiences of the CEO. Southwest Airlines will be forever identified with its long-term CEO, Herb Kelleher, and the company's culture and style, as well as the management practices and associated values that reflected Kelleher's philosophy, including putting employees first, customers second, and shareholders third. The sense of the company as a community or even a family is part and parcel of the company's way of operating, as Colleen Barrett, president and chief operating officer, explained:

> We've talked to our employees from day one about being one big family. If you stop and think about it for even 20 seconds, the things we do are things that you would do with your own family. We try to acknowledge and react to any significant event in our brothers' or sisters' lives, whether it's work-related or personal. We do the traditional things, like sending birthday cards and cards on the anniversary of their date of hire. But if employees have a child who's sick or a death in the family, we do our best to acknowledge it. We celebrate with our employees when good things happen, and we grieve with them when they experience something devastating. (Shin 2003, 19)

George Zimmer, founder and CEO of the Men's Wearhouse, was very much a child of the 1960s, and he talked about doing things to ensure he remained spiritual enough. Again, the humanistic values that emanated from Zimmer permeated the company and infused its specific management practices such as offering loans to employees having financial difficulties and giving employees second and third chances even when they had stolen a pair of socks or put a customer's deposit in their pocket for several days.

DaVita, a large operator of kidney dialysis centers, reborn under CEO Kent Thiry, reflected Thiry's values and orientation toward community. It is not every CEO, particularly a nonfounding CEO with fewer than 10 years of service, who would set up a family foundation to provide educational benefits to company employees' children, something that Thiry did. The company was referred to as a village, Thiry was the "mayor," and the ethos was very much one of community that emanated from Thiry and his close associates.

There is no question, particularly in America, at a time of strong, even dominant, CEOs, that the tone set at and by the top permeates much of the organization, and this is true whether that tone consists of the ethical lapses of Ken Lay at Enron and the abusive, take-no-prisoners ethos of "Chainsaw" Al Dunlap (e.g., McLean and Elkind 2003; Byrne 1999) or the humanistic, community-oriented tone of Thiry, Zimmer, and Kelleher. But what this explanation lacks, of course, is an account of precisely how these CEOs' values get formed and, perhaps as importantly, in the case of CEOs who were not the founders of their companies, how and why boards of directors selected them in the first place and then subsequently retained them and accepted their cultural values and management approach. Although leaders and their beliefs matter, an exclusively leader-centric account seems to leave out the explanation for how these leaders formed their particular view of what organizations should be and how they come to get selected and are able to remain in power.

An important additional factor, not often addressed in either research or theorizing, that may help explain the variation in the communal nature of organizations over time and across locales is the set of social values and norms that get embedded in particular theories and perspectives about people and organizations, perspectives that do not simply "arise" but that are promulgated by interest groups with particular agendas and beliefs. So, for instance, when George Zimmer gave a talk to a class of Stanford MBAs, the most frequently asked question was what other retail CEOs said about his unique and different philosophy and approach to running a retail business. Zimmer's response was that he did not spend much time talking to other retail CEOs (nor, one would suspect, listening to or benchmarking their ideas).

The question reflects the correct belief that there are socially accepted and valued ways of running a company, that these beliefs influence how leaders behave, and that in current times, such ways of managing do not much include thinking of organizations as communities or employees as important. A new question then arises as to how CEOs and companies with this approach are able to withstand the various pressures, including pressures from peers in business and pressures from the capital markets. But another equally important question is how social expectations and ideas about appropriate models of organization get established in the first place. As Zimmer also made clear in his talk, there were two ways of thinking about business and society: as places facing the need to allocate scarce resources and compete, or as places existing in a world filled with infinite love, compassion, and expandable resources. He remarked, with a smile, that he could predict which of the two views of the world the MBA program inculcated.

At the societal level, the waxing and waning of ideology that informs management practice is not exogenous but is, instead, driven by the political agendas of affluent groups with an ideology that they would like to advance (e.g., DeParle 2005). Therefore, management practices reflect general trends in beliefs about people, their responsibilities, and how they relate to each other, as well as what makes organizations effective. The rise of neoclassical economics with its assumptions of methodological individualism, the pursuit of self-interest (e.g., Miller 1999), individual choice and responsibility, and the importance of market-mediated exchanges (Kuttner 1996) is at once inconsistent with a view of organizations as communities of mutual responsibility and shared obligation and also helps to explain why a communal organizing model may be particularly scarce at times such as the present and in places, such as the United States, where such an ideology has gained ascendance.

Therefore, culture matters—not just or perhaps even primarily the national culture, but more particular social values embedded in people's implicit assumptions about human behavior and organizations and what makes each effective. As extensively documented elsewhere (e.g., Kuttner 1996), such beliefs and ideologies about human behavior are neither simply subject to empirical proof of their validity nor emergent from society, but instead, these points of view are promulgated by foundations and organizations that are active in the political discourse precisely to influence not only specific policies but also, more importantly, the language and assumptions that shape how people see the world, including the organizational world (Ferraro, Pfeffer, and Sutton 2005). In that sense, the waxing and waning of an organization as community model is a consequence of more general changes in views of human and organizational behavior that are the result of political action by advocates favoring a particular conception and point of view.

Needless to say, these explanations for variations in the prevalence of a communal model of organizing are not mutually exclusive. Moreover, their influence on organizing models ought to be studied rather than, as is almost invariably the case, simply asserted (e.g., Ouchi 1981). Most importantly, the explanations should be considered, to the extent possible, simultaneously in studies of management practices, to assess their joint and separate effects.

## Some Dimensions of Organizations as Communities

To talk about or to study the idea of organizations as communities, it is essential to develop some dimensions or indicators that might measure the extent to which organizations are, or are not, communal. A reading of the literature and a consideration of some companies that explicitly have adopted communal-like language and management practices suggest at least the following aspects for consideration in such a definition.

### Helping Employees in Need

One element of community is that people look out for and take care of one another. At DaVita, formerly Total Renal Care, one of the largest operators of dialysis centers in the United States, the CEO dresses up as one of the Three Musketeers to reinforce the idea of "one for all and all for one." Very much like Southwest Airlines, which has a similar arrangement, DaVita collects contributions from employees to help other employees facing unanticipated medical expenses or other family emergencies that strain their financial resources. At SAS Institute, the company provides much the same sort of assistance. There are no sick days at SAS, but employees who fall ill get sympathy, concern, and a paycheck. Employees who violate the company's trust in them and abuse their perquisites get removed from the organization. When an SAS employee drowned in a boating accident, leaving his two young children no longer eligible to continue in company-subsidized, high-quality day care, SAS did the humane and concerned thing and let the children remain until they were no longer eligible by reason of age. At the Men's Wearhouse, because most retail employees are fairly low paid, there are funds available to provide no- or low-interest loans to people who need help, for instance, financing automobile repairs so they can have transportation to and from their workplace.

The presence and extensiveness of this sort of mutual aid and company-provided resources to help employees through difficult and unanticipated life events is a hallmark of companies that feel like communities and that connect employees more closely to each other and to the corporation.

## Employee Benefits and Assistance

Another element of community is that the community, society, or organization takes care of people and their needs throughout the course of their life and not just in emergency situations. So, in cities there are schools for children and, presumably, social services and healthcare for the ill and the aged. In a similar fashion, more communal organizations typically offer a wider and more generous range of assistance and benefits to employees. SAS Institute is famous for its on-site subsidized daycare, on-site medical and recreational facilities, and the eldercare and adoption advice services it provides for its people and their dependents. SAS offers access to its cafeterias to families of employees so that, for instance, children in the on-site daycare can eat lunch with their parents. DaVita also offers medical benefits that are generous, considering its industry type and workforce composition, and provides ongoing training and education so that employees can develop their skills and progress in their careers. The Men's Wearhouse uses a relatively small number of part-time employees so a higher proportion of its workforce is eligible for its relatively generous benefits, including profit sharing.

Unlike the assumptions of neoclassical economic model in which people receive money and benefits for their labor and are expected to optimize the associated trade-offs between the various components of pay as well as among the different employment opportunities they could choose, organizations operating under a more communal approach seek to provide for employees' anticipated needs such as healthcare and retirement. There are obvious tax advantages to providing assistance in this way, but the primary motivating factor seems to be a sense of obligation to provide benefits to help employees in significant aspects of their lives. Companies with a communal orientation do not abandon these programs at the first sign of financial stringency or when others in their industries do.

## Nepotism and Dating Policies

In communities, people meet each other and form close interpersonal ties. In communities, neighborhoods, and ethnic enclaves, people become close friends and sometimes fall in love. Although only a small minority of employers have formal policies forbidding workplace dating, most discourage intimate relationships in the workplace in order to avoid "conflicts of interest, ethical trespasses and leaks of proprietary information," as well as time spent flirting (rather than working) and dealing with sexual harassment suits (Feeney 2004, 37).

Not so in Southwest Airlines, where, of the company's 35,000 employees, about 2,000 are married to each other (Feeney 2004). Nor SAS Institute, where both the current and the past head of human resources were married to other SAS employees, where people often meet at work, fall in love, get married, have children that they then send to SAS daycare, while both continue to work for the company. When I wrote a case on SAS, I interviewed a male programmer who responded to the question as to why he did not leave SAS at the height of the Internet frenzy to make more money elsewhere with the comment "my wife [a fellow SAS employee] would have left me."

*Company-Sponsored Social Events*

Communities have community activities—fairs, parades, holiday displays—that bring people together to celebrate accomplishments, mark the passage of time, and share significant milestones. One element of strong culture organizations is holding company-sponsored and -encouraged social events and other activities that bring people together (e.g., Deal and Kennedy 1982), and organizations that seek to build a more community-like atmosphere therefore do things to create opportunities for informal social interaction.

The Men's Wearhouse, the $1.4 billion retailer of tailored off-price men's clothing, has about 30 Christmas parties around the country where employees and their significant others come to celebrate with music, good food, and an awards ceremony. The company encourages its store managers to organize social outings and basketball or baseball games throughout the year so that employees enjoy recreation with each other. DaVita sponsors DaVita academies that offer not only learning and training but also games and socializing. SAS Institute encourages employees and their families to use the company's facilities and has numerous celebrations, including ones for new product releases. In the on-site recreational facilities, such as basketball and tennis courts, employees not only get their exercise but also literally "play" with each other. Southwest Airlines, too, is famous for its fun atmosphere and for the many celebrations and ways in which people get to informally interact with each other and with senior management.

The purpose of all of this is to encourage people to build deeper ties to each other and to create relationships fostered on mutual liking and interaction, not just on work-related interdependence. The idea is that by building a community feeling through informal social interaction, the company creates social capital that can be relied upon to build trust and to encourage people to work together to accomplish common goals.

*Resolving Work-Family Issues*

Inter-role conflict—the inconsistent demands of both being a family member and an employee—is pervasive in the U.S. workplace. Galinsky, Bond, and Friedman (1993) reported that 40 percent of employed parents experienced problems in combining work and family demands, and Frone, Russell, and Cooper (1992) found work interferes with home life three times as frequently as home or family responsibilities interferes with work. Bakker and Geurts (2004, 360) noted that "[e]mployees particularly experience negative interference between work and family life when they are exposed to a high workload and demanding interactions with clients."

Communal organizations try to resolve these issues in numerous ways, but most importantly by creating a culture and environment in which the activity of employees taking care of those outside of work for whom they are responsible is accepted and expected. The evidence is clear that the mere existence of formal policies permitting flexibility are insufficient, because employees are reluctant to take advantage of programs such as flexible work hours, maternity or paternity leave, the opportunity to work from home, or the opportunity to work part-time or job share (e.g., Evans, Kunda, and Barley 2004, 3). That's because "managers and peers interpret the use of flexibility programs as evidence of a lack of commitment, motivation, and productivity" and supervisors frequently deny requests for more flexible and family-friendly work schedules (Evans et al. 2004, 3). What matters are not formal policies but the organization's culture and its orientation and values about work-family issues.

SAS Institute is frequently on the list of the best places to work and has won many plaudits for its family-friendly environment. SAS employees can adjust their work hours to accommodate family needs, and more importantly, the company has a workweek of 35 to 40 hours, not the long days and weeks more typical of the software industry. The company recognizes that the people most important to its employees are those that they care for and are responsible for, such as their husbands and wives, children, domestic partners, and parents, and it makes available both benefits and work arrangements that make it feasible to have both a job and a life. As a consequence, SAS has been able to attract a large number of talented women employees into professional and managerial roles as well as people from families with children, much greater than the average for companies in the software industry. Accessing talented women gives SAS a competitive advantage in the challenging task of recruiting and retaining talent in an industry that is in the end all about intellectual capital.

## Long-Term Employment

One is presumably a member of a community for a long and indefinite period. Similarly, the idea of long-term employment is fundamental for those organizations that operate in a more communal fashion. Following September 11, 2001, Southwest Airlines, even as it prepared for the anticipated downturn, stayed clear of the knee-jerk reaction of immediately laying off workers, even as all of its industry competitors reduced their schedules and their workforces. SAS Institute tells its employees that it expects to see them have numerous careers and pursue various professional interests during the course of their work life, but it hopes that these changes will all occur at SAS. EADS, the large European defense and space agency that owns 80 percent of Airbus, also laid off no one following September 11, even though orders for new aircraft plummeted. Their head of human resources maintains that the goodwill engendered through that action has been instrumental in their overtaking Boeing and in avoiding the union conflicts and various production and quality programs that have plagued Boeing.

One reason this idea of long-term employment is so fundamental is that many of the other dimensions of community make sense only in the context of long-term mutual commitments. It is difficult and probably not very sensible, for example, to provide for employees over their life courses through pensions, medical benefits, and adoption and long-term care if the employees are not going to be in the company very long. But another reason for the emphasis on long-term employment is that it is fundamental to building a sense of permanence and attachment that communal-like organizations seek.

The irony is that although there is a pervasive sense of instability, fear of job loss, and increasing impermanence in the workplace, as Jacoby (1999) has argued, there is actually less evidence than one might expect that job tenures have actually shortened very much for most of the adult workforce or that career jobs are disappearing. In some sense, then, many companies have obtained the worst of both worlds—on the one hand, the costs and presumed disadvantages of long-tenured workforces such as higher benefit costs, and, on the other hand, people fearful of losing their

**Table 1.1**   Dimensions that might be Used for Characterizing the Degree to which Organizations are Communities

---

*Helping Employees in Need*
"Rainy day" fund
Low-interest or no-interest loans to employees having financial difficulties
Maintaining salary and/or benefits when not required to do so

*Employee Benefits and Assistance*
Pensions, including defined-benefit pensions
Health insurance and/or health care
Adoption and elder care assistance
Tuition reimbursement and educational assistance
Recreational facilities or health club membership

*Nepotism and Dating Policies*
Are employees married to each other allowed to work in the company?
Are there formal or informal policies precluding dating?

*Company-Sponsored Social Events*
Holiday parties
Travel and trips for recreation
Games and sports teams and leagues
Celebrations of accomplishments and milestones

*Resolving Work/Family Issues*
Use of parental leave
Maternity policies
Flexible work hours
Part-time work as an employee option, including job sharing
On-site childcare

*Long-Term Employment*
Voluntary turnover
Layoffs

---

jobs and not taking a long-term perspective on their commitment and attachment to the company.

Table 1.1 summarizes the dimensions and management practices that could form the basis for characterizing organizations in terms of their community-like nature.

## The Advantages and Disadvantages of Managing Organizations as Communities

Understanding the logic behind managing organizations as communities compared to managing the employment relationship in a more market-like fashion can help us understand how these models vary over time, across organizations, and across cultures, as well as the factors leaders must consider working on, should one or the other model come to be perceived as desirable.

### The Argument for Managing Organizations as Communities

The problem with the market-oriented, free agency-like model described by Cappelli (1999) as growing in prominence can be nicely seen by considering professional sports or investment banking, two labor markets that are probably the closest to this model in their operation. In each instance, the arrangement works well for the free agents, particularly those favored in the competition by their performance, but the employers tend not to do so well. When Warren Buffett stepped in to run Salomon Brothers after a bond trading scandal, one of the things he talked about was how the individual investment bankers were getting rich even though the returns to shareholders, measured by indicators such as return on shareholder equity, were quite poor for the firm. Most baseball teams lose money, at least in the absence of collusion to restrict players' salaries (e.g., Helyar 1991).

These results are scarcely surprising. In the absence of any form of attachment other than money, people will continually be assessing their alternative market opportunities, will always be at risk of leaving, and because of the social comparison aspect to the salary determination process, the upward pressure on salaries will often be relentless. Salaries are invariably set with respect to some market level, but almost all consider themselves to be above average in their skills and performance (e.g., Brown 1986). Consequently, there will be a tendency for average salaries to trend upward, unless there are severe downturns in the economy or enough foreign competition to fundamentally change the salary structure. This process accounts for the upward pressure on salaries in professional sports as well as the CEO labor market.

Moreover, turnover will be higher than it might otherwise be—again baseball, and for that matter other sports in the era of free agency, and investment banking provide good examples of this—imposing extra costs on the organization. These costs include the direct costs entailed in replacing the people leaving, costs in customer retention and satisfaction that come from having clients dealing with a perpetually inexperienced workforce, and the losses due to coordination failures or increased investment in the coordination and control required when people are working interdependently with others who are strangers.

Consequently, some companies seek to transform the employment relationship from one based strictly on money or other extrinsic incentives to one based on other things such as social relationships, purpose, and cultural fit as well. So, for instance, Apple Computer in its heyday early in its history recruited people, including former CEO John Sculley, by talking about its mission to change the world of computing.

Yet another way of deemphasizing the solely economic aspects of the employment relationship is to create a more communal-like feeling in the company, increasing the strength and importance of social bonds among people as well as the emotional connection between employees and the company. This is precisely the human resource strategy pursued by the MTW Corporation (now the Innovation Group), a Kansas City–based information technology contractor and developer of software for the insurance industry. By taking care of its people—providing more benefits and a culture that signaled that people were valued and expected to be part of the company and contribute to decision-making—turnover fell to about 7 percent even in the height of the labor market frenzy, and the company was consistently profitable and growing.

Because of the norm of reciprocity, commitment is mutual. To expect employees to be loyal to the company, the company needs to be loyal to them. To expect employees to see themselves as citizens or members of a community that they find attractive enough to work for, exert discretionary effort on its behalf, and remain in the company, organizations must do the various things already discussed to create a sense of community that would warrant such attitudes and actions.

There are some additional important advantages of building organizations as communities. In the market-like arrangements characteristic of many contemporary employers, negotiation over everything is frequent. These negotiations take time and effort and divert attention from developing products and services and serving customers. Trust, as it turns out, is much more efficient as a coordinating mechanism than to have to specify and haggle over every detail of work and the employment contract. Moreover, by incorporating more of the employee's life, including the parts outside of work, into the organization, employees are freed from external distractions and can focus on doing their work and making the company successful.

One of the reasons SAS Institute claims it can operate effectively with a shorter work week is that when its people are at work, they face no distractions. They do not have to worry either about their benefits or their children in day care. They do not have to worry whether the company is exploiting them and whether they need to be out looking at employment alternatives. Frictions and wasted energy are reduced, albeit never completely eliminated, in organizations that are more communal-like and are thereby able to build deeper and more trusting relationships with their people.

### The Arguments against Managing Organizations as Communities

There are, of course, many reasons why companies are reluctant to embrace, or at least fully embrace, a community-oriented perspective. One explanation comes from many executives' reactions when my colleagues and I teach cases such as Southwest Airlines or SAS Institute—the executives feel that the organizations are too "cult-like" and are uncomfortable with their strong cultures, even though those strong cultures have contributed in important ways to their success. The norm of individualism runs strong in the United States in particular, and in the West in general (e.g., Morris and Peng 1994), and community, at least in some of its aspects and implications, is almost by definition group-oriented and group-centered. The clash with general social values looms large in explaining companies' reluctance to adopt this management approach.

Another aspect of the same phenomenon of managerial discomfort with community can be seen in a *Fortune* television interview with James Goodnight, cofounder and CEO of SAS. The interviewer accused Goodnight of being "paternalistic," which both the interviewer and, at least initially, Goodnight took to be a pejorative term. Upon reflection, however, Goodnight responded that if paternalism meant that he cared about his employees and their well-being, then he just might be paternalistic.

The point is that paternalism, or caring about the total person throughout his or her life course, is something expected of family members and friends, but somehow we have gotten the idea that business is, and should be, different from the rest of life, operating using different norms, values, mores of interaction, and rules. Ethics and honest behavior, for example, are important in interacting with family, friends, neighbors, and in religious and civic organizations, but ethical behavior has to be defended on occasion at work, with special workshops and training to inculcate behavior that is more completely natural in other settings. As another example, internal competition and forced curve ranking is often lauded in business, but sibling rivalry, although a reality, is seldom held out to be a desirable state of affairs, and few child-rearing experts argue that pitting family members against each other in a competition for status leads to good outcomes.

This attempt to keep work and business separate and distinct from other domains creates problems and is, in the end, impossible. As Libby Sartain, former head of HR at Southwest and now running HR at Yahoo, noted, how can work be separate from the rest of life when, with cell phones, e-mail, PDAs, and so forth, one can hardly escape from work?

A second reason for avoiding more communal and inclusive relationships with employees is potential legal issues. For instance, to offer a pension plan makes the employer responsible for ensuring the integrity of the plan and its administration, and, in the case of defined-benefit plans, financially responsible for ensuring that promised benefits are, in fact, paid. Offering on-site daycare may make the employer responsible for what goes on in the daycare center, even if it is operated by a contractor, and legally liable for problems caused by the daycare employees. Talking about organizations as communities and about continued association or membership may create an implied promise of long-term employment and get the employer into trouble for violating implicit contracts if layoffs occur. All benefit plans impose reporting requirements. In an increasingly litigious world, labor lawyers basically tell employers to promise as little as possible, to expressly limit and to put in writing any obligations they do incur and, in general, to delimit the implicit and broad promises implied by the idea of organizations as communities.

Interestingly, there is little evidence that all of this legal maneuvering actually curtails the amount of employment litigation. In fact, by creating formalistic, legalistic, and distant relations between employers and their people, it is likely that legal action on the part of employees who feel they are wronged is actually encouraged, because there are no positive sentiments they hold toward the company to cause them to hold back. Anecdotally, companies such as SAS Institute or the Innovation Group (formerly MTW Corporation) that have deeper and less formal relationships with their people actually face fewer employee suits than comparable organizations. Nonetheless, the advice of labor lawyers looms large as an explanation for why a more communal model of organizations has not diffused.

Separate from, but ideologically related to, the legal issues, many organizations seek to delimit their obligations to their employees and, to the extent possible, devolve responsibility for nonwork aspects of employees' lives back to the employees. That's because organizations do not want to open the Pandora's box by beginning to be responsible for more than they absolutely need to order to get the work accomplished. As part of the move toward a market-like employment relationship, organizations seek to delimit their sphere of involvement in the life and well-being of their workforce—by the way, at the same time feeling free to monitor people's behavior at work, including their Internet and e-mail behavior, and to make demands on people even during their off hours. Nonetheless, the idea of a limited transaction carries over and thus limits what companies feel they are responsible for.

So the advantages of greater involvement and inclusion are balanced with social expectations, norms of separateness, transactional relationships, and concerns about legal liability and assumption of responsibility. Different companies at different times and in different countries balance these conflicting pressures to reach different decisions about what kind of organization to construct.

### The Role of Public Policy, Values, and Management Education

What should be clear from the foregoing discussion is that there is some degree of equifinality in employment models—different ways of organizing can be economically effective for organizations as long as they are implemented in an internally consistent fashion and fit the organization's business model and strategy (e.g., Cappelli and Crocker-Hefter 1996). In other words, to use a contemporary example, one can be either Wal-Mart or Costco and be economically successful (Maier 2005). However, different organizational models have different costs for employees and the broader society. After all, many of the functions assumed by organizations operating more as communities must be performed by other institutions such as government or private charities, or else these functions are left undone for employees who work in more market-like organizations.

To take just two examples, if employers do not provide medical coverage or pensions for their employees, those employees must somehow either acquire health insurance and retirement income on their own or, as is often the case, rely on the government to provide at least a limited safety net. And with respect to job satisfaction and commitment, employees who can rely on and trust their employers to look after more of their welfare are more likely to be satisfied with their employment—witness the difference in turnover levels, for instance, between Costco with its greater wages and benefits and Wal-Mart, which pays as little as possible given the local labor market, uses a higher percentage of part-time employees, and therefore provides benefits to fewer of its people (Shuit 2004).

Throughout the history of the modern industrial age, there has always been choice in how companies structured their relationship with their employees, from the time of welfare capitalism at the beginning of the twentieth century, to the era of the "organizational man" (Whyte 1956) in the 1950s, to the time of Theory Z and Japanese-style management in the 1980s, to the present-day emphasis on markets and labor market flexibility. As already noted, these choices are affected by values and beliefs, and also by public policy with its direct effect on management practices through law and regulation and its indirect effect through shaping norms about appropriate management behavior. Recent trends in values and beliefs and public policy regimes make the idea of organizations as communities less likely, regardless of the virtues of such an approach.

Management practice is affected by what is taught in business schools (Ghoshal 2005), in part because schools in the United States now turn out more than 100,000 MBAs per year, business education based in large measure on the U.S. model and U.S. literature is expanding rapidly around the world, and in addition to the people enrolled in formal degree programs, many other executives come into contact with business school through executive programs. As documented by Ghoshal (2005) and others (e.g., Ferraro, Pfeffer, and Sutton 2005), business school curricula are heavily influenced by economics and the assumptions and language of economics, including assumptions of self-interest, agency problems, and the virtues of markets as ways of allocating resources (see also Kuttner 1996). Although there are obviously other points of view—and one can find human resource management courses that offer organizational models emphasizing commitment, strong culture, and community (e.g., O'Reilly and Pfeffer 2000)—economics remains the mother discipline and an important influence on managerial thought, language, and practice.

The consequences of this economic orientation need not just be logically inferred but can be empirically seen in studies that explore how business school students' values and behavior change while in school. The Aspen Institute's (2001) study of values shows that over the course of their education, students come to place less emphasis on customers and employees and more emphasis on shareholders and creating shareholder value. McCabe and his colleagues (e.g., McCabe and Trevino 1995) have shown in numerous studies that business school students are more likely to report having cheated than students from other majors. And a study of corporate malfeasance found that while organizational size was positively related to the likelihood of corporate malfeasance, this relationship was even stronger for companies with a higher proportion of senior management with MBA degrees. Ghoshal (2005) has argued that all these consequences mean that business education and its language and theoretical foundations need to be fundamentally rethought and redesigned. Until this task is accomplished, however, business education and the dominant economic logic make building organizations as communities less likely.

Government, under the banner of an "ownership society" and making the economy more efficient by reducing regulation, has also invoked economic language, assumptions, and practices, thereby serving as a model to other organizations. Public employees, such as nurses and teachers, feel under attack and are called "special interests" as various states and cities try to introduce more variation in pay, less job security, and less generous staffing ratios. Ironically, government's relaxation of regulations that might constrain the choices of companies often does not encourage companies to behave responsibly toward their people.

So, there are no proscriptions on abandoning healthcare insurance for either employees or retirees, and competitive dynamics will virtually force companies to do so when enough others in their industry do, leaving those who want to maintain more generous communal benefits at a competitive disadvantage. The result is that 45 million Americans now have no health insurance, an increase of more than five million in the last five years, and the National Academy of Sciences estimates that 18,000 people die each year because they have no insurance and thus reduced access to care (Pear 2005). Companies are also free to change or abandon pension plans, again putting pressure on competitors to do likewise. This dynamic is currently playing out in the airline industry where companies in bankruptcy can renegotiate the terms of employment and can jettison pension obligations, almost forcing other companies not yet in bankruptcy to match these actions for competitive survival.

The irony is that government regulation, or its absence, lets companies off the hook for promises, but then government itself, through guarantees of minimum pension benefits and the need to provide healthcare to those who otherwise cannot afford it, winds up shouldering the costs offloaded by private sector employers. In fact, faced with their own pension obligations that strain their budgets, city and state governments have begun to contemplate changing their own retirement practices, to move away from defined-benefit plans that guarantee a certain percentage of income based on years of service, and instead to have their employees assume more responsibility for their own retirement income through defined-contribution plans. Thus, it is questionable whether public policy and public organization examples encourage the development of a more communal orientation toward the workforce.

Although the current zeitgeist is very much contrary to the idea of organizations as communities of shared fate, and much more consistent with an ethos of every person for him- or herself (get what you can when you can and how you can), this actually leaves an amazing competitive opportunity for the companies that operate differently. Just as in product markets, competitive advantage in labor markets comes from offering a better—and different—value proposition. Doing what everyone else does basically produces the same results as everyone else. Variation in performance, either positive or negative, comes from being different. So, the competitive advantage in attracting employees enjoyed by SAS Institute, Southwest Airlines, and DaVita, for example, only grows to the extent that their cultures and communal orientation are increasingly unique.

## Missed Opportunities

Work in America continues to be problematic in many dimensions, and maybe even more so than when the original volume was published (Special Task Force 1973). My reading of that original work is that in the 1970s, people were largely concerned about whether or not work itself had sufficient variety and autonomy—whether jobs were sufficiently enriched to motivate and engage the workforce (e.g., Hackman and Oldham 1980), the effects of alienating jobs on physical and mental health, and the need for worker training. Alienation from and boredom with work—often routine and deskilled work—was an important focus of attention.

The good news is that work requiring no skill, work that can be outsourced or off-shored, has been, or soon will be. The work that remains in advanced industrial economies is increasingly intellectual or knowledge work, requiring innovation and skill—except, of course, for personal services that cannot be provided at a distance. The bad news is that what seems to be more problematic is not just people's work, although autonomy and control over work remains a critical issue, but also employees' connections to their employers and each other.

People are now spending more time at work than ever before:

> The Japanese do not feel rich, Imada (1997) argued, because an over-emphasis on work and long hours has made it difficult for many Japanese to enjoy family life . . . . U.S. workers now work more hours per year than do workers in any other industrialized country . . . . Middle-class parents in dual-earner households worked a total of 3,932 hours in 2000, equivalent to more than two full-time jobs in most European countries. (Berg et al. 2004, 332–333)

Not only are people spending lots of time at work, but work roles also remain central to social identity and status, and the conflict between work and nonwork time and responsibilities remains pervasive (e.g., Barnett 1994; Bolger, Delongis, and Kessler 1989; Gareis and Barnett 2000). So the fundamental question is, what sort of relationship is forged between people and their employers within the workplace, the place where people spend so much time? There is certainly evidence that people want to do meaningful work, work that has purpose and that they find fulfilling in the sense of accomplishing something they believe contributes to achieving some important goal (Ashmos and Duchon 2000), as well as work that permits them to realize their full potential as a person (Mitroff and Denton 1999).

But people also desire a sense of belonging and community at work. People are social creatures and social interaction at work is important. For people spending more time and making more personal sacrifices for their work, not only what they do but also the relationship with their employer is psychologically important.

For a number of reasons briefly reviewed here, most organizations are not providing the sense of community and psychological attachment that most people seek. This leaves many people dissatisfied and reasonably uncommitted to their employers, which results in less discretionary effort and providing fewer ideas and innovation than might otherwise be the case. In sum, the story of work in America today, with respect to the communal nature of organizations, is a story of missed opportunities. There are many factors and forces at play in creating this situation, ranging from public policy to what we teach in business schools to general social norms, values, and expectations about the appropriate relationship between people and organizations. For work in America to change, each and all of these factors and forces will need to be both better understood and a target for intervention.

# 2

# The Transformation of Work in America: New Health Vulnerabilities for American Workers

*Richard H. Price*

The plate tectonics of work in the United States have shifted in the last 30 years, causing changes in the risks and vulnerabilities of worker health. The introduction of information technology in its various forms, the globalization of economies, changes in the nature of the employment contract between employers and workers, the emergence of the service economy, and the entry of women into the workforce all have affected the dynamics of working life for Americans. This chapter explores these changes and the ways they are consequential for the health and well-being of American workers and their families.

## Stress and Health in the American Workplace: Then and Now

The picture of the American workplace painted in the landmark report *Work in America* (1973) is one in which workers were faced with monotonous, regimented, and stressful work. These workers lived in an organizational world where little control over the nature and quality of their work was possible and where the work itself frequently lacked any larger human meaning. The report noted crucial links between worker discontent and worker health. More generally, the 1973 report argued that stressful conditions at work could have adverse effects on mental health and increase the risk of drug and alcohol addiction as well as increase cardiovascular risk.

Thus, improving the conditions of work could have health benefits. The report explained that there is an important difference between attempting to improve health by increasing spending for medical care and taking advantage of the opportunities for improving physical and mental health that reside in improving the conditions of work. For example, a considerable proportion of the unexplained risk of heart disease could simply be due to occupational stress, rapid changes in employment, lack of security, and lack of stability and support in the workplace (*Work and Health* 1973).

As we shall see, a body of scientific literature on the links between working conditions and health has emerged in the last 30 years. That literature has greatly enlarged our understanding of the processes and mechanisms that link working conditions to health. But to understand the American workplace today, and in particular to understand how changes in stressful work are related to health, we must first turn to a brief history of the evolution of work in America over the last 30 years.

## Changes in the American Workplace 1972–2002

While it is commonplace to acknowledge that dramatic social changes have occurred over the last four decades, it is less frequently acknowledged that the nature and conditions of work have undergone perhaps an even more dramatic transformation. Cooper (1998) has summarized the steps of the transformation of the regimented and monotonous workplace of the early 1970s into the workplace that we see now at the beginning of the twenty-first century.

The 1960s and early 1970s began as a period of optimism about the power of technology to transform workers' lives and to ease the burden of work. That early optimism has now been substantially tempered (Rifkin 1995). The optimistic 60s were followed in the 70s by worker and union struggles to maintain their position while management pressed for more efficiency and reduced benefits. The 80s saw the emergence of an "enterprise culture" (Cooper 1998), a strong movement for deregulation, and a new enthusiasm for privatization. Workers themselves were faced with reductions in job security and health benefits, and the workplace began to take on the atmosphere of a "free market." The 90s began with a period of economic downturn, with an accompanying downsizing of the workforce. Sometimes aided by technology, more work was being demanded of fewer workers, and the economy began to run 24 hours a day (Price and Kompier in press).

Perhaps one of the most important changes to have occurred in the 30 years between 1972 and 2002 is the large-scale entry of women into the workforce. Facing the demands of a workplace designed for men who are largely free of daily family responsibilities, women faced conflicts between the obligations of family and the demands of work. More and more couples struggled to deal with the challenge of "two people, three jobs" (Guerts and Demerouta 2003; Hochschild 1997).

Finally, in the midst of all of these other changes, the content of work had dramatically changed. Dull, repetitive manufacturing and laboring jobs that required a strong back were being replaced by information and service jobs that required greater cognitive skills as well as the capacity to manage one's emotions to provide pleasing service. This change in the psychosocial content of jobs meant that jobs provided more latitude in how work was done, and they also represented a crucial shift from manual effort to mental and emotional demands (Price and Kompier in press).

## The Quality of Employment Survey 1972 and 2002

In the late 1960s and early 1970s, a survey of American workers was conducted by the Institute for Social Research. The survey (Kahn and Quinn 1970; Quinn et al. 1973, 1975, 1979) provided an overview of conditions of employment in the United States in 1969, 1973, and 1977. The study, originally developed by the U.S. Department of Labor and the ISR Survey Research Center, was aimed at understanding the nature and distribution of working conditions and their effects on American workers. In 2002 the National Institute for Occupational Safety and Health (NIOSH) developed a quality of work life module (QWL) that was included in a national survey of U.S. households using many of the same survey items as the earlier surveys, allowing a direct comparison of worker experience over a 30-year period.

Tausig et al. (2004) and Murphy et al. (in press) reported comparisons in the results of the survey of American workers three decades apart. When Murphy et al. compared the workers of 1972 with their counterparts in 2002, some of the changes could be expected. There are more women in the workforce, and fewer workers are members of a union in 2002. On the other hand, in comparison with their earlier counterparts in 1972, workers in 2002 report that their work makes more use of their own skills and provides more opportunity to learn new skills. Workers in 2002 also report that they have more equipment to deal with their job adequately and that their autonomy at work is considerably higher than was the case in 1972. In addition, twenty-first century workers express a greater intention to find new jobs in the foreseeable future.

The QWL survey results suggest that some of the worst, most boring and repetitive jobs in manufacturing, the ones that produced worker discontent in the past, are now being done by foreign workers, as the jobs go offshore or become easier to perform by the introduction of new technology. It may also be the case that the shift from manual to service and information work requires the greater flexibility and autonomy workers report now as compared with 1972.

In addition, analysis of the 2002 QWL data (Murphy in press) showed that high workloads for non-healthcare workers and work/family interference were strong predictors of job stress, which can compromise worker health, as we will describe in detail later. At the same time, reports of stronger worker commitment to the organization and worker perceptions of organizational effectiveness were associated with the belief that they had supervisor support and that their skills were being well utilized, and also with the belief that they worked under good occupational safety and health conditions. Finally, supervisor support and good skill utilization were strong predictors of job satisfaction.

Ideally, one would find conditions of work that improve not only worker health but also organizational performance. Thus, it is particularly interesting that supervisor support appears to have broad impact and influence on both worker well-being and perceptions of effectiveness and commitment to the organization. It is also noteworthy that perceptions of good safety conditions are associated with perceptions of organizational effectiveness and employee commitment. These results have clear implications for improvements in working conditions that can improve worker well-being and productivity. Organizations with both supportive supervisors and explicit concern for worker safety appear to have the most beneficial combination of work environment characteristics to promote worker health.

*Common Threads in Conditions of Work since 1972*

Taken together, we might ask, what are the common threads in this history of change in the conditions of work over the last 30 years, and how might they have changed the nature of work stress and influenced health and well-being? First, there are clear changes in the content and demands of the work role. Much of today's work has replaced the physical and repetitive tasks of manufacturing and manual labor with the cognitive and emotional demands of service and information work. Second, the boundaries of work have changed. Rather than a clearly demarcated 40-hour week, for many workers the increased use of technology has meant that work is accessible everywhere and all the time. In addition, the emergence of nonstandard forms that jobs may take can mean that workers are expected to work overtime on the one hand or be unable to get a full-time job on the other. A third major change is in the resources and benefits a job provides. Many jobs now not only lack the security that they once did, but also lack health benefits. Finally, the dramatic increase of women in the workforce has introduced new demands on workers and their families, as conflict between the demands of work, home, childcare, and eldercare now take their toll in increased stress and diminished well-being.

## Health Risks for American Workers

Clearly, the working life of America's workers has changed in important ways that influence their health and well-being. At least four areas of research suggest themselves when we study the health risks to American workers today: (1) physical and psychosocial conditions in the workplace, (2) job insecurity, underemployment, and unemployment, (3) work/family conflict, with the entry of growing numbers of women in the workforce, and (4) vulnerability to health problems due to lack of health insurance.

### How Do the Conditions of Work "Get Under the Skin"?

One of the most important changes in the last 30 years has been our increased understanding of the mechanisms by which adverse conditions in the environment are transformed into health problems. In a wide-ranging review, Taylor and Repetti (1997) examined the growing evidence that events in the physical and social environment are the beginning of a chain of causation leading to negative health outcomes. They argued that unhealthy environments are those that threaten safety, undermine the creation of social ties, or are conflictual, abusive, or violent. By contrast, healthy environments are those that provide safety, opportunities for social integration, and the ability to predict and control aspects of the environment.

In the causal chain from environment to health, unhealthy environmental characteristics are translated into acute and chronic stress, which in turn influences affective responses and mental health, coping strategies, health habits, and finally, biological precursors of disease and disease itself. For example, Taylor and Repetti (1997) showed how depression, anxiety, and anger can be translated into cardiac illness through the activation of the sympathetic-adrenal-medullary (SAM) system and the hypothalamic-pituitary-adrenocortical (HPA) axis. This is one of many routes by which physical and psychosocial environments may "get under the skin." In what follows we will see the changing nature of work in the United States, and how its exposures, demands, and resources follow many different pathways to health outcomes.

### The Role of Working Conditions in Influencing Health

A wide range of working conditions have now been shown to be consequential for health, and some of the pathways leading from working conditions to health outcomes are only now being identified. Physical and chemical exposure in the work environment can lead to injury, cancer, and respiratory and cardiovascular risk (House and Smith 1985). Shift work disrupts circadian rhythms and is associated with elevated level of psychosomatic complaints (Frese and Zapf 1986).

But over and above physical exposures and shifting work schedules, the evidence is now fairly clear that stressful conditions of the work itself can have an adverse influence on people's health and psychological well-being (Kahn 1981; Kahn and Byosiere 1992; Beehr 1995; Karasek and Theorell 1990; Price and Kompier in press; Stellman 1997). Semmer (2003) succinctly summarized what is now known about the conditions that produce stress and adverse effects on health. Features of work tasks such as their lack of variety, complexity, and level of stimulation, as well as the conditions under which the tasks have to be performed such as speed, working time, and ergonomic conditions, all can produce stress reactions and jeopardize health. Role requirements, particularly when they are ambiguous or conflicting, can create stress and anxiety (Kahn et al. 1964). Social conditions in the workplace, including fairness and support or conflict, as well as wider organizational conditions such as job security or prospects for development, can all influence the experience of stress, psychological well-being and health. Semmer (2003) also noted that in all these instances a sense of control and influence plays a major role (Karasek and Theorell 1990).

A broad review of work conditions and health (Karasek and Theorell 1990) indicated that jobs with high levels of demand and low control are particularly likely to produce chronic stress and health problems. Furthermore, there is now growing evidence of the biological pathways linking psychosocial work stressors to health outcomes. Frankenhauser (1991) demonstrated that situations low in control produce catecholamine/cortisol imbalance. Other pathways involving coping skills and social support are also important in understanding how adverse work conditions can get under the skin. Taylor and Repetti (1997) noted that active coping and jobs that provide more decision latitude are more protective of health, and that social support from coworkers and supervisors (House 1981) can reduce the negative health effects of stressful work. Indeed, high blood pressure in stressful work situations can be moderated by social support (House 1981; House and Kahn 1985).

Many of the characteristics of work described above persist in the jobs of some American workers and influence their health. But over the several decades during which research linking working conditions to health was being conducted, the nature of work itself was changing.

## Underemployment and Unemployment

If the conditions of work can jeopardize health and well-being, so can resource poor, inadequate, insecure jobs, or the loss of a job altogether. Employers are changing the employment contract (Cooper 1998; Rousseau 1995) in ways that increase job insecurity, underemployment, and involuntary job loss. As the contractual conditions of employment change, workers are at risk for underemployment, involuntary job loss, and prolonged periods of unemployment (Price et al. 1998). The rise of contingent work, underemployment, organizational downsizing, and involuntary job loss produce a wide range of both physical and mental health effects in laid-off workers and their families (Vinokur 1997).

Underemployment can take several forms, including inadequate income, inadequate hours of work, mismatched skills and job requirements, and working in jobs below the qualifications of the worker. While few studies on the health effects of underemployment have been conducted, a recent longitudinal study of a national sample of U.S. workers (Friedland and Price 2003) found lower levels of health and well-being among underemployed workers. Underemployment defined in terms of inadequate income was associated with lower levels of functional health and increase in the incidence of depression, and working in jobs where qualifications were higher than the skills the worker was required to use was associated with functional health problems and higher levels of chronic disease. More research is needed on the health effects of nonstandard work, especially since we can expect its prevalence to increase in the years ahead.

Downsizing of America's firms in response to economic pressures and global competition, changes in technology, and the movement of American jobs offshore in the 1980s and 1990s is well documented (Baumol, Blinder, and Wolff 2003). The health problems associated with involuntary job loss and prolonged unemployment include anxiety, depression, alcohol abuse, child mistreatment, and marital disruption (Catalano et al. 1993a, 1993b; Price 1992, 2002; Vinokur et al. 1996). The social and economic burden associated with extended unemployment is substantial, including increased health-care costs, increased costs in the welfare system, increased crime rates, increased divorce rates, and a variety of other societal consequences (Vinokur 1997).

Economic hardship associated with unemployment is an important determinant of the health effects of unemployment (Kessler et al. 1987; Price et al. 2002; Vinokur et al. 1996). Economic hardship produces a cascade of secondary stressors, including loss of health benefits, family conflict and stress, inadequate diet, and loss of other critical resources (Price et al. 1998).

*Conflict between the Demands of Work and Family*

One of the most significant changes in workforce composition since the last report on *Work in America* in 1973 is the increase in a number of women in the workforce. As Geurts and Demerouti (2003) observed, dual-earner couples face household and caregiving responsibilities in addition to the demands of two jobs. A recent national survey of the U.S. workforce indicated that 30 percent of workers experienced a major conflict between family responsibilities and work demands (Bond et al. 1998).

There is emerging evidence that work/family conflict is associated with a range of physical and psychological health problems for dual-earner working families. For example, couples experiencing work/family conflict report higher levels of physical symptoms and distress (Allen et al. 2000). Guerts et al. (1999) also reported that work/family conflict is associated with higher reported levels of headache, backache, and other somatic symptoms. In addition, Alan et al. (2000) identified psychological strain, family distress, and increased levels of depression among the psychological symptoms associated with work/family conflict.

Understanding precisely the mechanisms by which work/family conflict influences well-being is not yet complete. The hypotheses include role strain (Kahn et al. 1964), negative spillover from work to family (Westman and Piotrkowski 1999), and the possibility that work/family conflict interacts with some of the stress producing characteristics of jobs already described. More research is needed on both the causes and the consequences of this emerging new source of stress for U.S. workers and their families.

*Working without Health Insurance*

In the United States today, having a job with health insurance benefits is one of the most important factors in protecting the health of working Americans. And yet, with the rising prevalence of nonstandard work, increases in underemployment (Friedland and Price 2003), and unemployment as a consequence of layoffs and downsizing (Price et al. 1998), health insurance benefits are a diminishing protective resource for American workers. A recent report by the Institute of Medicine (IOM) of the National Academy of Sciences (2001) made it clear that, in the United States, health and economic well-being are closely tied to whether a job carries health insurance as a benefit.

Several additional observations in the IOM Committee report (2001) powerfully illuminate the links between employment status and health protection in the United States. Full-time work throughout the year and a moderate income level offer families the best likelihood of having the protection of health insurance. But many work arrangements do not provide health insurance. The report observed that more than 8 out of 10 uninsured children and adults live in working families. Even individuals living in families with two full-time workers may stand a 1 in 10 chance of being uninsured.

Furthermore, the uninsured are much more likely to do without medical care that they need. Young workers between the ages of 19 and 34 are particularly vulnerable, because they are often not eligible for workplace health insurance, either because their firms do not provide coverage to employees or because they are too new in their jobs. Finally, employment status is one of the most important ways in which an individual may gain or lose health insurance. Job loss and subsequent unemployment are a direct threat to health insurance coverage and access to adequate healthcare.

Clearly, working life has changed markedly in ways that can compromise the health and well-being of American workers. While we know much more about the characteristics of jobs that make them dangerous or stressful, we are starting to understand new sources of vulnerabilities, including strains on families due to work/family conflict, underemployment, and unemployment, and the economic and health risks associated with lack of health insurance. We now turn to a discussion of interventions and policies that can change the stressful conditions of work and protect health.

## Interventions and Policies to Change Conditions at Work and Protect Health

Interventions or policies can be directed at different points in the causal chain linking conditions of work to health. Kompier and Kristensen (2000) have elaborated the ISR stress framework (Kahn et al. 1964) to point out opportunities for intervention. The opportunities include primary prevention efforts aimed at the work conditions themselves, secondary prevention efforts aimed at the short-term physiological and psychological reactions to adverse work conditions, and finally tertiary prevention, actual treatment rather than prevention of work related illness or disability. While all three intervention strategies are important and needed, clearly primary prevention efforts, if they can be shown to be effective and economically viable, are most desirable.

## From Programs to Policies

Murphy and Sauter (2004) have extended this basic prevention framework to distinguish between different levels of intervention ranging from interventions directed at the individual to policy and legislation. They classify interventions aimed at (1) the interface between the individual and the job, (2) the task or job itself, (3) the employer organization, and finally, (4) legislation and policy. So, for example, at the individual level, a primary of prevention effort might involve health promotion programs for exercise or weight control. Secondary prevention efforts might involve stress management, and tertiary treatment efforts might involve disease management or employee assistance programs (Cooper et al. 2003) to treat drug addiction, mental health, or chronic diseases such as high blood pressure.

Programs designed to reduce the stresses of the individual worker have been widely employed in recent years. Examples include programs to help employees manage stress, manage their time better, or reduce conflict in their work roles or between workers. Programs aimed at managing worker stress reactions employ a variety of techniques including muscle relaxation, behavioral skills training, meditation, and biofeedback (Murphy and Sauter 2004). Research on the effects of these individually targeted stress management programs indicate that they often produce only short-term reductions in distress along with increased knowledge of the sources of stress.

Interventions aimed at the job or task itself usually involve an effort to redesign poorly designed and stressful jobs (Kompier 2002; Parker and Wall 1998), or to enrich them by increasing task variety, or in some cases, job rotation. Murphy and Sauter (2004) reported that there has been considerable research in this area, but the results have not been encouraging in terms of improvement in health and reduction in stress. However, some studies (Kompier et al. 1998) have demonstrated that task redesign programs can improve absence rates, and that the benefits of the intervention outweigh the costs.

A seemingly obvious site for programs and policies to protect worker health and well-being is the workplace or employer organization. Organizational interventions to improve coworker and supervisor support have been developed and tested—interventions that involve improvement of communication and feedback and the management of conflicts, as well as training in group mutual support and teamwork (Heaney, Price, and Rafferty 1995a, 1995b). Heaney and her coworkers (1995) reported on a large-scale, randomized trial testing an intervention aimed at increasing the ability of teams of caregivers to mobilize socially supportive team behavior and problem-solving techniques in order to increase their coping resources and improve mental health (Price and Kompier in press).

In the last two decades, employers both in the public and private sector have instituted a wide variety of worksite wellness or health promotion programs for their employees. The rationale is that these programs can help employees at risk of health problems caused due to smoking, overweight, substance abuse, hypertension, or other conditions. The cost containment opportunity for employers is clear, particularly in light of rapidly increasing healthcare costs, and the health benefits for employees seem obvious. Furthermore, healthier employees should be more productive and have fewer absences.

The programs typically offered to employees, who engage in them voluntarily, include hypertension screening, stress management, smoking cessation, cholesterol screening, physical fitness, nutritional counseling, and weight reduction. Initial research suggested that these programs improved health and reduced healthcare costs, especially if they were delivered in a comprehensive format (e.g., Erfert, Foote, and Heirich 1991; Pelletier 1996). As a consequence, health promotion programs in the workplace have over the last two decades become a widely adopted innovation to improve worker health.

More recently, economic analyses of the cost-effectiveness of workplace wellness programs suggest that a more complex picture of the benefits of such programs is emerging. For example, a recent three-year study of 1757 employees (Haynes, Dunnagan, and Smith 1999) examined the relationship between health insurance costs and wellness program participation. These investigators found that voluntary wellness programs face an adverse selection problem, in that the less healthy employees are much more likely to select themselves into wellness programs. Therefore, employees that elect to participate in worksite wellness programs may incur higher, rather than lower, health claim costs.

Another economic study of health promotion programs (Musich, Adams, and Edington 2000) helps to illuminate the problem. In a six-year study of 1272 company employees, Musich et al. (2000) also found that increasing levels of program participation were associated with higher medical costs. The authors concluded that these patterns of participation may have reflected the fact that health promotion programming was more appealing to high-risk/high-cost employees. These investigators then contrasted employees who participated in comprehensive programs with those who participated in less comprehensive programs, involving, for example, only health education or screening efforts. They also subdivided employees into low- and high-cost groups. Over time, high-cost employees still remained substantially higher in healthcare costs than low-cost, healthier employees.

However, while the health costs of high-cost employees continued to go up over time, the rate of increase was moderated if they participated in a comprehensive rather than a limited program. Taken together, these results suggest that worksite wellness programs are more likely to be used by less healthy employees, whose healthcare costs will still be high, but that comprehensive programs can moderate increases in healthcare costs for these employees.

There is little doubt that health promotion programs in the workplace are of benefit to both workers and employers. However, some of the more optimistic expectations of their impact on worker health and healthcare costs employers bear may be in need of some revision. As mentioned, recent studies suggest that workplace wellness programs are used more by less healthy workers who have higher healthcare costs. But comprehensive programs can moderate increasing healthcare costs for these workers over time. Thus, modest gains in cost containment are possible through worksite wellness programs if they are well implemented and comprehensive in scope rather than piecemeal.

In addition, at the organizational level, work/family programs have emerged in the United States in the last 15 years as an important response to the increasing numbers of women in the workplace. Work/family programs take a number of different forms, and most usually involve flexible work schedules, provision for childcare, part-time work or job sharing, and in some cases provision of eldercare. Research on the effects of these programs on worker health and well-being is in its early stages (Geurts and Demerouti 2003), but there is little doubt that provision of these services for working families has grown substantially and is seen by companies as a tool for improving recruitment and retention of employees (Murphy and Sauter 2004).

We have already described the health risks of involuntary job loss and unemployment. Normally, employers who are reducing their workforce may provide severance pay, and in some cases outplacement programs to help laid-off workers find reemployment. Usually, however, programs providing job search assistance are conducted by state governments in unemployment offices. Programs to aid in job search have been developed, and research shows that participants find jobs sooner, receive higher pay, are less likely to suffer from depression (Caplan et al. 1989; Price et al. 1998; Vinokur et al. 1995), and that the programs themselves are cost effective (Vinokur et al. 1991).

Policy level interventions in the United States and legislation to reduce stress and protect worker health are much less prevalent than they are in Europe. However, Murphy and Sauter (2004) noted that there are significant exceptions. One is the Family and Medical Leave act of 1993, which allows workers to take up to six weeks of unpaid leave per year to attend to family members in need of medical care. Examples of secondary preventive efforts at a legislative level involve worker compensation programs, and tertiary prevention or treatment is represented by the Social Security Disability program.

## The Rise of Occupational Health in the United States

Professions offer expertise, encourage new social arrangements, and respond to issues that concern the public. An index of change in the American workplace is the rise of the field of occupational health. Cullen (1999) chronicled the rise and fall of the occupational health movement over the twentieth century and judged the last 30 years as a striking success. Among the clear achievements he cited are the establishment of health and safety regulations for most forms of work, development of occupational medicine as a professional field, diffusion of occupational health services into American industries, the development of occupational epidemiology, expansion of the concept of occupational disorder to musculoskeletal pain and dysfunction and to reversible reactions to chemical exposures, provision of safety risk information to workers and their families, and the development of surveillance measures and data bases. Furthermore, the available data suggest that these developments have contributed to reductions in occupational injuries, fatalities, and illnesses over the last three decades (Karrh 1983; OSHA 1998).

However, Cullen observed that the "public oversight of private working conditions" has been very much a cyclical affair over the last century in America, with periods of social movement and reform followed by periods of neglect and apathy. It is worth asking whether we might be entering such a period of neglect now after three decades of progress. Cullen noted, "It is easier to investigate or close a restaurant after a case of food poisoning than to investigate or close a factory after the outbreak of an occupation-related disease" (1999, 11).

## The Occupational Safety and Health Administration

Concern about workplace safety and health was growing rapidly at about the same time the original report on *Work in America* was published. In 1970, President Nixon signed the Occupational Safety and Health Act, which established specific standards to reduce accidents, injury, and hazards, and outlined employer and employee responsibilities. The Occupational Safety and Health Administration (OSHA) was established in 1971 to receive complaints about work hazards, provide for inspection of industries, keep records to assure compliance, and levy fines on employers for violations.

Under OSHA, a number of milestones in workplace safety and health have been achieved. In the early 1970s, initial standards for safety and health were established, training programs for workplace inspectors were developed, state programs were created to accompany the federal program, new cotton dust exposure standards protected workers from brown lung disease, and lead exposure standards in the workplace were introduced. By the mid-1980s, hazard communication standards were established for training workers and inspectors about toxic materials, and hazardous waste operations and emergency response standards were devised. By the 1990s, new threats from blood-borne pathogens such as hepatitis B and AIDS elicited safety standards for worker exposure, and asbestos standards were updated to cut down permissible exposures in light of new evidence of its harmful effects (*OSHA 30-year milestones*, http://www.osha.gov).

There is general agreement that even as the workforce has expanded since 1970, occupational fatalities have been falling steadily (Fleming 2001). Specific initiatives against severe hazards, such as reduction of cotton dust exposure and exposure to vinyl chloride (which causes liver cancer) are clear successes. Furthermore, OSHA regulations provide a broader societal benefit, not only reducing health risks for workers, but also reducing the negative economic externalities associated with job related injuries and deaths not usually borne by employers, but passed on to society.

Still, there are sharp debates over the impact of OSHA from advocates for employers on the one hand and advocates for workers on the other. For example, Hood (1995) argued that firms already have strong economic incentives to improve worker safety because of pressure from insurance companies and that OSHA regulations raise production costs with little influence on worker health. He added that OSHA inspectors visit a firm only once in 10 years on the average and could therefore have little impact on worker safety and health.

The National Academy of Sciences/Institute of Medicine (*Musculoskeletal disorders and the workplace* 2001), however, has concluded that new regulatory initiatives, such as ergonomic standards, are needed because of the changing nature of work and an aging workforce. Legislation has not been forthcoming on this issue. While a strong case can be made for the impact of OSHA on worker health over the last 30 years, the future may be less certain. Current policies and budgets in OSHA are shifting away from earlier enforcement practices in high hazard areas to compliance assistance, which provides government funding to employers for making needed workplace changes.

### Opportunities and Challenges for Workplace Intervention and Policy

While there has been some progress in the development of policies and interventions in the last several decades, several opportunities now present themselves and deserve comment. First, working in a stressful social environment increases not only the risk of psychological distress, but also the risk of work-related injuries and accidents. Cooper and Clarke (2004) have observed that much of the treatment of stress and health in the workplace has ignored the issue of workplace safety. They called for an integrated approach, which encompasses both safety related outcomes and health, and noted that behavioral modification programs aimed at changing specific safety related behaviors have a real record of success.

Second, at the organizational level, one may ask whether programs of the sort we have described to reduce stress and protect health are taken seriously and with the high-level commitment necessary for effective organization-wide implementation. Shannon (2004) suggested that organizations will be most often committed to change when there is a crisis or disruption in productivity. It may be that we need to look for organizational intervention opportunities where management sees the need for change and is committed to making it happen.

Third, Semmer (2004) observed that almost all workplace interventions involve trade-offs between multiple outcomes. For example, efforts at job enrichment may raise job satisfaction while at the same time increasing the complexity of the job. Most job interventions aimed at reducing stress and improving health may involve trade-offs and should thus be evaluated based on trade-offs among multiple outcomes rather than focusing on a single criterion of success.

Finally, it is often tempting to call for organizational or policy level interventions in the environment because they appear more comprehensive. On the other hand, Semmer (2004) noted that it is also the case that the more remote the intervention is from the worker, the less likelihood there is that it will filter down to the individual level. He added, "The effects of policy interventions therefore are often difficult to predict, due to the creativity of the actors involved in complying with, or working around, the rules" (2004, 89).

## Conclusion

The balance has shifted in the interplay of work and health in America. Three or four decades ago a job was more likely to be a 40-hour-a-week agreement with an employer to exchange effort at what might be a dull, repetitive, and possibly dangerous job for pay, health benefits, and a pension at the end of 30 to 40 years of work. Today the job may involve only a short-term contract, and the work tools are more likely to be a computer, a telephone, and whatever communication skills the employee can muster to work with project team members or customers (Rousseau 1995). The most dangerous jobs have become somewhat safer. But jobs today are also less secure, will involve more health compromising transitions in and out of employment, and carry with them fewer safeguards such as health insurance for workers and their family members.

This new American workplace offers challenges for research. Continued surveys like the Quality of Work Life survey are needed to monitor changes in working conditions and in worker health as work for Americans continues to change. Surveys of this kind can provide not only information about health compromising conditions of work, but they can also identify health protective practices and policies that can be incorporated into new programs and be disseminated more widely or incorporated into legislation and policy.

Researchers also need to cast a wider net when measuring outcomes of innovative programs or managerial actions. Research on programs and policies to protect worker health in the past has often focused on a single health or economic outcome.

This narrow focus fails to recognize that managerial actions and program innovations seldom have a single impact and that there are usually trade-offs between various outcomes, improving one type of outcome at the expense of another (Grant, Christianson, and Price in preparation; Semmer 2004). For example, programs to enhance individual goal setting skills may also reduce spontaneous helping and social support among workers. Job enrichment programs may increase job satisfaction, but they also increase workload because mental demands of the job increase as well (Campion and Thayer 1985).

Employers and policymakers need to attend more seriously to some of the most salient features of the new workplace and the modern job. Work/family demands, job insecurity, loss of insurance, and increased time demands dominate the lives of many American workers. Cullen (1999) persuasively argued that the occupational health movement has improved worker safety and reduced exposure to harmful chemical and physical substances at work; now it is time to take the psychosocial risks of American workers more seriously.

Just as work redesign programs are being introduced (Parker and Wall 1998) to respond to the health compromising aspects of monotonous repetitive work, the content of work is shifting in the new service economy that makes often stressful interpersonal and cognitive demands of many U.S. workers. It may be that the influential demand-control model (Karasek and Theorell 1990) of work stress is becoming less relevant to today's workers and that, as Cooper (1998) suggested, it is time to look for another model linking work conditions to health. That model will need to expand the conceptual boundaries of what we mean by a job beyond the task itself, to encompass the larger web of resources and demands on worker health and well-being.

The new model of work will focus not only on the immediate concrete task at hand, but it will also expand to include the larger network of contractual and personal relationships between the worker and employer, worker and coworkers, worker and family, worker and insurer, and their implications for health. It is this broader network of relationships and exchanges, constraints, and resources, both material and psychosocial, that must be mapped if we are to fully appreciate the research and policy implications of the new American workplace for worker health.

# 3

# Restoring Voice at Work and in Society

*Thomas A. Kochan*[1]

It is probably fair to assume that the authors and background researchers involved in the original *Work in America* report shared a view that a strong, independent, and forward looking labor movement is critical to a democratic society. Unfortunately, three decades later, America is questioning this assumption. Since the publication of *Work in America*, the labor movement has declined in membership density and power to the point where it is no longer able, despite its best efforts, to provide workers and their families with an influential voice in the affairs that affect their most vital interests.

Partly as a result, the economic welfare of American workers and their families has declined over these three decades. As other chapters in this volume report in more detail, real wages have stagnated or declined for the average worker, incomes have become more unequal, pension and health care benefits have declined and/or become less secure, and families are working longer hours to make ends meet.

The quality of our democracy has also declined. For more than a quarter century, a political impasse between business and labor has kept policymakers from updating badly outmoded labor and employment policies. Dialogue between labor and management leaders in civil society has also deteriorated, as longstanding forums for bringing together leaders from these groups have been disbanded.

The good news is that there is now widespread consensus that the labor movement is in deep crisis and needs to change if it is to be a vital force in the economy and society of the twenty-first century. Indeed, in summer 2005, unions representing approximately one-quarter of the AFL-CIO membership split off to form their own coalition. This has set off the most important public and active debate over the future of the labor movement since the 1930s, when John L. Lewis stormed out of the convention of the American Federation of Labor (AFL) and formed what was to become the Congress of Industrial Organizations (CIO). The current debate was initiated by Andrew Stern, president of the Service Employees International Union (SEIU), and leaders of several other AFL-CIO unions who called for a more streamlined structure in which existing unions would merge, specialize on specific sectors, and focus on organizing strategic companies and communities.

To date, however, the debate is too narrowly focused on the structure of the labor movement. How many national unions should there be and what should be their jurisdictions? Should there be one union per industry or not? How do occupation-based unions and professional associations fit into the future structure? Who should be responsible for organizing the workers? What power and resources should reside in the AFL-CIO relative to national, state, and community-level bodies?

These are all important questions. But none of the proposals for reform challenges or questions whether the basic underlying organizing strategies or processes unions used to represent workers in the heyday of the twentieth century industrial economy are capable of giving workers the voice they need and want in this century's knowledge-based economy. This question will confront whoever emerges to lead the labor movement, under whatever structural arrangements are created.

So in this chapter I will lay out what I believe to be the deeper challenges and issues that must be addressed by local and national labor leaders and others committed to providing workers a voice at work and in society. In summary, these include the need for unions to (1) develop a new vision and strategy for recruiting and organizing and retaining members, (2) build and draw on new sources of power, (3) build sustainable coalitions and networks that cut across traditional unions and other groups and organizations that advocate for workers, and (4) reshape public policies governing worker voice and representation. Moreover, a deeper question must also be addressed: Will workers find their voice within the labor movement as we know it today or through other more varied groups, processes, and organizational arrangements that either complement or compete with traditional unions?

### Multiple Levels of Worker Voice

This chapter draws heavily on the conclusions my colleagues and I have reached through 30 years of research and involvement in efforts devoted to updating policies, practices, and institutions governing employment relations to better fit the changing workforce and economy. Deeply embedded in this work is the view that workers need a voice at four levels: (1) at the workplace, where they work, learn, and utilize their talents on a day to day basis; (2) through collective bargaining or some other means operating at the level of the firm, industry, or occupation where their basic terms of employment (wages, benefits, schedules, etc.) are set; (3) at the highest levels of the firms or organizations where the key strategic decisions affecting their long-run welfare are made; and (4) in the larger social and political processes in which decisions affecting all citizens are made. Before turning to how to restore workers' voice, we need to briefly review the current state of affairs at each of these levels.

### Voice at the Workplace

At the workplace, two sets of facts pose an apparent paradox. First, the number and percentage of people who want to join a union has been rising over the same time period that membership has been falling. In the 1970s, the first time a representative national sample of unorganized workers was asked whether they would vote in a union election if one were held on their job, 33 percent of the responses were in the affirmative (Kochan 1979). By the mid 1990s, this number rose to approximately 43 percent (Lipset and Meltz 2004; Freeman and Rogers 1999), and some more recent polls now put this number at around 50 percent (Hart and Associates 2002). Second, over this same 30 years, twice as many workers as those who would like to join a union consistently expressed a desire for alternative forms of worker voice that do not require taking the risks of organizing in the face of managerial opposition (Kochan, Katz, and Mower 1984; Freeman and Rogers 1999).

The paradox, then, is that today between 40 and 50 million American workers would prefer to be represented by a union but do not have access to representation, and perhaps as many as 60 to 80 million would like to have a more cooperative, consultative discussion with their employers over workplace issues but lack access to such a forum or process. These stark numbers reflect both the size of the representation gap present in American workplaces today and the potential support base for an alternative approach that addresses today's workers' aspirations and needs.

### Collective Bargaining

Throughout the twentieth century, collective bargaining served as the main tool for advancing the economic conditions of union members and of those non-union workers whose employers felt the need to match union gains. Collective bargaining has been most successful in advancing worker interests when two conditions were present: (1) unions organized, or served as a credible threat to organize, a sufficient part of the relevant labor and product market to "take wages out of competition," and (2) unions could mount a credible strike threat as a key source of power.

Today, both of these conditions are problematic. Global competition and the rise of domestic non-union competition in all but a few industries make it difficult to take wages out of competition, especially in situations where employers have the ability to locate, move, or threaten to move operations to alternative domestic or international locations. Moreover, since 1980, the strike, with some notable exceptions that I will discuss later, has largely turned into a defensive weapon used only as a very last resort to ward off aggressive employer demands for concessions. Prior to 1980, strikes were positively associated with wage gains; after 1980, the relationship between strikes and wage increases turned negative (Kochan, Katz, and McKersie 1986). Clearly, some alternative sources of power will be needed to advance worker interests in today's economy.

### Voice in Strategic Decisions and Corporate Governance

Recognition of the limits of traditional collective bargaining led us to argue that a broader transformation of labor management relations was needed to provide workers a voice where the real power lies and the key decisions that shape employees' long term security and welfare are made—that is the inner circle of executive decision-making and corporate governance. We envisioned a transformational model that combined direct forms of employee participation and flexible team-based work systems at the workplace, with greater emphasis on training and contingent compensation and employment security in collective bargaining, and various forms of union participation and partnership with management at strategic levels of firm decision-making (Kochan, Katz, and McKersie 1986).

Since this strategic level of management decision-making has traditionally been off-limits to workers and their unions under the National Labor Relations Act, we predicted that it would take significant reforms of this law to make this happen on any large scale. These reforms were not forthcoming. Thus, it is not surprising that recent national survey data show that less than 10 percent of bargaining relationships in the private sector have integrated innovations across these levels of activity in ways that approximate what we described as a transformation in labor management relations (Cutcher-Gershenfeld and Kochan 2004).

Unions have engaged in a variety of other efforts to gain power over management and corporate strategies. These include seeking seats on corporate boards (steel, trucking, airlines), negotiating commitments to neutrality in organizing campaigns (telecommunications, autos, aerospace), and mounting capital strategies aimed at using the leverage of union pension funds to mount shareholder resolutions on specific topics and/or to pressure companies to change specific antiworker practices (the AFL-CIO, several national unions, several state employee pension funds). All of these have had some successes and some show considerable promise. But none have penetrated more than a small fraction of the corporate world.

### National Affairs

Signs of the absence of labor's voice in national political affairs are abundant. Consider the now quarter-century-old impasse over whether and/or how to reform labor law. There is widespread recognition among independent experts that fundamental reforms of the National Labor Relations Act are warranted (Commission on the Future of Worker Management Relations 1994, 1995). The law simply no longer delivers on its promise to provide American workers with the ability to join a union for the purposes of collective bargaining if that is their desire. But the reality is that despite efforts by some of our profession's most respected scholars and policy officials, Congress and the president failed three times over the past three decades to address the demonstrated failures of labor law. Each time political considerations and forces blocked reform, and each successive time reform advocates came less close to success (Mills 1979; Kochan 1995).

Today, labor law reform is completely off the political agenda. In fact, the actions taken by the Bush administration have further weakened worker voice and set back positive labor management relations—ending of project agreements in construction, ending labor management partnerships in the federal government, eliminating rights to union representation and civil service protections for over 60,000 federal employees under the guise of concern for national security, and so on. So there is little or no prospect for constructive policy reform at the national level for the foreseeable future.

Dialogue among top business, labor, and government leaders has also dissipated to perhaps its lowest level since the 1930s. Unlike his predecessors, President Bush has to date seen no need and shown no interest in asking national labor leaders to join him and business leaders to work together to help pull the country through a prolonged period of national crisis and the war on terrorism (not to mention the war in Iraq). Longstanding forums for business/labor dialogue such as the National Policy Association (formerly the National Planning Association), the Collective Bargaining Forum, the Work in America Institute, and several private labor management groups have disbanded. The demise of these forums signals a perception on the part of business and government leaders that it is no longer necessary to build and maintain communications and personal relationships with America's top labor leaders.

## Out of the Ashes: Reinventing Unions and
## Professional Associations

John Sweeney won the first ever contested election for the presidency of the AFL-CIO in 1995, promising to renew the labor movement's commitment to organizing. He attempted to reinvigorate organizing efforts by expanding and strengthening the AFL-CIO's Organizing Institute, recruiting talented and dedicated young people to the labor movement, and urging national unions to put more resources into organizing. But these efforts have not produced a resurgence in membership, in large part because the traditional organizing model is incapable of turning the labor movement around.

Following the traditional organizing model under the NLRA, it takes a majority of workers in a given location or bargaining unit to vote to join and be represented by a union for collective bargaining. If a majority is not achieved, none of those who prefer to be represented gain representation. It is an all or nothing, high-risk venture. To get a majority to vote for a union, the evidence shows that workers must be deeply dissatisfied with and distrust their employer, risk their jobs or career prospects, and hold on for two to three years before any benefits are likely to be realized (Kochan 1979; Wheeler 1985). Their chances of winning an election are on average about 50 percent, and considerably lower if the employer resists or delays the process, as they are counseled to do by their lawyers and consultants (Brofenbrenner and Juravich 1998). And even if they gain certification, these workers face another 30 percent chance that their union will not be able to achieve a first contract or sustain a relationship with the employer (Commission on the Future of Worker Management Relations 1994).

The basic value proposition unions offer under the traditional organizing model is that if they can get and sustain collective bargaining relationships over time they are likely to deliver to their members a 10 to 15 percent wage and benefit premium, increased protections and rights for more senior workers, protections against unfair disciplinary action or discharge, and a labor contract with clear rules enforceable through grievance arbitration. But achieving these benefits is not certain, and it will likely take at least a year, and considerably longer if the employer resists strongly, and may require a threatened or actual work stoppage.

These threshold conditions for gaining access to representation via the traditional organizing model are simply too high and the potential gains too risky and limited for all but the most desperate workers. Thus, it is not surprising that for many years this approach has not come close to yielding the 500,000 or more new union members needed to keep constant, much less increase, union density, given the slow growth in the labor force and the attrition of union jobs (Freeman 2003). In 2004, for example, the National Labor Relations Board held 2,299 certification elections. Unions won 53 percent of these, yielding a total of approximately 160,000 new members. Another 420 decertification elections were held, however, and unions lost 65 percent of these, resulting in a loss of approximately 13,650 workers.

These numbers, the proportion of wins and losses, and certification/decertification ratios have been relatively stable over the past decade (National Labor Relations Board 2004). Since one of the strongest predictors of union success in organizing is the degree of managerial opposition encountered, the ultimate irony is that by following this traditional organizing approach, it is largely American *managers and their consultants*, not American workers or unions, who decide who will be organized.

**Table 3.1**   What Attracts Employees by Age

| Top Attractors | U.S. Overall | 18–29 | 30–44 | 45–54 | 55+ |
|---|---|---|---|---|---|
| Competitive Base Pay/Salary | ● | ● | ● | ● | ● |
| Competitive Health Care Benefits Package | ● | ● | ● | ● | ● |
| Opportunities for Advancement | 1 | 1 | 2 | | 3 |
| Work/Life Balance | 2 | 2 | 1 | 2 | |
| Competitive Retirement Benefits Package | 3 | | | 1 | 1 |
| Pay Raises Linked to Individual Performance | 3 | | 3 | 3 | 2 |
| Learning and Development Opportunities | | 3 | | | |

Source: Towers Perrin Talent Report 2001: New Realities in Today's Workforce
Key: ● Core rewards that rank at the top for all groups, 1–3 Top differentiators in rank order

So how might this organizing model be changed to better fit what workers need and want today? A place to start is to recognize how workers needs and priorities change as they move through different stages of their careers at work and family life. Table 3.1 summarizes this point vividly, by showing the common and different priorities workers of different ages and family situations bring to work. Good wages and benefits remain as important as ever to today's workers. Regardless of age, these are expected to be part of any good job and, therefore, the first responsibility of any institution that seeks to represent workers is to address these needs.

But that is not enough. Young workers are especially concerned about gaining access to opportunities to learn and advance on their job. Balancing work and family life is a high priority throughout normal child bearing and raising ages, and it rises to the top priority as people move through middle age. Retirement security rises in priority as people advance in age and approach the later stages of their working years.

### Positive Vision and Strategy

To interest and mobilize these modern workers, the next generation unions will need a positive vision and strategy that addresses these common and varied needs. That means going beyond the traditional organizing model that relies on deep dissatisfaction, frustration, and distrust of one's employer before turning to collective representation. Unions must offer a hopeful, positive vision of how workers themselves can realize their aspirations over the course of their careers and family life stages. Some unions are already doing so.

The organizing slogans of the HUCTW (Harvard Union of Clerical and Technical Workers) illustrate this approach quite nicely: "You don't have to be anti-Harvard to be pro-Union" and "Harvard works because we do" (Hoerr 1997). The union backs up these slogans with an organizing strategy that emphasizes building a supportive community and network among employees, before seeking collective bargaining certification.

This same approach has been successful in organizing predominantly female healthcare workers in Massachusetts, Minnesota, and elsewhere. The fact that women respond well to such an organizing strategy should not be surprising. For many years, women have expressed significantly greater interest in joining unions than their white male counterparts (Kochan 1979; Freeman and Rogers 1999; Lipset and Melt 2004). In fact, women accounted for nearly three-fourths of all new union members in the 1990s. So addressing the needs of women is clearly a necessary condition for restoring voice at work and meeting the needs of working families. Strategies such as those followed by the HUCTW and other unions that have been successful in organizing large numbers of women need to be pursued more extensively.

While work/family balance and integration are not solely women's issues, the reality is that women have been on the forefront of this movement, are likely to respond with more enthusiasm to organizations that champion this cause, put it high on their agenda, and provide leadership to such efforts. Women are a prime constituency and potential source not only of new union members, but also of new creative ideas, energy, and leadership.

Some critics of the HUCTW approach say it is too expensive and takes too long to achieve majority representation status. It took nearly a decade for this union to gain majority status and formal recognition at Harvard. One labor law scholar (Morris 2005) has proposed a solution to this problem by suggesting labor law that recognizes and protects workers' right to be represented by a union even before it demonstrates it has majority support. So perhaps the National Labor Relations Act is not as rigid and difficult to use in organizing workers as conventional wisdom and practice would have us believe.

## Lifetime Memberships

Under the standard industrial organizing model, union membership and representation are linked to a specific job or bargaining unit. Once a worker leaves the job, representation is lost. Given this, it is not surprising that today there are twice as many former union members in the country as there are current members.

An alternative approach, better suited to today's mobile workforce, would be to build on a craft or professional organizational model and recruit individual workers and family members independent of their workplace and employer and outside of the process built into labor law. Once recruited, the relationship with members could be maintained for life by providing the labor market and educational services and benefits that individuals and families need as they move through different stages of their careers and family lives. Consistent with the history of the way many unions began, these types of organizations might serve as mutual benefit organizations by providing workers with health insurance, savings programs that build retirement security, lifelong education, work/family supports, the social networks and information needed to find jobs when required, and quick and effective advice and representation to solve problems and, if necessary, representation of workers in trouble, individually and collectively.

A good deal of experimentation is already underway with this approach. Clearly, craft unions in the building trades and professional associations such as the Screen Actors Guild and others have followed this approach for many years. Both the National Education Association and the American Federation of Teachers recruit and provide an array of representational services and benefits to teachers under collective bargaining contracts and also to those unable to obtain formal bargaining recognition. Working

**Table 3.2**   Working America

---

WORKING AMERICA is people like you—working women and men, retirees, people who want to set America's priorities straight.

WORKING AMERICA, a community affiliate of the AFL-CIO, is a powerful force for working people. With the combined strength of 13 million union men and women and millions of nonunion workers who share common challenges and goals, we fight in communities, states and nationally for what really matters—good jobs, affordable health care, world-class education, secure retirements, real homeland security and more.

And we work against wrong-headed priorities favoring the rich and corporate special interests over America's well-being.

WORKING AMERICA uses professional research, communication, education, canvassing, lobbying and community organizing to demand that politicians address the priorities that matter most to working people—not just wealthy special interests. Make a difference for your community, for America and for your working family.

---

*Source*:  http://www.workingamerica.org

America, an innovative organization described in table 3.2, follows this approach in providing an array of healthcare supports, networking, and other benefits and services to independent contractors in New York's media industries. The Communications Workers of America (CWA) has experiments underway such as Washtech, the Alliance at IBM, and an internal organizing effort called WAGE at General Electric. An increasing number of unions and professional associations are championing lifelong learning for their members. Joint funds for this purpose have been negotiated by unions from several industries, namely communications, aerospace, auto, steel, and most recently healthcare. These build on the longstanding role that craft and professional unions and associations have played in providing apprenticeships, continuing education and certification credits, and related programs. Clearly, this is a major area of need for the America workforce, and an opportunity for unions and professional associations to both recruit and serve future members.

As noted, table 3.2 describes Working America, another approach to recruiting individuals developed by the AFL-CIO. Approximately one million individuals have joined this organization in its first two years of operation, largely in response to door to door canvassing in selected states and communities. Working America's executive director thus summarizes his organization's goals and the means of achieving them:

The key to our success so far is that we tap into the central economic concerns of working families both nationally and in the communities we target. We have been especially active on overtime pay and the exporting of jobs. Our members delivered 35,000 letters to President Bush protesting his new overtime rules. Our "ask a lawyer" page on our Web site got 50,000 inquiries on the new rules. Our "job tracker" feature—where a member can enter a zip code and find out who is exporting jobs in their community—has had 500,000 visits in the past three months. The long-run goal of Working America is to provide a political voice for people who do not have a collective bargaining relationship. We want to create a new source of worker power that is geographically based and that makes full use of the Web to activate workers and encourages them to get involved in electoral and legislative affairs and to hold elected officials accountable.

## Direct Participation

Today's workers want a direct voice. They no more want to be told how they are being represented by a centralized bureaucratic union or association than they want to be told to trust that management will take care of their interests. Having a direct voice in how to do one's job, how to improve the flow of work, and how to build a collaborative, high-trust work environment increases job satisfaction, dignity, and self-worth. Worker participation, combined with other appropriate workplace innovations and investments in technology, has also been associated with increased product and service quality and productivity.

Moreover, Black and Lynch (2001) demonstrated that these positive performance benefits are higher in settings that combine transformed union/management relationships with direct participation than in non-union settings, both participatory and non-participatory. So any modern system of worker voice and representation must be based on a foundation of employee participation in the day-to-day affairs, particularly in the processes of taking decisions that affect how they do their jobs and how they can better contribute to the success of the enterprise.

American industry has developed lots of ways to do this, dating back to the ideas for improving the quality of work included in the original *Work in America* volume, through the circle movement of the early 1980s, to the broader use of team-based work systems introduced in recent years (Lawler, Mohrman, and Ledford 1998). The challenge with these processes lies in sustaining them through turnover of managers and others who championed their creation or through the first budget crunch, layoff, or other normal crises that one can expect to occur.

Some unions have been in the forefront in promoting opportunities for their members to gain a stronger voice in how they do their work. In the 1980s, unions in the auto, steel, telecommunications, and apparel industries were all active in various efforts to negotiate and co-lead efforts to create team-based work systems. Some of these have survived, some have not. More recently, similar efforts have been made in healthcare. Kaiser Permanente and its coalition of healthcare unions have made active joint efforts to promote joint workplace initiatives aimed at the quality and efficiency of healthcare delivery and the availability of new career opportunities and ladders for employees.

However, too many labor leaders still tend to view employee participation as a two-edged sword. On the one hand, most now recognize that the majority of their members want a direct voice, and that if properly structured, these processes can produce higher job and union satisfaction and improved economic performance (Kochan, Katz, and Mower 1984; Appelbaum, Bailey, Berg, and Kalleberg 2000). On the other hand, they have seen firms use employee participation as a strategy to prevent possible union formation and/or to undermine existing unions. This ambivalence continues to constrain efforts to diffuse and institutionalize participation processes in American industry. Overcoming it will require legal reforms that both protect workers from managerial efforts to use these processes to substitute for or undermine unions and to give *workers and their unions* the ability to initiate and sustain a direct dialogue at the workplace, with or without managerial champions.

On this score, Europe is ahead of America by several decades. Most European countries, including recently all member countries of the European Union, provide all employees in an enterprise the right to elect representatives to a "works council," a representative body that meets, consults, and works with management on issues of workplace and workforce. I will come back to discuss the public policy changes needed to support this type of workplace representation in the last section of this essay.

## Building New Sources of Power

Where will the power come from to deliver tangible benefits to workers and their families? If the strike threat is too narrow and limited a source of power, what else is there? Just as social scientists have long recognized that there are multiple sources of power available to individuals (French and Raven 1962), so too the labor movement needs to see its potential power as coming from varied sources and work to build and leverage them.

### Knowledge and Skills

The most important sources of power workers can bring to their jobs today are their knowledge and skills and the readiness to put them to work. Knowledge is a necessary prerequisite for workers to have the individual bargaining power to navigate success-fully in today's labor markets. Thus, unions need to expand current efforts to provide workers with the lifelong education and training needed to keep their skills current. Lifelong educational opportunities can be one of the key benefits and services unions offer to recruit and retain lifelong members. If unions and professional associations take up this role, it will help society wean itself from dependence on individual firms and help overcome the market's failure to supply the optimal amount of training in marketable skills.

### Information and Communications

Today, information is one of the most important sources of power available for exploitation. Consider the successful efforts of the coalition of forces that have come together to expose and publicize exploitation of labor in the supply chains of transnational companies. The campaigns to fight child labor and to achieve fair labor standards for employees of Nike and other highly visible transnational firms came about because of the publicity given to exposés of violations of basic human rights of workers in these companies' supply chains in developing countries (Locke 2003). The few successful strikes that have occurred in recent years, such as the IBT-UPS strike in 1997 and the various Justice for Janitors' efforts in cities such as Los Angeles and Boston, were successful in part (perhaps in large part) because they were able to gain broad public understanding and support for their cause. A sustained and effective, multichannel information and communications strategy is essential to any modern organization, including a modern labor movement.

The Internet is one obvious tool to support using information and transparency as a key source of power for labor. Freeman and Rogers (2002) used the term "open source unionism" to emphasize this point. Clearly, the Internet is a tool that all modern organizations and social movements need to master and incorporate into their strategies. Labor is no exception.

More traditional media channels are equally important. Often labor leaders complain that the existing media is biased against them, only covers labor when there is a conflict, and therefore misses the good things labor does on an ongoing basis. By and large, this is an accurate critique of the current media. Changing this bias and increasing exposure to the concerns and perspectives of working families will require a significant investment of talent and resources on the part of the labor movement.

Workers and their families need their own counterpart to report on developments in the business and financial markets, one that captures the ups and downs of working in America today. This media counterpart would mix positive examples and pragmatic tips on what it takes to navigate today's careers and labor markets and to get ahead with examples of the injustices that continue to prevail and ideas for what can be done to remedy them. The fact that books such as *Nickel and Dimed* (Ehrenreich 2002) have been so popular and widely acclaimed suggests that there is a large ready audience for this type of information about work—something that we are already witnessing in today's world.

### Exit

Industrial unions have emphasized voice over exit as their bread and butter strategy. That emphasis fit the stable workplace and long-term employment relationships many union members both wanted and experienced. And for many this will continue to be the dominant way unions improve the working conditions and lives of their members.

But for a significant portion of the workforce, particularly for more educated, mobile professionals, the ability to move from a job that does not meet their needs or expectations to a better one is equally important. And, over time, reducing the costs of mobility and making exit a more viable option serves as a key source of power not only for the employees who move but for those who stay. As any manager (or dean) will attest, nothing focuses the mind or generates improved conditions like a credible alternative job offer. Thus, reducing the costs of inter-firm or geographic mobility by providing information on job opportunities, contacts and referrals, and portable benefits could be an increasingly important source of power for unions and professional associations. Clearly, this is not a new idea or development. But it is one that labor organizations may want to focus on more intensively in the future.

### Labor's Capital Investments

American workers' investments are a sleeping giant that, when mobilized, has enormous potential for exercising power. A recent example described by John Sweeney illustrates this potential. Following publication of a message from a Morgan Stanley analyst that warned against investing in unionized companies, John Sweeney wrote Morgan's CEO a letter (with a copy to union pension funds that use Morgan's services) indicating labor's strong disagreement with this point of view. The response from Morgan's CEO was quick and decisive: a personal visit to John Sweeney, a clarification that the analyst did not represent the view of Morgan Stanley, a public clarification of the firm's view of unions, and an engagement with the analyst on the productive contribution that unions make to a firm's financial performance (Morgan Stanley 2003). Morgan Stanley understood immediately the potential power of a large, unhappy client.

The AFL-CIO and several unions have been active in developing shareholder resolutions and other capital strategies. The evidence from these efforts is that they are more successful when they focus on governance issues or executive compensation rather than traditional workforce or labor/management issues and when they are done in coalition with other groups, such as Institutional Shareholders Services (Chakrabarti 2004). Specific pension funds, such as CALPERS and those in strong union states such as New Jersey and Wisconsin, have also been supportive and active in shareholder resolution campaigns. Clearly, this is a direction for the future.

### Corporate Governance and Accountability

Engagement in governance processes is not likely to become widespread unless a different conception of the role of the corporation in society is articulated and pursued. As long as the view that corporations exist to maximize shareholder value prevails over a view that corporations should be held accountable to shareholders, workers, and communities, workers will not have a legitimate claim to having a direct voice in strategic decisions or governance processes. Unfortunately, even at the peak of the debate over what to do about recent corporate scandals, labor did not join this issue directly. Yet there are even some CEOs and other leaders in civil society who make this point in their speeches and rhetoric. Labor needs to take them at their word and become the champion for getting a direct and influential voice in corporate management and governance.

Articulating this point of view clearly, forcefully, and creatively could provide a vision for the twenty-first century corporation that is both well grounded in theory and resonates well with the workforce. Economists and organization theorists have argued that knowledge and human capital will serve as the critical sources of competitive advantage in corporations today and in the future (Blair 1995; Blair and Stout 1999). If this is true, then workers have just as legitimate a claim to have a voice in corporate governance as do investors of finance capital. Workers invest their human capital in their companies, and each day they stay they put more of their capital at risk. Yet unlike investors of financial capital, they are not afforded a role in governance. Like investors, workers who invest and put at risk their human capital in corporations need access to information regarding the decisions being made that affect their long term investments—the stability of their jobs, pensions, benefits, and careers.

This could be achieved in various ways, ranging from providing workers legal rights to information, to allowing or requiring American-styled works councils that would receive and share information and consult on human resource issues, to providing workers' seats on pension funds and corporate boards. All of these would require changes in labor and/or corporate laws. These are the types of reforms of labor and corporate law that are more likely to resonate and build support among a cross-section of the workforce and voting public than calls for more narrowly focused labor law reforms.

### Coalitions and Networks

Labor cannot go it alone. Labor's biggest wins in recent years have come when labor unions in specific communities have built coalitions with community, religious, civil rights, women and family advocates, and other groups. Labor has formed coalitions with local affiliates of organizations such as the National Interfaith Alliance, the

Industrial Areas Foundation, and ACORN. Working together, these coalitions have passed living-wage ordinances, supported "no-sweat" campaigns, implemented school reforms, and created employment and training programs. Osterman (2003) has documented one such highly successful effort in South Texas that he argued could serve as a model for rebuilding the tradition of progressive politics in America. These examples point out the importance of building networks and coalitions with diverse grassroot groups and expanding the reach and influence of the labor movement. Union leaders have as much to learn and gain from working with these community organizers and grassroot groups as these groups have to learn and gain from union support.

### Complementary or Competing Forms of Worker Voice

So far I have focused on efforts to restore workers' voice by rebuilding and revitalizing labor unions. But this is not the only way in which this voice is exercised at work today and it is not likely to be the exclusive means in the future. Labor has historically had a schizophrenic attitude toward other forms of worker representation. Part of this reflects an egotistical view that organized labor is the only legitimate institution for representing workers and their families. But as noted earlier, it partly reflects the insecurity of the labor movement, given its vulnerability to historic efforts of employers to undermine independent unions with company-sponsored unions or participation processes. Yet, since alternative forms of representation will continue to prevail in the future, the question is whether these alternatives are treated as complements or competitors to unions. Several of the more visible forms will be discussed briefly below.

#### Passion with an Umbrella

Scully and Segal (2001) used the term "Passion with an Umbrella" to describe the growing number of informal groups arising in corporations that seek to bring about change by working within the prevailing culture of an organization. Some of these are known as "identity" groups, since these are formed around specific racial, gender, ethnic, or other personal or social attributes. One of the earliest and most successful of these was the Black Caucus at Xerox that started as far back as the 1970s (Friedman 1993). More recently, women faculty groups demonstrated the power of this type of effort for raising awareness of and addressing gender equity and advancement issues at MIT and in other universities (Bailyn 2003).

This approach will very likely continue to grow in the future, since it matches the preferences a majority of the workforce expresses for collective action by employees who share a commitment to the overall goals and values of their employer but are not afraid to raise tough issues that need attention and that do not encounter strong management resistance. While these groups are most prevalent within professional and white-collar employees, others, such as the Korean Immigrant Workers Advocates, have successfully mobilized Koreans working in restaurants and other service jobs in selected cities (Cho 2003). Others are allied with various workers' centers located in various cities (Fine 2003).

These networks use race, gender, national origin, or other sources of personal or social identity as the community of interest around which to organize. As such, they pose an interesting question: Are the bases for mobilizing workers shifting from a common economic community of interest (same occupation, production unit, employer, and so on) to a personal or social base? If so, will these serve as coalition partners with unions, as has been the case in some organizing drives among Haitian nursing-home workers (Yu 2005), or will they operate informally and separately, as is the case for a Latino group known as La Raza that has been negotiating with major food processing firms to improve the working conditions of newly arrived immigrants (Kochan 2005)? Whichever pattern dominates, clearly these types of groups will be part of the mix of institutions providing employees a voice and representation in the future.

## Nongovernmental Organizations (NGOs)

As noted earlier, a variety of NGOs have been formed in the past decade to pressure transnational firms to comply with core labor standards. Some of these are working in coalitions with existing unions. Others are operating independently. Clearly, the labor movement has a lot to learn from the successes of these organizations and has a lot to offer them in return. NGOs have been very successful in using modern communications, networking, and, information as means of engaging large, visible, consumer-market companies. Many unions are working in partnership with NGOs, but some have chosen to pull out of these coalitions over disagreements over tactics or other issues (Bernstein 2005). In turn, some NGOs have sought support from unions, while others have stayed at arm's length. As with other such groups, it is unclear how NGOs will coexist with more traditional unions in the United States or in other countries around the world.

## Professional Associations

The line between a union and professional association has become blurred in recent decades, as various associations of teachers, nurses, engineers, entertainers and other media specialists, athletes, and other professionals have taken up the process of collective bargaining. Professionals report strong interests in representation and in the *form* that representation takes. Specifically, professionals prefer organizations limited to their specific occupation/profession, those that are led by members of their profession who identify and understand their values, needs, and technical work, uphold professional standards and service quality, and actively promote their professional interests in public policy debates affecting their profession (Department of Professional Employees 2005).

Moreover, since they see these as issues that transcend the boundaries of their specific or current employer, they prefer to see these issues addressed outside the workplace, and if addressed within the workplace, they want to see them addressed in what they perceive as a "professional manner." That is, they expect their employers to engage them without strong resistance or high levels of conflict. At the same time, professionals expect to be compensated fairly, and so they also expect their organizations to advocate basic wage and benefit improvements.

This profile leads to wide variations in the preference for or against traditional collective bargaining across professional groups. For example, teachers and nurses indicate a higher preference for collective bargaining than do engineers and information technology specialists. Where collective bargaining is used, a majority of professionals prefer labor/management partnership modes of interaction rather than more traditional arm's-length or positional forms of negotiations (Eaton, Rubinstein, and Kochan forthcoming).

For professional, this profile has profound implications for how employee voice and representation is likely to evolve. Many professional associations that currently do not engage in formal collective bargaining neither consider themselves nor are counted as "unions," yet they do engage in various forms of collective action and provide many of the lifetime labor market services, such as job referrals, continuing education, certification, and networking that were suggested as part of a new organizing model for labor unions. Thus, these associations are likely to play a growing and significant role in the mix of institutions and processes for providing voice and representation for this professional segment of the labor force.

## Politics and the Law

Union representation has risen and fallen in long cycles in the United States. Declines tend to be gradual and extended; rebirths and resurgence, like the rise of the CIO in the 1930s and the emergence of public sector unionism in the 1960s, tend to come in abrupt and unpredictable bursts. Each time, labor's resurgence tends to coincide with the emergence of a new vision and strategy for how to rebuild unions in line with a changing economy and workforce and a shift in public policy to support the new forms of representation. The rise of industrial unionism in the 1930s was supported by the passage of the National Labor Relations Act, and the rise of public sector unions in the 1960s was supported by new federal and state policies providing collective bargaining for public sector workers.

This suggests that the reforms and shifts in strategy outlined above are a necessary, but not sufficient, condition for restoring workers' voice at work and in society. A fundamental overhaul of labor and employment policies will be needed to support and protect employees who seek to reassert a voice at work in ways that fit the needs and preferences of today's workforce and economy. This means that the demonstrated failures of basic labor laws to protect workers who want to join a union need to be fixed. But this is just a necessary starting point. Also, labor and employment laws need to be updated to provide workers with the ability to create and sustain the more cooperative or collaborative forms of participation and representation that they consistently indicate they want and that have demonstrated their value to both employees and the economy. As noted earlier, most European nations (and the European Community) do this through works councils. Some American adaptation of this approach will be needed if the preferences of the workforce and the needs of the economy are to be met.

The lessons from failed efforts to break the business/labor deadlock of the past quarter century are clear. The American public will need to see a rebuilding of worker voice as critical to dealing with the problems they face at work and in their families and communities, and their voices will need to be added to those of the traditional business/labor interests (Kochan 2005). In short, breaking the impasse will require mobilization of political support among the American public.

## Summary

The cumulative effects of labor union decline have left a void in worker voice at work, eroded the standard of living in America, and weakened our democracy. If the decline in unions continues, American workers and American society in general will increasingly be at risk. Workers will have less job security, more exposure to arbitrary treatment and dismissal, and diminished retirement and healthcare benefits. Those pressuring for redress of workers' grievances will continue to seek relief in the court system, leading to a situation where only the high-income workers capable of attracting contingency-fee lawyers will have access to workplace justice. This is clearly not the type of society or employment relations system that serves our values or our economy well.

Standard calls for union resurgence—to put more resources into traditional union organizing, to reform labor law, or even to promote greater dialogue, cooperation, or consensus between business and labor—have not worked and will not work on their own to reverse the decline in worker voice.

More fundamental changes are needed, ones that build on a vision capable of addressing the aspirations and expectations workers bring to their work, careers, and families, a strategy for recruiting individuals into lifelong membership in unions, structures that support community, state, and national initiatives and coalition building, and a broadening out of the sources of power that unions see as part of their tool kit.

Many of the pieces of this alternative approach are already being tried out in isolated experiments within individual unions around the country. The time appears ripe for such an effort, given the pressures on working families today, the void in political leadership and discourse on these issues, the loss of confidence in corporate leaders and market forces, and the toll that is being exacted on current and future generations by the war on terror, and the domestic and international tensions that will very likely continue to be with us in its aftermath.

America is once again at a historic crossroads with respect to worker voice. We can begin by working collaboratively to fashion the next generation organizations, institutions, groups, and forums for engaging the voice of today's workers and their families in constructive ways that can produce mutual gains for workers, families, and the economy and society. Or we can continue to ignore and suppress efforts to restore voice at work and in society and wait for the pressures on working families to put us in a perilous quandary. The longer we wait for the crisis, the more we risk recreating the adversarial culture and modes of interaction that characterized the industrial era.

# 4

# Work and Family in America: Growing Tensions between Employment Policy and a Transformed Workforce

*Ellen Ernst Kossek*

Housekeeping may still be the main occupation of American women, but it is no longer the only occupation or source of identity for most of them. In the past, a woman's sense of identity and her main source of satisfaction centered on her husband's job, the home, and the family. Today, there are alternatives opening to increasing numbers of the female population. In addition to the fact that half of all women between the ages of 18 and 64 are presently in the labor force, Department of Labor studies show that 9 out of 10 of women will work outside of the home at some time in their lives.

The clear fact is that keeping house and raising children is work—-work that is, on the average as difficult to do well and as useful to the larger society as almost any paid job involving the production of goods or services. The difficulty is not that most people don't believe this or accept it (we pay lip service to it all the time) but that, whatever our private and informal belief systems, we have not, as a society, acknowledged this fact in our public system of values and rewards. *Work in America* 1973:56–57, 179

About 30 years ago, the *Work in America* (1973) report noted the countervailing trends of growing numbers of women juggling work and family (W–F) coupled with ambivalence over societal support of domestic and caregiving work. Kanter (1977) articulated the "myth of separate worlds" between work and family—the notion that workplaces often are designed as if workers do not have families that compete for their attention and identities during working time.

Now, in the twenty-first century, these same issues are still largely unresolved and increasing in scope and complexity, while work-family tensions have risen for virtually all demographics and occupations across the nation. The need for policy innovation on a national level is highlighted by statistics showing trends where all workers will have some responsibility for managing care for a child, an elder, or a disabled family member (including self) at some point during their lifetime (see table 4.1).

**Table 4.1**  Summary of Demographic, Legal, and Social Trends Increasing Work-Family Tensions

| Trend | Supporting Statistics |
|---|---|
| 1. Transformati on of family economic household configuration: Dual earner family is modal American family | Employment Status of Parents with Children under 18 (rounded):<br><br>• Two parent dual earner (41%), single mother employed (16%),<br>• Two parent, husband sole earner (21%), two parent, mother sole earner (4%)<br>• Single father employed (5%), unemployed single mother (7%), unemployed two parent (4%), unemployed single father (1%) (CPS, Bianchi, and Raley 2005) |
| 2. Growth in nontraditional families | • A majority of adults will cohabitate with another adult for some life period.<br>• One-third of all births occur now outside marriage<br>• 40% of children will live in a cohabitating family and 50% of all children will live in a single parent household (usually female) before reaching 18 years old (Cohen 2002)<br>• 15% of the workforce between 40–65 years are "sandwich generation" employees, who must manage care for both aging parents and financially dependent children or grandchildren (Ingersoll-Dayton et al. 2001; Nichols and Junk 1997) |
| 3. Increase in employee caregiving responsibilities | • 80% of U.S. wage and salaried workers live with family members and have immediate day to day family responsibilities when away from the workplace (Bond et al. 2002)<br>• *Child care*: 43% workers report they have a child under 18 years living at home at least half the year<br>• *Elder Care*: A third (35%)had significant elder care demands in the past year (reported by equal proportions of men and women) (Bond et al. 2002) |
| 4. Population decline in replacement workers: From pyramids to pillars | One of the fastest growing U.S. population segments is individuals over 55 years old, and a workforce shortage is also predicted as baby boomers are reaching retirement. A 2003 SHRM report indicates that over the ten years leading up to 2010, the number of workers between 25 and 54 will increase by 5%, and the number of workers over 55 years will increase by 46.6%; 2003 fertility rates declined to 1.9 children in U.S. compared to 3.1 in 1976 (Riche 2006) |
| 5. Rise in work hours and loads and work-family conflicts and intensification | • Couples in dual earner households averaged of 3932 hours in 2000, an increase of 300 hours (7.5 additional work weeks per year) since 1989 and equal to more than 2 full-time EU jobs (Mishel, Bernstein, and Boushley 2003)<br>• U.S. workers worked an average 1,978 hours per year in 2001 (Berg et al. 2004). Americans work the longest work hours in the world except Korea (OECD 2004)<br>• 38% NSCW respondents state they must choose between advancing in their jobs or devoting attention to their families (Bond et al. 2002) |
| 6. Growth in participation of women in labor force and key occupations, but varying by age of | • Since 1975, labor force participation of U.S. women with children under age 18 has increased from 47% to 78% (U.S. Dept. of Labor 2004)<br>• Changing occupational profile of women in workforce; 39% of professional and managerial positions were held by women compared to 24% in 1977 (Bond et al. 2002) |

Continued

**Table 4.1**  Continued

| Trend | Supporting Statistics |
|---|---|
| children and marital status | • One-third of mothers with working husbands and children under age six did not work at all in 2002 compared to 80% of married women with children between 5–18 years (U.S. Bureau of Labor Statistics 2003; Riche 2006) |
| 7. Increase in new work and career structures | • Growth in preferences for part time or reduced load work for some segments, e.g., NSCW shows that 25% of working women held part time jobs or jobs with reduced schedules as their main job compared to 9% of men. About two-thirds of women work part time and half of men do so by choice, even though 61% of part time jobs often received pro-rated health care and lower pay (Bond et al. 2002, 10) <br> • Growing numbers of workers are delaying retirement or working part time in second career until their 1960s or 1970s as opposed to an up and out thirty-year career (Moen 2003) |
| 8. Changing beliefs about gender roles and work-home relationships | • A Radcliffe Center and Harris poll (2000) stated that over four-fifths of men in their 20s and 30s believed that a work schedule that allowed for family time was more important to them than a challenging or high-paying job, a dramatic shift from earlier generations <br> • In 1977, 74% of NSCW men believed that men should earn the money and women should stay home to take care of the children & the house compared to only 42% in 2002 <br> • In 1977, barely half (49%) of men surveyed in the NSCW believed that employed mothers could have just as good relationships with their children as mothers who only work in the home in 1977. In 2002 that number had risen to nearly two thirds of men surveyed (Bond et al. 2002) <br> • Men do between 38% and 40% of the domestic chores, if the statistic counts child care and not just housework (Lee and Waite, in press) |
| 9. Technology and 24–7 global work blurring boundaries between work and home | • 15% of employed workers work or telework from home at least once a week (U.S. Census Bureau 2002) <br> • Increase in major U.S. companies operating work sites overseas (e.g., India, China) |

This chapter will show that while over the last 30 years employed workers' responsibilities for managing caregiving and domestic life have generally increased and some policies have been formally adopted, an implementation gap remains where U.S. public and private W-F policy is out of sync with labor market developments. The failure of the U.S. to develop a coordinated W-F policy through federal and state, public and private partnerships and to move toward some new collective cultural solutions for W-F conflicts may impact the long-term competitiveness and resilience of its workforce.

This chapter unfolds as follows: I provide a brief overview of the current U.S. W-F policy approach. I then discuss historical, demographic, and legal, developments since the 1973 report. I review three main content areas of organizational support for work and life and discuss implications for employment policy. Overall, I argue that administrative, legal, and cultural employer practices pertinent to work and family are significantly lagging behind societal changes (Kossek 2005).

## U.S. Work and Family Policy Overview

### U.S. Macro Approach

Relative to other industrialized countries, the United States is unique in providing limited public supports for employees' work and family demands and in heavily relying on a patchwork system of voluntary private employer supports (such as flexible work schedules, leaves, childcare and eldercare, vacation and sick time, healthcare) that are mostly available from larger firms (Kelly 2006). The main national U.S. policy, the Family Medical Leave Act (FMLA), which provides only 12 weeks of *unpaid leave* to care for a child, elder or self, because of workforce size (minimum 50 employees) and other limitations, in practice covers only about 11 percent of the U.S. workplaces, which employ about 58 percent of workers (Canter et al. 2000). In contrast, countries in the European Union (EU) provide 14 weeks *paid* leave to mothers, and most offer additional partially paid parental leave (Kelly 2006). In most EU countries, childcare for children under age three is a public service, and the government often trains, employs, and subsidizes childcare workers (Kelly 2006).

Internationally, the United States is distinctive in following what Block, Berg, and Belman (2004) refer to as "a minimalist market-based employer approach," where an unregulated free-market labor economy is viewed as efficient and fair. Employers have wide latitude to determine the degree to which they will support workers' family needs. Block and colleagues see the U.S.'s individualistic cultural generally valuing a limited role for government regulation, with caregiving decisions left up to the discretion of individual employees and employers, as a barrier to policy innovation. Today, in the United States, the lack of a strong collective voice (like the voice the unions in the EU provide) that speaks for workers' social issues at corporate or government levels is identified as another barrier.

Leaving the nation's W-F policy to the voluntary *noblesse oblige* of employers presents long-term risks to labor-force quality and the nation's health. While some workplace practices such as flexible work schedules have the potential to directly increase employer competitiveness, raising talent attraction and retention and reducing absenteeism, others, such as investing in the quality of childcare and eldercare in a community, are unlikely to be self-funded. The direct payoffs to individual companies from improving the quantity and quality of care in a community and investing in the well-being of elders and children has diffuse, long-term, and indirect impact on the bottom line.

Without a significant national public policy initiative, corporate leaders and workforce experts are unlikely to see the urgency or economic benefit of significantly redesigning and changing workplaces to place family and job demands on more equal footing as employee investment and retention strategies, let alone as a social responsibility. The need for employers to more fully adapt to the transformation of work and family relationships is occurring at a time when many face hypercompetitive global markets and eroding profits. Employers are cutting headcount, pensions, and healthcare obligations and reconfiguring employment structures to reduce long-term relationships (Tsui and Wu 2005).

*Workforce Needs, Access, and Utilization*

As table 4.1 in the preceding section shows, the problem of effectively managing breadwinning with caregiving has become a critical concern across the entire gamut of contemporary U.S. workforce. It is important to note that most labor market segments are simultaneously facing both cross-cutting and distinct issues. Crosscutting workforce issues include (1) the cultural mainstreaming of W-F tensions as a shared employee concern, (2) growing financial costs of caregiving, (3) a time famine, (4) rising employee workloads at work and home, and (5) tensions over scheduling conflicts and boundaries between work and nonwork life. Distinct issues pertinent to specific laborforce groups are (1) diversity in job and family demands and control over work hours and schedules, (2) disparities in access to personal, employer, or governmental supports for W-F integration, and (3) the effects of these discrepancies on physical and mental health, labor market readiness and participation, and performance at work and home.

Much of this variation correlates with the workers' gender, family type, socioeconomic background, disability status, race/ethnicity, occupation, and employer (DHHS 2004). For example, the working single mother of a newborn child is actively involved in caregiving and domestic life while off the job, and she may rush from work to breastfeed an infant, while her coworkers may not. Thus, some employees get off work and arrive home to work an intense "second shift" (Hochschild 1989). As work demands or hours increase, they limit the time, energy, and emotional resources workers have to devote to taking care of their family demands, and their abilities to recover from the previous day's work to be able to focus on the next.

Employers' provision of flexibility in working schedules, workloads, leaves, and careers can ameliorate some of these tensions, yet there is wide variation in the workforces' access to policies—for example, adoption of W-F policies varies by job groups and industry. According to the BLS National Compensation survey (2000) employers in service industries are 2.5 times more likely to offer childcare assistance than those in manufacturing. BLS also reports that professional and technical employees are twice as likely as clerical and retail employees and 5.5 times more likely than blue-collar and service workers to have access to childcare assistance. Overall, lower-paid jobs (such as retail or clerical) with less flexible schedules and lower pay and benefits are disproportionately held by people of color, women, and low-income workers, thereby resulting in less access to resources for W-F integration (DHHS 2004). Many workers with the greatest needs for employer support are likely to find it least available.

It is important to emphasize that even with growing interest in W-F policies in the United States, the adoption of formal policies does not necessarily create a family-friendly workplace. In many workplaces, there are gaps in management and organizational cultural support, and uneven in implementation across work groups. Further, well-intentioned policies (such as FMLA) may not meet the specific needs of workforce segments. For example, low- and middle-income workers may not be able to afford to take unpaid leave to use the policy. Career-oriented workers face backlash from using available flexible career policies. Professionals and managers often have careers that require high commitment, and the need for constant updating of skills may create barriers to using leaves or reduced-load work followed by reentry into the fast track. Another example involves, jobs with direct customer contact or on the assembly line which often have limited flexible scheduling.

Many human resource structures are based on outmoded conceptions of "ideal workers." Ideal workers are defined as those who do not let family and personal responsibilities influence their hours at work and their commitment to the job, are rarely late to or absent from work, and do not interrupt or slow their careers (Williams 2000; Moen 2003). More critically, there is a disconnect in effectively linking W-F policies to other essential employment policies, ranging from pensions to healthcare to the daily management of coworker and client interactions. For example, allowing workers to have phased retirement or to work part-time at other periods in their careers may have implications for wage penalties due to gaps in employment, benefit eligibility, and pension computation.

Developing job sharing, cross-training, and back-up support is needed to redesign work systems to allow flexibility and work group effectiveness. Yet most policies are implemented as individual initiatives rather than as a group interventions. In order to develop strategic directions that U.S. employment policy needs to take, it is important to first understand historically where we have come from over the last three decades.

## Work and Family since 1973: The Rise of a Major Employment Concern

### Historical Background

Managing daily stress between work and family, though portrayed in U. S. culture and media as a relatively new and unusual problem, has for long been a part of the American workplace, a part that is neither new nor unique (Pitt-Catsouphes, Kossek, and Sweet 2006). Historians remind us that from colonial times, many Americans from colonialists to slaves to Native Americans had little choice but to juggle family and economic pursuits (Boris and Lewis 2006). What has changed dramatically since early times and even since 1973, though still in its infancy, is the emergence of "work and family" as a defined and mainstreamed employment issue. It is no longer viewed as a problem limited to a small female labor force segment, families in poverty, or single parents who have no choice but to combine breadwinning with caregiving.

Though this change in the popular meaning of employer responsiveness to work and family can be a positive force for workplace change, it is important as we move forward not to discount the unique challenges faced by specific workforce segments (such as single and dual earner parents, older workers, welfare-to-work participants, high-talent professionals, and so on). The challenge for policymakers is to recognize that workplace solutions need to not only be broad-brushed and comprehensive, but also implemented in ways that can be customized to empower and meet the special needs of individuals and particular labor market sectors.

### Work and Family as Depicted in Work in America Reports

Using examples from the landmark reports (O'Toole 1973, 1974) to depict the U.S. policy framework 30 years ago, we can say that references to what would be considered "work and family" issues today were thinly scattered across several chapters. W-F was just beginning to appear on the radar screen of workforce experts, but it had not coalesced as a coherent employment policy domain. For example, in her chapter on "work, well-being and family," Rainwater (1974) considered part-time work, childcare, and flexible hours to support family life, with a focus on these policies' relevance for a "central provider." The assumption was that if someone worked and needed flexible work schedules, she was a primary and often single breadwinner.

Another chapter, by Furstenburg (1974), titled "Work Experience and Family Life," centered on the effects of poverty and family instability (such as divorce or unemployment) on poor families, and the impact of a father's occupational status on economic and family well-being. A father's main role was seen as an economic provider. A third chapter considered increased labor participation of women, but little attention was devoted to professional or managerial jobs, as Sawhill (1974) observed that most of these were still held by men.

### Quality of Work Life: W-F Policy Connections

O'Toole (1974, 1) aptly titled his edited book to emphasize "work and quality of life linkages," as "the institution of work was seen as a lever to improve the quality of an employee's overall life." Similarly, I see the effective implementation of "work and family policies," defined as formal and informal employer support for the integration of work and family life, as a key subset of quality of work life. W-F policies send a critical message regarding the level of respect for the employee's individual needs and the degree to which workers are seen as valued resources. If one is experiencing constant stresses and tensions between work and nonwork and unable to develop positive relationships between these roles, then one is not likely to have a high quality of work life (QWL). As discussed below, much of the QWL movement focused on issues of relevance to work-family and work-nonwork integration.

An excellent book by Bohen and Viveros-Long (1981) captured the thinking of policy experts at the time that lead to the creation of a Federal Family Impact Seminar in 1976. The seminar was created in recognition of the dramatic changes in relation-ships between work and family, the central "role of work in the whole of peoples' lives" (60), and the critical linkages between "the well-being of families and the well-being of society as a whole" (37). Its goal was to examine the impact of employment policies on families of government workers. As the largest employer of the United States, the government was seen as a key field site for employment policy analysis and the implementation of model practices to promote change. Initially, four employer policies were seen as critical for study: childcare, working hours and work schedules, job relocation and transfers, and "quality of work life" (QWL).

QWL analyzers asked, "What is the environment of the job—intellectually, physi-cally, socially and physically?"; and "How do these job qualities and policies affect family well-being?" (6; 98). QWL became a symbol of work redesign initiatives that enabled employees who lacked strong empowering voice to suggest improvements that would humanize their working conditions and enhance job quality. Central con-siderations to designing work for job enrichment involved greater worker control over job conditions and autonomy. Greater flexibility for workers' scheduling needs and facilitation of worker-dependent care and child-rearing demands were also a key to many of these efforts. Ironically, these same calls to link improvement of the inter-action between work and family to work redesign efforts are even today being viewed as somewhat revolutionary concepts (see Rapoport et al. 2002).

Over the next few decades, the federal government became a leader in providing on-site childcare and workplace flexibility (e.g., the U.S. Post Office and World Bank).

But eventually the Family Impact Seminar decided to abandon focus on QWL, as it was seen as "too amorphous" and "basically the Boy Scout Oath . . . applied to work organizations" (Bohen and Viveros-Long 1981, 8). Paradoxically, the statistics provided in the next section show that these same issues—of the need for greater employee control over work conditions and schedules, increased availability of quality and affordable dependent care, and difficulties in rallying policy reforms around a broad and ambiguously defined problem—remain, despite heightened relevance.

### Moving From QWL to Work-Family to Work-Life

The term "QWL" has now been replaced with "work-life," the accepted moniker indicating that all employees, even those without families, may experience tensions between work and personal life (Kossek and Lambert 2005). This mainstreaming of work and life as an employment issue is useful for gaining broad acceptance and increasing resource allocation to institutionalize policies. It is somewhat reminiscent of early diversity efforts that first started to appear in the 1980s. Employers adopted publicity efforts to garner support for diversity policies by indicating that all employees are diverse in one way or another and can benefit from better management of multiculturalism.

However, policy experts should take care not to downplay the cogent fact that employees with dependents (elder, spouse, or children) or personal health disabilities face significant unmet caregiving challenges and constraints both at work and home. One problem that limited W-F policy development on the employer side of the equation is the field's lack of clear boundaries coalescing around well-defined interventions and outcomes (Lambert and Kossek 2005). This lack of definition runs the risk of work-family/life policies being called everything and then nothing, not unlike some of the problems in institutionalizing and developing focused national policy for the QWL movement.

In the 1970s, leading employers became cognizant of labor market shifts that suggested that work and family relationships were intertwined, and so they began providing support systems ranging from flexible work arrangements to caregiver replacement benefits while the individual worked. Although growing in availability on paper, as noted, many of these formal policies are not well linked to the way work is carried out or to important outcomes from the business, family, and health research literatures such as productivity, performance, stress, well-being, health, and safety (Kossek and Ozeki 1998; 1999; Hammer and Kossek 2005).

Further, the prevailing policy view of W-F supports is a somewhat simplistic treatment—the mere existence of policies in an organization is seen as leading to positive outcomes for both the organization and the individual (Ryan and Kossek 2003). Overall, despite increased employer interest in work and family, formal workplace support is uneven, linkages between job design and working conditions are minimal, and policy implementation is often ineffective.

### National Statistics on Demographic Shifts: Rise in U.S. Labor Force's Work and Family Tensions

The most recent National Survey of the Changing Workforce (NSCW), conducted by the Families and Work Institute every five years since 1977, shows that most individuals are juggling work and care for children, spouses, or elders, and about half (45 percent) reported some or a lot of interference between work and personal life (Bond et al. 2002).

Table 4.1 summarizes nine main trends explaining the rise in work and family as a national policy concern with supporting statistics. The overall implications of these trends are that there is a dramatic increase in workers who are experiencing increased W-F stresses, in an era of rising work demands, potential future labor shortages, and transformed relationships between work and home. These trends are seen in the transformation of the American parental household, where the dual earner family is the modal American family; growth in nontraditional families; increasing caregiving responsibilities for all workers at some point over their lifetime; decline in the population of replacement workers; rise in work intensification and hours; growth in women's labor force participation across occupations; growing acceptance of new work structures and ways of working; changing beliefs about gender roles and work-home relationships; and the rise of technology and with it the blurring of boundaries between 24-7 work and home.

The latter issue, the increased blurring of boundaries between work and home for many individuals, is a problem that has been underexamined by employers (Kossek, Lautsch, and Eaton 2005a and b) and merits additional discussion here. Although most policy experts have focused more on how to reduce barriers between work and family, it is important to also consider the potential downsides of increased interspersion of work and family. Technological tools such as e-mail, pagers, laptops, cell phones, and global 24-7 workplaces have made work constantly accessible to employees and encourage overwork. These same technologies also make most workers more accessible to their family members, enabling workers to try to multitask work and family roles. Individuals can try to stay connected to family when at work (e.g., managing an elder or child caregiver problem via a cell phone). Conversely, employees can stay connected to work when at home (e.g., checking e-mail while cooking dinner or watching the kids outside). Though this has the potential to increase emotional, physical, and behavioral conflicts between work and home, more and more individuals are trying to multitask work and personal needs.

All these technological changes have led to a general intensification of the pace of work and the pace of family life in United States. We are at risk of becoming a society that is much overloaded and knows not how to relax. For example, a recent *Fortune* magazine article reports that firms in consulting, law, and investment banking have built 80-hour weeks into their businesses (Miller and Miller 2005). The United States is renowned for taking fewer vacation days (average 13 days per year) compared to other industrialized countries such as Italy (42), France (37), or the U.K. (28) (WTO 2005).

Many firms have adopted a "use it or lose it policy" on vacation time, which has resulted in many workers not using their vacation. Workers are afraid to take their whole vacations, and some may even feel pressured to work during vacations (Kossek et al. 2005a). These individuals fear losing their jobs or being overwhelmed when they return from vacations to face thousands of e-mails and piled up work (Kossek, Lautsch, and Eaton 2005). For lower-level workers, lack of vacation is also a problem, as many firms have a minimum seniority policy before workers can even qualify for vacation and sick time. This means less senior workers have problems in caring not only for themselves, but also for their families during the workweek.

Even the elite labor force of the United States— its future top talent and leadership—has concerns about how to juggle work and personal life. Recently, the

*New York Times* ran a front-page story quoting a survey that found that despite making up half of the current student body, most female undergraduates at Yale planned to put their careers aside in favor of raising children (Story 2005). Similarly, the national media has featured articles about high-powered career women who voluntarily "opt out" of the rat race to become full-time mothers (Belkin 2003). U.S. Census Bureau reports show that the growth in women's labor market participation is slowing as the number of children being cared for by stay-at-home moms is increasing slightly, with the percentage of new mothers who went back to work falling from 59 percent in 1998 to 55 percent in 2000 (U.S. Department of Labor 2004). This trend, is perhaps indicative of the problems with the current effectiveness of employer work-family supports.

## Legal Developments

The United States has generally become more supportive of women's participation in paid employment and of fathers' involvement in early childcare over the last few decades (Lewis and Haas 2005). However, as noted at the beginning of this chapter, compared to other industrialized countries such as those in the EU, the United States is the only one that does not provide federal paid leave or public support of childcare for the general population (Stebbins 2001). Despite these gaps, under the guise of "gender equality" in employment, the policy of increased access to unpaid and paid maternity leave and flexible hours became more common starting in 1970s and 1980s (Cobble 2004).

Table 4.2 lists some of the main federal laws, and their coverage and concerns over implementation. For example, one of the main issues with FMLA is that many caregivers cannot afford to take unpaid leave and thus do not use the policy. Other problems noted by Block et al. (in press) are that of litigation. Given that most leaves are for personal health reasons and the term "serious illness" is ambiguous, it is not surprising that nearly one third of litigation has occurred over this issue. Wisensale's (2001, 172) survey of appellate cases filed in the late 1990s found that one fourth (25 percent) of cases challenged the seriousness of the employee's illness and another 6 percent questioned the seriousness of the illness of a family member being cared for.

Block et al (2006), noted that federal law generally preempts state law, but states may adopt more generous legislation. So far only one state in the nation, California, has done so by adopting paid family leave in 2004. California law mandates employers to provide partial paid family leave to bond with a new child (birth, adoption, or foster), or care for a seriously ill relative (parent, child, spouse, or domestic partner) for up to $728 dollars per week for up to six weeks (Milkman and Appelbaum 2004; California Code).

As table 4.2 suggests, some of the problems with other laws is that only pregnancy discrimination is protected, yet many caregivers desire protection after they assume responsibility for the new dependent. FLSA does not regulate the right to refuse overtime, and more workers are being exempt from being paid for overtime. Besides ERISA's limiting part-time workers access to pensions, part-time work, which is one solution that enables caregiving, as well as phased retirement for older workers, faces many barriers. National Compensation 2002 Survey indicates that part-timers earn an average of 44 percent less per hour, $8.89 per hour compared to $15.77 for full-timers. Only 17 percent of part-timers have health insurance benefits. Another

**Table 4.2**  Overview of U.S. Work-Family Laws and Policy Implications

| Law | Coverage | Effectiveness Concerns |
|---|---|---|
| Pregnancy Discrimination Act in 1978 | • Passed as amendment to Title VII of the 1964 Civil Rights Act<br>• Clarifies how employers should treat pregnant workers, such as not firing them during pregnancy if they want to work, viewing pregnancy as a temporary disability, and not setting arbitrary dates for unpaid maternity leave (Kulik 2004). | • Does not protect discrimination against parents<br>• Does not enable flexible or part time hours<br>• Many barriers to filing suit. Career oriented workers may not file lawsuits for fear of hurting reputation; low income workers may lack resources to file and fight employer |
| Family Medical Leave Act (FMLA) 1993 | • Amended to allow most individuals at firms with at least 50 employees to be able to request up to 12 weeks of unpaid leave during any 12-month period.<br>• Leave can be taken in any increments to care for a newborn or adopted child, a sick spouse or parent, or to cope with one's own illness.<br>• Employers are mandated to continue health insurance coverage while person on leave, & must offer the same or equivalent position once an individual has returned from leave (U.S. Dept. of Labor, undated). | • Although primary FMLA Congressional rationale was to enable workers to take time off to care for a newborn or adopted baby without losing job security or health care insurance, in reality, act does not effectively cover what it was intended to cover (Block, Malin, Kossek, and Holt, in 2006.)<br>• Reviewing Dept. of Labor Surveys, Canter et al. (2000) found the most frequent reason for taking a leave during last18 months was due to one's own health (52.4%). Less than one-fifth (18.5%) took a leave to care for a newborn, newly adopted, or newly placed foster child; 13% were taken to care for an ill parent, followed by an ill child (11.5%), and then for maternity-related disability (7.8%.)<br>• Highest paid 10% workers not covered and may lose jobs if use.<br>• Employers have discretion on how year is counted- calendar or actual; Many workers cannot afford to take unpaid leave. |
| Fair Labor Standards Act 1938 | Requires employers to pay nonexempt employees 1.5 times wages for overtime work | • Does not enable workers to control work hours or place a cap on hours they work or refuse overtime<br>• Numbers of workers of workers exempt from overtime pay is increasing (Kelly 2006)<br>• Does not require payment for time not worked, such as vacations, sick leave or holidays (federal or otherwise). Benefits are under the discretion of employee and employer) http://www.dol.gov/dolfaq |
| Employee Income Retirement Security Act of 1974 (ERISA) | Regulates minimum standards for most voluntarily established pension and health plans in private industry. http://www.dol.gov/dol/topic | • Has thresholds of at least 1000 hours that prevent part-timers from receiving pensions<br>• Only 21% of part-time workers are included in their employer's pension plan) http://www.mothersandmore.org/ |

59 percent receive health insurance through their spouses, but often pay for the extra coverage (http://www.mothersandmore.org).

Having reviewed these labor force, social, and legal developments, in the remainder of the chapter I review the three-legged stool of private approaches to work and family (policies, job conditions, and culture). I integrate implications for future employer policy with discussion of current firm policies and conclude with federal policy suggestions.

## Employer Work and Family Support: Workplace Developments

From an employment perspective, "work and family" refers to three main policy areas (Kossek 2005; Kossek and Friede 2006). These domains influence the extent to which a workplace is designed to reduce conflicts and stresses between work and employees' caregiving and nonwork demands. They are (1) formal human resource policies and practices, namely work-family policies, and related benefit and career systems, to support the integration of paid work with other significant family demands; (2) job conditions and the structure of work, namely job design, work schedules, and terms and conditions of employment; and (3) informal occupational and organizational culture and norms.

### Formal Policies

Examples of formal policies include but are not limited to flexibility in work time, place, or load; direct work life services for childcare, eldercare, or self-care; and information and social supports related to work and life integration. Some employers define work-family very narrowly and initially focus W-F policies on the most visible family needs such as parental roles. Progressive employers and those that become more experienced with work and family over time often broaden policies to support participation in many nonwork roles and identities. These include eldercare, community service, school age children's extracurricular activities and supervision, personal healthcare and fitness, military, political and religious activities, domestic partners, and household care (Kossek 2005).

Employer support for work and family may have been overstated in the current media and as noted earlier varies greatly in terms of access across workforce groups (Kossek 2005). Most research is conducted at large employers, yet 80 percent of U.S. firms have fewer than 100 employees (U.S. Bureau of the Census 2001) and are less likely to provide family-friendly supports. For example, the National Compensation survey conducted by the Bureau of Labor Statistics (2003) shows that 25 percent of employers with more than 100 workers provide some assistance for childcare, compared to only 5 percent for firms with less than 100 workers.

Using childcare benefits as an example, to be counting as providing, "employer childcare benefits" can be as minimal as providing an employee with lists of state licensed childcare providers. Twenty percent of individuals in white-collar occupations have access to childcare support compared to only 8 percent of individuals in service and blue-collar occupations. Sixteen percent of employers in metropolitan areas provide childcare assistance compared to only 4 percent of rural employers. Overall, wide variation exists in employer support based on size, location, and worker wage level and occupational status.

There are considerable problems in the way in which many employers approach the work-family issue. For one, many companies view W-F policies as a support system that mainly benefits the workers and not the company. This leads companies to resist wanting to innovate in times of cost-cutting. Also, many companies heavily outsource W-F policies to benefits consultants. This may result in W-F issues becoming disconnected from mainstream human resource strategy. These benefits-consulting firms, while well intentioned, are receiving millions of dollars for services that are not open to government or academic scrutiny. Many companies adopt W-F policies that are being sold by consultants without conducting a needs assessment of their particular workforce or having some serious management conversations as to how W-F supports relate to HR strategy and how these will be valued in the corporate culture or linked to the way work is being managed and carried out.

Employers must be willing to be more open to public research scrutiny and collaboration. Currently, considerable research is being conducted by work-life consultants and nonprofit research organizations, which are not strongly attached to universities or the public sector. While most of these research institutes and consulting firms have made significant contributions to the work and family field and in some cases provided some of the best existing research on work and family (e.g., the NSCW), more public and university research partnerships need to be integrated with these endeavors if we are likely to make major advancements in national policies. There is a lot of data on companies that is simply not in the public domain and measures of effectiveness are not being shared to benchmark firms.

As a result of the way current policy evaluation is done, much of the research on work and family is heavily flawed in several ways. The research studies are cross-sectional in nature and lack control groups of users and nonusers of different policies. Studies often lump all work family policies in a bunch and fail to distinguish effectively between the work and family effectiveness of different policies (Kossek 2005). This should cause employers great concern—they are spending a lot of money on programs or consultants who have little accountability to ensure policy effectiveness. Notwithstanding these weaknesses, there are potential benefits to employers when policies are effectively implemented.

Studies show that W-F policies can positively affect employee loyalty (Roehling and Moen 2001), organizational productivity (Konrad and Mangel 2000), turnover intentions (Rothausen 1994), absenteeism (Dalton and Mesch 1990), and commitment (Grover and Crooker 1995); flexibility to take on new assignments, help others, and make suggestions (Lambert 2000); and organizational performance (Perry-Smith and Blum 2000). One study comparing users and nonusers of quality, employer-subsidized, on-site childcare found users were much less likely to turnover and more likely to return from maternity leave within a few months (Kossek and Nichols 1992). Another study on linkages between employer policies and return to work after maternity leave found that the willingness to refuse mandatory overtime and supervisor and coworker support predicted employee retention (Glass and Riley 1998).

I believe flexibility policies that give workers more control over their schedules, loads, hours of work, and the right to refuse overtime hold great promise for improving attraction and retention, for worker morale, and for reducing fatigue and detrimental work behaviors such as accidents, stress, and mistakes. Absenteeism may also be reduced, because workers can restructure their day to squeeze parent conferences and medical and domestic appointments into their days off. I would also like to see employers receive incentives for supporting the availability and quality of dependent care in their community. Pensions and healthcare systems need to be reconfigured to enable flexibility in work hours, workload, and careers without undue penalty.

The way to make W-F policies work is to link them to work-redesign efforts that enable policies to be implemented as part of an organizational and work group cultural intervention. That means cross-training for workers, rewarding and socializing employees to volunteer to learn others' jobs and provide back up, and teaching managers how to plan ahead and redesign jobs to work well in a flexible work environment.

Employers also should start more systematically conducting their own policy evaluation following the old adage "what gets measured gets done." If W-F policies are not evaluated for effectiveness, there is little motivation to improve them. One way to do this would be to identify users and nonusers who have equal need for specific W-F supports and assess them for productivity.

Before adoption, needs assessments must be done to make sure the policies fit workforce needs. Once adopted, supervisors and employees must be trained in how to use and implement the policies, in ways that link them to how the work is carried out. Connections to existing HR systems are also needed, such as performance appraisal and pay systems. For example, a worker working part-time should not be expected to do the same amount of work as one working more hours, yet some companies may not adapt HR systems accordingly (Kossek and Lee 2005b).

As an example of this debate on linking study of the effectiveness of policy implementation to study of organizational culture, colleagues and I looked at managerial and HR systems from a research project funded by the Sloan Foundation on managing professionals in new work forms (Lee and Kossek 2004; Kossek and Lee 2005a; 2005b). Many human resource managers and departments are unaware of the degree to which flexibility policies were actually implemented in work units, since implementation is done according to management discretion (Friede, Kossek, Lee, and MacDermid 2004). Because of this, we focused on interviewing managers and organizations that had experience implementing these policies (Kossek and Lee 2005a; 2005b). Reduced-load work was found to be increasing in 60 percent of the firms interviewed six years later. Enabling professionals to have greater control over work hours or loads for a proportionate cut in pay was highly effective.

Part-time and reduced-load work hold great promise for retaining talent if companies can figure out how to offer employees the ability to switch back to full-time from part-time when they wish, or remain at part-time while still being seen as valued and high talent. Linkages to bonus systems, pay, promotion, and training needed to be reconfigured. For particularly large jobs, combining reduced-load work with a job share, even for managerial work, was highly successful. Companies that embraced new ways of working saw cost savings from the pay cuts, and they enabled departments to gain innovation from this talent as burnout was reduced and more creative suggestions were elicited from these workers. What is clear is that managers and workers need resocialization and help in implementing new ways of working in changing organizations.

*Job Design and Employment Conditions*

Job design and employment conditions include but are not limited to pay, work hours, job demands, health benefits, pensions, which may dictate the manner in which work and family roles can be combined, controlled, or performed in ways that create psychological and/or physical distress as well as enrichment (Kossek and Friede 2005). For example, a single parent who works the second shift may find that her job design makes it virtually impossible for her child to participate in after school activities that require parent involvement. Or she may find that sick-care policies are not available unless she has minimum tenure, and even then she is reluctant to use them if she is not paid. Or pension systems may be designed to emphasize full-time employment with no breaks and upward movement. All of these policies are examples of working conditions that have adverse impact on employees with family demands. They create barriers that keep many employees from being able to work schedules or loads that enable them to dually care and financially provide for family.

Alternative work schedules (such as flextime, leaves, flexible place, flexible careers, and reduced time) are examples of policies that have been viewed as being both family-supportive and a term and condition of employment. According to the 2002 NSCW, in the United States, 74 percent of workers work regular day or night shifts, 9 percent evening or night shifts, 8 percent rotating shifts, 7 percent on call, and 2 percent split shifts. Fourteen percent of those considered to be working day shifts work at least one weekend per month. Overall, one in four workers works at least one weekend (Galinsky, Bond, and Hill 2004). NSCW also reports that about half (49 percent) of all U.S. employees would prefer to have a different shift from the one they have. Thus, not all alternative work schedules or nonstandard hours are necessarily preferred by workers or thought of as being family friendly. What seems to matter for well-being is workers' autonomy or latitude to truly control their hours, and their own and family members' satisfaction with their work schedules.

Another issue that has received mixed media reports is overwork. Gerson and Jacobs (2004) reported that some professional and managerial couples work a combination of more than 100 hours a week. Galinsky and colleagues (2004) found that time spent on unscheduled work hours (such as overtime, being called in at the last minute, working informally from home) has raised total work hours to the highest level ever. The average total weekly work hours was 46 hours in 2002 for men. (This included five hours more than the regular scheduled hours of 39.3 hours per week.) For women, the average was 39.8 hours, which was 3.8 hours more than the regular schedule. Galinsky and colleagues (2004) also reported that employees worked longer hours than scheduled in order to be able to keep up with their workloads (47 percent), be successful on the job (43 percent), make ends meet (37 percent), or keep their job (34 percent).

It is important to note that the workforce work and family needs vary across economic strata. Many low-skilled or unskilled workers would like to work more hours in order to be able to provide better for their families. The 2002 NSCW showed that 14 percent of workers needed to work two different jobs in order to be able to provide for their families. Another problem that low-wage workers face is that they can work for an employer that has award-winning policies on paper, but they cannot use these policies due to job or family constraints. This phenomenon has been termed "organizational stratification" of work and family policies (Lambert and Waxman 2005).

Yet studies have found low-wage and low-income workers are less likely to seek jobs with other employers when they have health insurance and childcare benefits (Bond 2003). Although low-wage workers are generally less satisfied with their jobs and more likely to seek other jobs than middle- and higher-wage workers, Bond (2003) argued that with access to flexible work schedules that they feel they can use without hurting job security or advancement, these differences virtually disappear.

Batt and Valcour (2003) examined relationships between general access to work-family policies, human resource incentives such as salary or work hours, and job design. They found that salary and work hours had a stronger relationship to W-F conflict and turnover than access to policies. These findings suggest that when implementing policies, employers need to consider the effectiveness of W-F policies as part of high performance work contexts (Berg, Appelbaum, and Kalleberg 2003). They need to think about how to implement W-F policies not as a separate benefit, but in terms of how they interact with overall work systems and conditions of employment ranging from work schedules to pay to job design to benefits.

Emulating Equal Employment Opportunity research on the adverse impact of seemingly neutral employment practices, employers should do an audit on the adverse impact of seemingly neutral employment policies and job conditions on the ability to care for or provide for one's family. For example, the pension example mentioned above may affect family retirement income and the ability to work part-time and accrue healthcare and other life benefits. The inability to participate in extracurricular activities may have a variety of negative consequences such as causing childhood obesity, family health problems, and parental stress. All of these gaps may hurt the bottom line by affecting healthcare costs and productivity.

## Organizational Cultural Support for Work and Family

Organizational cultural support for work and family refers to organizational and professional cultures and norms that create stresses, social supports, and parameters shaping the ways in which individuals are able to carry out work and nonwork demands. Although the W-F literature has more often studied their negative effects, it is important to note that some of these effects can also be positive (e.g., healthy, safe, or diversity-friendly climates).

Organizational culture regarding W-F issues is defined as the "shared assumptions, beliefs, and values regarding the extent to which an organization supports and values the integration of employees' work and family lives" (Thompson, Beauvais, and Lyness 1999, 394). Organizational culture influences employer demands for long work hours, perceived job and career consequences for using informal work practices, and supervisor support of family needs. Thompson and colleagues (1999) found that a W-F supportive work culture was associated with increased employee use of W-F benefits, increased organizational commitment, decreased W-F conflict, and decreased intention to turnover. Kossek, Colqiutt, and Noe (2001) focused on positive cross-domain climate relationships between work and family and found that the ability to share concerns about work when at home or about home when at work was related to better performance and well-being. O'Driscoll et al. (2003) found that higher and more significant effects on employee well-being were more due to positive work and family culture than to the availability of formal policies.

Although many employers introduce work and family initiatives as mechanisms for reducing employee stress, by themselves these policies can be insufficient to result in significant reduction in stress. The fostering of an organizational culture that is widely perceived by employees as being supportive of work and family integration is a necessary condition for the reduction of work and family conflict and effective policy use.

Many employers have been slow to effectively implement formally adopted policies into the workplace culture (Kossek 2005). Since supervisors are often the gateway to policy use, a critical challenge for companies is to more clearly define ways that supervisors can behave, ways that will enhance employees' overall feelings of support for family. Hammer and Kossek (2005) noted that it is not clear what behaviors supervisors should adopt and how to operationalize these to create employee perceptions of a supportive work and family culture. This is important for employers to understand in order to design and implement meaningful workplace interventions to support effective utilization of W-F benefits. Supervisors are the pathways to effective policy use.

Employers also need to change prevailing cultural assumptions that take for granted that if an employee is highly effective and has invested in a particular realm, such as work, then he or she will be less effective in the other due to a win-lose relationship. Yet it is important for employers to shift cultures to focus on how work and family can also enrich each other. For example, a positive experience at work or skills learned at work can shape effective behaviors at home—this is the idea of accumulative effects of work and family. Companies need to recognize that more and more of the workforce is dual-centric (Lobel 1991). Many individuals are placing work and family roles on an even keel. In their daily lives, it is increasingly important to many workers to be successful in both work and family roles simultaneously. Changing cultures to enable people to work fewer hours more effectively may increase productivity in the long run. Companies could use the cost savings to pay others, and workers might be more energized and engaged when at work.

Although unions are declining in percentage of the workforce, garnering cultural support from unions and culturally embracing access to W-F support as a collective benefit is important for future policy (Kossek and Berg 2005). Unions remain a powerful political force in this country, and an even more powerful force abroad as U.S. employers continue to globalize workforces. In the United States, unions historically have been slow to embrace flexibility, as it is viewed as mainly serving employers' interests. And effectively introducing flexibility may require treating workers individually rather than collectively. Consequently, interest of unions in the provision of W-F benefits (such as childcare, pay, healthcare) has been greater than in flexible work schedules. An exception is found in service industries such as healthcare that employ large numbers of women.

Overall, applying some concepts from a union perspective could be valuable for advancing cultural support for the implementation of flexibility and W-F policies in many firms. A union perspective will be more likely to be interested in ensuring equal access to publicly negotiated benefits to all workers who need them and in ensuring their equal treatment. Currently, some employers have preferred to provide access to flexibility to only the best workers. While flexibility should be viewed as a two-way street between employee and employer, its availability needs to be wider— encompassing all employees, not just the highest performers.

Companies need to culturally embrace a dual agenda, where workplaces are redesigned to benefit improvement in both productivity and in responsiveness to individual needs (see Rapoport et al. 2002). Lee and Kossek (2005), for example, found instances where reduced-load work was implemented into entire departments, at the same time that work systems were redesigned to actually improve productivity. In some cases, these new ways of working were linked to cultural shifts in the management system to have made a narrower span of control, such as job sharing in a managerial job. This prevented managerial overload and enabled better relationships between managers and workers.

Effectively implementing work-life policies requires a fundamental cultural change in the assumed hegemony of work and nonwork. Successful work-life policy implementation is an ongoing process and demands major culture change—referred to as second- and third-order culture changes (Bartunek and Moch 1987). Thus, it involves moving beyond the mere adoption of policies on paper to relearning how to work in new ways to link flexibility to, for example, how clients are served or workers are managed.

### Suggestions for Future Federal Policy

A major national legal and public policy effort is needed. A key first step toward any future policy initiative is to simply educate employers and the public on what constitutes work and family policies and practices, and what are the indicators of effectiveness. We then need more visible national demonstration projects. It might be useful to offer development certification awards, following the success of the Total Quality Management and the Affirmative Action Movement. Employers who get large government contracts may be given incentives to show that they are going beyond the minimum legal requirements and are employers of choice in supporting work and family. Following the work of the seminar on early family impact, tool kits and training could be developed to help companies assess the direct and indirect effects of work practices on families.

The FMLA should be expanded to provide partial paid leave. Legal protections need to be developed to protect workers from losing their jobs by caring for an ill family member. Berg (2004) argued that the FMLA should be expanded to include regular school and medical appointments, and those related to domestic violence, even if the leave is unpaid. Berg (2004) also noted that some U.S. political leaders would like to see an expansion in the definition of family (to include domestic partners, for example) and monies provided to states to encourage experimentation with wage replacement during leaves.

Case law involving employer interpretation of employment policies that discriminates against parents and caregivers is growing (Williams 2000), and legislation protecting employees' parental and caregiving rights is needed. A key problem is that some of the legal policies that do exist are ineffective or out of date with current societal changes. For example, despite the increase in cohabitating families noted in table 4.1, many work and family policies still assume legal definitions of family, marriage, and parental responsibility based on formal birth or adoption rights. Legal gaps also remain for eldercare policy. Although most employed women provide eldercare for in-laws, the FMLA allows leave for the care of only one's parents, not one's in-laws. These legal definitions of family must be updated to account for the diversity of employees' family and personal relationships.

We need to improve the effectiveness of existing legislation and develop national, regional, state, and community initiatives to foster more effective support for work and family needs of the workforce. One way to improve support for caregiving is by providing public incentives for employers to subsidize quality care and other workplace supports that are customized to what workers want in their communities. For example, Steelcase had a program where they provided training and resources to increase the number of licensed family day care providers located in the community. The first group of recruits comprised of spouses and friends of Steelcase employees.

There could also be a national government initiative to give regional and employer awards for excellence in work and family policies and the development of national certification systems, not unlike the TQM movement of the 1980s. In order to be considered for some federal grants, the workplaces would need to be certified as being family-friendly. There also needs to be an increased federal funding for after-school care and childcare related to welfare, limits on work hours and mandatory overtime, mandated vacation and sick time, and pro-rated pension and health benefits for part-time workers (Appelbaum 2004; Berg 2004).

A focused national initiative must be conducted to distill the many statistics from all government sources to simply lay out the state of W-F policy and identify where policy gaps occur. This is necessary to make the case that change is needed clearer and more accessible to policymakers and the public. It might also eventually enable government monitoring, not unlike EEO and AA statistical tracking.

## Conclusion

Leaving the responsibility to provide employer support for working families mainly dependent on the goodwill and economic health of U.S. companies may not be a wise national public policy. Kanter (2006) pointed out that if families do not perform their roles well (e.g., reproducing and socializing the next generation of workers), employers and the economy will suffer. The challenge that remains is how to create work environments that truly support, welcome, and include those who have different ways of working due to their family and nonwork demands. This objective is related to notions of the "inclusive workplace"—a growing concept in diversity management.

How do we enable all employees to bring the best of themselves to work when they are there, feel as if they are included in the workplace culture, and feel capable of focusing and caring about work outcomes? At the same time, how can employers address vital personal and caregiving needs that affect the development of our future workforce and the health of our nation? We need to bring the family more into the organization, while at the same time enable workers to control their personal lives as separate from work, so as to be able to focus on the family when needed—a particular concern in a 24-7 world. It is clear that significant gaps in the structural and cultural design of workplaces vis-à-vis the workforce's growing needs to have regular participation during the "established work day" in caregiving (childcare, eldercare, self-health care) and other nonwork demands not only remain, but are increasing.

# 5

# The Effects of New Work
# Practices on Workers

*Michael J. Handel and David I. Levine*[1]

The study of work and employment in the 1970s was shaped by a widely cited report that took stock of the current workplace and proposed broad changes (*Work in America* 1973). Some of those changes came under the heading of employee involvement (EI) practices. In this chapter we review research on how EI practices affect job quality and assess the extent to which they have delivered on their promise. Overall, we find that new workplace practices increase employee satisfaction and (on average) increase wages by a small amount. Effects on employee injury rates are less clear. It is also unclear if the small and inconsistent findings across many studies reflect variation in the seriousness of implementation (with many workplaces making few real changes), variation in the quality of the studies and measures, or true variation in effects. We conclude with an analysis of some considerations of policy options.

Appearing after nearly 30 years of prosperity and economic growth, the *Work in America* (1973) report focused on how work could be made more satisfying, skilled, and participatory. Similarly, the 1990s also began with a widely cited report advocating fundamental changes. However, *America's Choice: High Skills or Low Wages!* (National Center on Education and the Economy 1990) focused on the need to restore American competitiveness and wage growth through tougher education standards, structured school-to-work transitions, one-stop job service and information centers, and incentives and assistance for firms adopting high-performance work systems to compete on quality rather than low wages.

Although policymakers paid a lot of attention to these issues, policy changes were modest. Perhaps in spite of this relative neglect, the economy did very well in the 1990s in terms of job growth. But the economic recovery in the 1990s left one agenda item conspicuously unresolved: securely improving the quality of jobs for the middle and lower segments of the workforce. Thus, as the 1990s boom ended, inequality remained extraordinarily high, living standards improved little for the vast majority (Mishel, Bernstein, and Allegretto 2005), and doubts lingered as to whether a credible model of high-quality employment had emerged to compensate for the waning influence of unions.

New work practices with higher levels of employee involvement and skill were viewed favorably by academics, policymakers, and firms, to judge by the various studies of their prevalence (Osterman 1994, 2000; Frazis, Gittleman, Horrigan, and Joyce 1998; Cappelli 1996; Cappelli and Neumark 2001; Freeman and Roger 1999). While definitions vary, most would agree that EI practices include job rotation, quality circles, self-directed teams, and most implementations of Total Quality Management (TQM), as well as supportive practices such as enhanced training and nontraditional compensation (such as pay for skill, bonuses, gain sharing, and profit-sharing).

A number of arguments suggest that employee involvement can help workers. Workers have insights into how to improve their jobs, and most find that the opportunity to influence their work environment is intrinsically satisfying; employers find they enhance productivity as well. Management and workers can both gain if workers receive higher pay, greater job security, and improved working conditions in return for their contributions. In fact, such involvement appeared to be one of the keys to Japanese manufacturing success in the 1980s.

The difficulty in sustaining traditional American industrial jobs has only increased in the last few years, as low-value-added jobs are moving abroad. Many have argued that American manufacturing workers can retain jobs in high-value-added operations, particularly those serving rapidly changing markets and using information technology, high skills, and high employee involvement (Piore and Sabel 1984; Zuboff 1988; Appelbaum et al. 2000, 10f.). However, studies also support a more cautious view, noting middle and lower management resistance to change (Zuboff 1988), token or faddish adoption (Abrahamson and Fairchild 1999), and poor execution (Vallas 2003). The harshest critics describe workplaces in which management uses employee involvement to control workers and intensify work (Graham 1993; Barker 1993) as part of a more general strategy to control labor cost, which may also include real wage reductions, union avoidance, outsourcing, offshore production, and less stable employment arrangements.

Adding to these theoretical disagreements are methodological challenges and differences in the execution of research on how new work practices impact worker outcomes, particularly wages. We will summarize the research on wages and other selected outcomes and conclude with suggestions for how future research and policy can build on the lessons learned.

## Theories Relating Workplace Practices and Employee Outcomes[2]

There are at least five theories that might explain why workplaces with employee involvement, profit-sharing, and other new workplace practices might have different outcomes for employees than more traditional workplaces: human capital, compensating differences, efficiency wages, incentives and complementarity, and theories centering on conflict over distributive issues within the firm.

### Human Capital Theory

Human capital theory argues that workers with higher skill levels receive higher compensation because they are more productive. Employee involvement may require workers with more general skills to perform more complex tasks, which might result in more rigorous selection and hiring criteria and increase the demand for and wages of more educated workers. New practices may also require more firm-specific skills, which would increase employer-provided training and wages as well.

### Compensating Differences Theory

This theory argues that workers who face particularly desirable (undesirable) working conditions will receive lower (higher) wages (Williamson 1985, 268 ff.). If employees regard employee involvement as a benefit because problem-solving tasks and job redesign relieve the tedium of traditionally organized work (Hackman and Oldham 1980), then firms that have it could offer lower wages and workers would not be worse off. Conversely, if employee involvement requires extra effort and tighter work demands, then plants with employee involvement might offer better compensation.

### Efficiency Wage Theories

Efficiency wage theories predict that paying higher wages may increase workers' productivity through three main channels (Katz 1987 and Levine 1993 review this literature). A higher wage may increase worker effort due to the greater cost of job loss, so workers would want to reduce the chances of being dismissed for low effort. A higher wage may also increase effort by increasing workers' loyalty to the firm, which may be especially important in systems that require greater discretionary effort from employees and in group activities such as problem solving, in which effort and output are costly to monitor (Akerlof 1982; Milgrom and Roberts 1995).

Indeed, the core concept of the mutual gains enterprise or high commitment systems (Walton 1985) is consistent with Akerlof's (1982) theory of labor contracts as partial gift exchange and the role of fairness conceptions in the determination of expectations, effort, and wages. Finally, a higher wage may reduce firms' turnover and recruitment costs, which might also be important if EI requires more careful recruitment or increased firm-specific training.

### Incentives and Complementarity

The prescriptive literature on organizational design emphasizes the importance of aligning decision-making rights with incentives to make good decisions. If undertaken seriously, the use of greater employee involvement involves substantial changes in decision-making rights when frontline employees collect and analyze more data to suggest and implement improvements. In these circumstances, it makes sense to structure incentives in ways that reward quality and improvement and align frontline workers' goals with their new authority (Milgrom and Roberts 1995; Levine 1995).

Because workplaces with greater employee involvement depend more on employee initiative, the theory of complementarities between involvement and incentives implies that pay practices such as gain sharing, profit-sharing, and stock ownership plans will be more common. If these forms of variable compensation substitute for base pay, shift earnings risk to workers, or are introduced in the context of concession bargaining (Bell and Neumark 1993), then one would expect to observe lower regular wages in their presence, though perhaps less employment variability as well in some cases. However, if the firm's strategy is to introduce a supplement, or at least to avoid putting current pay levels at risk, then total earnings may be no different or slightly higher. If the practices work as intended and increase motivation and productivity, earnings may be significantly greater, assuming firms share gains with workers.

## *Conflict Theories*

These theories emphasize that employee involvement can shift bargaining power within the enterprise. To the extent employers become more dependent on hard-to-monitor discretionary effort of employees, employees' bargaining power can increase. High-involvement workplaces with just-in-time inventory make it easier for employees to disrupt the production process, so that worker noncooperation or other reactions to perceived unfairness are more costly to the firm.

At the same time, several authors have referred to high-involvement systems as "management by stress," positing that employee involvement is simply a method of sweating the workforce and curbing worker power and influence. Firms reduce employee and union power by using ideological appeals, suggestion systems, and peer pressure in small work groups to instill a culture of company loyalty, appropriate workers' tacit knowledge, and enforce discipline (Graham 1993; Parker and Slaughter 1988; Sheahan et al. 1996). This view predicts increased workloads, faster work pace, closer monitoring, and more job stress, without offsetting compensating differences such as higher wages.

Case studies provide examples of firms that devolve responsibilities to workers but refuse to increase wages (Bailey and Bernhardt 1997, 30f.; Zuboff 1988, 298f.). Press reports indicate that some employers, particularly when times are tough, ask for wage cuts, more skills, and increased participation simultaneously; such an effect implies that employee involvement might be correlated with wage declines, but not cause them. Other press reports, though, suggest that participatory workplaces are willing to pay higher wages.[3] Some researchers argue that workers require union representation to give them the leverage to compel firms to share gains resulting from EI programs, given the unequal bargaining power of firms and workers in the current environment (Black, Lynch, and Krivelyova 2004).

TQM and standardized work pose additional threats to worker safety and health. TQM emphasizes reduction in variation and is often combined with just-in-time inventory practices that eliminate buffer stocks and worker control over work pace in order to maximize total work time. The result can be twofold—more standardized and repetitive work, and increased workloads that raise the risk of repetitive motion injuries such as carpal tunnel syndrome, confirming the suspicions of many that TQM represents a more developed form of Taylorism (Adler, Goldoftas, and Levine 1997; Brenner, Fairris, and Ruser 2004).

The possibility of conflict was most apparent with the reengineering movement in the 1990s, where the redesign of jobs (often involving both new information technology and increased worker autonomy) was explicitly tied to laying off the workers no longer needed after the resulting increase in efficiency (e.g., Hammer and Champy 1993).

## Methodological Challenges

While theory and intuition suggest numerous hypotheses regarding EI's effects on workers, there are several difficulties to testing them conclusively. For example, new work practices are not randomly assigned to employers or to workers; thus, statistical analyses can be biased. In some cases, prosperous firms both pay high wages and are more likely to introduce new work practices. In other cases, desperate firms both try new workplace practices and cut wages (Caroli and van Reenen 2001, 1475). In addition, firms that enjoy above-average success with their workplace innovations may be more likely to respond to surveys than are those that are less successful. Thus, we cannot even be sure whether the average selection bias is positive or negative.

Selection effects exist on the worker side as well, because new work practices may lead firms to use more rigorous selection procedures and hire workers with greater human capital. Such selection can induce a positive correlation between wages and involvement, even if the employees would have anyway earned the higher wages without the involvement.

Cross-sectional data, which is a single snapshot of conditions at a number of workplaces, make it very difficult to rule out the possibility that preexisting differences between adopters and non-adopters account for observed differences in worker outcomes. Data collected before and after an organization adopts different practices would help isolate the effects of introducing the change. However, longitudinal data can compound problems with measurement error and raise questions regarding the lag that is expected between treatment and outcome.

Measurement problems may be great because surveys almost always rely on a single informant per workplace. Multiple respondents in the same workplace typically have very different views of the same workplace practices (Wright et al. 2001). Even when respondents agree, they may each use different definitions from those at other workplaces; thus, at one firm a "semi-autonomous work team" may be a totally autonomous group without outside direction, while at another it may be a traditional workgroup with a supervisor who held a single team meeting six months ago! Such measurement error can make it very hard to detect true effects of new workplace practices.

Most of the different theories reviewed earlier imply that the different dimensions of employee involvement—increased task complexity, responsibility, autonomy, training, and gain sharing—are interdependent and mutually reinforcing. For example, it may be far more effective both to train frontline employees in problem solving and to permit them to solve more problems on their own than to make only either of the changes. This interdependence implies that correctly specifying "high" versus "low" levels of employee involvement is quite difficult.

However, there are many EI practices, and theory does not provide clear guidance as to which bundles may be most effective, whether some practices are substitutes (e.g., employee stock ownership or profit-sharing) or complements, or even how to measure bundles (e.g., interaction effects, additive indices, factor analysis, cluster analysis, or *ad hoc* indexes). It is difficult to identify which workplaces have introduced a theoretically sound bundle of practices and which have not.

Some studies suggest the confusion extends beyond researchers to employers themselves. Most workplaces adopt only a few practices (Osterman 1994; Gittleman, Horrigan, and Joyce 1998; Forth and Millward 2004; Blasi and Kruse forthcoming), not the coherent bundle of practices recommended by theory (Levine 1995; Milgrom and Roberts 1995). When employee involvement is not tried seriously, its lack of effects is not surprising. The research challenge is to identify a subset of workplaces with meaningful changes for workers.

### Research on the Relationship between EI and Wages

In a companion piece (Handel and Levine 2004) we have reviewed in detail the results of more than 20 academic studies of the effects of various EI practices and bundles on wages. The results of the various studies (including a few more recent studies) are summarized in table 5.1 according to effect size and study characteristics. In Panel A, we distinguish whether the studies use nationally representative samples (which have an advantage, in that the results generalize to the whole economy) or focus on particular industries, firms, and establishments (which have an advantage, in that the measures of workplace practices can often be measured more precisely). In Panel B we divide the studies based on the several measures of employee involvement.

Because most studies estimated multiple models, there is no single best way to summarize the different studies. However, every effort has been made to include the best estimates from those studies for as wide a range of practices as possible. Where the EI variable was a standardized scale, the effect size equals the coefficient (that is, the effect of a single standard deviation), and where the EI variable was in percentage form, the effect size was based on multiplying the coefficient by 100.

Although three-fifths of the coefficients are positive, a majority of both nationally representative and more focused studies indicate no statistically significant effect of EI on wages. The results from industry- or firm-specific studies tend to be slightly more favorable than those based on nationally representative samples (Panel A). This result may be because the restricted sample controlled more effectively for unrelated inter-organization differences, such as specific industry affiliation, that are associated with both the tendency to adopt innovative practices and workers' wages. Studies restricted to one industry or firm may also use more context-appropriate survey items that reduce measurement error. However, if these studies focused disproportionately on industries in which EI is intrinsically more effective, their results would not generalize to the overall economy.

In studies where the effects of new workplace practices on wages are statistically significant, effects tend to be small and their causal status clouded by the possibility of selection effects. Most studies do not eliminate the possibility that high-wage establishments may adopt more high-involvement practices or that high-involvement establishments may hire workers who would receive high wages at low-involvement workplaces. Almost all the negative effects are insignificant and the point estimates are small. A reasonable reading of the evidence suggests that EI's average effect is somewhere between 0 and 5 percent, though larger effects have been found in a small number of cases. These estimates are well below those for the union wage premium (Freeman and Medoff 1984), but problems with measurement error biasing coefficients toward zero are also greater in research on employee involvement.

In Panel B, the small number of studies for most practices and the heterogeneity of measures across studies prevent strong conclusions. Results are most consistently positive for TQM, with all four studies finding positive effects and two reaching statistical significance. Conversely, three of the four studies examining job rotation

**Table 5.1**    Effects of Employee Involvement Practices on Wages

| | Negative Effects[a] | Positive and Insignificant Effects | | Positive and Significant Effects | | | |
|---|---|---|---|---|---|---|---|
| Point Estimates | | >0–5% | ≥6% | >0–5% | 6–9 % | ≥10% | Total |
| **A. Study type[b]** | | | | | | | |
| *Nationally Representative Samples* | | | | | | | |
| Percent | 39.6 | 35.8 | 3.8 | 9.4 | 7.5 | 3.8 | 100 |
| N | 21 | 19 | 2 | 5 | 4 | 2 | 53 |
| *Industry, Firm, or Establishment Studies* | | | | | | | |
| Percent | 14.7 | 32.3 | 5.9 | 26.5 | 8.8 | 11.8 | 100 |
| N | 5 | 11 | 2 | 9 | 3 | 4 | 34 |
| *All* | | | | | | | |
| Percent | 29.9 | 34.5 | 4.6 | 16.1 | 8.0 | 6.9 | 100 |
| N | 26 | 30 | 4 | 14 | 7 | 6 | 87 |
| **B. EI Measures[c]** | | Percent of Studies | | | | | |
| Job Rotation (n = 4) | 75.0 | 25.0 | | | | | 100 |
| Quality Circles (n = 4) | 25.0 | 25.0 | | | 50.0 | | 100 |
| TQM (n = 4) | | 50.0 | | 25.0 | 25.0 | | 100 |
| Teams (n = 22) | 27.2 | 36.4 | 9.1 | 9.1 | | 18.2 | 100 |
| Alternative Pay (n = 11) | 27.3 | 45.4 | | 9.1 | 18.2 | | 100 |
| EI Scales (n = 9) | 22.2 | 22.2 | 11.1 | 44.4 | | | 100 |

*Note:* Teams and alternative pay include all varieties of these practices; this pooling may account for some variation across results.
a. Almost all negative effects were statistically insignificant.
b. In Panel A the Pearson $\chi^2(5) = 10.27$, P = 0.068, providing suggestive evidence that results from national and establishment studies differ. If the order of the columns is meaningful (which requires assuming that statistically significant estimates of 0–5 percentage point increase are "more" in some sense than insignificant estimates of over 6 percent) ) it is appropriate to use an ordered test. Fisher's exact test shows the rows differ at the 5 percent level.
c. In Panel B the Pearson $\chi^2(25) = 33.74$, P = .011 which cannot reject that the patterns of results of the six work practices are drawn from identical distributions. The sample size of studies in Panel B is larger than in Panel A because many studies provide estimates for multiple programs.
*Sources:* Appelbaum, Eileen, Bailey, Berg, and Kalleberg 2000; Arthur 1992; Azfar and Danninger 2001; Bailey and Bernhardt 1997; Batt, 2001a; Batt, 2001b; Black, Lynch, and Krivelyova 2004; Bauer and Bender 2001; Cappelli 1996; Cappelli and Neumark 2001; Colvin, Batt, and Katz 2001; Forth, and Millward 2004; Hamilton, Nickerson, and Owan 2003; Handel and Gittleman 2004; Helper, Levine, and Bendoly 2002; Hunter and Lafkas. 2003; Kelley 1996; Osterman 2000; Rénaud, St-Onge, and Magnan 2004; Tullar 1998

found negative, but statistically insignificant, effects. None of the other programs (quality circles, teams, alternative pay systems, or scales of employee involvement and other new work practices) show patterns that are distinctive compared with the overall average. Given the small number of studies of job rotation and of TQM, we cannot conclusively state that one set of programs is or is not consistently better or worse for employees (the test of similar distributions of outcomes across programs is distributed $\chi^2(25)$ and is not significant at the 10 percent level).

Some notable findings from the different studies are worth highlighting. Despite the focus on the importance of bundles, stimulated in part by Ichniowski, et al. (1997), Cappelli and Neumark conducted one of the most thorough and thoughtful tests of the bundling thesis and concluded that "there is not consistent evidence of statistically significant effects of bundles of work practices" (2001, 760).

Osterman conducted an initial longitudinal study and concluded, "The bottom line is that there is very little evidence that HPWOs [high performance work organizations] have delivered on their promise of 'mutual gains' " (2000, 190f.). However, in more recent work, Osterman (2006) found a wage premium for blue-collar manufacturing workers of just under 4 percent to be consistent with our prior conclusions. Appelbaum et al. (2000) also found positive effects of a similar magnitude in their thorough survey of the steel, apparel, and medical electronics industries.

A final hypothesis from conflict theories is that employee involvement might benefit workers most when unions are present and, therefore, can bargain for a share of any productivity increases. While plausible, the results remain mixed (with support from Black and Lynch 2000, 2001, but not Handel and Gittleman 2004).

## Other Outcomes

While economists have emphasized studies of wages, psychologists more often look at the relation between EI and job satisfaction. These results are more consistently positive than those for wages (Cotton 1993; Freeman and Rogers 1999; Appelbaum et al. 2000; Hodson 2001, 190; Hunter, MacDuffie, and Doucet 2002). Thus, not all increases in wages can rightly be explained as compensation employees receive for the burden of autonomy. Given the very large emphasis that the original *Work in America* report gave to the link between repetitive jobs and employee dissatisfaction, these results are encouraging.

There have been fewer studies of the effects of employee involvement on safety and on job security. Safety professionals consider employee involvement a key element in reducing injuries (e.g., Ariss 2002). The skills of problem identification and problem solving that are the basis for EI can help reduce hazards as well as improve quality. At the same time, while quality programs often increase employee involvement, they also try to routinize and standardize tasks. High rates of repetition and increased monitoring can increase stress and repetitive motion injuries, potentially worsening the safety record of plants with quality programs (as found by Brenner, Fairris, and Ruser 2004).

The relationship between employment security and new workplace practices promoting higher employee involvement remains less well studied, in part due to the scarcity of longitudinal data. Methodological issues described previously, such as selection effects and the indeterminate length of lagged impacts, also complicate efforts to establish causality.

With these cautions in mind, some evidence suggests that new workplace practices reduce involuntary turnover and lengthen employment spells, although all results are somewhat ambiguous. On the one hand, organizations trying to involve employees in decision-making are more likely to provide formal promises of employment security than do other organizations (Levine and Parkin 1994; Helper, Levine, and Bendoly 2002; Brown et al. 1997; Ichniowski, Shaw, and Prennushi 1997). On the other hand, such promises remain the exception (see, e.g., Forth and Millward 2004).

Moreover, in a national sample (Osterman 2000), employee involvement in the early 1990s was associated with *higher* probability of layoffs between 1995 and 1997, while it had no effect on survival among auto suppliers over a similar time period (Helper, Levine, and Bendoly 2002). Lawler, Mohrman and Benson (2001, 171) found no relation between downsizing and employee involvement in a sample of very large employers. Cappelli and Neumark (2004) found that high-involvement practices are associated with below-average employee turnover in manufacturing but not in other sectors. Black, Lynch, and Krivelyova (2004) found that different high-performance work practices had positive and negative effects on the probability of employment reductions within manufacturing. Batt (2004) found that installation and repair workers in the telephone industry who worked in self-managed teams felt greater subjective job security than workers who are otherwise similar, while supervisors of such teams expressed less job security than their counterparts in traditional systems. In Australia, Drago found that high-involvement practices are associated with above-average employment security but are also found in some "disposable" workplaces with low employment security (1996).

## Summary and Implications

### Summary

The recent growth of research interest in employee involvement reflects both the growing use of employee involvement within the workplace and hopes that it might be a source of good jobs for workers. From the current evidence, it appears that if the reforms are serious, EI can improve organizational outcomes. The evidence on workers' compensation is mixed. Our reading is that most involvement plans have no effect on pay, in large part because the efforts were not that serious and not much changed in the workplace. At the same time, the average wage effect appears to be an increase of a few percentage points.

There is no evidence that EI programs decrease compensation and no consistent evidence that compensation rises by more than perhaps 5 percent. The evidence is too weak to know where in that range the average effect lies, although we suspect that more serious efforts would be at the high end of the range.

As noted above, EI's effects on employee satisfaction are more consistently positive than are the effects on compensation. Unlike the original *Work in America* report, this review puts more emphasis on compensation than on satisfaction—largely due to the composition of the research literature. That shift in the literature, in turn, partly reflects the training of economists; as they have increased their research on this topic, their standard economic outcome of compensation looms larger. The increased emphasis on pay also reflects the slow growth of median pay since the *Work in America* report was released. Pay was perhaps less salient a concern in 1973, given the rapid compensation growth in the 20 years prior to that report.

Despite proponents' hopes, the wage effect of new workplace practices remains significantly below the union wage premium (Freeman and Medoff 1984), though the new practices also cover a larger proportion of the workforce. To increase the number of high-wage jobs, EI may be necessary, but not sufficient.

Though EI advocates argue that a wage premium due to improved productivity is more sustainable than, for example, a premium originating in union bargaining power, the evidence is (perhaps surprisingly) mixed on the relationship between employee involvement and employment security. Each of the theories discussed earlier may have some explanatory power, but there is little evidence for strong effects. EI appears to have modestly positive human capital implications, though effects may be somewhat suppressed if training reduces starting wages, as human capital theory predicts.

Similarly, firms may pay efficiency wages after implementing EI in order to elicit higher commitment and discretionary effort and minimize loss of training investments due to turnover. However, the small size of the EI premium also suggests that employers feel limited pressure to pay efficiency wages, perhaps reflecting workers' weak bargaining position.

The evidence on satisfaction suggests that wages may be held down by many workers' preference for high-involvement jobs, but there is little consistent evidence of greater employment security associated with EI that might also function as a compensating differential. The evidence on injuries suggests that a wage premium for EI may sometimes be a compensating differential for more negative working conditions in some cases.

Existing research suggests more strongly that when EI is not used as a form of speed-up it gives workers more autonomy, recognizes the value of their contributions, improves job satisfaction and feelings of voice, and often lowers quit rates. By mitigating the more negative aspects of hierarchy, EI represents another positive step in the evolution of management practice comparable to the earlier restrictions on the "foreman's empire" (Nelson 1975) that transformed the supervisory role from, at times, that of a petty dictator to the more constrained "man in the middle" (Whyte and Gardner 1945).

These findings do not support the most positive views of EI, that EI by itself it can create a "high-road" solution to the problems of poor wage growth and increased inequality. At the same time, these findings do not indicate that management-by-stress is typical (because EI usually raises job satisfaction), nor do they suggest that higher demand for skills at high-involvement workplaces (what economists call "skill-biased organizational change") is a significant cause of inequality growth.

All conclusions regarding the effects of EI must be qualified by the recognition that existing research has not eliminated potential problems such as measurement error and selection bias. Indeed, to some extent it is not surprising to find such disparate results, given the lack of agreement on the best measures of EI. Future research requires standard and more behaviorally concrete measures of various EI practices to improve comparability across studies, minimize measurement error, and distinguish strong from weak adopters. More attention must also be given to understanding organizational performance and worker quality prior to adopting EI, in order to exclude the possibility that wage effects are biased by any preexisting differences between the wages of adopters and non-adopters.

*Policy Implications*

Everyone would like to see the quality of American jobs improve. A generation ago, optimists thought that new workplace practices were the most attractive way to achieve that goal because of their potential to increase productivity, share gains, and increase satisfaction. There have been many private-sector permutations of these ideas since Quality of Work Life programs began to be adopted in the 1970s, encouraged by the original *Work in America* report and the social trends it documented.

Complementary public-sector initiatives initiated in the late 1980s also supported strategies of skill upgrading and employee involvement. These included school-to-work programs that promised to create high-skill workers direct from high school, the Baldrige Quality Award that promoted TQM with some upgrading of skills and employee involvement, national voluntary skill standards in many industries and states that were intended to lower the cost of hiring and acquiring high skills, the Manufacturing Extension Program that was supposed to upgrade skills, and many others.

Unfortunately, despite these efforts, our knowledge of their effectiveness remains inadequate, and the quality of jobs in the United States (as measured by wages, stability, or skills) has not improved consistently. Median earnings and job security remain disappointing, and inequality is still elevated (Mishel, Bernstein, and Allegretto 2005). Manufacturing employment has continued to decline, even as many U.S.-based firms have prospered using overseas assemblers.

What remains unclear is whether the new workplace practices were ineffective or never brought to scale. Measuring the extent of genuine employee involvement in the workplace in a nationally representative fashion remains difficult. Most of the supportive public-sector initiatives were small, poorly funded, and affected few students or workplaces. We also do not know what would have happened to American jobs if these efforts had not been made; perhaps the situation would have been significantly worse. Thus, the question remains: Do we need *more* of the same medicine (more training, more employee involvement) or *different* medicine?

American living standards are tied to the value of what we produce (not the value of negative externalities such as pollution). For working people, living standards are also tied to high employment rates and institutions that ensure the fruits of higher production are shared. Unfortunately, we have no quick answer for how to raise productivity, maintain employment, and increase wages. It seems clear that better data is needed if we are to understand whether recent efforts are on the right track. In the absence of more definitive answers, we next propose ways to improve our understanding and discuss how this information might be leveraged to promote change.

### Better Measurement for Researchers

Progress on understanding the effects of new work practices on both employers and employees is slow in part because we lack basic data. We do not even know the incidence of training or gain sharing, nor do we know how levels of employee involvement vary over time or sector. Understanding the effects of these policies remains even more remote.

While a number of nations have repeated workplace surveys, the United States has only a series of ad hoc surveys that do not use common definitions; thus, we cannot even identify basic trends (e.g., the datasets analyzed in Osterman 2000, Lawler et al. 2001; Freeman and Rogers 1999; Cappelli and Neumark 2001; Bureau of Labor Statistics 1996a, b ).

The United States needs a repeated survey of American workplaces. The ideal measure would have a longitudinal component (presumably with workplaces rotating in and out of the sample). To address measurement error, the survey would need two or more employees per workplace.

### Better Measurement for Workers and Employers

Because shreds of employee involvement are ubiquitous but serious implementations seem rare, the government may have a useful role to play—although not one of just mandating how workplaces should be organized. The government's role could be to make it easier for employers, customers, and investors to see which employees and suppliers are constantly solving problems. As researchers identify patterns of workplace practices that reliably predict better outcomes for workers and firms, customers will shift demand to those firms that are implementing the (now observable) effective practices.

This recommendation would provide coherence to the dozens of disjointed policies the government already has that affect the workplace, including accounting rules that fail to measure training as an investment, skills standards that define problem solving differently in different states or industries, and procurement policies that emphasize low bids over quality. The win-win approach of measuring who solves problems can make the goals of government, business, and employees reachable.

As noted above, many governmental policies in the last generation have attempted to make the nation's workplace-related policies more friendly to high-skill workplaces. Nevertheless, much more can be done.

In the computer industry, the saying is, "Standards are wonderful, there are always so many to choose from." Certifying what our students and workforce have learned is becoming as complicated as computer industry standards. Currently, the electronics and retail industries (among others) and a number of states are each creating separate standards that measure skills in problem solving and working in groups—the key skills that employers say they need. Thus, someone who has good skills at solving problems in one industry might receive no credit for these very same skills when he or she moves to another industry.

Our skill standards should be created from a common set of building blocks that measure these key skills. Standards for measuring how well students work together in groups and solve problems have the additional benefit of helping schools. Clear standards in these areas would help schools understand what they need to do in their move away from "chalk and talk" toward making education both more interesting and more relevant.

Companies face the same problem as employees when trying to certify the quality of their goods or services—a profusion of standards and certifications. A company that hires workers who solve problems and that collects data from its customers to always improve its products and services is a good supplier. Nevertheless, it has to jump through different hoops to sell to a car company than to sell to an airplane company—and different hoops again to sell to different parts of the U.S. government.

The federal government must work with other large customers to create standard certifications that measure which companies are high-quality producers and are organized to further improve their quality. The good news is that the federal government is already beginning to copy the private sector's best practice; specifically, the government is starting to rely on existing supplier certifications (such as those given by the automobile and computer industries) as one factor when choosing suppliers. This move should improve the quality and lower the lifetime cost of the goods and services bought by our government. Suppliers of high-quality goods and services tend to rely on their workers for help in improving quality. Thus, buying higher-quality goods should not only save the government money but also increase the quality of U.S. jobs.

Investors face the same problem as customers: How do they know whether the company is investing in building a high-quality reputation or is depreciating its customers' and employees' good will? Unfortunately, current accounting rules do not measure the investment managers make in building a high-quality workforce and in producing high-quality goods. Instead, in the short run, such spending shows up only as lower earnings.

The government should restructure its accounting rules to put investment in people and in quality on a more even footing with investment in plant, equipment, or research. It can work with industry and the accounting profession to create standard measures of workplace investments that are comparable across time and across companies. Only then can investors understand which companies are investing for the long term.

All of these efforts must be tied to careful evaluation. Jobs with high skill requirements and high employee involvement involve continuous learning and improvement. We can ask no less of the policies that are supposed to support such jobs.

The bottom line is that American workplaces will continue to slowly expand their use of high-skill, high-involvement strategies—if only because low-skill jobs will increasingly be located overseas. At the same time, these shifts can be accelerated if government policies removed obstacles and addressed market imperfections. Just as important, workers would share more of the fruits of any gains if the government promoted the flow of information on the characteristics of workers and workplaces.

# 6

# Trends in Jobs and Wages in the U.S. Economy

*Alec Levenson*

In this chapter, I review the changes in the U.S. labor market over the past four decades, focusing on the economic trends that have had the greatest impact on work as viewed from the employee's perspective: wages, hours, job stability, and demographics.

## Wages

Economists like to use hourly wages to measure how skill is valued in the labor market, because it enables the comparison of labor market outcomes for people whose jobs and demographics may be very different from those of the majority. Entire volumes have been written on how and why wages have changed since the 1970s. What follows are the key changes.

### Aggregate Wages versus the Wage Distribution

The Bureau of Labor Statistics (BLS) monthly reports focus public attention on changes in average earnings for all workers. But this focus on averages masks significant differences in trends for lower- versus higher-wage workers. Thus, many researchers and policy analysts prefer to compare different points in the real (inflation adjusted) wage and income distributions. We follow that convention here.

Table 6.1 shows real hourly wages for men and for women at three points: 1973, 1995, and 2003, as originally reported by Mishel, Bernstein, and Allegretto (2005). The year 1995 is significant because it represents the general time (mid-1990s) when there was a marked shift in trends in the male wage distribution. Consequently, the numbers in table 6.1 are constructed to show how wages changed over the 30 years between 1973 and 2003, and how those changes, at least for men, can be divided into two distinct periods. For greater details on the trends (including the year-by-year changes) see Mishel et al. (2005).

**Table 6.1** Changing Real Wage Distribution for Men and for Women

|  | Percentile of the Hourly Wage Distribution | | | | | | | |
|---|---|---|---|---|---|---|---|---|
| **Men** | | | | | | | Male Wage Ratios at Certain Percentiles | |
| Year | 10th | 30th | 50th | 60th | 80th | 95th | 50–10 ratio | 80–50 ratio |
| 1973 | $7.73 | 11.70 | 15.20 | 17.23 | 21.83 | 33.51 | 1.97 | 1.44 |
| 1995 | 6.58 | 9.88 | 13.93 | 16.28 | 22.87 | 37.29 | 2.12 | 1.64 |
| 2003 | 7.46 | 10.90 | 15.04 | 17.79 | 25.50 | 43.48 | 2.02 | 1.70 |
| *Subperiod* | *Change in Wages by Percentile of the Hourly Wage Distribution* | | | | | | *Wage Ratio Change* | |
| 1973–95 | −14.9% | −15.6% | −10.3% | −5.5% | +4.8% | +11.3% | +0.15 | +0.20 |
|  | 10.3% | 5.5% | +4.8% |  | +11.5% |  |  |  |
| 1995–2003 | +13.4% | +10.3% | +8.0% | +9.3% | +11.5% | +16.6% | −0.10 | +0.06 |
| *Overall* | *Overall Wage Change for Men by Percentile of the Hourly Wage Distribution* | | | | | | *Overall Wage Ratio Change* | |
| 1973–2003 | −3.5% | −6.8% | −1.1% | +3.3% | +16.8% | +29.8% | +0.05 | +0.26 |
| **Women** | *Percentile of the Hourly Wage Distribution* | | | | | | *Female Wage Ratios, Certain Percentiles* | |
| Year | 10th | 30th | 50th | 60th | 80th | 95th | 50–10 ratio | 80–50 ratio |
| 1973 | $5.44 | 7.61 | 9.60 | 10.80 | 14.03 | 20.50 | 1.76 | 1.46 |
| 1995 | 5.80 | 8.09 | 10.69 | 12.32 | 17.88 | 28.56 | 1.84 | 1.67 |
| 2003 | 6.67 | 9.22 | 12.18 | 14.29 | 20.20 | 33.40 | 1.83 | 1.66 |
| *Subperiod* | *Percentile of the Hourly Wage Distribution* | | | | | | *Wage Ratio Change* | |
| 1973–95 | +6.6% | +6.3% | +11.4% | +14.1% | +27.4% | +39.3% | +0.08 | +0.21 |
| 1995–2003 | +15.0% | +14.0% | +13.9% | +16.0% | +13.0% | +16.9% | −0.01 | −0.01 |
| *Overall* | *Overall Wage Change for Women by Percentile of the Wage Distribution* | | | | | | *Overall Wage Ratio Change* | |
| 1973–2003 | +22.6% | +21.2% | +26.9% | +32.3% | +44.0% | +62.9% | +0.07 | +0.20 |
| Gender Wage Ratio | *Female/Male Wage Ratios by Percentile of the Wage Distribution* | | | | | | *Ratio of Gender Wage Ratios** | |
| Year | 10th | 30th | 50th | 60th | 80th | 95th | 50–10w/50–10 m | 80–50w/80–50 m |
| 1973 | .70 | .65 | .63 | .63 | .64 | .61 | .89 | 1.01 |
| 2003 | .89 | .85 | .81 | .80 | .79 | .77 | .91 | .98 |
| *Overall* | *Change in Female/Male Wage Ratio* | | | | | | *Change in Ratio of Gender Ratios* | |
| 1973–2003 | +.19 | +.20 | +.18 | +.17 | +.15 | +.16 | +.02 | −.03 |

* Ratio of gender wage ratios: (i) (50–10 female ratio)/(50–10 male ratio); (ii) (80–50 female ratio)/(80–50 male ratio).

*Source*: Real wage values taken from Tables 2.7 and 2.8 in Mishel, Bernstein and Allegretto(2005). Percentage changes and gender wage ratios are author's calculations.

The top panel has the male wage distribution and the middle panel has the female wage distribution. Within each panel, the first three rows report the real hourly wage at various points of the wage distribution (columns 2 through 7), and the ratio of wages for the fiftieth versus tenth percentiles (column 8) and for the eightieth versus fiftieth percentiles (column 9). The latter are measures of inequality for workers at the bottom versus middle versus top of the wage distribution at a given point in time. The bottom three rows in each panel report percentage changes in hourly wages for two sub-periods (1973–1995 and 1995–2003) and overall (1973–2003); these figures are in columns 2 through 7. Columns 8 and 9 in the bottom rows of the top and middle panel report changes in inequality for the two sub-periods and overall.

The bottom panel reports female/male wage ratios, indicating how women's wages fall short of men's wages at each point of the wage distribution. Note that the gender wage ratios in this context are not designed to describe "comparable worth," which is a measure of wage ratios for women and men working in similar jobs. Rather, the gender wage ratios in this case provide a way of summarizing the relative economic progress of women (compared to men).

## Changes in Wage Distribution

### Changes in the Hourly Wage Distribution for Men

Wages for men in the bottom half of the distribution (fiftieth percentile or lower) in 2003 were slightly below their counterparts' wages in 1973: –3.5 percent for the tenth, –6.8 percent for the thirtieth, and –1.1 percent for the fiftieth percentiles. Wages in the top half of the distribution (sixtieth percentile or higher) were higher in 2003 compared to 1973: 3.3 percent for the sixtieth, 16.8 percent for the eightieth, and 29.8 percent for the ninety-fifth percentiles. Thus, jobs at the lower end of the wage distribution lost ground during 1973–2003, while jobs at the upper end gained in both absolute and relative terms.

The overall trend during these three decades masks two very different trends, before and after the mid-1990s. Prior to the mid-1990s, wages for the bottom half of male wage earners fell in real terms, with a majority of the decline occurring during the 1980s (Mishel et al. 2005). Other measures of wage and income disparities also show a marked increase in inequality during the 1980s (Card and DiNardo 2002; Jones and Weinberg 2000). During the rapid economic expansion in the latter half of the 1990s, in contrast, wages rose throughout the income distribution, though the gains tapered off after 2001 for lower-paid workers and continued to rise at a more moderate pace for higher- paid workers (Mishel et al. 2005).

Reasons for the increased dispersion in wages include skill-biased technical change (a relatively larger increase in demand for skills that already commanded a pay premium, such as knowledge work), loss of highly paid industrial jobs, and institutional changes (erosion in the real value of the minimum wage, deregulation and increased competition in industries such as transportation and services, and continued erosion of union power). While the debate over the relative importance of each of these has not been resolved, the most likely scenario is that each plays a contributing role. (For further discussion of these changes, including international comparisons, see Blau and Kahn 2001, 2002; DiNardo and Pischke 1997; Johnson 1997; Juhn, Murphy and Pierce 1993; Katz and Murphy 1992; Levy and Murnane 1992.)

*Changes in the Hourly Wage Distribution for Women and the Gender Gap*
The middle panel of table 6.1 reveals a different story for women. Wages throughout the female wage distribution rose in both periods. This led to a marked closing of the male-female wage gap (bottom panel of table 6.1). When gender wage ratios are constructed for workers at different life cycle stages, the differences and changes over time are more stark. According to Blau and Kahn (2000), in 1978 women aged 18–24 earned 82.4 percent of the wages of their male counterparts in the same age range, which contrasts with 62.3 percent for women versus men aged 55–64. By 1998, the gender earnings gap for 18–24 year olds had narrowed to 94.2 percent, while for those aged 55–64 it narrowed, at a slower rate, to 69.3 percent.

One of the more striking features of women's wage gains in the 1980s is that they were achieved at the same time that the overall distribution of wages widened substantially, which hit many traditionally low-paid, female-dominated occupations. Blau and Kahn (1997) quite appropriately called this "swimming upstream" against economic forces that otherwise might have widened the gender wage gap.

Volumes have been written on the progress women have made in the labor market. As summarized by Blau and Kahn (2000), the leading explanations include occupational shifts toward white-collar and away from blue-collar jobs, technological change, and increased computer usage, all of which indicate the rising importance of knowledge-based work, decreased discrimination by employers, and increased female labor force attachment and dedication to professional and managerial occupations. With respect to the latter, women now spend greater fractions of their adult years in paid work outside the home, including those immediately after childbearing, and they are much more likely today to work in occupations that traditionally have been male dominated.

Educational attainment has changed significantly. According to Blau, Ferber, and Winkler (2002), between 1966 and 1997 women's share of professional degrees increased in a range of areas including medicine (from 6.7 to 41.4 percent), law (from 3.8 to 43.7 percent), business (from 3.2 to 38.9 percent), and dentistry (from 1.1 to 36.9 percent). These trends continued through 2002: Women account for two-thirds of veterinary medicine and pharmacy degrees and more than 40 percent of the degrees in both medicine and business (Cox and Alm 2005).

Increased education leads to occupational achievement: Between the early 1970s and 1999, the share of women working in administrative support and service occupations fell from 53 to 41 percent, while the percentage of managerial jobs held by women increased from less than 20 percent to 40 percent (Blau and Kahn 2000). The percentage of female college graduates who go on to become teachers fell from almost half in 1960 to less than 10 percent by 1990 (Flyer and Rosen 1994). (For further details on these changes, see Berman, Bound, and Griliches 1994; DiNardo and Pischke 1997; Krueger 1993; O'Neill and Polachek 1993; and Weinberg 2000.)

*Changes for Racial and Ethnic Groups*
Both blacks and Hispanics earn, on average, much less than whites. In 2003, those earning wages at or below the poverty line were 20.4 percent of whites, 30.4 percent of blacks, and 39.8 percent of Hispanics (Mishel et al. 2005).

Among nonwhites, there are some dissimilarities for the gender-based subgroups (Mishel et al. 2005). The share of black men earning wages at or below the poverty line declined slightly in the 1970s, rose in the 1980s, and then declined further in the 1990s; by 2003, the rate stood at 26.2 percent, down from 31.9 percent in 1973. Hispanic men's wages had a similar up-and-down pattern (as did white men's wages), yet over the 30-year period they lost ground: Those earning wages at or below the poverty line rose from 31.7 percent in 1973 to 35.7 percent in 2003.

The improvements for black and Hispanic women mirror that of their white counterparts. All three groups saw continual improvement over the 30 years (Mishel et al. 2005). The percentage of white women earning wages at or below the poverty line fell from 46.1 percent in 1973 to 26.0 percent in 2003. For black women, the improvement was even stronger, falling from 58.2 percent in 1973 to 33.9 percent in 2003. For Hispanic women, in contrast, the gains were more moderate, though still substantial, with those earning at or below the poverty line falling from 60.6 percent in 1973 to 45.8 percent in 2003.

*Changes in the College Wage Premium*
College-educated workers have always earned more on average than high school graduates or dropouts. But the premium rose significantly in the 1980s and again rose slightly further in the 1990s (Card and DiNardo 2002; Mishel et al. 2005). In 1979, the college wage premium was approximately 29 percent for men and 32 percent for women; by 1999, it had risen to approximately 45 percent for men and 50 percent for women (Card and DiNardo 2002). This was a significant reversal from the 1970s, a time when a falling college wage premium led some to worry about "overeducated" Americans (Freeman 1976).

Today it is clear that a college education is a primary determinant of labor market success *on average*. Yet the average obscures significantly different outcomes among workers with similar levels of education. In short, having a college education does not guarantee high wages, nor does lack of advanced schooling doom high school graduates to a life of poverty. But in general more education is a good thing. And the fact that the benefit to having more education has increased so strongly over the past two decades is compelling evidence of the shift toward knowledge work in today's society.

*Executive Pay*
The most widely cited measure of inequality is the ratio of CEO pay to average worker pay, which has increased dramatically from 24-to-one in 1965 to 185-to-one in 2003 (Mishel et al. 2005). Much of the criticism of the inequality focuses on whether the CEO alone creates firm value, particularly because CEO compensation continues to increase at fast rates regardless of firm performance.

If the increase in pay were limited to CEOs alone, it would not merit discussion here: The CEOs of the *Fortune* 1000 firms constitute only 0.0000008 percent of a total U.S. workforce of more than 130 million. Rather, the increase in CEO pay has coincided with a sharp increase at the upper tail of the income distribution (table 6.1): The upper 5 percent of income earners collectively have realized the greatest gains over the past couple of decades.

Is this just a striking coincidence, the simultaneous increases in pay both for CEOs and for the bulk of the highest-paid people in the workforce? It is not likely. One possible explanation is the trend toward flatter organizations with fewer middle management layers (Lawler, Mohrman, and Benson 2001; Rajan and Wulf 2003). A flatter organization implies that the people who were highly paid 30 years ago (those higher up the corporate hierarchy) today have greater responsibilities (bigger spans of control). Increased responsibilities in turn can be used to explain even higher within-company wage differentials, comparing those at different levels of the hierarchy, and this appears to have occurred (Rajan and Wulf 2003).

In such a world we might see the wages of lower-level workers remain relatively constant in real terms (assuming their job responsibilities did not change appreciably), while the wages of higher-level workers would rise to compensate for the greater responsibilities. Other factors undoubtedly have contributed to the complex changes that have taken place in the labor market, but this pattern is consistent with the general changes in the wage distribution shown in table 6.1.

*Rising Within-Group Dispersion*

The increased dispersion evident in table 6.1 holds good even within groups of workers who share similar demographic characteristics. For example, today there is more variation in wages and earnings among people with similar levels of education, not just between levels, more dispersion among high school graduates, more dispersion among those with only some college education, more dispersion among four-year college degree holders, and so on. This pattern also appears among employees holding the same job title (Groshen and Levine 1998; Levine, Belman, Charness, Groshen, and O'Shaughnessy 2002; O'Shaughnessy, Levine, and Cappelli 2000). This means more relative economic winners and losers among groups of people who previously had economic fates that were much more closely aligned.

Three human resource practices are consistent with increased wage dispersion. Rising within-occupation pay dispersion (O'Shaughnessy, Levine, and Cappelli 2001) is consistent with increased use of competency-based pay (Lawler and McDermott 2003), which differentiates rewards among employees in similar jobs based on their knowledge, skills, and abilities (Lawler, 2003; Spencer and Spencer, 1993). Increased use of merit pay and bonus pay create rewards based on actual performance, with impacts that are both long-lasting, in the case of merit-based increases, and transitory, in the case of one-time bonuses; the use of both forms of pay appears to have increased (Lemieux, Parent, and MacLeod 2005; O'Shaughnessy et al. 2001). Thus, compensation policies of the current era appear to differentiate pay among job incumbents more than the compensation policies of the previous era did.

## Job Stability

In the mid-1990s, when the United States was in the middle of the first "jobless recovery," concern was raised that jobs had become less stable, marking the end of lifetime employment. One potential cause was the corporate restructurings that started in the late 1970s, causing setbacks for many icons of U.S. industry (U.S. Steel, IBM, AT&T, and General Motors, among others).

The concerns about job stability led to a flurry of research on job tenure—that is, how long a job lasts, where a "job" is defined as the particular role a person has while working for a company. This research echoed an interest from a previous era in the number of jobs people would have over their working lifetimes. Of course, it is impossible to forecast with any certainty how long a particular job will last. Thus researchers instead have focused on the distribution of job tenure.

*Trends in Overall Job Stability*

Despite common perceptions, the research through the mid-1990s found little change in the overall distribution of job tenure (Jaeger and Stevens 1999; Neumark, Polsky, and Hansen 1999). That this research has not been updated is likely due to two factors: (1) the lack of a strong downward trend in job durations through 1996, and (2) the booming labor market of the late 1990s, which temporarily shifted the balance of power toward workers. Thus, while workers today may, for other reasons, perceive that they are in a tougher labor market than the generation before them, shorter job duration for the "typical" workers does not appear to be part of the problem.

One reason for the gap between perception and reality is the attention paid to the fates of large corporate icons and a corresponding reporting bias in the media. Job losses often happen episodically and rapidly, making for good press material. In addition, actual jobs cut often fall short of the announced number, because the latter include unfilled positions; thus, over time, not all cuts necessarily occur. Further, despite the fall of corporate icons of the last era, new icons have risen to take their place—companies such as Microsoft, Intel, and Wal-Mart. These new icons all have employees who have spent their entire careers in the service of the company, but none was on "the list" of icons in the late 1960s and early 1970s. Moreover, other companies, such as Procter & Gamble and UPS, have always preserved their icon status and have continued to offer the chance for lifetime employment. Finally, hiring often is much more incremental than job cuts, and it does not garner headlines.

Another issue is large firm reporting bias: 1000 layoffs at one firm make a bigger splash than 1000 layoffs spread evenly over 10 smaller firms. This means that media reports of announced layoffs (weighted heavily toward large companies) offer little evidence on the nature of job stability for the "typical" job, which is just as likely to be at a small firm as a large one, using the cutoff of 500 employees as defined by the U.S. Small Business Administration. Still, in reality, jobs are less stable at smaller companies than at larger ones: Small businesses have greater rates of both job creation and destruction (Davis, Haltiwanger, and Schuh 1998).

### Job Stability Winners and Losers

Despite the lack of change in the average duration of jobs, there have been notable changes in the experiences of certain subgroups. Through the mid-1990s, there was an increase in job stability for women, and for men with shorter job tenures; at the same time, job stability declined for men with less formal education, for men with longer job tenures, and for blacks (Neumark, Polsky, and Hansen 1999). Cappelli's chapter in this volume provides evidence that the declining trend for older men continued through the late 1990s.

Decreased job tenure does not necessarily indicate negative labor market outcomes, especially if employees initiate the separations for better jobs. Yet both high school–educated men (at all levels of experience) and college-educated men with more than 15 years of labor market experience had falling real wages in the 1990s (Card and DiNardo 2002), so their reduced job tenure indicates either involuntary loss of desirable jobs or voluntary separations from less-desirable jobs. On the other hand, wages for women and men with less experience increased or stayed approximately the same in real terms, and they had relatively stable job tenure in the 1990s. Thus, changes in job duration seem to be positively correlated with changes in average wages.

### Changes in Hours of Work

The publication of Juliet Schor's *The Overworked American* in 1991 served as a clarion call for people worried about the burden of work on employees. The debate that followed the book's publication was intense, in a pattern similar to the debate over job stability. With the benefit of more than a decade of additional data, the evidence can be summarized as follows (Coleman and Pencavel 1993a, 1993b; Jacobs and Gerson 2004).

Average hours worked per week barely changed for both genders between 1970 and 2000. Yet the flat trend masked growing dispersion in the distribution of hours worked. For both genders, there was a decline in the percentage working 40 hours a week, and an increase in the percentage working 50 or more hours. A growing dispersion in hours worked along education lines mirrored changes in the wage distribution: College-educated workers are working longer hours, particularly at the top of the hours distribution, while hours worked for less-educated workers have fallen. Moreover, gender today appears to be growing less important than education in distinguishing hours of work: College-educated workers, regardless of gender, are increasingly more likely to have similar patterns of hours worked, relative to high school-educated workers (Coleman and Pencavel 1993b).

The workers with the longest hours (50 or more per week) are professionals and managers: 37.2 percent for men and about 15 percent for women, in contrast to men's 21.3 percent and women's 7 percent in other occupations. College-educated workers have always worked long hours on average, and that gap has grown since 1970; they are precisely the group more likely to be professionals and managers. Thus, the picture painted by Coleman and Pencavel (1993a, 1993b) and by Jacobs and Gerson (2004) is one in which the demands on employees' time have increased over the past four decades, at least for more highly skilled employees.

The situation for those with lower levels of skill is opposite, however, at least for 1967–1989. During this period, Juhn, Murphy, and Topel (1991) documented that both unemployment (not working but actively looking for work) and nonparticipation (neither working nor looking for work) increased significantly for lower-skilled men—the group with falling real wages. This meant, in large part, increased spells of joblessness during the year—that is, for many lower-skilled men, increased rates of unemployment and nonparticipation mean a lower number of hours worked during the year (versus not working for the entire year). Thus, one response to falling wage opportunities appears to be withdrawal from the labor market altogether.

### Business Cycle Changes

The most recent recessions have been more "white collar" than in the past: A larger percentage of white-collar workers lost jobs in 1991–1992 and 2000–2001 compared with earlier recessions (Mishel et al. 2005). This is consistent with the media's coverage of the last two recessions. Yet I believe that the media tend to focus too much on the fate of the more-experienced, higher-wage workers and ignore the fate of the less-skilled, lower-wage workers who traditionally have borne the disproportionate burden of labor market adjustments.

Part of this is probably just the "old news" phenomenon: Lower-skilled, lower-paid workers have always had it harder, in both good times and bad, so editors may have gotten tired of publishing the same old stories about who loses jobs in a recession. The other cause, however, I believe lies in reporters' self-centered view of the world: It is their friends and family members who are more likely to be white collar and higher paid, so recessions in the past happened to "other people," not people like them (the reporters). When the structural adjustments that took root in the 1990s started to impact their friends and family, reporters took notice.

The most recent data indicate that the 2000–2001 recession had a fairly significant negative impact on higher-paid, white-collar workers (Farber 2005). Specifically, there has been a relative shift in job loss such that college-educated workers experienced their highest job loss rates in over 20 years. In contrast, other groups' recent job loss rates are either the same or lower than in the period during and immediately following the early 1980s recession. Consequently, between 2000 and 2003, the share of long-term unemployment accounted for by workers with a bachelor's degree or more rose from 14.2 percent to 19.1 percent. Yet despite this, the overall unemployment rate for this group is still lower than it is for other workers.

## The Consequences of Job Loss

Up to this point in our analysis we have not differentiated between voluntary and involuntary job loss. One reason why such a distinction often is not relevant is that people often leave jobs voluntarily when the job-compensation match is no longer rewarding, be it due to performance or non-performance related reasons. Thus the dividing line is blurred.

In order to identify the economic impact of true job loss, economists have focused on "job displacement"—the subset of firm-initiated separations that are not performance related (due to a plant closing, layoff, abolition of a job, and so on). The trend data on job displacement are relatively short, dating to the early 1980s. Yet some interesting patterns nevertheless emerge.

According to Farber (2005), following the early 1980s recession, the job displacement rate tracked the unemployment rate very closely, both falling with economic growth. The trend after the 1991–1992 and the 2000–2001 recessions differed, however: Between 1993 and 1995, the job displacement rate increased while unemployment fell; while in the years 2001–2003, both the displacement and unemployment rates rose after the recession ended. Thus, the latest two recessions have had high job destruction rates extend past the end of the recession.

Along with the greater job displacement, the last two recessions have also been followed by relatively slow rates of job growth (Groshen and Potter 2003), introducing the "jobless" recovery notion. Low job growth and high displacement indicate a higher degree of structural adjustments in the period following a recession. Yet both of the latest recessions were characterized also by relatively low unemployment rates: Jobs were easier to find for a greater percentage of the working population. Considering all these aspects together, it appears that over the last two decades the U.S. economy became less likely to experience deep, short structural adjustments, and more likely to experience less deep, but longer lasting, structural adjustments.

Finally, we consider whether the consequences of job loss are greater today. People displaced from jobs typically suffer significant declines in their earnings, partly because they earn lower wages on subsequent jobs and partly because they lose earnings while out of work. According to Farber (2005), between 1981 and 1993 the average total earnings loss for displaced workers was relatively constant, ranging between 10 and 15 percent. In the mid- to late-1990s, however, the earnings loss fell below 10 percent, but then it rose significantly to a two-decade high for people displaced from jobs between 2001 and 2003. Thus, the consequences of job loss today are as high as they have been in a generation, indicating that there is a substantial economic hardship from structural adjustment. Unfortunately, it is too early to tell whether recent experience indicates a new reality for displaced workers.

Similarly, there has been a recent shift in who bears the larger brunt of the economic burden from job displacement. Among workers who lose full-time jobs and eventually find one, before the most recent recession, it was workers with less education (particularly high school dropouts) who experienced the greatest percentage loss of total earnings, compared to workers with a four-year college education or more. Between 2001 and 2003, however, the situation reversed: Now the workers who realize the greatest percentage reduction in total earnings are those with at least some post–high school education (Farber 2005).

## Shifting Income Risk onto Employees

### Variability

Up to this point in our analysis we have considered how employment and earnings vary across jobs at a point in time. However, changes in employment and earnings variability or uncertainty within a job also impact job quality.

One indication that incomes within a job may be more variable today is the increased use of bonus pay for salaried workers. On the positive side, greater use of bonus pay can preserve jobs by shifting revenue fluctuation risks from firms to workers. On the negative side, it can be used as a way to keep overall compensation costs down, either inadvertently or on purpose. According to Lemieux et al. (2005), the percentage of salaried jobs that received bonus pay at least once during the employment relationship increased steadily during the 1980s, and it stood at around 50 percent in 1998, up from about 30 percent two decades earlier. The percentage of jobs receiving bonus pay in the current year, however, increased much more slowly during that period and lagged considerably behind, rising from about 12 percent in the mid-1970s to about 20 percent in 1998. The fact that an increasing fraction of jobs is bonus eligible (having received a bonus at some point in time) but the bonuses are not granted in the current year indicates that some earnings variability has been successfully shifted from firms to workers.

### Trends in Health and Retirement Benefits

Two other trends that have shifted income risks onto employees are falling healthcare coverage and changing retirement plans.

Between 1979 and 2003, the share of workers covered by employer-provided healthcare plans dropped by 11.6 percentage points, from 69 percent in 1979 to 56.4 percent in 2003 (Mishel et al. 2005). This significantly shifted the income risk of unforeseen health expenses from companies to employees. Greater coverage loss occurred for high-school educated workers (down 16 percentage points) than for college-educated workers (down 9.2 percentage points), further exacerbating the inequality trends in wage compensation (Mishel et al. 2005). Thus, including healthcare coverage provides a starker picture of widening total compensation inequality (including fringe benefits) than the analysis based on wages alone reveals.

Employer-provided pension coverage also declined over the 1979–2003 period, though not in a linear fashion, first falling in the 1980s, then rising through 2000 before declining again through 2003. According to Mishel et al. (2005), the net loss was 4.7 percent (from 50.6 percent in 1979 to 45.9 percent in 2003), which also represented a shifting of (old age) income risk from companies to employees. Interestingly, the less-than-sharp aggregate decline masked big gender differences: Coverage for men dropped substantially, from 56.9 percent in 1979 to 47.2 percent in 2003, while coverage for women *increased* from 41.3 percent in 1979 to 44.3 percent in 2003. Thus, the pension coverage gender gap almost disappeared.

The education gap, however, widened: High school–educated workers' coverage fell from 51.2 percent to 40.9 percent; college-educated workers' coverage fell and then rose, so that it ended up virtually unchanged, at 61.0 percent in 1979 versus 60.2 percent in 2003. So adding this second component of total compensation to healthcare benefits and wages paints an even starker picture of rising inequality along educational lines.

Among those who remain covered, costs and risks shifted as well. For healthcare benefits, this meant rising premiums and co-pays. For pension benefits, this meant large-scale substitution of defined contribution for defined benefit plans (Mishel et al. 2005): In 1980, defined benefit plans covered almost 40 percent of the workforce, versus less than 10 percent for defined contribution; by 1998, defined benefit plans covered about 20 percent, while defined contribution covered more than 25 percent. Moreover, with the recent insolvencies of large defined benefit plans such as United Airlines, there is every reason to believe the trend continues through today and will continue into the future.

### Shifting Employment Risk onto Employees: "Contingent" or At-Risk Jobs and Outsourcing

One of the biggest developments in recent decades in the debate over the nature of jobs and how they are changing is the perceived growth in "contingent" jobs. There is no single definition of contingent jobs; for example, some people include part-time jobs, others do not. Most observers would agree that contingent jobs are those that are most tenuous and susceptible to being cut when times are difficult. This includes temporary staffing positions and project-based jobs with no guarantee of continued employment beyond a fixed date.

One view is that firms today are more likely to take a core versus periphery approach to managing their workforces, in which the core is made up of the employees who uniquely or disproportionately contribute to the bottom line and the periphery includes the employees whose jobs are more like commodities to be bought and sold on the open market. Periphery jobs are prime candidates for outsourcing to other firms that specialize in providing commodity labor, such as janitorial work and food service (Abraham and Taylor 1996). Outsourcing of periphery jobs is part of the trend toward focusing on core competencies that accompanied the breakup of large industrial conglomerates in the 1970s and 1980s. An increase in outsourcing happens as firms embrace the concept of core versus periphery and apply it to jobs within business units.

Periphery and contingent jobs are similar, but not the same. For employees, holding outsourced periphery jobs does not necessarily mean that their employment prospects worsen, *so long as the job stays in the same general geographic location.* Workers in both the "sending" firm (the outsourcer) and the "receiving" firm may remain just as likely as before to have their positions eliminated due to organizational restructuring. Because labor appears on the balance sheet only as a cost and not an asset, there always is a tendency for organizations to look to labor cost savings as one of the first options to improve financial performance.

Apart from the longevity of the job, an employee's career trajectory may be either worsened or improved by outsourcing too. Consider the case of janitors working in a knowledge-intensive firm. Before outsourcing there may be little upward mobility, because of a lack of an internal labor market in the sending firm. The receiving firm, in contrast, may specialize in janitorial services, and therefore offer more of a career ladder. For janitors working in a blue-collar firm, however, being outsourced may increase the difficulty of moving into related occupations in the sending firm, an option that previously might have led to better career trajectories.

Thus, outsourcing does not necessarily worsen workers' employment prospects *so long as the job does not move and continues to exist.* If the job changes geographic locations, however, or if it is eliminated altogether because of technological changes, then the worker falls into the category of being displaced, the general consequences of which we discussed above. With this in mind, it is worth noting the recent media and business focus on offshoring of knowledge-based, higher-level white-collar jobs, such as accounting, engineering, and so on. This outsourcing has been aided by high-speed Internet connections and a ready supply of highly skilled English-speaking workers in less-expensive labor markets, such as India and Eastern Europe.

These changes have the potential to lower wages and increase employment insta-bility for workers previously sheltered from international wage competition. Many labor market changes over the past two decades are consistent with higher-wage, higher-skilled workers facing more turbulence and competitive pressures in the labor market. Yet despite the fact that such workers are more likely to suffer long-term unemployment than in the past and take longer to recover from the negative impacts of job displacement, it is this same group of workers that on average has reaped the greatest labor market gains, at least in terms of wages.

Further, it is unclear how much of the economic impacts are due to offshoring per se, versus the more "ordinary" organizational restructuring that had previously impacted first blue-collar jobs in manufacturing and then lower-level white-collar jobs, such as data entry, receptionists, and call center operators. Given that the esti-mates of jobs lost due to offshoring are miniscule in proportion to the total number of jobs created and destroyed annually in the United States—amounting to about only 1 percent (Bhagwati, Panagariya, and Srinivasan 2004)—the reality is that off-shoring likely is a contributor, but only a very minor contributor, to the U.S. labor market changes that have impacted higher-skilled workers recently.

One likely factor that will limit offshoring's ability to materially impact the aver-age U.S. worker is the difficulty in integrating work of interdependent teams when team members are in distant locations. The research on distributed work reveals pro-ductivity limitations that often offset the hourly labor cost savings (Gibson and Cohen 2003).

Because peripheral jobs are not necessarily contingent, we need to focus on jobs that more narrowly fit the definition of contingent. Thus, we define contingent jobs to mean those jobs in which the organization has shifted employment risk onto employ-ees who otherwise would be hired as "regular," or "indefinitely employed," workers.

In the extreme, organizations may treat almost all jobs as contingent, as in many parts of Hollywood and aerospace. Yet these models are interesting because they represent the *promise* of what might happen in other sectors, not the *reality* of what has happened. To my knowledge, there is no data to gauge the spread of *organization-wide* contingent employment models. However, we still can address whether contingent employment has increased in the less extreme cases where companies make use of contingent or project-based jobs alongside a core of noncontingent, or "regular," jobs. The BLS defines three categories of contingent jobs: temporary help agency workers, independent contractors, and on-call workers.

*Temps*

Of all three groups, the most comprehensive data and research are available for temporary workers. The temporary help services industry has certainly evolved since the 1970s. A generation ago, temps were epitomized by the "Kelly Girl," a female working in administrative support occupations, such as secretary or receptionist, who was called in for short periods to cover for employees who were sick or on leave. Segal and Sullivan (1997) referred to these as the stereotypical "pink-collar" occupations. As Segal and Sullivan (1997) documented, however, in the 1980s the growth in temporary employment was disproportionately concentrated in blue-collar occupations. The 1980s also was a period of rapid expansion in the temporary staffing industry, though from a very small base (Levenson 2000). Despite the rapid growth, today only one to two percent of the workforce at any point in time works as a temp.

Anecdotal accounts suggest that the percentage of higher-skilled, white-collar workers employed as temps expanded during the 1990s, though it is more likely that such people were working as independent contractors (see below) rather than for staffing firms. By 2005, pink-collar occupations accounted for 25 percent of people employed by temporary staffing agencies, while 37 percent were in blue-collar occupations, 20 percent were in management and professional occupations, and 18 percent were in service and sales occupations (BLS 2005). It should be noted, however, that these figures include the "permanent" or core staff of agencies, so the percentages in the non-blue-collar categories are likely to be at least slightly overestimated.

During the boom years of the late 1990s, temporary staffing firms accounted for a disproportionate percentage of net job growth (Katz and Krueger 1999). Yet despite this, in 1995, in 2001, and in 2005, the fraction of the workforce whose primary jobs meant working for staffing agencies did not change (BLS 2001, 2005). The flat trend is likely due to two factors. First, a certain percentage of temporary jobs are held as second jobs to supplement income from a main, nontemporary job. If this type of temping increased in the late 1990s, it would show up in the establishment survey payroll statistics, but not in the Current Population Survey (CPS), which classifies workers according to their main job; it is the CPS that the BLS (2001, 2005) uses to analyze temporary jobs.

Second, temporary employment is just that—temporary. It often is used by companies to screen for regular positions (Houseman 2001), and it is used by workers as a short-term strategy when dealing with job displacement (Farber 2000). Consequently, more than half of people who are temping in any one year typically end up in "regular" jobs one year later (Segal and Sullivan 1997). As many as two to three times more people temp at some point throughout the year than are found temping at any given point in time within the year (Finegold, Levenson, and Van Buren 2003).

Thus, the concerns that have been voiced about larger and larger numbers of people being forced into temporary employment do not appear to be well founded—at least if we define temporary employment as a long-run phenomenon from which workers cannot extricate themselves. That said, temporary employment does appear to have become much more pervasive in the U.S. economy, serving as the new port of entry for many workers who today must first work as temps before being offered a regular job (Houseman 2000; Finegold et al. 2003).

Firms' increased use of temps is motivated at least partly by rising costs associated with the erosion of the employment-at-will doctrine and the associated increased cost of firing regular employees (Autor 2003). Many of these same workers in previous generations would have been hired directly by the company; for them, the new regime arguably is worse. But for a different, and likely smaller, group of workers, the ability of temporary staffing agencies to provide points of entry and free training for more marginal workers (Autor 2001; Finegold, Levenson, and Van Buren 2005) likely represents an *improvement* in their labor market prospects relative to what might have happened in the absence of staffing agencies.

For others, particularly youths who are trying out different occupations and those who are committed to finding work in a specific occupation, temporary agencies may create a more liquid market for job search that enables better matching of workers to jobs and provides a "try-before-you-buy" option for workers who want to learn more about a specific organization before committing to stay on for the long term. For these workers, temping can help them to avoid the stigma associated with having a large number of short duration jobs on one's resume. On the downside, however, workers employed with a temporary agency are much less likely to receive benefits, lowering the value of their total compensation relative to that of other workers. Thus, many temps prefer to have regular jobs and make that transition within a year (Segal and Sullivan 1997). Firms appear to use temps as part of a successful financial strategy (Nayar and Willinger 2001), suggesting that their use is not likely to revert back to the lower levels of the previous generation anytime soon.

### Independent Contractors

Independent contractors have received much less attention from both the media and researchers. Yet according to the BLS (2005), they are much more common, representing 7.4 percent of the workforce in 2005, versus 1 percent for temps (as defined by the person's "main job"). Also, independent contractors are much more likely to be older white male and college educated, compared to temps.

The demographics of independent contractors and the self-employed are very similar. This is not surprising, because there should be a lot of overlap between the two groups, particularly the two-thirds of self-employed who are unincorporated (Hipple 2004). Because of the similarities, we can use the self-employment research to make some extrapolations.

Self-employment rises with age (Evans and Leighton 1989); greater labor market experience leads to more successful self-employment. This is driven by a relatively constant rate of entry into self-employment, but a sharply declining hazard rate for leaving self-employment. Thus, over their life cycle, people learn how to not fail in self-employment, suggesting a link between accumulated labor market experience (and/or the ability to finance an attempt at self-employment) and self-employment success. The same likely is true of independent contractors, who probably are willing to enter that state of employment only after accumulating sufficient labor market experience to be able to negotiate effectively for satisfactory employment terms.

Independent contractors are twice as likely as temps to be managers and professionals, and four times as likely to be in construction and extraction occupations.

Being an independent contractor is preferred by 80 percent of the incumbents, much more than the 32 percent of temps who prefer to stay temps (BLS 2005). This probably means different things for different occupations. For managerial and professional independent contractors who prefer that role, being an independent contractor likely represents a real choice, because these skilled workers have other traditional job options to choose from. For the manual labor jobs such as construction, however, an independent contractor preference may reflect the fact that the entire industry is seasonal, and that there are relatively few benefits to being a regular employee who is laid off every year when work slows down, rather than being an independent contractor who is hired on a project basis.

The recent evidence shows that the percentage of independent contractors has not changed much, rising slightly from 6.7 percent in 1995 (Cohany 1996) to 7.4 percent in 2005 (BLS 2005). This might be surprising, given the explosion in Web-based job search sites. But despite the expansion in such job search capabilities, it is not clear that the role of informal networks has diminished in importance, since a majority of jobs traditionally are filled through informal channels, such as word-of-mouth through friends and family or professional contacts (McDonald and Elder 2005). And finding jobs through professional contacts is more important for older, managerial workers, precisely the group more likely to be independent contractors. So it is doubtful that the Internet plays a role in the current incidence of independent contractors.

Rather, if independent contractors are a relatively new phenomenon for the current generation, as compared to the 1960s and 1970s, it is more likely that they are an outgrowth of companies' efforts to save on wage and benefits costs for a group of employees whose skills put them in a position of relative strength (compared to temps) to bargain for a more transactional relationship that is viewed as favorable by both sides—organization and employee.

*Female Self-Employment*
Over the past 30 years, female self-employment has gained in importance (Devine 1994): Between 1975 and 1988, women's share of self-employment grew from 24 to 32 percent, even as the overall rate of self-employment grew. This was the "swimming upstream" period when women made wage gains in regular jobs even as rising wage inequality worked against them by lowering the real value of (disproportionately female) lower-paid jobs. Then, in the 1990s through 2003, the overall rate of self-employment fell slightly, but more so for men than women, so women's share of self-employment grew further to 34 percent.

Some commentators have said corporate "glass ceilings" lead women to strike out on their own. The relatively minor gains in female corporate board and top management team membership are consistent with this. Yet discrimination may not be the only cause of rising female self-employment. Gender differences in wage and hours worked imply converging work patterns, and the same trend may help close the self-employment gap: Rising female self-employment may be due as much to rising levels of labor market experience.

Despite any such convergence, however, women—both self-employed and non-self-employed—remain much more likely to work part-time than their male counterparts (Devine 1994). Thus, women's demands for more flexible or reduced hours schedules may partly be driving their increased self-employment rate, even as the rate of working part-time among wage and salary workers for women has declined (figure 6.1). Consequently, it is likely to be the case that glass-ceiling factors

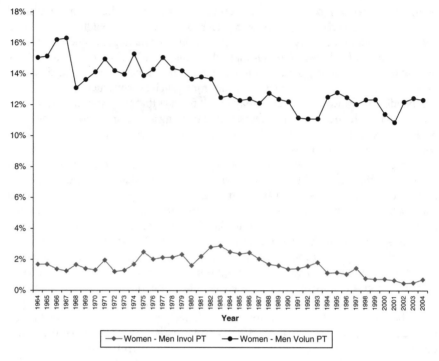

**Figure 6.1**    Gender Differences in Part-Time Employment

contributed to rising self-employment among the most successful women in very large organizations, but only marginally contributed to the rise in self-employment for women overall.

*On-Call*
On-call workers account for 1.8 percent of all jobs. This may not seem like much, except for the fact that on-call workers have been virtually ignored in discussions of the labor market, even though they account for twice as many "main" jobs as temps. The BLS defines on-call workers as those who are called to work only as needed, although they can be scheduled to work for several days or weeks in a row.

On-call workers are like temps who are hired directly by a company, instead of using a temporary staffing company as intermediary. As of 1995, there were approximately three direct-hire temps for every temp hired through a staffing agency (Polivka 1996). Just like agency temps, a majority of on-call workers would prefer to have a regular job than remain on-call.

*Contingent versus Alternative Work Arrangements*
The BLS distinguishes between alternative work arrangements (temp, independent contractor, on-call) and contingent jobs. The latter refers to jobs that are not expected to last longer than a year. Almost 40 percent of temporary help agency workers are *not* contingent. Even if we allow for overcounting due to the inclusion of core agency staff (who themselves are not temps), this would suggest that a non-negligible percentage of "temporary" assignments last for more than a year. For on-call workers and

independent contractors, the vast majority are not contingent, with fully 75 percent and 97 percent, respectively, reporting that they expect their jobs to last at least a year (BLS 2005).

Thus, like outsourcing, more alternative work arrangements, particularly independent contractors, does not necessarily imply greater job instability. Of particular importance is the fact that the percentage of independent contractors who are not contingent is virtually identical to the percentage of workers who are not contingent within "traditional" arrangements (96.6 percent versus 97.1 percent).

*Part-Time Jobs*

Part-time jobs do not equate to contingent jobs, because many people are voluntarily part-time and remain in that state from year to year. A part-time job is one that typically averages less than 35 hours per week, and thus it may be ideal for students who are in school, people (most often women) who are responsible for taking care of their dependents, and the elderly who wish to remain active in the workplace but who do not want to work a full schedule.

Despite the fact that part-time does not equal contingent, people still often equate part-time jobs with bad jobs (Blank 1990). A main reason for this is that, on average, part-time jobs pay lower wages and are less likely to offer benefits than full-time jobs. Given that the profiles of people who are better matches for part-time jobs (women, youth, elderly) all tend to earn comparatively low wages in the labor market in full-time jobs, standard human capital models find that much of the part-time/full-time wage gap is due to the different demographic characteristics of part-time workers. At issue is whether part-timers earn lower wages because of the job (that is, the job is the cause) or whether people with lower wage opportunities choose to take part-time jobs (hence, lower skills are the cause).

The reality is that both these hypotheses are probably true. Aaronson and French (2004) found evidence that working part-time produces a wage penalty for men but not for women. It also is the case, however, that lower-wage men are more likely to report that they are part-time "involuntarily," which may be partly because they refuse lower-wage full-time jobs as they hold out for higher-wage full-time jobs that may not be available (Levenson 2000). And being involuntarily part-time is a relatively temporary state, compared to being voluntarily part-time, as the former are at least 50 percent more likely to make the transition to working full-time (Stratton 1994). Finally, the rate of involuntary part-time employment is highly cyclical, rising in slack labor markets and falling in tight labor markets. Thus, while involuntary part-time work may be an inferior labor market state, it typically is not long lasting.

Moreover, the vast majority of part-time workers are voluntary, not involuntary: Only about one in seven part-time workers is involuntary. This means that trends in the overall rate of part-time employment are driven primarily by changes in voluntary part-time job holding. The trend from the 1960s through the early 1980s was slightly upward, but then it turned slightly downward through 2003.

During the last two decades, however, the gap in part-time work patterns between men and women has narrowed (figure 6.1). In the early 1980s, women's voluntary part-time employment rate exceeded men's by 14 percent; that gap narrowed during the 1980s by two percentage points (one-seventh of the overall gap) and stayed roughly constant during the 1990s. Similarly, women's involuntary part-time employment rate exceeded men's by three percentage points in the early 1980s, but it fell to less than one percentage point by 2003. Thus, as seen using other measures of economic success (wages, self-employment), the work patterns and the labor-market outcomes of men and women are becoming more similar.

### The Graying Workforce: Greater Vitality and the Aging Baby Boomers

Social scientists and social commentators have spent five decades examining how the baby boom has changed society in both the economic and noneconomic terms. The impending retirement of the baby boomers portends changing work-related norms among older workers as well.

Perhaps the most important work-related issue of relevance to both organizations and employees is the changing supply and demand of workers who in previous generations would have retired by age 65. With rising average incomes and wealth, for decades after World War II, the trend was toward earlier and earlier retirement. The pattern of increasingly earlier retirement stopped in the mid-1980s; what is unclear is what will happen next.

In one camp are those who argue that increased lifespans, improved health, and less generous Social Security benefits will lead older people to want to work for more years than in the past. Countering this argument is the research showing that previous episodes of increased health and changes in Social Security benefits did not materially impact the overall trends toward increased early retirement (Costa 1999). Thus, based on past experience alone, there is no reason to believe that we should see increasing labor force participation among people 65 and older just because the baby boomers are entering their golden years.

Yet there are a number of reasons why I believe that businesses should not assume that current employment practices, most of which are not designed with older workers in mind, are the best way to deal with the aging baby boomers. First, changing norms about work and vitality mean that the baby boomers are liable to be the first true exception to the trend toward earlier retirement—future generations will likely be more inclined to continue working at older ages. Second, the increased prevalence of defined contribution retirement plans means that the fraction of the workforce that makes poor investment decisions may increase the need to work at older ages in order to make up for shortfalls in their expected retirement income.

Third, even if the trend toward early retirement does not reverse, even if it stabilizes, a constant percentage of the population at each age will, however, continue to keep working at least into their early 70s. The baby boomers getting older means that a larger and larger percentage of the total workforce will be over 65—and even older. Indeed, instead of stabilizing, the recent data indicate *increasing* labor force participation among older cohorts, particularly men in the 62–69 age range and women in the 55–69 age range (Korczyk 2004). Thus, it is reasonable to expect greater demand for work by elderly baby boomers who will in the near future account for an increasing fraction of the labor force.

### Bridge Jobs

Many older workers make the transition to retirement by working in another job and/or working part-time after spending much of their careers in one full-time job (Gustman and Steinmeier 1984; Quinn, Burkhauser, and Myers 1990). This may become more and more important as the baby boomers enter the traditional retirement years, leading to an upsurge in demand for "bridge" jobs: In the 1990s, more than 20 percent of full-time older workers (with 10 or more years of job tenure) took transition jobs (Chen 2004).

One interesting pattern in the recent data is that individuals leaving career jobs in larger companies are more likely to take on part-time jobs elsewhere, compared to workers leaving smaller companies (Chen 2004). This suggests that large firms already may be missing important opportunities to offer part-time bridge jobs to older workers as a retention strategy for critical talent. Demand for such flexible employment options may increase significantly in the coming years.

## Summary of Findings

### Changes in Wages and Total Compensation over the Past Three Decades

- There has been increased dispersion in wages throughout the economy. This means more wage winners and losers than in the last generation.
- Lower-wage, less-educated male workers have not fared well. Their inflation-adjusted wages have fallen. Wages for men in the top half of the income distribution and for women throughout the income distribution, in contrast, have increased faster than inflation.
- Women's wage gains are partly due to greater educational attainment and occupational advancement, accounting for more and more professional degrees and jobs in previously male-dominated fields such as medicine, law, and business/management. A generation ago of all the female college graduates 50 percent went on to become teachers; today, fewer than 10 percent.
- Racial and ethnic wage trends track the gender differences, for the most part. Black men saw moderate improvements and Hispanic men fell further behind to a moderate extent. Black and Hispanic women, in contrast, had continual gains.
- Falling healthcare coverage, shifting of healthcare costs among those covered by insurance, and the substitution of defined contribution for defined benefit plans all have shifted risks from firms to workers, thereby lowering the value of total compensation relative to what it would have been otherwise. These shifts are most pronounced for lower-wage and less-educated workers, which exacerbates the trends in wages.

### Changes in Job Stability, Hours of Work, and Job Loss

- Older and less-educated men have shorter job tenure than in the past. Women, more-educated men, and younger men have longer job tenure than in the past.
- Changes in hours of work mirror changes in the wage distribution. College-educated workers are working longer hours, particularly at the top of the hours distribution; less-educated workers work decreased hours.
- Gender today appears to be growing less important in distinguishing hours of work than is education. College-educated workers, regardless of gender, are

increasingly more likely to have similar patterns of hours worked, relative to high school–educated workers.

- Demands on highly skilled employees' time have increased over the past four decades. The opposite is true for lower-skilled employees.

### Changes in Contingent Work

- The fraction of the labor force working as temps has increased, though it remains relatively low at any given point in time. Employers' use of temps to screen for regular positions appears to have increased, which partly explains why a larger fraction of the workforce is serving as a temp at some point or the other during the year than at any specific moment. There are about twice as many people working "on call" at any given moment—another reserve pool of flexible labor.
- Firms' use of independent contractors is even more widespread, accounting for 7–8 percent of all jobs. There is little evidence of this trend because of limited data. Even if the trend has been up sharply, most independent contractors appear to be happy with that kind of employment relationship and have job security on par with "regular" employees.
- The trend toward retiring at an earlier and earlier age stopped recently. It is too soon to say for certain whether the trend has stopped for good, will continue again, or will reverse itself. However, it is reasonable to conclude that a larger and larger fraction of the labor force will consist of people working past the "normal" retirement age and into their elderly years. This may create demand for jobs that "bridge" regular employment and retirement.

## Conclusion

What are the implications of these trends for individuals and for organizations?

The past 30 years have produced an increased shifting of economic risks onto workers, both in the form of greater dispersion in compensation and lower guaranteed benefit levels (both health and retirement). People today have to take care of themselves, more so than they did in the past, because organizations are shouldering less of the burden.

Older and less-educated male workers, who traditionally had careers in organizations, have shorter job tenure and lower compensation than they did in the past. These losses have been balanced by gains for women, for shorter-tenure men, and for better-educated men. Thus, the traditional longer-term career appears to have been replaced by shorter-term engagements; some groups have gained, while others have fallen behind where they were a generation ago.

The overall impression is that the employment relationship appears to have become more transactional, more "what-have-you-done-for-me-lately." People are more likely than their parents were to be working as temps and independent contractors. They appear to be under greater pressure to constantly prove their economic value to organizations—sufficiently high productivity to justify their compensation—to get and/or keep a "regular" job.

The national economic trends are consistent with organizational performance management and reward practices that more closely tie individual economic outcomes to organizational economic outcomes, leading to both more variability among workers who previously were rewarded similarly, and more variability for any given worker over time. It is not clear that these changes are necessarily good or bad from a productivity standpoint, particularly if the workers whose skills are in high(er) demand are willing to go along with a more transactional employment relationship. But if organizations increasingly are creating haves and have-nots among demographically equivalent workers, are they undermining the community and commitment that might be needed for long-term success?

Given the relative lack of sophisticated HR metrics and analytics within organizations (Lawler, Levenson, and Boudreau 2004), it is uncertain whether organizations are targeting the right workers with rewards, development, and career advancement. The pendulum may have swung too far toward differentiation. Would organizations guarantee themselves a better set of skills in the future—through both development and retention—if they were to go back to the earlier practices of less individual-based and more group-based rewards and development?

Even in cases where organizations correctly identify and reward the "right" employees, the trend appears to be toward greater and greater responsibility and demands being placed on their shoulders. What are the limits of this trend? At some point will these employees refuse to shoulder this burden, opting instead for shorter-term engagements (that might be shorter than what the organization needs) or for not engaging at all in the first place? What then would be the long-run implications for organizations' competitive advantage? These are important issues that organizations should take into account as they weigh their options on job and organization design in today's labor market.

# Part 2

# Careers in the New American Workplace

# 7

# Is Education The Answer? Trends in the Supply and Demand for Skills in the U.S. Workforce

*David Finegold*

To treat a host of economic ailments—from reducing income inequality and unemployment to boosting productivity and innovation—the favorite prescription of policymakers across the world is more education. This was never more apparent than in the last of the 2004 U.S. presidential debates. First, President George Bush was asked whether he supported raising the minimum wage, which was at its lowest level in real terms since the 1930s. His response was that "the best way to increase earnings for this group was through more and better education." Later, he was asked what he would do about the growth in the offshoring of U.S. jobs to India and other nations. To this he responded, "We need more and better education."

The arguments in favor of a high-quality education and ongoing opportunities for skill development appear unassailable in today's rapidly changing, knowledge-based economy. However, as demonstrated by the experience of numerous well-qualified, yet underemployed, computer programmers and other IT workers in the last few years, a high level of education is no longer a guarantee for obtaining well-paying, secure employment (Levenson this volume). And most Americans are not highly educated: only a little more than one quarter of the workforce has a four-year college degree; of those who did not attend college, relatively few have any form of skill certification that is rewarded well in the labor market. In contrast with Germany, where a large majority of the population completes an apprenticeship before entering the workforce, the supply of certified apprenticeships in the United States has dwindled to fewer than 20,000 (Crouch et al. 1999).

A key factor in the strong economic performance of the United States over the last 50 years has been access to a larger supply of highly skilled workers than its main economic rivals. Starting with the GI Bill following World War II, the United States was the first nation to create a mass higher education system. The relative economic advantage generated by this high-skilled labor supply began to increase dramatically during the 1990s: technological change and globalization brought about a shift toward a more knowledge-based economy, and a growth in the demand for college graduates and higher salaries for those with bachelors' or advanced degrees (Shaw this volume; Levenson this volume).

While the need for a highly educated workforce has continued to grow, a number of trends appear to be undermining the educational advantage that the United States has had for so long. This chapter focuses on four of these trends:

- a relative deficit in the production of basic skills for the majority of the workforce;
- a loss of the country's lead in the supply of college graduates, as other nations have substantially expanded their higher education systems;
- a decline, following 9/11, in the supply of highly educated immigrant students coming to, and remaining in, the United States to work;
- reduced incentives for employers to invest in developing the skills of their workforce.

## Basic Skill Deficit

As early as 1983, with the publication of the landmark report *A Nation at Risk* (NCEE 1983), American policymakers recognized the failure of the education system to prepare the majority of America's young people for the challenges of an increasingly global, knowledge-based economy. They chose inflammatory Cold War rhetoric to frame the problem:

> Our once-unchallenged preeminence in commerce, industry, science, and technological innovation is being overtaken by competitors throughout the world. . . . If an unfriendly foreign power had attempted to impose on America the mediocre educational performance that exists today, we might have viewed it as an act of war. As it stands, we have allowed this to happen to ourselves . . . We have, in effect, been committing an act of unthinking, unilateral educational disarmament.

The two decades that followed saw a nearly continuous series of educational reforms. These ranged from the introduction of more rigorous standards for high school graduation to a variety of experiments to introduce more market mechanisms into K-12 education, including school choice (charter schools, vouchers) and hiring for-profit companies to manage failing school districts (the Edison Project). Despite these reform efforts, a high percentage of young people in the United States remain educationally at risk. In international comparisons of math, science, and reading proficiency, American students consistently trail behind their main European and Asian competitors. In the most recent comparison, conducted in 2003 by the Organization of Economic Cooperation and Development's (OECD) Program for International Students' Assessment, U.S. tenth graders' scores (see table 7.1) were average in reading, below the OECD average in science, and very poor in practical math and problem solving, ranking twenty-fourth out of 29 nations (OECD 2004). More than one quarter of the U.S. high school students tested failed to reach even the most basic standard of math proficiency.

The problem is particularly acute among the most rapidly growing segments of the U.S. population—Latinos and African Americans in inner-city public schools. It

**Table 7.1** PISA 2003 Mean Scores in Mathematics—OECD Countries

| | Mean Score | S.E. | OECD countries | |
|---|---|---|---|---|
| | | | Upper Rank | Lower Rank |
| *OECD countries* | | | | |
| Finland | 544 | (1.9) | 1 | 3 |
| Korea | 542 | (3.2) | 1 | 4 |
| Netherlands | 538 | (3.1) | 1 | 5 |
| Japan | 534 | (4.0) | 2 | 7 |
| Canada | 532 | (1.8) | 4 | 7 |
| Belgium | 529 | (2.3) | 4 | 8 |
| Switzerland | 527 | (3.4) | 4 | 9 |
| Australia | 524 | (2.1) | 7 | 9 |
| New Zealand | 523 | (2.3) | 7 | 10 |
| Czech Republic | 516 | (3.5) | 9 | 14 |
| Iceland | 515 | (1.4) | 10 | 13 |
| Denmark | 514 | (2.7) | 10 | 14 |
| France | 511 | (2.5) | 11 | 15 |
| Sweden | 509 | (2.6) | 12 | 16 |
| Austria | 506 | (3.3) | 13 | 18 |
| Germany | 503 | (3.3) | 14 | 18 |
| Ireland | 503 | (2.4) | 15 | 18 |
| Slovak Republic | 498 | (3.3) | 16 | 21 |
| Norway | 495 | (2.4) | 18 | 21 |
| Luxembourg | 493 | (1.0) | 19 | 21 |
| Poland | 490 | (2.5) | 19 | 23 |
| Hungary | 490 | (2.8) | 19 | 23 |
| Spain | 485 | (2.4) | 22 | 24 |
| United States | 483 | (2.9) | 22 | 24 |
| Portugal | 466 | (3.4) | 25 | 26 |
| Italy | 466 | (3.1) | 25 | 26 |
| Greece | 445 | (3.9) | 27 | 27 |
| Turkey | 423 | (6.7) | 28 | 28 |
| Mexico | 385 | (3.6) | 29 | 29 |

is compounded by the more than one million illegal immigrants in U.S. schools, most of them not native English speakers, who place a large, unfunded burden on already overcrowded urban schools. In California, which has the highest concentration of illegal immigrants, the public school system is in dire shape. Only 60 percent of Latinos and 57 percent of African Americans graduated on time from high school, compared to 84 percent of Asian Americans and 78 percent of whites. The situation was even worse in the Los Angeles Unified School District, where only 39 percent of Latinos and 47 percent of African Americans graduated with their cohorts (Helfand 2005).

The Bush administration's "No Child Left Behind" policy and many state reform efforts have sought to address the problems of underachievement by raising educational requirements and testing to ensure that students demonstrate proficiency in core subjects before being promoted to the next grade level or graduating from high school. But there are concerns that the failure to fund local school systems to meet these new requirements and the raising of the attainment bar may have the reverse effect—forcing the most disadvantaged students out of the system even earlier (Tomsho 2005). Currently, 70 percent of U.S. eighth graders are failing to meet the proficiency levels in math, science, and reading on national achievement tests set by the Bush policy (RAND 2005).

## Loss of Higher-Education Advantage

The U.S.'s large higher-education system has compensated for the relatively poor educational preparation of the average high school graduates. Throughout the latter half of the twentieth century, the system generated a larger supply of college graduates, than the systems of the main competitors of the United States. This helped to fill the growing number of managerial, professional, and service jobs that were created as the U.S. economy continued its long-term shift away from agricultural and manufacturing. In the last two decades, however, other nations have significantly closed the graduate gap, dramatically increasing their levels of college graduates while the overall percentage of the U.S. population obtaining a bachelor's degree has grown at a slower rate, from 23 percent of all 25 to 29-year-olds in 1980 to 28 percent in 2003 (Peter, Horn, and Carroll 2005, 11).

The shift in relative educational advantage is perhaps best illustrated by comparing the United States with South Korea. At the end of the Korean War, South Korea had virtually no higher-education infrastructure, and the majority of the population was illiterate. Today, South Korea has almost universal literacy, and more than 80 percent of school-leavers go on to higher education, compared to 59 percent of their U.S. peers.

The 30 percent difference between those attending higher education in the United States and those completing a degree is accounted for by two factors: (1) the dramatic growth in community college enrollments over the last 30 years, and (2) the high college dropout rate.

The percentage of the U.S. workforce that is aged 25 and over with some college education, but not a four-year degree, has grown from 11 percent in 1970 to 27 percent in 2003 (EPF 2005, 74). The number of individuals completing an associate's degree is roughly half the number completing a BA, with women (up from 227,739 in 1980–1981 to 357,024 in 2001–2002) far outnumbering men (up from 188,638 in 1980–1981 to 238,109 in 2001–2002) (Peter and Horn 2005). But there is an alarming attrition rate at all levels of the higher-education system: 42 percent of those seeking a bachelor's degree, 47 percent of those seeking an occupational certificate, and 56 percent of those enrolled for an associate's degree fail to complete (Bailey et al. 2004, vii). For those who do complete a qualification, the returns are substantial, ranging from 67 percent higher earnings for women with four-year degrees and 37 percent for men matched with comparable high school graduates, to 39 percent for women and 16 percent for men completing a two-year occupational degree (Bailey et al. 2005, 8).

Alongside the U.S. higher-education system's failure to keep pace with the growth of its competitors, there has been a dramatic change in the gender mix of those in college: the percentage of young men completing a degree was almost completely stagnant over this 23-year period, edging up from 24 percent to 26 percent of the age cohort, compared to a growth of nearly 50 percent in the number of young women obtaining a BA (from 21 percent to 31 percent of the age group) (Bailey et al. 2005, 8).

As a consequence, women now make up 56 percent of all college graduates, up from 42 percent in 1970 (Freeman 2004).

Although the expansion of career opportunities and accompanying incentives to pursue higher education for women is a very positive development, the flip side is much more worrying—that is, the stagnation in the number of young men attending college during a period when many of the manufacturing jobs that used to offer them relatively high wages and benefits have been disappearing rapidly from the U.S. economy.

Differences in the educational qualifications of different ethnic groups in the United States are stark: more than 44 percent of Asian Americans aged 25 and over have a bachelor's degree or higher, compared to 24 percent for this age group in general (U.S. Census Bureau 2003). There is a strong correlation between such educational differences and earnings: the average Asian American family's income was more than $9,000 above the U.S. average of $50,046 in 2000. In contrast, there are more young African American males in prison than in college; the African American prison population has increased five-fold since 1980, when young black men were three times more likely to be in college than incarcerated (Talk Left 2002).

Differences in educational attainment are as dramatic within broad ethnic categories as they are between groups. Among Asian Americans, close to 64 percent of those aged 25 and over with Indian origins have at least a BA, compared to only 7–9 percent of Cambodians, Laotian, and Hmong, and the Indian American average family earnings are nearly twice as large. Research suggests that these differences are not due to innate intelligence, but rather to differences in culture, family emphasis on education, and the quality of the schools and surrounding environment in which young people are growing up.

The loss of comparative advantage in higher-level skills for the United States is most pronounced in the fields of science and engineering. Graduates in these fields have been one of the key resources fueling the growth of U.S. high-tech industries (Finegold 1998). Since the publication of the original *Work in America*, there has been a dramatic decline in the relative strength of the U.S. technical workforce. In 1975, the United States ranked third internationally in the percentage of 24-year-olds completing a science and engineering degree, trailing only Finland and Japan (Grimes 2005). By 2000, the United States ranked seventeenth, because of the decline from more than 5 percent to less than 4 percent of young Americans graduating in science and engineering, while the supply of technical manpower more than tripled in such countries as Finland, France, Taiwan, and South Korea to more than 10 percent of each cohort. Although the quality of science and engineering education and research from U.S. universities remains world-class, leading Asian nations now produce eight times as many technical graduates as the United States (Friedman 2005); there are some questions about the quality of many of the new graduates being produced in China and other Asian nations, some of whom may be more comparable to graduates from U.S. community colleges (Gereffi and Wadhwa 2005), but the much higher growth rates in individuals seeking to enter technical fields is unquestionable.

Moreover, demographic trends suggest that the gap is only likely to grow: the most rapidly growing segments of the U.S. school population, including the women who are a clear majority of those going on to college, have historically been underrepresented in science and engineering, with many of those who do complete high school lacking the math and science foundation to pursue technical courses at a university.

The high attrition rate of those who enter a university hoping to pursue college-level technical work is another sign of the inadequate preparation in science and math: only half of the 120,000 U.S. students who enroll for an engineering degree complete their studies (Grimes 2005). The appeal of pursuing careers in science and engineering has declined further compared to those in law and finance, which offer higher salaries and require less time to become qualified (Teitelbaum 2002).

## Reduced Supply of Immigrant Talent in the United States

The United States has historically supplemented its own supply of graduates by attracting the best and the brightest from other countries. Since colonial times, immigrants have played a vital role in building the American economy. Thanks to a skill-bias in immigration law, there has been a sharp increase in the educational qual-ifications of the legal immigrant workforce. (Illegal immigrants, however, tend to have a much lower skill profile.) In 1990, one quarter of all Ph.D. scientists working in the United States were foreign-born, and up to 50 percent of graduate students currently being trained in U.S. science and engineering graduate programs are for-eign-born (Stephan 2002). The percentage of foreign-born new doctorates working in the United States grew 760 percent between 1973 and 1997, more than twice the growth in American-born doctorates during this period (Stephan 2002). Indeed, by the 1990s, the odds of a new infant receiving a U.S. engineering PhD were greater for a Taiwan-born child than an American one (North 1995).

These immigrant scientists outperform their American-born counterparts on a range of measures of research productivity, from publication of the most influential research to membership in the National Academy of Sciences (Stephan 2002). They also play a key role in creating new high-tech enterprises, with Indian and Chinese immigrants alone accounting for more than 25 percent of new start-ups formed in Silicon Valley (Saxenian 1999).

In the post-9/11 environment, this vital source of technical workers has been threatened, as concerns about terrorism have led to visa restrictions that make it sig-nificantly harder for foreign-born students to come to the United States and to stay on to work when they have completed their studies. In addition, the annual quota of H-1B visas (issued for highly skilled immigrants to obtain long-term jobs) was cut in half. These policy changes, along with harder-to-quantify shifts in international per-ceptions of U.S. attitudes toward foreigners, have had a chilling effect on foreign-student demand for U.S. education: between 2003 and 2004, U.S. universities experienced the first decline in international student enrollment since 1971–1972 (AACU 2004). The overall decline was a relatively small 2.4 percent, with a more sig-nificant 8 percent decline from the Middle East.

The decline in foreign student applications, however, has been far more significant, with a drop of 28 percent in 2003–2004, and an even sharper drop of 45 percent in applications from China (Dillon 2004). At the same time, a growing number of other countries—most notably Australia, Singapore, Canada, Great Britain, and India—are competing aggressively to attract international students and to keep their own brightest students at home (Simkins 2005). In 1990, for example, significantly more students from Taiwan, South Korea, and China came to the United States for their doctorates than those who remained home; by 2000, the situation had been reversed. The most dramatic change occurred among the Chinese, with more than 8,000 students earning doctorates in China compared to just over 2,000 in the United States (Colvin 2005).

### Declining Incentives for Companies to Invest in Developing the U.S. Workforce

The economic theory of human capital suggests that companies should be unwilling to invest in the development of general skills because such skills are transferable to other employers; hence, the companies run the risk that they will lose their investment when workers they have trained are hired away by competitors (Becker 1964). This theory appears to imply that companies would be unwilling to invest time and effort to improve the quality of U.S. schools and colleges, since the education they provide is inherently a "public good" and since no company is likely to hire a sufficient number of graduates from these institutions to justify the investment.

Despite this theory, there is clear empirical evidence that U.S. companies *are* devoting substantial resources to developing the general skills of their workforce. A recent survey of U.S. firms with more than 100 employees indicates that, overall, U.S. companies spent more than $50 billion on workforce development in 2004, with three-quarters of the money going to salaries of trainees and trainers (*Training Magazine* 2004). Included in such company-sponsored workforce development activities are

- informal, on-the-job learning (the most prevalent type of workforce development);
- formal company training and leadership development programs (whether delivered in-house or through outside providers);
- tuition reimbursement programs (where the firm pays all or part of the costs for employees who take for-credit courses in their own time);
- e-learning (the use of the Internet and other associated multimedia technologies to deliver training wherever and whenever the learners desire, and at the pace at which they prefer to learn);
- corporate universities, a relatively recent creation, where firms provide managers, employees, and sometimes suppliers and customers with a wide range of course offerings. The member organization for corporate universities has 131 members, with 75 percent located in the United States (Corporate University Xchange 2001).

Despite the large aggregate expenditure and diverse array of activities, such employer-sponsored education and training programs are unlikely to address the deficiencies of a significant segment of the U.S. workforce, which leaves the education system without an adequate foundation of general skills. One reason is that a high proportion of employer training expenditure goes to individuals who already have the highest levels of education. In addition, the average amount of time employees spend in firm-sponsored development activities is relatively small. The most recent training data from a nationally representative sample of U.S. employers found that, in establishments with 50 or more workers, employees reported receiving more than a week's worth (44.5. hours) of training in a six-month period (May–October 1995), but that only 13.4 hours were in formal training, with the rest coming through informal on-the-job learning (BLS 1996b).

A parallel survey of employers found that even less formal training was offered, averaging 10.7 hours-per-employee (BLS 1996a). Computer training was the most common form of job-specific skills training (received by 54 percent of all employees), while occupational health and safety training was the most common type of general training, followed by development of communication skills. In terms of more general education, less than 3 percent of establishments (19 percent of large establishments) offered remedial training in areas such as reading, math, or English as a second language, and the average spending on tuition reimbursement was just $51 per employee, with larger establishments again making a significantly greater investment. The most common reasons that employers cited for offering formal training included "providing skills specific to the organization (75 percent of establishments), keeping up with changes in technology, and retaining valuable employees (both >50 percent)."

Several major long-term trends appear to be reducing the incentives for companies to invest in developing workers' skills, including

- a long-term decline in the percentage of the workforce represented by labor unions (the BLS survey found that unionized establishments offered more training than non-union ones);
- the rupturing of the old employment contract between companies and workers, a contract that implied a long-term employment relationship (if neither side is committed to a long-term relationship, the up-front costs of general skill development, with benefits then spread over the subsequent work life, make firms less likely to be willing to invest in individuals (Rousseau 1997));
- the dramatic recent growth in the offshoring of high-skill work to lower wage nations, most notably India (see below).

*Training Magazine*'s annual survey of U.S. employers provides some evidence suggesting that these trends are beginning to have a negative impact on education and training activity. For the first time since the survey began in 1982, the level of company training expenditure dropped for two consecutive years between 2002 and 2004, from $56.8 billion to $51.3 billion (Dolezelak 2004). Although the decline in overall expenditure of just under 10 percent may not seem overly significant, salary costs of $37.5 billion remained almost constant during this period, while spending on seminars and conferences, custom and off-the-shelf materials, and other expenditures dropped by 28 percent, from $19.3 to $13.9 billion.

Whether this represents a short-term response to the downturn in the business cycle that followed 9/11 and the dot-com crash—or the start of a longer-term shift by U.S. firms to put more emphasis on hiring workers with the needed skills rather than investing in developing their own workers—is too early to assess. The fact that one-third of U.S. *Fortune* 500 companies now have a policy of forced ranking employees and managing out the lowest performers, however, suggests that they are not committed to long-term employment relationships and the training of all workers.

## Offshoring

Historically, corporations have had deep ties to their country of origin and have been heavily dependent on their home country's population to fill their key leadership and technical positions. For example, an average of 90 percent of a typical firm's R&D investment has been located in the same country as its corporate headquarters (Galbraith 1998). The embeddedness of a firm in a particular national context gave it a strong interest to ensure that the quality of educational outputs in its home country met its workforce needs; if they did not, it had an incentive to invest in, and work for, the reform of the educational system.

The transformation of the global economy in the last decade, fostered by the spread of the Internet and other information technologies, has significantly changed this equation. Offshoring of work has been occurring for centuries and is part of the wider system of international trade; what is new is the geographic mobility of the most highly skilled work. The ease with which firms can now move information instantaneously, and nearly without cost, around the world has meant that many segments of knowledge work—call centers, accounting, web design, claims processing, medical diagnosis (such as reading a CAT-scan or X-ray)—can be relocated to wherever a supply of labor with suitable skills can be found at the best price.

India, with a population now exceeding one billion and an education system that has produced millions of English-speaking graduates who are particularly strong in computer programming, engineering, and other technical areas, is a leading source of offshore human resources (see Foulkes this volume). India has attracted many top U.S. high-technology companies, including IBM, General Electric, and Hewlett Packard, among others, to set up operations in Bangalore and Hyderabad and to take advantage of the available high-quality, but relatively low-cost, workforce. Call center operators, paid an average of $10 per hour in the United States, earn an average of $1.50 per hour in India (Meredith 2003).

Similar salary differences of 10:1 are found in many technical and service occupations. With this supply of high-quality, low-cost workers, Indian firms such as Infosys and Wipro are leading the way in the provision of comprehensive outsourcing services for multinational corporations. But lower labor costs are not the only attraction. Many corporations are organizing "virtual teams" that take advantage of the time difference between the United States, India, and Europe to offer round-the-clock technical support, and to expedite new product development.

With the IT infrastructure in place, the pressures of global competition served to accelerate the offshoring trend. India has more than 850,000 people working in IT and business services, with roughly three-quarters of those jobs originating from U.S. firms. Experts estimate that the United States, Europe, and Japan will continue to shift 600,000 jobs per year to lower-wage nations over the next decade, with as many as ten million U.S. jobs, many occupied by college graduates, under threat (Meredith 2003). As the growth of high-tech work continues to attract many emigrant Indian technical experts and investors back home from the United States, it appears likely that India will continue to move rapidly up the value-chain, creating its own companies that will be generating new innovations in products and services. At the same time, many other countries—Malaysia, the Philippines, China, Hungary—are entering the offshoring business, providing alternative low-cost suppliers to U.S. firms.

The offshoring trend is well illustrated by the experience of IBM. In May 2005, IBM announced the laying off of some 10,000 employees in Europe and the United States as part of its ongoing global restructuring efforts. Meanwhile, it continues the rapid growth of its Indian operations, which already include over 20,000 employees performing a wide variety of programming, consulting, and back-office functions. But it is not just companies who are embracing offshoring: state and local governments, which might be expected to resist the movement of jobs away from their voter and taxpayer base, have begun to move work offshore because of budget pressures. And now entrepreneurs have given a new meaning to offshoring, creating a company,

SeaCode, that can house 600 foreign software engineers on a cruise ship anchored off the California coast, combining the benefits of a lower-cost workforce with greater proximity to U.S. clients (Hiltzik 2005).

Although U.S. job losses associated with offshoring have generated many head-lines and much anxiety among workers, it is important to recognize that there are many benefits from offshoring. In addition to the obvious benefits to developing nations in raising their standards of living, there are other gains for the United States: access to cheaper goods and services, direct creation of high-value-added U.S. jobs to manage a global labor force, and indirect job creation through the growth of a large middle class in China, India, and other nations, a growth that generates greater demand for U.S. goods and services.

Then, too, access to a highly skilled workforce in other nations may prove essential for U.S. firms to offset shortages of managerial and professional talent in the coming decades if baby boomers retire as projected (Levenson this volume). Thomas Friedman (2005) has even suggested that the benefits may include helping to preserve world peace; his "Dell Theory of Conflict Prevention" posits that no country that is part of a high-tech supply chain has ever gone to war. In support of this theory, he cites the strong pressure that India's IT firms placed on its government in 2002 to avoid escalation of a conflict with Pakistan, recognizing that a war would likely cause the permanent relocation of the good jobs that they had worked so hard to create.

## Tying It All Together: the Case of the Biotechnology Industry

The driving force in innovation and job creation in the latter half of the twentieth century was the global diffusion of information technology. Many are predicting that the twenty-first century will be the age of Biology. Advances in biotechnology are likely to have profound impacts on health, agricultural, the environment, and indus-try, affecting as much as 50 percent of global GDP in the coming decades (Shahi 2004). A quick look at the evolution of this heavily knowledge-intensive industry illustrates some emerging challenges and opportunities for the American education system and workforce.

The United States created the world's first biotechnology companies in the late 1970s—Cetus, Genentech, Biogen, Amgen—and has dominated the biotech industry during the first 25 years of its existence. A set of interrelated factors sometimes referred to as a high-skill ecosystem (Finegold 1998) or the Silicon Valley model (Saxenian 1994) has helped the United States to develop clusters of successful bioen-terprises that other countries have had difficulty emulating. These factors include

- cutting-edge innovations and highly skilled graduates produced by top U.S. uni-versities and research institutes,
- strong legal protection for intellectual property (IP), the Bayh-Dole Act of 1980 that gave universities strong incentives to patent and commercialize the results of their research through spinout companies or licensing agreements,
- access to the large amounts of capital needed to develop highly risky technolo-gies, and the world's largest and most profitable market for biomedical and bioagricultural products.

Although U.S. companies currently have a dominant position in the global bioscience industry, all of the major developed and newly industrialized nations are seeking to close the gap and build their own strong presence in this industry. The small island nation of Singapore, for example, has invested billions of dollars to create a biotech cluster that seeks to combine many of the elements of the high-skill ecosystem described above (Finegold et al. 2004). While the number of biotech firms in the United States has remained relatively stagnant at about 1,500 over the last 15 years, Europe and Asia have seen an explosion in bioscience start-ups; they now surpass the United States in the number of biotech companies.

With the entry of India and China into the WTO, and the adoption of the TRIPS agreement for IP protection in 2005, two huge new competitors are likely to emerge on the world stage. India alone has more than 400 bioscience companies, most created in the last decade (Finegold, Shakti, and Shahi 2005). Even though many of these firms are likely to fail, it is clear that the United States will face growing competition going forward in this most knowledge-intensive of all industries (employing more Ph.D. holders as a percentage of the workforce than any other sector).

At a time when the competition for bioscience leadership is increasing, it is not clear that the U.S. education system is preparing the population effectively for this challenge. A majority of the U.S. population has low levels of scientific literacy—for example, not knowing that tomatoes have DNA—and is ill-equipped for the coming world of genetic-based medicine and biology-driven industry (Nelson 1999). And while some states are experimenting with programs to improve science education, others, such as Kansas and Pennsylvania, are considering changing their biology curriculum in ways that will hinder the teaching of established scientific facts.

At the other extreme, the long time required to complete a biomedical PhD (six to seven years on average), followed by multiple post-docs and often relatively low-paying research positions, makes this career track unappealing to students entering top universities (Teitelbaum 2002). As a consequence, the United States may find that scientific leadership and accompanying employment opportunities in the biotechnologies that will underpin many key sectors of the economy will gradually migrate to Asia, where the talent is available.

### Ongoing U.S. Competitive and Education Advantages

Despite many signs of deterioration in America's historical educational advantage, there are a number of other important areas where the United States retains a competitive edge in the knowledge economy. Notable among them are being native speakers of English, the global business language; having one of the most diverse populations in the world and the creativity that this diversity of perspectives and cultures brings; the openness to risk-taking; access to capital; a culture of entrepreneurialism that helps turn this creativity into new businesses; and a stable set of political and economic institutions and constitutional protections for the free sharing of information that create an environment in which new knowledge-intensive businesses can thrive.

On top of that, the United States continues to enjoy a number of educational advantages for the knowledge economy. It is home to the world's most vibrant and diverse higher education sector, including more than a third of the world's colleges and universities, and a very high percentage of the world's top-ranked research institutions (Friedman 2005, 244). As Asian countries such as Singapore and China that seek to expand their own educational elite have recognized, creating a new world-class research university is a very slow and expensive proposition, although this has not deterred them from making the investment. These research universities not only prepare the brightest students to enter high-paying professional, scientific, and managerial positions, but they also generate the research breakthroughs and patents that are vital to the success of biotechnology and many other high-tech sectors.

In addition, while they now have significantly more competition than in years past, U.S. research universities and the opportunity-rich U.S. high-tech economy continue to exercise a strong magnetic attraction for the world's top technical talent. Clear evidence of this came in 2004, when the entire annual allotment of H-1B visas was filled within the first few hours of it being made available.

Another key skills advantage for the United States is Americans' conviction that education is an investment. Individuals and families are prepared to devote their resources to education because they believe it will yield a high return. This stands in contrast to most European and other developed countries where higher education has traditionally been perceived as an entitlement for the top performers in secondary education. The state is expected to pay for the education of these young people, which tends to limit levels of university enrollments to what governments can afford. While this situation has started to change in countries such as Great Britain and Australia, it is difficult to change popular perceptions, and these perceptions may act as a deterrent to higher education participation, particularly for the working class.

Treating education as an investment is likely to be even more important in the twenty-first century because, with the move toward a more knowledge-based economy, the returns to education have been increasing significantly. Moreover, the accelerating rate of change in work demands caused by technological innovation and global competition is reducing the shelf-life of skills and, hence, the need for frequent retraining and reinvention of individual careers.

## Ways Forward

To leverage its strengths while dealing effectively with the many educational challenges facing the American workforce in the twenty-first century, the United States needs nothing short of a national skills strategy. Asian competitors such as Singapore and South Korea are already aggressively pursuing such national skills policies, but it is not something that the U.S. has traditionally undertaken; there are two reasons for this: (1) the U.S.'s federal system, where education has historically been overwhelmingly a state and local responsibility (accounting for 93 percent of the K-12 funding); and (2) the strong market orientation of the United States, an orientation that limits any government efforts at industrial or skills policy for those in the workforce.

There are, however, a few historical U.S. precedents for such large-scale interventions (Colvin 2005). At the turn of the last century, the United States recognized that the shift from an agricultural to an industrial economy required higher levels of education and created a system of universal high school education. Then, in 1958, following the launch of Sputnik, the United States recognized that it was in danger of losing its technological leadership and undertook a massive investment in science and engineering research and education that culminated in sending a man to the moon, an act that underpinned the success of U.S. high-tech industry for the next two generations.

Great Britain offers a more recent example of large-scale education and training reform that suggests what can possibly be done where there is sufficient national will and resources. In contrast with the United States, England retained an elite education and training system through the mid-1980s, with only 7 percent of the working population possessing a university degree, and one of the lowest participation rates in post-compulsory education among OECD countries (Hayes et al. 1984).

Over the following 20 years, however, the education and training system was transformed, with large increases in participation in further and higher education. By 1995, more than 20 percent of young people were completing bachelor's degrees; by 2004, Britain had surpassed the United States, with more than 33 percent of young people completing a bachelor's degree. The Blair government has set a target of 50 percent of young people completing a higher education qualification by the end of the decade (see Leitch, 2005).

These dramatic improvements were achieved starting in the 1980s with a highly decentralized education system quite similar to that of the United States. Under Margaret Thatcher, Great Britain began a complete overhaul of its system, including the creation of a national curriculum and assessment, empowering head teachers (principals) to manage their schools, reform of the examination system, dramatic expansion of higher education, with funding targeted at institutions that were most able to grow enrollments while maintaining low dropout rates, creation of a National Vocational Qualifications (NVQ) framework, and investments that now total £8 billion annually in lifelong learning for those in the workforce (Finegold 1992). While the reforms have undergone many iterations over two decades, and are still not without their problems, they have succeeded in dramatically increasing the preparedness of all young people for entering the modern world of work.

Given the differences in the structure of government, any major U.S. reform will require more of a partnership approach among federal, state, and local government, and between the public and private sectors. While the study of a full-scale strategy is beyond the scope of this chapter, let us conclude by examining some of the options that research suggests may help government policymakers, companies, and individuals better prepare America's workforce.

### Government Policymakers

The members of America's future workforce must be equipped with the tools to operate in a knowledge-intensive economy. To help accomplish that, in the 1960s, in a bold stroke of public policy, California set up the Kerr Commission, which designed a three-tier higher education system to meet the needs of anyone who could benefit from higher education—community colleges offering open access to all citizens, the California State Universities to provide mass undergraduate education, and an elite tier of world-class research universities, including UC Berkeley, UCLA, and UC San Diego.

However, two generations later, the subsequent failure to invest in California's public school system means that nearly half of the most rapidly growing segments of the state's population cannot take advantage of this opportunity, since they are not even graduating from high school. Nationally, the level of investment in basic schooling has been declining in real terms, and the level of high school dropouts is higher than it was two generations ago, with the problem particularly intense in the inner cities (Levy and Murnane 1995).

A major new national initiative to prepare all Americans for the challenges of the knowledge economy is needed. In this case, the challenge may be even more daunting than beating the Russians to the moon—returning the U.S. to the position it enjoyed after the introduction of the GI Bill, with the best educated workforce in the world. Given how rapidly the competitors of the United States are improving their own education systems, attaining this objective will require setting some very ambitious targets and then putting in place major reforms and the resources—from all levels of government, companies, and individuals—to meet them. An example of some stretch goals would be, by 2015, to:

- provide all Americans with the basic skills needed to function in a knowledge economy;
- enable 75 percent or more of the U.S. population to participate in some form of higher education;
- have 50 percent or more of young people completing a bachelor's degree;
- have 25 percent or more of the working population with some form of advanced qualification.

Meeting such lofty targets requires not only major improvements and radical innovation in the public education system, but also the focusing of investments where they can yield the greatest return. As Shaw (this volume) notes, the returns are highest (17–20 percent) at the earliest stages of life, when individuals have the greatest learning capacity, and core foundation knowledge and interpersonal skills are formed (Carneiro and Heckman 2002; Karoly and Bigelow 2005). Based on a large body of research on education and learning, as well as major demographic and economic trends, some of the specific reform options to consider are:

- support for pregnant women and newborns to ensure their nutritional and health needs are met and stimulation for their infants starting in the womb (e.g., extending Georgia's program to distribute Mozart CDs to pregnant women) and continuing throughout childhood;
- using a combination of public and private provision to provide high-quality universal pre-school education for 3 to 5–year-olds (currently only 38 percent of children whose mothers dropped out from high school take part in pre-school compared to 70 percent of children of college graduates (Karoly and Bigelow 2005));
- examining other models. Although the decades of education reform that followed *A Nation at Risk* have failed to generate system-wide improvements in the U.S. K-12 system, they have generated a large number of successful local and state initiatives that could serve as models for more systemic change in public schools (Glennan et al. 2005). Among the promising examples that could be extended with sufficient resources are:
  - creating smaller schools or schools within schools/academies with a mission sufficiently focused and an environment intimate enough for teachers to be aware of the progress of all learners;
  - extending programs—such as Teach America, America Reads, and America Counts—to get more new college graduates and volunteers and well-qualified

teachers into the classroom to help provide at-risk students with more individualized attention. This could be expanded to include the growing number of baby boomers who are retiring, but who are still interested in working and contributing to society and have a wealth of real-world experience and subject expertise that is too often lacking among elementary school teachers;

- creating targeted programs to encourage the most rapidly growing segments of the future labor force—women, Latinos, and African Americans—to pursue science and engineering careers. This means reaching them early in their schooling (no later than middle school, but ideally earlier) to excite them about technical careers and ensure they take the courses needed to enable them to qualify for science and engineering degree courses. Programs that provide guaranteed college admission and scholarships for all students who meet the necessary standards have been shown to have a strong motivating effect;

- raising the status of the teaching profession by creating awards, financial bonuses, and mentoring opportunities for the best-performing teachers, while making it easier for principals to remove teachers who do not meet minimum performance standards;

- expanding higher education enrollments by ensuring that the double-digit annual increases in tuition that have occurred over the last decade do not deter individuals from attending. This can be done by increasing existing federal student loans and private scholarships and targeting resources to those institutions that do the best job of controlling costs and reducing dropout rates. The United States might also consider replacing the student loan system with a graduate tax (as in England and Australia) where individuals can have the full cost of college education covered and then pay back tuition through the tax system once they cross a certain earnings threshold. The lifetime earnings of college graduates are, on average, more than one million dollars greater than high school graduates' earnings, generating a high return on this investment;

- creating nationally recognized technical and vocational education, delivered through community colleges, in partnership with local employers, that can attract close to half of each cohort currently not attending higher education;

- maintaining the world-class research infrastructure of the United States, one that can fuel the next generation of innovation and high-skill jobs, by

  - restoring growth in investment in basic research. At a time when the main competitors of the United States are investing heavily to expand their higher education and research efforts, the Bush Administration's budget for the next four years projects no growth in spending on research that is not related to security and cuts the budget for the National Science Foundation by 1.9 percent (Schiffries et al., 2005). In contrast, the European Union has proposed to increase government R&D spending by one-third from 2007–2013;

  - adopting venture capitalist's John Doerr's suggestion of providing all international students who successfully complete U.S. graduate programs with a green card to work permanently in the United States if they so desire (Colvin 2005);

- providing high-quality retraining opportunities to all Americans whose jobs are lost to offshoring. This would entail expansion and reform of the existing Trade Adjustment Assistance (TAA) Act, a one billion dollar federal program that assists 75,000 people per year, to include workers in the service sector as well as manufacturing.

### Stimulating the Demand Side

Any comprehensive national skills strategy will have to tackle the demand as well as supply side of the skills equation; it must examine what measures are necessary to maintain the U.S. lead in technology innovation and to generate high-skill, high-quality jobs, as well as to prepare the workforce with the skills to fill them. Projections are that virtually all of the roughly 20 million new jobs likely to be created in the United States between now and 2014 will demand at least some college education, with the majority requiring a B.A. or a higher qualification (Employment Policy Foundation 2004, 75). These projections, however, are based on demographic trends and likely economic growth rates, ignoring the potentially destabilizing effects that the growing offshoring of knowledge work may have on job opportunities for those without an advanced, distinctive skill set. A few years of college or an average U.S. bachelor's degree are unlikely to provide these.

Although newly created positions are likely to be concentrated at the high end, many of the job vacancies will be for lower-level workers to replace retirees in the service sector, which accounts for 76 percent of the U.S. labor force. The main concern with these jobs, typified by the work at the largest employer of the United States, Wal-Mart, is not offshoring, but the fact that many have no educational requirements, offer little opportunity for further skill development, and fail to provide even full-time workers with a decent standard of living and healthcare coverage. Significant improvements in the minimum wage and working conditions require not just better education, but also reforms of government policy for the most disadvantaged in the labor market (Crouch et al. 1999).

At the opposite end of the labor market, what is needed to stimulate the creation of whole new industries and high-end jobs in the United States, while simultaneously tackling many of the most pressing problems facing the world, are bold investments in science and technology. In California, for example, despite a budget deficit larger than the other 49 states combined, a large majority of voters decided in 2004 to spend three billion dollars over the next decade on stem cell research, a promising, yet controversial, area of biology. This may not have represented the most rational way of making public policy, but it did signal Americans' continued willingness to make major public investments in scientific research when they believe it will produce long-term economic and social benefits.

Other such initiatives might include providing food and clean drinking water to a projected global population of nine billion people by 2050 (when 96 percent of arable land will already be under cultivation), promoting sustainable development, developing feasible energy alternatives to a carbon fuel-based economy, providing healthcare coverage to all Americans, and eradicating AIDS and infectious diseases that kill millions and cripple the economies of many developing nations. The combined resources of its state and federal governments and numerous private foundations place the United States in a unique position to lead global initiatives in these and other areas.

## Companies

Although it is not the responsibility of U.S. firms to address the structural problems identified with the U.S. education system, there are a several strategies that they can adopt—both individually and collectively—to help improve the system. Three promising approaches for firms are:

- jointly lobbying for strong public investment in education and training, and maintaining the country's position as a magnet for top talent from around the globe;
- partnering with educational institutions at all levels;
- building a "learning contract" with employees.

### Lobbying for Improvements in Skill Supply

Corporations, particularly when they act collectively, have a powerful influence over U.S. policy. A clear example of this power was shown recently when a number of the world's most prominent CEOs—including Bill Gates, Jeff Immelt, and Rupert Murdoch—objected publicly to the changes in U.S. immigration policy and called attention to the negative consequences this would have for U.S. high-tech industry. This quickly prompted a response from federal policymakers who launched a campaign to clarify that they were not trying to restrict the flow of foreign students to U.S. colleges and universities, although the H1-B quotas were not raised.

In addition to continuing lobbying efforts to keep the United States as the premier site for top technical and entrepreneurial talent from around the world, it will be vital for industry to press federal, state, and local policymakers to sustain their long-term investment in education—for both high-quality research and teaching—during a period when the government is facing large budget deficits.

### Educational Partnerships

There are partnerships between companies and education providers at all levels of the U.S. education and training system. Strengthening these relationships could provide a low-cost way to enhance the skills of the future American workforce. Firms can assist local schools by donating surplus equipment and a few hours of their employees' time to volunteer in the classroom. Encouraging volunters can yield a variety of benefits: improving instruction by providing real-world examples, making young people aware of different career options, enhancing the firm's image in the community, and providing leadership development opportunities for their employees.

At the higher education level, companies can save significant resources by outsourcing some of their education, training, and research needs to educational partners. Many community colleges are well positioned to develop customized offerings tailored to the needs of local employers. This is a win-win proposition: firms are able to prepare young people to meet their skill needs while saving the largest portion of training costs (the trainee salary), and colleges gain additional resources and higher placement rates for their graduates. Similarly, by partnering with top universities—through sponsored research, internships, and/or including professors on their scientific advisory boards—companies gain access to cutting-edge technologies and top graduate student talent.

## A Learning Contract

The uncertainty and ultra-competitiveness of global markets make it hard for firms to offer long-term employment security as a way to attract, motivate, and retain the talent they require. In its place, the most plausible basis for an employment bargain appears to be a learning contract (Finegold 1998), where companies offer ongoing investments in individual employabilities—whether with the firm or elsewhere—in return for individual commitment to invest effort to keep his or her skills up-to-date and to use these for the benefit of the organization (see table 7.2 for the elements on the learning contract).

Recent research by the Center for Effective Organizations (Benson et al. 2004) in a large technology company, TechCo, suggests that benefits from making a learning contract the focal point of the organization's talent strategy can accrue to both companies and their workers. TechCo offered employees an unusually generous tuition reimbursement program as part of the CEO's goal to "develop the best-educated workforce on the planet." The program covered all costs for virtually any courses the employee chose, offered up to three hours' paid time off to study per week, offered a stock bonus equivalent to approximately $10,000 for completion of a degree, and had no requirement that individuals pay back to the company the costs of their education if they left the firm.

Over a five-year period, 38 percent of TechCo's more than 12,000 salaried employees participated in the program. It produced a number of benefits for the firm, such as creating a powerful differentiator in recruiting graduates from the nation's top universities, greatly expanding the supply of general skills, and improving employee retention. The improvement in retention occurred for two groups—those who were

**Table 7.2**    The Learning Contract

| Employer Responsibilities | Employee Responsibilities |
|---|---|
| • Provide ongoing opportunities and support for education and training | • Invest in developing their own competencies |
| • Structure work and career paths to foster ongoing development | • Use competencies to help organization achieve its objectives |
| • Reward individuals who build new skills and use them effectively | • Help build competencies of co-workers |
| • Help individuals whose skills are less in demand find new opportunities, internally or externally | • Contribute to organizational learning |

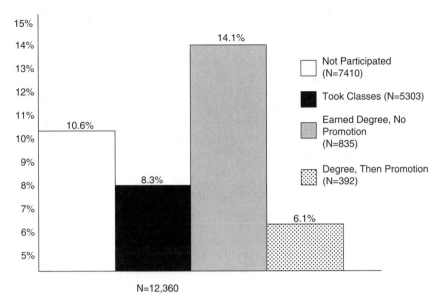

**Figure 7.1** Participation in Tuition Reimbursement and Voluntary Turnover, 1996–2000

taking classes toward a degree, which often took four years or more to complete on a part-time basis, and those who were promoted after completing the degree (see figure 7.1). The research also showed that the turnover rate was highest for those who completed a degree, but were then not promoted. This suggests that when a firm invests in the general education of individuals but then does not find new ways for these employees to use their new skills, they risk losing a major investment in human capital.

## Individuals

In *The World is Flat*, Thomas Friedman quips that when he was growing up, his mother used to say, "Finish your dinner, people in China and India are starving." Now he tells his daughters, "Finish your homework, people in China and India are starving for your jobs." As a father of two, I too share his concern about what career advice to offer my children to prepare them for a world of growing global competition and the opportunities and the insecurities that it brings. President Bush may have been correct that the answer starts with education. But, as we have seen, just getting into a good college is unlikely to be a guarantee for success in the workplace. Young people need to be prepared to be lifetime learners and to be their own career counselors, continually reassessing their skill needs and investing in keeping their knowledge and skills on the cutting edge.

It is also important to encourage our children to follow their passions, to find what it is in life that excites them most, and to become truly expert at finding it. The same technological and economic trends that have intensified global competition by enabling three billion people to take part in the global economy since 1990 are making it far easier than before for individuals to connect with others around the world who share their passions and then to find new ways to make a living out of it. Today's economy is increasingly rewarding those who are world-class in a given field, while penalizing those who are average or worse (Levenson this volume). Thus, it is vital to find better ways to help young people identify areas where they can excel and then, as Tom Peters suggests, equip them with the tools to create their own employment brand around their unique set of competencies (Peters 1999).

Finally, it is vital to prepare our children to be global citizens if they are to spot the opportunities available in the economy of the twenty-first century and be prepared to take advantage of them. This means encouraging them to travel, to build global social networks, and to learn languages besides English. Most of all, it means enabling them to see trends and issues not just with American eyes, but also from the perspective of other nationalities around the world.

# Bringing Careers Back in . . . The Changing Landscape of Careers in American Corporations Today

*Elizabeth F. Craig and Douglas T. Hall*

In 1973, when *Work in America* was published, we were just beginning to see the first signs of corporate interest in employee career development. In this chapter, we will make the argument that we are at a similar point in corporate America today. After significant economic and social upheaval dramatically changed the organization of work and careers, companies are once again beginning to appreciate the strategic importance and value of investing in employees' careers. This time around individuals and organizations have different assumptions and expectations, and both parties face new challenges and enjoy new possibilities for those careers.

The similarities and differences beg the question: Are people better off in their careers today than they were in 1973? This is difficult to answer in a global sense. Better or worse for whom? The current career context is probably more favorable for younger, well-educated, more adaptable individuals with the resources to use the freedom they have today. But it may be worse for employees who lack the skills to adapt to new and changing demands. Overall, the state of affairs for organizations is probably better than it was in the past, because now employers have more flexibility to deploy their human resources. But that is only a short-term view, and companies could be losing out on employee motivation and creativity if employees do not feel that their development is being supported by their employers.

It is our impression that the mean level of organizational career development activity today may not be much different from that of 1973, but the variance across companies may be higher. That is, overall, there is simply a wider range in the quality of career experiences that employees have today and in the quality of an organization's career management practices than was the case when *Work in America* was published. And that increased variability introduces a number of new dilemmas for individuals and organizations managing careers today.

We start by reviewing the approach to careers in recent decades, beginning with the publication of *Work in America*. Then we zoom in on the current state of the art in organizational career development. We are not examining the full range of career practice, such as the work of career counselors in schools and universities, career and outplacement consultants, and instructors in career workshops and courses. Rather, we will look at career practice in organizational work settings. Thus, our target is the adult population employed in organizational settings.

We next reflect on these current organizational practices and trends and consider several ways that changes in careers create dialectical dilemmas in the career tasks that individuals must cope with and reconcile in their careers.

## The Changing Landscape of Careers

### The 1970s

Before we get into discussing where we are today in corporate work on careers, let us look at a "timeline of career activity," starting with *Work in America* in the 1970s. The book's index contained a modest number of references for "career," most of which dealt with retraining and mid-career development. The major focus, of course, was on job redesign, but it was clear that if jobs were to be redesigned to allow for greater employee discretion and decision-making, it would also require concomitant employee training and development.

As employees became more involved in their jobs, and as they experienced "psychological success" from taking more responsibility and making bigger job-related decisions, they experienced a "success syndrome" (Hall 2002) in which their needs for growth and achievement as well as their career aspirations increased. For many people this awakened a concern for longer-term career development, not just satisfaction in today's job. As a result, companies began to attend to employees' career aspirations and to create programs and processes for career exploration and development. At the same time, the spirit of the times was oriented toward personal self-discovery, liberation, and development.

Looking back over this period, Hall (2004) described the environmental context for careers in the mid-1970s as follows:

> . . . Although the prevailing view of careers was still something out of . . . *The Organization Man* [Whyte 1956] . . . , with the stress on upward mobility in organizations, there were the beginnings of a reaction, a counter-trend. There was a strong counter culture . . . [for example, Reich's (1970) *The Greening of America*], and the postwar baby boom cohort were just starting their careers, wanting freedom, personal choice, and values expression in their work. The theme of change was definitely in the air. Robert J. Lifton wrote about the "protean style of self-process" as "one of the functional patterns of our day" (Lifton 1968, 17, quoted in Hall 1976, 291). The first edition of *What Color Is Your Parachute?* (Bolles 2005) had just been published in 1970 and was picking up steam. Eugene Jennings was writing about the "mobicentric manager," and *Psychology Today* had lots of articles about careers. In fact, a companion magazine was introduced to the market, *Careers Today*.

### The 1980s

In the 1980s, with the rise in global competition, American industry entered a period of restructuring and downsizing that continues to this day. This process was originally seen as more of a one-shot deal, an adjustment to make an organization more competitive, and the hope was that the resized organization could then return to a more stable operational pace. However, it soon became apparent that this restructuring was going to be a continuous learning and change process, and that the company would always be in some form of transition.

This intensive and recurring downsizing and restructuring transformed employment relationships (Cappelli 1999; Cappelli et al. 1997). The traditional model of stable, long-term employment centered around a career of advancement within a single organization became the exception rather than the rule, as many organizations eliminated guarantees of employment security to increase their internal flexibility. Companies began to promise to provide skills and experiences to ensure an individual's continued employability in the external labor market, rather than offering employment security with the firm. As employability contracts replaced job security contracts, measurable performance replaced seniority as the basis for professional rewards (Useem 1996). Careers of achievement and the "accumulation of reputational capital" became more important than careers of advancement and the "accumulation of organizational capital" (Kanter 1991, 76; Zabusky and Barley 1996).

Another major issue for many people working in organizations in the 1980s was plateauing—that is, reaching a career dead end, with little prospect of upward mobility (Hall and Rabinowitz 1988). As organizational growth leveled off and downsizing and restructuring increased, organizational career ladders changed (Jalland and Gunz 1993). People's career advancement necessarily became less certain. Fewer positions in the managerial ranks meant increased competition for opportunities and slower career advancement. Companies were beginning to search for practices that would continue a person's career growth but not necessarily require a promotion (Hall 1993). Examples of such alternative career development activities included lateral moves, temporary assignments, varied project or task force assignments, mentoring activities (both giving and receiving) (Kram and Hall 1991), cross-functional moves, and even downward moves (Hall and Isabella 1985).

This is also the period when outplacement activity took off. Some companies, such as Ford, began programs to help people with self-assessment so that they could decide for themselves whether the best path for them was to stay or to leave—and if they decided to leave, the organization was perfectly okay with that.

### The 1990s

This awareness of continuous change became more a part of the American worker's mindset in the 1990s. As Hall and Moss (1998) found, there was a change in the perceived "career contract," in which executives and workers seemed to go through three stages of adjustment. The first stage was one in which there was great uncertainty about what was happening and what the future might hold. In interviews with employees in organizations that had to change long-standing practices of long-term employment (companies such as IBM, AT&T, Digital Equipment Corporation, and Polaroid), there were many comments to the effect that it was hard to see the forest (the underlying causes of economic stress) for the trees (layoffs, loss of business, and other current crises). This stage was labeled "lost in the trees." In the second stage, the dust was beginning to settle- and people were becoming clearer on the underlying problems, such as global competition. This was called "sees the forest." The final stage, called "continuous learning," was one in which people understood that everyone was going to have to remain in a state of constant environmental analysis, self-assessment, and adaptation. This last stage was one in which it was clearer to individuals that they would have to become more "protean," or self-directed, and more clear on what direction their own "internal compass" dictated.

In the late 1990s, with continuing restructuring even in the face of a thriving U.S. economy, the culture in many companies had shifted strongly from organizational careers to a more protean (or as some people have dubbed it, "roll your own") model. Along with the downsizing of the human resources (HR) function, there was little support for employee career development beyond the recruiting and early career stages. Individuals were expected to assume responsibility for managing their careers within and across multiple organizations.

Cappelli and Hamori (2005), in their study of temporal shifts between 1980 and 2001 in the composition of the executive work force in Fortune 100 companies, discovered evidence for this shift from an organizational career model to more of a self-directed, free-agent model. Their research found that companies are more likely now to hire from outside rather than promote from within, and contemporary executives are less likely to have spent their full career with one company. Cappelli and Hamori also reported that the new generation of corporate executives is younger (average age 52 in 2001 versus 56 in 1980), more likely to be female (11 percent versus none), less likely to have an Ivy League degree (10 percent versus 14 percent), and more likely to have gone to a public college (48 percent versus 32 percent). In an editorial titled "Farewell, Organization Man," the *Wall Street Journal* drew the following conclusion about these trends: "In short, he (or she) is not your daddy's Organization Man, slowly working his way up the corporate ladder one rung at a time" (December 31, 2004).

Cappelli and Hamori argued that this increased interorganizational mobility and more rapid promotions are the result of global competition, recessions, restructuring, and the shareholder value movement. All of these influences put more pressure on companies to become more competitive and to raise share prices and profits. To do this, they need to recruit and develop the best talent, regardless of gender, age, or school.

### The 2000s

In recent years, along with this need to nurture and retain the best managers, there has been an increase in top management concern for talent management and increasing employee "engagement." Research has shown that employee loyalty and retention are significantly related to a firm's financial performance (Reichheld and Teal, 2001). Pfeffer (1998) has also presented considerable evidence that companies such as Southwest Airlines that put employees first (even above customers) are more likely to be successful than companies that do not. The theory is that if the company takes care of its employees, then the employees in turn will be motivated to take care of customers. Other companies with this philosophy include Starbucks, IBM, eBay, Nucor, and Wells Fargo. The leadership and development processes that generate this level of employee loyalty and commitment are described in detail in Collins' *Good to Great* (2001) and in Reichheld and Teal's (2001) *The Loyalty Effect*.

Thus, it appears that the pendulum of corporate concern for developing employee involvement and commitment has begun to swing back toward more of an organizational focus on employee careers, even though there may still be an awareness that the company is developing free agents. What this means is that the company's time span for career development might be a few years rather than an entire career. This is not unlike the practices of well-managed sports teams that devote a lot of energy to developing the skills and team loyalty of a player over the three- to four-year span of his or her contract. It is understood by all parties that at the end of the contract, the player could be playing for another but everyone's focus is on the present and near future.

For example, the Boston Red Sox put together a highly cohesive group of players that called themselves "The Idiots" in the 2004 season and proceeded to stage one of sport's greatest comebacks after trailing the Yankees 0–3 in the league playoffs to win the American League Championship. They followed up this triumph with a World Series victory for the first time since 1918, breaking the infamous "Curse of the Bambino." And then in 2005, some of these World Series stars, such as Derek Lowe and Pedro Martinez, were playing for other teams. Similar positive results from developing strong team cohesion have been obtained by the New England Patriots, winning three Super Bowls in four years. The team feeling is very strong, although everyone recognizes that each year some of the top players will probably leave for other teams.

Corporations have abandoned the traditional implicit employment contract in which company loyalty was exchanged for long-term employment security. Seeking flexibility, they have instead offered "employability"—the notion that the work assignments, while not necessarily leading to advancement within the company, would give workers the skills and experience they would need to advance their careers anywhere. Despite fears that employees would "take the training and run" if companies invested in their development, research has shown that when firms invest in their employees' career development, they can actually engender loyalty (Benson, Finegold, and Mohrman 2004). Craig, Kimberly, and Bouchikhi (2002) found that executives who are satisfied with their opportunities to learn new skills, take on new responsibilities, and make new professional contacts were much more committed and intended to stay with their companies longer than executives who were less satisfied with these career development opportunities. Moreover, organizational investments in the executives' careers had a stronger relationship with commitment and intentions to stay than did employment security and stability.

One might argue that what we are seeing is a shift back in the direction of the old career contract that was based on a long-term relationship with the organization. However, as we just pointed out, the time frames are now shorter, so it seems that the pendulum has not swung all the way back to the traditional organizational career model. Rather, we seem to be at a midway point, where it is more of a relational-transactional career contract. It is understood that the relationship between the person and the organization is still a transaction in which the person might remain for three to four years, but during that time both parties are valuing the relationship, developing it, and contributing to the success of the individual and the common venture. Both parties are acting as if the relationship will continue indefinitely, showing mutual loyalty - and making contributions to the common enterprise.

Thus, we appear to be in a period where we are seeing both individual self-direction (or agency, as career specialists sometimes call it) and organizational career initiatives being practiced. As organizational career systems and practices have changed, new norms of individual responsibility for defining and managing careers have compelled people to be more actively engaged in constructing their careers throughout their working lives (Mirvis and Hall 1996). These changes represent a call for *greater individual agency* with respect to one's work career in the context of *shifting career structures.*

Careers have always been, by their nature, a product of the interactions between individual goals and actions and organizational systems and structures (Barley 1989). Yet, the changing landscape of careers in American corporations has caused several contradictions inherent to careers in organizations to become increasingly problematic. For example, the downsizing, delayering, and restructuring of the 1980s and 1990s were in contradiction with the existing practice of long-term employment security (Benson 1983, as cited in Ford and Ford 1994). The opposing principles of employment security and human capital flexibility created conflicts between individual career expectations and behaviors and organizational career values and practices. As organizations attempted to reconcile these opposing principles within their systems and practices, many abandoned the traditional employment relationships and organizational career systems for market-based, free agency, and employability approaches. Yet, a decade of experience has revealed that neither the view of individual careerists as unrestrained free agents nor the view of organizational career systems and structures as deterministic is complete or practical.

A number of individual-societal dilemmas emerge when increased individual career action occurs in a context of changing organizational career structures and systems. In the next section, we apply a dialectical lens to contemporary careers to identify several significant dilemmas resulting from the often competing principles and interests underlying individual and organizational career actions.

## A Dialectical Perspective on Contemporary Careers

A dialectical perspective on contemporary careers focuses on the opposing principles, or internal contradictions, inherent in self-directed careers in organizations. Careers are constructed through the dialectical interplay between the individual and the social system (Hughes 1937; Schein 1978). The dialectical nature of careers has long been recognized by careers scholars (for a review, see Barley, 1989), as has been the danger of valuing one perspective over the other. As Van Maanen (1977, 8) has observed,

> To seriously study careers requires a profound respect for the dialectic quality of human experience. Man is both the creator and the determined. An excessive commitment to either a position emphasizing an ordered world of constraint, manipulation, and conformity, or a position accentuating man's capacity for growth, vision, and originality, would be a mistake.

Taking a dialectical perspective on careers focuses directly on the internal contradictions created by individually defined careers played out in organizational contexts. When faced with potentially incompatible practices, such as self-directed careers and organizational career ladders, people often gravitate to one principle or the other. At one extreme are individuals who act as self-interested free agents with little concern for the organization. At the other extreme are employees who mechanically follow the structured career paths in organizations without consideration for their own capabilities and interests.

Without thoughtful, planned intervention, counterproductive behavioral patterns can develop. On the one hand, the experience of discomfort or ineffectiveness with a particular principle may lead people to simply try harder to make that approach work for them, effectively locking them into an extreme and ineffective position. For instance, Baker and Aldrich (1996) observed mid-career employees showing increased loyalty to their employers as the firms restructured, downsized, and eliminated promises of employment security. Instead of adapting their career expectations and behaviors to the changing environment, these employees coped by attempting to regain control by clinging to familiar behaviors that were no longer as effective as they once were.

On the other hand, ineffectiveness and frustration with a principle may push people toward the opposite extreme in search of increased effectiveness. An individual who is unable to construct a personally meaningful, authentic career in an organizational setting characterized by rigid job ladders and career norms may adopt a free-agent perspective and either detach from the organization in order to pursue career possibilities elsewhere or pursue self-interested actions while remaining with the organization—potentially at the expense of organizational goals or effectiveness.

Over time, individuals and organizations may simply vacillate between the two poles. In the end, none of these solutions is particularly satisfying or effective. Ultimately, it is only through the reconciliation, or synthesis, of the opposing principles, that escape from the perpetual conflict and ineffectiveness associated with operating at either extreme becomes possible. Meaningful and rewarding careers for individuals and productive and competitive organizations will only come from creating synthesis of conflicting principles. But synthesis is not easy. Even when individuals and organizations are able to recognize and frame the dilemmas, they still must overcome the deep ambivalence inherent in these dilemmas that keeps people locked into the extremes. The challenge for people constructing careers and organizations managing careers is to adopt new career practices that represent a skillful synthesis of the seemingly contradictory principles of self-directed and organizationally structured careers.

In the next section, we identify several dilemmas that individuals face as they construct their careers and discuss how skillful synthesis of the seemingly contradictory principles at play in those dilemmas might be achieved, using examples from organizations to illustrate what synthesis looks like in practice.

## Bringing Careers Back in: Reconciling Dilemmas in Contemporary Careers

As we have said, just as when *Work in America* was published, there now seems to be a growing sense of the importance of *people* (also known as "talent," "human resources," "human capital," and "employees") in business today. The effectiveness of a firm's people management practices determines its capacity to achieve and sustain a competitive advantage. The popular current buzzword that is often used to describe competitiveness is "execution," and what really enables a firm to execute strategy effectively is the way it deploys and develops its people.

What is effective people management? It is creating clear and compelling links between an organization's purpose and strategy, its core capabilities and values, and employees' capabilities, talents, and aspirations. It's about discovering, developing, and deploying talent in organizations. In other words, it is about managing careers in organizations. Unfortunately, many companies have gotten out of the business of managing their employees' careers. The push for human capital flexibility and the subsequent emphasis on personal responsibility for careers created ambiguity and ambivalence in many companies about the role they should play in shaping employees' careers. Yet, the combination of unbridled individual agency and nebulous organizational career practices is unlikely to generate productive and competitive organizations or meaningful and rewarding careers for individuals.

For this reason, we believe that companies need to bring careers back into the organization. This does not mean that organizations can or should resume responsibility for providing long-term, stable careers. Instead, organizations need to establish career practices that facilitate individual growth and development while enabling organizational flexibility and change. To create careers in American corporations that are both meaningful and rewarding for individuals and productive for organizations, companies need to get back into the career management game. In order to facilitate career self-direction that supports organizational goals and values, companies must first appreciate the challenges individuals face in managing their careers. We believe that by understanding the nature of the dilemmas individuals face and dealing directly with them, organizations can engage in career practices that help individuals better cope with their career management challenges and transcend the conflict created by the underlying dilemmas.

We identify three fundamental dilemmas that individuals are presented with as they construct their careers. Constructing a career is a process of organizing and giving meaning to work roles and experiences (Van Maanen 1977). Far from being a choice that people make once at the start of their work lives, constructing a career is an ongoing process throughout the course of a person's life (Hall 2002). Hall and Mirvis (1996) have proposed a model of the contemporary career as a lifelong series of short (3–5-year) learning cycles. Every learning cycle involves three core developmental tasks, each of which presents individuals with a fundamental dilemma between individual needs and interests and societal needs and interests. Table 8.1 lists the three core developmental tasks individuals confront during their careers and the dialectical dilemmas associated with each career task: (1) finding a purpose (self-definition vs. social-determination), (2) finding a place (authenticity vs. loyalty), and (3) finding a path (agency vs. structure). Figure 8.1 illustrates the three dialectical dilemmas—with individual choice and freedom at one extreme, and social structural constraints at the opposing extreme.

Individuals repeatedly face these fundamental dilemmas as they cycle through these core tasks in the process of constructing their careers. These are by no means the only dilemmas individuals face when constructing and directing their careers, but these are issues that almost all individuals encounter. In the rest of this section, we describe each dilemma, identify the challenge those dilemmas present for organizations involved in career development (see table 8.2), and suggest general recommendations for organizational practices that could assist individuals' efforts to reconcile these dilemmas. We also present examples of actual company practices that, in different ways, achieve skillful synthesis of the competing principles at play in the dilemmas. The company examples are drawn largely from Karaevli and Hall's (2002) survey of 13 leading organizations including BP, Dell Computer, Eli Lilly, Motorola, Southwest Airlines, and the U.S. Army.

**Table 8.1** Developmental Tasks and Dialectical Dilemmas in Contemporary Careers

| | | Dialectical Dilemmas | | | |
|---|---|---|---|---|---|
| Core Developmental Tasks for Individuals | Individuals' career actions | Individual | vs. | Societal | Organizational actions that enable synthesis |
| Finding a Purpose | Exploring new possibilities and meanings | Self-Definition<br><br>Construct personally relevant career goals and meanings | vs. | Social-Determination<br><br>Adopt organizationally defined career goals and meanings | Valuing Careers:<br><br>Organization adopts a career mindset |
| Finding a Place | Trying on various roles and experimenting with new areas | Authenticity<br><br>Leverage personal strengths, capabilities, and interests | vs. | Loyalty<br><br>Take on roles and experiences as dictated by organizational needs and interests | Investing in Careers:<br><br>Organization gives priority for learning and development |
| Finding a Path | Becoming established and achieving mastery in the new area | Agency<br>Organize a series of work experiences that advance personal goals | vs. | Structure<br><br>Follow institutionalized career paths | Supporting Careers:<br><br>Organizational provides supports for employability |

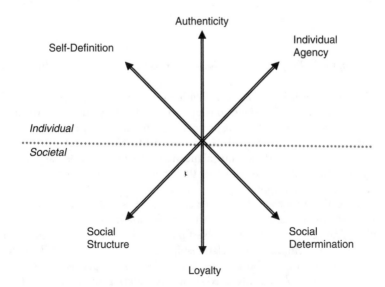

**Figure 8.1** Dialectical Dilemmas in Contemporary Careers

**Table 8.2**   Career Management Dilemmas Related to Core Career Tasks

| | Core Tasks in Career-Learning Cycles | | |
|---|---|---|---|
| | *Finding a Purpose (Exploration)* | *Finding a Place (Trial)* | *Finding a Path (Establishment)* |
| Career Dilemmas for Individuals | Self-Definition vs. Social-Determination | Authenticity vs. Loyalty | Agency vs. Structure |
| Organizational Challenges | Prioritizing people | Prioritizing learning | Prioritizing employability |
| Organizational Career Management Capabilities | Valuing Careers: Linking careers to organizational purpose & values <br>• A meaningful organizational purpose. <br>• Clear and compelling organizational capabilities and values <br>• A career mindset | Investing in Careers: Discovering and developing employees' strengths and capabilities <br>• A motivating, dynamic, learning-based culture <br>• Strong development focus throughout organization | Supporting Careers: Create enabling processes—not constraining structures—for deploying talent <br>• Career management practices focused on building employee meta-competencies of self-awareness and adaptability <br>• Creative approaches to deploying employee capabilities in job assignments |
| Company Examples | Southwest Airlines Johnsonville Foods | Staples, Inc. Millennium Pharmaceuticals | Semco SA U.S. Army |

*Finding a Purpose: Self-Definition versus Social-Determination*

With each new career learning cycle, individuals go through a process of "finding a purpose" in their careers. The dilemma here is related to the tension between giving meaning to one's career by looking to external sources, such as organizationally defined career goals and values, and looking inward to personal goals and meaning. Organizational pathways and the cultural meanings of careers define the frame of reference within which individuals construct their careers, but individuals make choices about their careers based upon their personal goals and motivations. Through their choices, people may adopt socially defined career models and meanings, or they may depart from existing models and construct more self-defined careers.

Socially defined careers were quite powerful during the second half of the twentieth century. Traditional employment relationships in post–World War II industrial America were characterized by long-term, stable relationships between employers and employees, in which employees advanced along job ladders, gaining status with seniority and trading loyalty for security, while they built their careers within the firm. Along with the assumption of a continued relationship, employers offered individual rewards designed to increase employee commitment to the organization, especially opportunities for advancement within the firm's internal labor markets (Tolbert 1996). In organizational careers characterized by stable and secure employment within an organization, title and status, regular promotions, steadily rising salary, and tenure are the primary indicators of career success. At the same time, affiliation with an organization provides strong subjective meanings in the form of work and personal identity. Weick and Berliner (1989, 321) have described it thusly: "In a traditional organization, the external career is defined by positions in the organizational structure, and movement through this structure is often adopted by people as their subjective career."

In recent years, the declining influence of traditional employment relationships and organizational careers has reduced the capacity of socially defined career models to organize people's careers (Barley 1989). As a consequence, individuals have greater latitude in organizing and giving meaning to their careers. As approaches to organizing employment increasingly favored flexibility over stability and security, and as career opportunities and expectations were altered, individuals began to devise new career forms and even redefine the notion of "career" to encompass new, personally meaningful alternatives. People constructing individualized careers lend meaning to their work experiences through self-defined interpretive schemes rooted in cultural ideologies of individualism, personal fulfillment, and the pursuit of passion (Craig 2002). For example, many managers and executives now define their career success in terms of personal achievements and accomplishments, rather than organizational advancement (Hall 2002; Kanter 1989).

People pursuing personal meaning are essentially constructing their lives and selves through their career choices (Ezzy 1997). Hall (1976; 2002) has argued for some time that individual goals and psychological success were becoming increasingly important for guiding career choices and defining career success. The self-directed careerist is something of a consumer of work experiences, a stance rather distinct from that of the old "organization man" as a producer of work (Berger 1972; Langer 1996). Rose (1989, 103) has compellingly described the self-defining approach to finding a purpose in one's career:

> The worker is portrayed neither as an economic actor, rationally pursuing financial advantage, nor as a social creature seeking satisfaction of needs for solidarity and security. The worker is an individual in search of meaning, responsibility, as sense of personal achievement, a maximized "quality of life," and hence of work. Thus the individual is not to be emancipated from work, perceived merely as a task or a means to an end, but to be fulfilled in work, now construed as an activity through which we produce, discover, and experience our selves.

Meaningful and productive careers in organizations will occur at the nexus of self-defined individual careers and organizational career structures and systems. The first step that organizations can take to bring careers back in, then, is to link employees' personal career purpose to the organization's purpose and mission.

### Organizational Challenge: Prioritizing People

To maximize the meaningfulness and effectiveness of individual careers, organizations must help—not hinder—employees' efforts to reconcile the self-definition versus social-determination dilemma. The organizational career management challenge related to this dilemma thus becomes strategically linking the organization's purpose with employees' aspirations and capabilities. Doing this requires that organizations view their employees' aspirations, talents, and capabilities as a potential source of competitive advantage. Organizations must adopt a career-centered mindset in which (a) the company recognizes the importance of career development to the employee, and (b) employees' capabilities, talents, and aspirations are seen as strategically critical for defining and achieving organizational goals.

Organizations with a career mindset do not view people as human "capital" or "resources" that are means to an end. These companies believe that investing in people is the best way to maximize organizational capabilities. Pfeffer (1998) has made a compelling argument that putting employees first has been strategically advantageous to organizations competing in a wide range of industries and sectors. Bartlett and Ghoshal (2002, 37) have gone so far as to argue that organizations are competing for investments of people's "talent and dreams," not for mere "human resources."

The basic requirement is a meaningful organizational purpose or vision, accompanied by clear and compelling organizational capabilities and values. The company's leaders and the organization's culture must embrace and encourage a career mindset throughout the organization. The career mindset sets the stage for the creation of a people strategy and people management capabilities that are the mechanisms that link the development of employees' talents and the realization of employees' aspirations to the accomplishment of organization's purpose and goals. The implementation of this approach is best understood by examining two exemplars of linking careers to strategy and performance: Southwest Airlines and Johnsonville Foods.

### Southwest Airlines

Southwest Airlines is well known for its founder and long-time CEO, Herb Kelleher, as well as for its low-cost, high-involvement culture. Although Southwest has been the target of many other low-cost airlines (such as Jet Blue), it remains to be seen whether these companies are able to match Southwest in its ability to attract, train, and motivate employees in a way that truly aligns talent and business strategy. In particular, Southwest is a strong example of what Karaevli and Hall (2002) found to be a key element of best practices in current succession planning processes: a focus on developing large pools of talent, rather than on a small group of crown princesses and princes—also called "hi-pos." The downside of focusing on hi-pos is that the talents of the remaining 98 percent of the workforce remain underdeveloped and underutilized.

In Southwest's view, every employee has potential. Southwest's philosophy is that the customer does not necessarily come first. The employee comes first. The idea here is that if management focuses on managing and developing the employee well, the employee will feel well cared for and motivated. And, in turn, the employee will be willing and able to take care of the customer. So their philosophy is that the best way to take care of the customer is by taking care of employees, who provide the service to the customer.

As a result of this philosophy, Southwest's strategy in recruiting and selection is to "hire for attitudes; train for skills." They reason that it is much harder to develop a positive, cheerful, customer-oriented attitude than it is to train people how to do the tasks of a flight attendant or a ticket agent. Southwest is regularly near the top of various "best companies to work for" lists.

*Johnsonville Foods*

Employee capabilities are the core source of competitive advantage at Johnsonville Foods (Stayer 1990). Johnsonville was a small sausage company that in the late 1980s was doing fairly well financially, but one that was not well positioned to compete effectively in the coming consolidation of the food industry, according to the CEO, Ralph Stayer. They were of an awkward size—too big to be a custom, gourmet producer, and too small to match the efficiencies of the major firms. As Stayer (1990, 2) put it,

> In addition to our big national competitors, we had a host of local and regional producers small enough to provide superior service to customers who were virtually their neighbors. We were too big to have the small-town advantage and too small to have advantages of national scale. Our business was more vulnerable than it looked.

As Stayer worked toward growing the company, employees were feeling stretched to do more work and to work longer hours, which resulted in alienation and demotivation, that showed up in decreased quality. As he analyzed the situation, Stayer realized that *he* was the problem. By exercising tight control at the top, he was depriving employees of the opportunity to take responsibility for making decisions and solving problems. And this lack of employee involvement was putting limits on the growth of the firms.

So Stayer started by making simple changes to get the employees more involved, such as having plant workers take responsibility for quality testing. Before that, his top management had done the testing. Then he started organizing the workforce into teams, which took responsibility for hiring and training their own people. Then they introduced a team performance evaluation system. And in this way, success bred more success, as employees developed more sense of ownership and more capabilities. A professor from a local college was brought in to train employees in using the tools of quality control, for example. Employees reported that they no longer felt that they had to "check their brains at the door" when they reported in for work.

Johnsonville has been described by the Society for Organizational Learning as a strong example of a learning organization. The story of their success starts with the realization by Ralph Stayer - that he would have to learn a new style of leadership, changing from "command and control" to one of commitment. As he learned and developed new leadership capabilities, he created new structures and processes that required employees to learn to perform in new ways. Through this training and learning, the employees developed feelings of psychological success and intrinsic rewards (Honold 1991). And these positive attitudes led to greater involvement and more learning. So, although the attitudes were important, the causes of the company's growth and business success were the new skills and capabilities of the employees.

By valuing and prioritizing people, both Southwest and Johnsonville Foods facilitate individuals' efforts to find a purpose in their careers. They do this not by presenting people with readymade careers or by abdicating all responsibility for careers, but by adopting processes and practices that enable individuals to reconcile the self-definition versus social-determination dilemma. Specifically, they enable people to pursue personally meaningful activities in organizationally relevant ways. Both companies reap significant benefits from their employees' sense of purpose and engagement in their work.

*Finding a Place: Authenticity versus Loyalty*

A second core task that individuals confront with each new career learning cycle is finding a fit between their strengths, interests, and values and the requirements and characteristics of the opportunities and roles they take on. The dilemma associated with "finding a place" is around the degree to which individual careers are defined by organizational needs and interests versus their own strengths and interests. There is a constant tension between being true to oneself by developing and deploying one's authentic talents and interests and being loyal to the organization's needs.

In the past, organizational needs were almost always prioritized. Traditional organizational career systems based on job ladders, internal mobility opportunities, and long-term employment security were designed to link individual career goals to organizational goals and systems in order to secure employee commitment to the organization (Tolbert 1996). Little consideration was given to other individual needs and interests. Employees were expected to adopt the organization's goals and values as their own, or, at a minimum, to put their authentic strengths and interests to work for the organization by somehow fitting them into the existing opportunity structure.

More recently, as the pendulum has swung toward individual career self-direction, individuals have assumed responsibility for seeking out opportunities to develop their unique strengths and capabilities and for finding career opportunities that fit their personal values and interests. The assumption behind this logic was that both individuals and organizations would be better off with more of a market-mediated matching process. However, the reality is that people have learned how to manage their own careers much better than organizations have learned how to support employees' learning or career process. Much of the information that companies make available to employees, such as career progression information on company Web sites, is aimed at recruits and new employees. And databases such as job boards, although helpful for job placement and intracompany transfers, are not especially useful in helping the employee become clearer on her or his longer-term career interests and plans. Organizations need to do a better job of connecting HR planning systems to individual career planning and learning processes. With such tighter integration, the company would be better able to keep up with employees who are cycling faster as they seek to continually discover and develop new strengths and interests.

*Organizational Challenge: Prioritizing Learning*
The career management challenge around this career task is to find the synthesis between personal authenticity and loyalty to the organization. Companies can help accomplish this by prioritizing learning and development. The temptation for organizations has been to abdicate responsibility for discovering and developing employee capabilities under the assumption that individuals have taken over that task. In the 1990s, more than a few organizations were eager to embrace a more market-based career model because it would minimize risk to the organization from investing in individual development and careers. Without an assumption of long-term relationships between the individual and the organization, employers saw little need to concern themselves with systems and processes for facilitating employee development and helping employees craft career paths that were a good fit for their ambitions and talents.

But even the most self-directed careerists, focused on discovering and developing their authentic strengths to ensure their ongoing employability and career coherence, still need structured developmental experiences and learning opportunities in order to accomplish their career goals. Unfortunately, organizations that took themselves out of the career development game narrowed their focus to the more immediate concerns of employee performance. This shortsighted shift in priorities can hamper organizational learning and effectiveness as it interferes with individual learning.

Learning and personal development are experiential and relational and cannot effectively be accomplished by a lone self-directed individual. In fact, 70–80 percent of career development occurs on the job (Hall 2002; McCall 1998), meaning that one of the highest-leverage forms of development is the strategic use of job assignments as a form of talent management. Karaevli (2003) has shown that a major factor in the success of a senior executive, and, in fact, of a company, is the extent of variety in that person's earlier career history. Being exposed to a wide range of corporate functions, industry sectors, and types of roles (such as start-up, turn-around) requires the person to stretch and expand his or her capabilities and thus develop a variety of skills and competencies. And Karaevli and Hall (2004) have argued that for this reason, career variety produces a higher level of adaptability in the individual.

Some of the organizations that are well known for their use of job assignments for development are IBM, Pepsico, Altria, Boeing, and GE. Boeing[1] is taking this form of talent management one step further by conducting longitudinal research on the effects of different assignments, the types of learning they engender, and the resulting outcomes for the individual and the company. According to Dr. Paul Yost, manager of Leadership Research, Boeing's research has replicated major findings from early research from the Center for Creative Leadership (CCL) on the lessons of experience (McCall, Lombardo, and Morrison 1989). At Boeing they identified similar types of assignments and similar lessons (Yost and Plunkett 2002). But in this research, since it is longitudinal (the CCL work was cross-sectional), it is possible to see the long-term effects of different patterns of assignments. This project, called the Waypoint Project, has also produced planning guides that show what types of learning are produced by different types of assignments. These tools, then, can be used to assist in making assignment decisions that will lead to career development, as well as good performance.

Organizations that prioritize learning, as evidenced by a motivating, dynamic learning-based culture and a strong development focus throughout the organization, can help employees to find a synthesis between their authenticity and loyalty. The task for organizations lies in creating processes that facilitate employee growth and development in ways that contribute to organizational performance as well. Organizations must embrace, encourage, and accommodate individual's strengths, capabilities, and interests, while ensuring that individual learning and development also contribute to the organization's strategic objectives. Similar arguments have been made by Kimberly, Bouchikhi, and Craig (2001) in their call for a "customized workplace" and Rousseau (2001) in her proposed "idiosyncratic deal." It is critical for organizations to get back into the career management game, but the future is in developing a motivating, dynamic context for learning, development, and career growth rather than rigid career structures.

Organizations can help employees begin to reconcile the authenticity versus loyalty dilemma by creating processes that enable individuals to develop their careers to the mutual benefit of the organization and the individual. Two companies that have created effective processes for cultivating career capabilities are Staples, Inc., and Millennium Pharmaceuticals.

*Staples, Inc.*

Staples is a strong example of a company where talent development is seen as a key element in the strategy for business growth. Staples has created a very entrepreneurial career management process in which job assignments and developmental relationships are key mechanisms for talent development (Hill 1998). The company selects people for their "eagerness to learn and stretch themselves" and then moves employees around the company frequently to keep them focused on learning, on becoming comfortable taking risks, and on being accountable for the outcomes (Hill 1998, 3).

The case of Jeanne Lewis offers an excellent example of Staples' capacity for supporting and encouraging individual career development in ways that also benefit the organization (see Hill 1998). Lewis first started with Staples in 1991 as a summer marketing intern. After completing her MBA, she took on a wide range of jobs and assignments, first outside and then within Staples. Through a series of vertical and lateral career moves, Lewis accumulated knowledge about herself and the organization, while developing valuable skills and capabilities through "stretch" experiences. Each of the roles she took on not only provided crucial developmental experiences but also presented her with valuable opportunities to invest in relationships throughout the organization. Her effectiveness in each of these roles established and added to her professional credibility. The learning from the various experiences and relationships fueled her career success in the organization. In 1999, Lewis was appointed president of Staples.com.

*Millennium Pharmaceuticals*[2]

An organization with a strong learning culture and a quite different approach to developing employee capabilities is Millennium Pharmaceuticals. Millennium is a young (11 years), small firm based in Cambridge, Massachusetts, with 1500 employees in research, development, commercial, and corporate operations. According to Carol Yamartino, senior director of Learning and Development, the company's vision is to transcend the limits of medicine. Their slogan is "Breakthrough science. Breakthrough medicine." The mission is to create a leading biopharmaceutical company.

To execute this ambitious strategy, the company has a leadership development mission to improve organizational and leadership effectiveness and to build workforce capabilities to substantially improve performance. Millennium's approach to development is very focused on employee learning. The core principles for building their workforce capabilities are (1) using measurement to improve, (2) learning by doing, and (3) learning by teaching.

One of their main methods of promoting this employee learning and development is a process of facilitated peer coaching groups. These are small peer groups or intact teams of three to five people. All participating groups are volunteers or sponsor-driven, and there are no direct reporting relationships within a group. All members make a commitment to participate over a six-month period. In a group session, each person comes prepared with a project or issue that he or she would like assistance with. The group spends time listening to each person's issue, engages in inquiry to fully understand the issue, and then offers suggestions, support, or whatever specific form of assistance the person needs. In this way, the peers are acting as consultants or coaches. Then, when they are finished discussing that person's issue, another person presents his or her issue for assistance. Members take action between meetings, and at the next meeting they report back what progress they have made and what additional assistance they might need.

This peer coaching process, while still new, has gone through three phases or generations of groups. What Millennium has learned so far in this process is that some of the key enablers of success are a high level of trust, ongoing commitment, good training and facilitation, strong managerial support and sponsorship, high potential participants, and scheduling meetings based on group need rather than at set intervals. The process does not work so well when participants fail to see value and do not commit, when they are too pressed by other work commitments, and when there is a lack of sponsorship.

According to one participant, Dr. Ping Li, director of Protein Sciences, the process is one that gives busy people a chance to slow down and reflect on what they are doing, to focus more clearly on an important project or task, to learn new ways of framing problems and to get new insights and suggestions. Thus, if careers are becoming a series of short learning cycles, rather than one lifelong cycle (Hall 2002), Millennium is in the forefront of finding new ways to promote this short-cycle learning.

By prioritizing learning, both Staples and Millennium Pharmaceuticals facilitate individual efforts to find a place in which their commitment to developing their authentic strengths, interests, and values is integral to the success of the organization. They do this by cultivating a motivating, dynamic, learning-based culture and practicing continuous learning and development throughout the organization. By prioritizing learning and investing in employees' development, companies such as Staples and Millennium ensure an engaged, productive, and loyal workforce.

*Finding a Path: Agency versus Structure*

The third core career task involves constructing a career path by organizing and finding meaning in a series of career experiences over time. The dialectical dilemma at play in "finding a path" is the degree to which *agency*, an individual's self-directed career action, or *structure*, institutionalized career paths and practices, should play a more significant role in shaping careers. People's career paths are always structured by organizational policies and practices, and they are also shaped by people's expectations, aspirations, and decisions (Buchmann 1989). As individuals make choices about their careers, they may simply follow established paths (that is, have a career path determined by structure) or they may depart from the existing models to construct more individualized paths (that is, a path determined more by agency) (Giele 1998; Barley and Tolbert 1997).

The breakdown in traditional institutions that historically provided structure for careers has now created the opportunity for increased agency in the career construction process (Kohli 1986). Changes in employment structures, including the elimination of long-term employment security and stability and the introduction of more flexible and market-driven employment arrangements, have altered the organization of work and employment (Cappelli 1999; Cappelli et al. 1997). At the same time, changing family structures, characterized by delayed and reduced marriage and childbearing, weakening boundaries between education and work, and the declining importance of retirement as an institutionalized life stage, are altering how people think about how work fits into their whole lives and how they allocate work and other activities over the life course (Favennec-Hery 1996; Gardyn 2000; Goldscheider and DaVanzo 1985; Hareven 1994; Riley 1988).

Meanwhile, the increasingly prevalent cultural ideology of individualism places responsibility on people for organizing and giving meaning to their own work experiences, with unclear and often competing models for how to put it all together (Giddens 1991). In essence, the contemporary context amounts to a "weak situation" for organizing careers, increasing the potential for and impact of individual preferences and choices (Weick 1996). The dilemma individuals face is in reconciling the need to exercise personal agency and work with existing career structures.

For individuals, there are clear advantages to following highly structured paths and relying on organizational career structures and systems in defining their career path. Organizational career structures provide stability, security, and predictability, while reducing ambiguity and uncertainty by providing people with readymade, accessible pathways and meanings for a wide range of possible careers. Thirty years ago, these benefits were unquestioned. Now, stable career structures are no longer so prevalent; they are, however, still evident to some degree. Where there are organizational or occupational structures to organize and give meaning to career experiences, career action is far less problematic than when structures are incomplete, inadequate, or ambiguous. For this reason, the pull to rely on structured paths is powerful.

On the other hand, career agency brings new benefits to individuals—the potential for greater freedom, autonomy, and self-direction. The highly structured organizational careers constrain individual careers in a variety of ways. The appeal of self-directed careers is considerable. Of course, with opportunities for increased self-directed action and career freedom come increased stress, uncertainty, and risk. Research has shown that having to choose from many possibilities can actually reduce people's effectiveness and satisfaction in their lives (Schwartz, 2004). Iyengar and Lepper's (1999–2000) research on choice and self-determination has shown that people feel overwhelmed and overloaded by too many options. At the extreme, people are effectively paralyzed by many possibilities and become less likely to take action (also see Schwartz 2000).

### Organizational Challenge: Prioritize Employability

The career management challenge around this dilemma is how to support individual career self-management in a way that benefits individuals and organizations. Operating at either extreme—unbridled individual agency or overly deterministic organizational career structures and systems—is ultimately disadvantageous for both employees and employers. Offering little in the way of career structures or systems and requiring considerable individual agency might minimize the risk to an organization from investing in individual development and careers when employees may not stay with the firm long enough for the company to recoup their investment. However, not investing in employees virtually guarantees that they will look elsewhere for the career development and experiences they want and need to remain marketable (Hall, Zhu, and Yan 2001).

Moreover, while limited structure will bring to the fore desirable characteristics such as autonomy and initiative in some employees, many employees will struggle considerably with too little structure and security. Extensive employment structures limit organizational flexibility and individual adaptability. For individuals, continuous learning and adaptability are the keys to continued employment with a firm as well as to future employment opportunities (Hall 1976; 2002), and adaptable employees enable organizational flexibility. So, organizational processes that develop employees' adaptability will also develop valuable organizational capabilities.

The strategic course of action must come from the skillful synthesis of the two poles. The career management challenge for companies is to create *enabling processes* rather than *constraining structures*. Employees of the future will not benefit from rigid bureaucratic job ladders. Rather, they will benefit from developing an acute understanding of their personal strengths, interests, values, and career aspirations and having access to the resources and supports that will enable them to leverage their capabilities in ways that contribute to their career goals and develop new knowledge, skills, and competencies, all the while contributing through these actions to the organization's goals.

We would argue, then, that one answer to the structure-agency dilemma is for the company to support the development of *employability* for the individual. Developing employability entails helping the employee increase self-awareness, adaptability, and social capital (Fugate, Kinicki, and Ashforth 2004). This includes supporting processes related to identifying and matching employees with job assignments that provide developmental experiences that will be most critical. Other supporting processes include performance management activities such as feedback and coaching and other relational supports, such as mentoring and developmental networks. In contrast, annual performance appraisals are more of a constraining structure.

Career practices and resources that enable employees to increase their self-awareness or develop new skills are also examples of effective supporting processes. One example of such a process is the one in place at AT&T for seasoned employees who have reached a plateau in their careers and are exploring for new challenges. AT&T is attempting to retain these employees through a program called Resource Link. This is an in-house "temp" service that lets employees make themselves available to other departments so that they may "sell" their skills for short-term assignments. Other companies use electronic job boards to match people with jobs, but the unique feature of the process at AT&T is its focus on plateaued employees and on short-term assignments.

In conducting our research for this chapter, we were impressed with the range of career development programs that are available in American companies today. It is also impressive how much information on these programs can be found on the Web. These are obviously intended for recruiting purposes, but they do reflect an attempt at making the process of career development and career movement more transparent than it had been in the past (see, e.g., Johnson & Johnson's Information Management Development Program (IMLDP) and other programs described at http://www.jnj.com/careers/imldp.html).

*The U.S. Army: Career-Long Self-Assessment*
Although one might think of a military organization as being so highly structured and institutionalized as to provide little room for individual self-direction, quite the opposite is true. As part of its transformation process, the Army now has incorporated two of what Hall (2002) has called "metacompetencies" that enable individuals to be self-learners: self-awareness and adaptability. Adaptability has always been provided through various ongoing training activities and combat training centers. Self-assessment, however, is a relatively new activity. Under the new Individual Assessment and Development Program, at key points in the Army officer's career, he or she now uses various self-assessment tools (such as MBTI, Strategic Leadership Development Inventory, a 360-degree feedback tool) to become clearer about values, interests, strengths, and approaches to learning. Assessments are taken at five different points in an officer's career, starting with the Basic Officer Leadership Course and culminating in a senior officers' course, and they contribute to an Individual Learning Plan, jointly developed by the individual and a faculty advisor. This plan is designed to help the person stay focused on his or her career goals, sort through a wide range of structural

opportunities, and make an informed commitment. According to Col. James Oman, chairman of the Department of Command, Leadership and Management, and Col. Charles Allen, director of Leader Development, both at the U.S. Army War College (2005), all of the data from these assessments and learning plans become part of the person's Leader Development Portfolio, which is a secure digital, self-initiated electronic summary of his or her career and professional identity statement.

As a result of the increased self-awareness resulting from these self-assessment tools, the individual becomes clearer on the path that she or he wants to pursue, as well as which paths would fit his or her capabilities the best. The result is a better person-organization fit. Thus, we see a resolution of the agency-structure dilemma: The structure of the Army organization, its opportunity structure, and the greater clarity of self-structure that results from this self-assessment work provide levers that the individual can use to better pursue his or her most preferred path.

*Semco SA*

A more extreme example of encouraging career self-direction by reducing constraining structures is Semco SA, a $160 million Brazilian company that is involved in a range of businesses. When legendary CEO Ricardo Semler took over the business from his father, he dismantled managerial structure to create a sense of ownership among employees and to encourage their active participation in the business. There are no career paths, no career structures at all. As Semler explains, "It's as free market as we can make it. People bring their talents and we rely on their self-interest to use the company to develop themselves in any way they see fit" (Caulkin 2003). Employees are seen as entrepreneurs, and they are encouraged to seek opportunities to contribute to the business in ways that leverage their strengths and engage their interests. This degree of customized career development is possible because of the creative, performance-oriented culture and the lack of structures and systems of control that tend to inhibit productive relationships.

The U.S. Army and Semco SA are both leaders in supporting individual efforts to find career paths. They do this by facilitating protean career construction in ways that develop organizational capabilities and flexibility, one through processes supporting the development of self-awareness and the other through processes encouraging agency and adaptability. These processes enable individuals to reconcile the agency versus structure dilemma because they encourage employees to be self-directed and pursue opportunities that enhance their employability while contributing to larger organizational goals. In the new career landscape, organizations do not need to promise long-term relationships to reap benefits from investment in individual careers. Research has shown that opportunities for career development strengthen the employees' commitment and intentions to stay with their organizations, even more than guarantees of job security can (Craig, Kimberly, and Bouchikhi 2002).

## Conclusions

To summarize a major theme of this chapter, it appears to us that the organizational career development pendulum is swinging back in the direction that it was moving when *Work in America* was originally published. That is, American companies are waking up to the fact that it is necessary to value, invest in, and support employees' careers even though people are unlikely to spend their entire careers in any one organization. They are beginning to focus on what the company can do to help employees attend to and develop their careers because they are coming to understand that doing so will increase the organization's effectiveness.

The challenge that a company has in the contemporary business environment is to know exactly *how* it should work on career development in a systematic way. The 1970s-style long-term career development program remains where it was—in the 1970s. It will not resurface in the 2000s. The new organizational career development initiative will be much more streamlined, much more focused on specific strategic initiatives, and much shorter-cycled. The returns for both parties, employer and employee, will have to be realized continuously, rather than reaped only in the long term. An initiative aimed at employee learning and development will have to build individual capabilities and yield clear results on today's projects and job assignments; no one will wait for development to show up ten years later in a higher-level job.

In this chapter we stress the fact that the employee development and career development processes are happening in much shorter cycles than those that existed in the 1970s. We still see the basic career stages of exploration, trial, establishment, mastery, and disengagement (Super 1957; Hall 1976), however; we see these stages as embedded in a continuous person-organization alignment process. Hence, instead of progressing through each of these stages only once over the career span, we see people cycling through them repeatedly during their careers. We see the career construction process as confronting and reconciling a set of core developmental tasks. Each individual must repeatedly find a purpose for his or her career activities, find a place in which to realize his or her personal potential, and find a path to new growth and opportunities. To illustrate the strategic centrality of these processes in organizations and to suggest how organizations can support individual efforts to complete these career tasks, we have discussed several examples of current organizational career development activity.

As we reflect on these current career activities, it appears to us that the process of doing a good job on career management involves coming to terms with several paradoxes, both for the organization and for the individual. These paradoxes include self-direction versus social-determination, authenticity versus loyalty, and agency versus structure. Grappling with these paradoxes is what drives learning and development, for both the individual and the organization. The metacompetencies of self-awareness and adaptability, again at both levels, are keys to success.

As a result of these new short-cycle career development processes, we expect to see a return to a new form of career contract between the employee and the organization. A cartoon that ran in the *Wall Street Journal* a few years ago wittily captured the essence of this new contract. It showed a picture of a conversation among a few corporate executives with the caption, "True, you can't buy loyalty. However, you certainly can lease it." The new career contract is not based on loyalty for its own sake or on job security that comes with length of service. Rather, it is based on loyalty that is built upon performance and mutual contributions, not upon seniority. That is, it is not a pure relational contract (Rousseau 1995), nor is it a purely transactional contract. Rather, it is a relational-transactional contract, in which both parties desire to have the relationship last for a long period of time, so that each side's investments in the relationship can yield good returns.

Yet, at the same time, each side understands that there are no long-term commitments or guarantees. Both parties know that employees will remain as long as they are learning and growing and being fairly treated and that the employer will continue in the relationship as long as the employee delivers good performance and has an ability to learn and adapt. With this short-cycle, performance- and learning-based loyalty, the organizational career contract is alive and well. And among the players in the employee career development process, employers are getting back into the game.

# 9

# The Shifting Risk for the American Worker in the Contemporary Employment Contract

*Denise M. Rousseau*

Since *Work in America* (O'Toole et al. 1973) was originally published, there has been a radical change in the relationship employers have with their highly skilled employees, workers such as scientists in R&D firms, software designers in IT companies, and consultants in professional service partnerships who contribute to the firm through their distinctive competencies, knowledge, and skills. The change is even evident in the approach taken by the U.S. government to the recent invasion of Iraq. This first American war of the twenty-first century has been fought by an army heavily populated by civilian reservists and part-time National Guard members—the result of massive downsizing in the military during the 1990s (Davey 2004; McGinnis 2005).

The erstwhile civilians now deployed are a striking contrast with the full-time military personnel who populated America's twentieth century wars. In Iraq, America's soldiers have been supported by outsourcing, with contract laborers from private companies responsible for duties such as policing and security, logistics, and food service formerly performed by military personnel (Eckhom 2005). Perhaps not unexpectedly, the citizen soldiers in Iraq have sometimes acted in ways they acquired in their civilian jobs—where innovation in accomplishing the mission is commonly rewarded. One soldier's story is a good example.

Reservist Major Cathy Kaus, who had served both in Iraq and in the Gulf War, was convicted in 2004 of theft and related charges for taking abandoned U.S. Army vehicles. An employee of the bicycle manufacturer Huffy Corporation of Dayton, Ohio, Major Kaus was found guilty of taking two tractors and the stripped parts of a truck, equipment used by Kaus's unit to carry out its mission in Iraq—supplying fuel to everything from helicopters to tanks. Seventy-two hours before the Iraq invasion, Kaus's company arrived in Kuwait, where they unloaded 60 trucks and tankers, each capable of transporting 5,000 gallons of fuel. The company was provided with no vehicles or other means to transport tools, no protective gear, weapons, or other supplies important to the unit's safety and mission. So members of her unit cannibalized abandoned vehicles to get the necessary equipment, acts that Major Kaus failed to communicate to or seek permission for from her superiors. She was one of six Ohio reservists from her unit court-martialed for their actions.

The court-martial occurred at a time when American troops were still complaining that they had to scrounge for equipment. "What we did, we did at that time because we thought we needed to do that," Kaus said, adding that she would "do it all over again" if put in the same circumstances (this and other quotes are from the *Dayton Daily News*, Kaus's hometown newspaper). Cathy Kaus's company "routinely operated over the most dangerous stretch of road in the Sunni Triangle," an Army evaluation concluded, yet performed the "lion's share" of fuel hauling and "never missed a mission." For this, prior to her prosecution, Kaus had been awarded the Bronze Star for "exceptionally meritorious service" and "initiative and courage" during "the time of hostilities in support of Operation Iraqi Freedom." Reflecting from prison, Kaus was proud that her company had traveled 1.8 million miles and hauled 33 million gallons of fuel. Ten members were awarded Bronze Stars, four received Purple Hearts, "and everyone walked back," she said.

In this contemporary event we can observe the two signal features of new American employment relationships: First, highly capable workers are faced with challenging and heretofore unheard of performance demands; and second, risk has migrated from the employer organization and its senior executives to lower level managers and other workers who must then manage risk under conditions in which organizational support is inconsistent or absent. Although these features have become pervasive, they are not yet fully institutionalized. Gaps and inconsistencies remain in how companies, workers, and society respond to the demanding and risky new features of employment. Thus, the same incident warranted a combat medal *and* a court-martial!

Building on such contemporary experiences, this chapter highlights features of new employment relationships and their impact on life in America, both on the job and in society at large. By focusing on *new* employment relationships, this chapter addresses one major segment of the American workforce, the labor market's first tier (St. Paul 1997), those professional or knowledge-oriented workers (many of whom are managers), especially those in firms competing globally, whose conditions of employment have changed drastically in response to ever-evolving business strategies. The firms employing them increasingly depend on these highly capable people to provide competitive advantage (Coff and Rousseau 2000; Rousseau and Shperling 2003).

There are, of course, other segments to the American labor force. This chapter's focus excludes members of the labor force's traditional second tier, the less-skilled and the working poor who are often immigrants or occupants of lower social economic ranks, for whom the more transactional employment pattern remains substantively unchanged (St. Paul 2003).

Since the original *Work in America* was written, it is first-tier workers, the "permanent employees" of yesteryear, who show the greatest change—specifically the professional, skilled, or semiskilled employees who formerly benefited from stable employment in large corporations and industrial firms. (Second-tier workers seldom enjoy stable employment, unless protected by unions or government statutes, conditions largely irrelevant on the American scene.) The essence of this change is the shift of risk, formerly shouldered by employers, to core employees, who once were buffered from market volatility by labor contracts and long-standing norms regarding seniority (Lazear 1981).

This chapter is divided into three sections:

1. The *allocation of risks* from American employers to American workers from Boston to Baghdad in the form of changing performance demands, reduced odds of long-term employment, more variable pay, and erosion of benefits;
2. The *consequences and the coping strategies these risks generate*, including questions of worker mobility and creation of work alternatives, the emergence of the working family as a central unit in employment relations, escalating bargaining by individual workers, and an emerging new form of psychological contract; and
3. The *unresolved dilemmas* this shift in risks creates, threatening sustained worker well-being, employer competitiveness, and societal stability.

### The New Allocation of Risks from Employer to Worker

Risk allocation is a central element in the relationship between worker and employer, an allocation that has changed substantially since the original 1973 *Work in America*, but most particularly during the period since 1990 (e.g., Farber 1997). In common usage, the word "risk" refers to the likelihood of some event seen to be undesirable. Yet in its broadest sense, risk refers to the volatility in a situation where alternative outcomes are possible, positive as well as negative, each with measurable probability (Yates 1992, 4–5). Two fundamental changes have occurred with respect to risk in American employment: First, its absolute level has escalated for both firms and workers in response to global competition and declining U.S. dominance in world markets; and second, employers have passed more of the risk they once shouldered to workers with respect to the returns to be gained from employment.

Historically, employers absorbed more risk than did workers and thus could pay them less in exchange for a guaranteed wage (Knight 1921). In the industrial firms of the twentieth century and in places such as the government's civil service where their practices were emulated, seniority benefits motivated workers to accept wages lower than their current economic contributions in anticipation of both security and higher wages in the future (Rousseau and Shperling 2003, 563, an argument consistent with Lazear 1981). Contemporary workers have fewer guaranteed conditions of employment and greater exposure to market volatility, making them increasingly conscious of risk (e.g., Leana and Feldman 1992; Herriot, Hirsch, and Reilly 1998). The new risk allocation takes the form of lower job security, more variable wages, and escalating job performance demands.

Today, considerable variability exists across employers in terms of pay, benefits, and other employment practices to a degree that employment statistics suggest is unprecedented (Mishel et al. 2005). These differences arise from alternative ways in which companies have responded to their own changing business environments. But despite the company differences, a broad trend is evident in the employment conditions of professional and knowledge workers. The features of the trend are apparent in the ways risk is allocated to workers, affecting the performance demanded of them on the job, their personal finances, their on-the-job conduct, their non-work life demands, and their futures.

*Changing Performance Demands*

Contemporary American employers demand more from their employees than the employers in the past. More, newer, better, and faster characterize many of the deliverables employees are pressured to provide (e.g., George, Works, and Watson-Hemphill 2005). Balanced scorecard approaches tie multiple and simultaneously assessed employee performance indicators to business results (e.g., Yeung and Berman 1997). Longer hours (Bureau of Labor Statistics 2004), shorter deadlines (Sethi, King, and Quick 2004), and many more explicitly demanded performance contributions (e.g., Marscke 2002) have become the norm. Labor productivity has grown substantially compared with earlier eras from the early 1990s until today (Hansen 2001; Bureau of Labor Statistics 2004). Hansen found evidence of a structural break in labor productivity growth between 1992 and 1996, meaning that substantively different forces from those that operated previously are driving the growth in productivity to a new phase of escalation. In effect, a confluence of forces has created a tipping point (Gladwell 2002), resulting in unheard of levels of labor productivity on a mass scale.

Although as yet there is no clear consensus as to the factors behind this accelerated labor productivity, a variety of forces are likely contributors, including the role of information technology informatting work and improving its coordination, enabling worker efforts to yield greater economic payoffs for their employer. This productivity growth represents an increase in the value workers add to the firms that employ them (Pfeffer 1994).

The critical contributions that workers make are evident in the demands for service quality and innovation (George et al. 2005; Peters 1999), requirements that cannot be imposed upon a machine or an assembly line. First-tier employees exert considerable control over their performance because their efforts are neither highly standardized nor easily monitored. Unlike assembly-line work, for example, knowledge work allows employees to control their own work processes and output. This control extends from shaping the information and analyses used to solve a design problem to the quality of the relationships built with customers and clients. Very often higher-level managers do not know how to accomplish such tasks, and may provide little in the way of active support or assistance, trusting their capable workers to figure out for themselves how to get the job done (Miles and Creed 1995).

Insofar as our opening story about reservists in Iraq is concerned, it is clear in hindsight that Kaus should have reported the cannibalization of military equipment up the chain of command. But the "prevailing attitude was that if it gets me into the fight, and allows me to stay in the fight, then in the bigger picture it is OK," her battalion commander explained (*Dayton Daily News* 2004). This "results focus" is evident in contemporary American work of skilled independent contractors (Meyerson, Weick, and Kramer 1996; Barley 2004) and high-involvement team members (MacDuffie 1995), and also among outsourced workers (Shir and Li 2005), where management specifies what needs to be accomplished and workers determine how.

Worker contributions are expanded via the demands that employees in highly competitive firms face to deliver on many objectives simultaneously. These typically take the forms of efficiency, cost-effectiveness, product or service quality, customer satisfaction, and growth in market share. The values expressed in corporate mission statements have become heuristics to help employees keep in mind their charge to fill multiple, concurrent performance demands. The broader mix of goals competitive firms pursue necessitates more complex forms of performance management.

For example, Bain, a global management consulting firm, advertises its dedication to "making companies more valuable." Each year it surveys how firms make use of 20 popular management tools. In 2005, these tools included Total Quality Management (TQM), business process reengineering, balanced scorecard, and mission statements along with management of change, loyalty, and knowledge. It is worth noting that the executives who responded to Bain's survey indicate lower satisfaction with their efforts regarding the latter three management practices than with tools of an economic nature, such as activity-based accounting, or with those tools that are more familiar and well-established, such as TQM. Tools directed toward managing the complex performance demands made of the first-tier workforce are the ones employers find most difficult to use (Bain and Company, http://www.bain.com/management_tools/tools_overview.asp?groupCode=2).

One crosscutting feature of contemporary management tools is their focus on metrics. Metrics are specific indicators, typically of a quantitative nature, that can be used to monitor performance and evaluate individual, team, and organizational success. Since many of these metrics are of a financial nature, we see evidence of increasing business literacy among workers, who are today more likely to be able to read their organization's balance sheets, understand its status in the stock market, and comprehend its drivers of cost and competitiveness (Ferrante and Rousseau 2001; Nadler 1998). What is measurable and gets measured becomes what employees and their managers pay attention to, while what goes unmeasured tends to be ignored.

This measurement focus gives rise to the need for better analysis of the factors underlying organizational performance in the first place, so that the factors that truly matter to performance can actually be managed (Goodman 2001). Unless the linkages to important organizational outcomes are well-understood, the employer risks demanding contributions from workers that ultimately interfere with the organization's success, as seen in the case of firms that demand short-term revenue growth where long-term investment in customer-supplier relations would be more effective.

First-tier workers also have experienced a change in their exercise of authority. As professionals and knowledge-workers in dynamic and demanding environments, first-tier workers exercise more of their own authority, relying less on supervisors for direction or permission (Fisher 1993, 2003)—as the incident with Kaus's unit exemplifies. Informal mechanisms such as worker initiative and peer pressure influence how workers serve customers, manage work-family conflict, and otherwise conduct themselves in performing their jobs.

This extrahierarchical authority is the result of employee expertise and competence as well as the informal influence trusted employees exert. It also reflects the need for the individual worker to reconcile how best to pursue multiple goals on the spot, without time to seek out management to resolve the matter. This complexity of work may contribute in part to the trend toward greater employer trust in workers (Miles and Creed 1995). In the day-to-day work world, these informal, sideways, and upward manifestations of authority help flesh out the otherwise incomplete employment arrangement. As a result, hierarchical, top-down authority tends to be reserved for resolving those disputes not settled through nonhierarchical means (Simon 1997). In place of hierarchical authority are the metrics, goals, and performance targets broadly applied across the firm—the very management tools that can be tough to apply in practice.

### Reduced Odds of Long-Term Employment

The notion of a "permanent employee" is a thing of the past. Long-term employment with the same firm is less and less the norm for American workers. Farber (1997) investigated changes in the incidence of long-term employment in the United States using data spanning from 1979 to 1996. After controlling for demographic character-istics, the fraction of workers reporting more than 10 years of service fell sharply between 1993 and 1996, to the lowest level since 1979. Layoffs targeting senior workers did not account for this trend. The greatest decrease in job tenure occurred in two occupations: managers and professional/technical workers. It is important to note that reduced job tenure occurred not only in financially troubled firms, but in successful ones, too. Hence, a recent advertisement placed by the Communication Workers of America denounced the job loss of 3000 Verizon employees following a year of $4 billion in profits ("Verizon's profits shouldn't be our loss," http://www.cwa-union.org/news, 2005).

Reduced organizational tenure is both a cause and effect of the declining value of seniority for American workers. There is little reason to keep faith in the broad value of seniority across workers and firms in the United States in an era where it brings fewer financial rewards. Further, because of hostile takeovers and acquisitions, employees are at much greater risk than commonly assumed in economic theory (e.g., Zardkhooi and Paetzgold 2004) because a new employer is less likely to honor commitments made by a previous management team (Shleifer and Summers 1988, 250). Changes in the employer itself, including turnover among managers, can undermine an existing deal's sustainability. In consequence, first-tier employees mak-ing substantial contributions to their employers, without expectation of seniority benefits, often expect instead some portion of that wealth premium typically reserved in the past for entrepreneurs and financial investors.

In contrast to the decline of property rights associated with seniority, American law provides greater protection for investors who hold equity stakes in firms (Ritter and Taylor 2000). Claiming a share of their employer's profits and stock provides workers a way to balance risk and reward between themselves and the firm's investors, entrepreneurs, and managers (Rousseau and Shperling 2003, 2004)—and gives them a reason to remain committed to the firm.

### From Fixed to Variable Pay

As first-tier employees experience less income growth due to erosion of seniority, the fixed component of their pay, such as wages or salary, has remained relatively stag-nant. In the 1990s, wages grew rapidly in the United States, but in the early years of the twenty-first century labor market slack has had a negative impact on wages and income for all workers (Mishel, Bernstein, and Allegretto 2005). Proportionately more worker compensation takes the form of pay that is contingent upon either indi-vidual performance (bonus) or firm performance (profit-sharing) (Rynes and Gephart 2000). Because contingent pay ties compensation to results, workers can win big rewards when they or their employers are successful; this induces them to share in the negative consequences that follow poor performance. It is important to note that while first-tier workers potentially can score big wins (or losses), other workers tend only to lose because their pay is fixed and has remained flat.

What real income growth there has been recently has been tied to contingent pay. In the capital sector, "since the first quarter of 2001, virtually all (98.5 percent) of the real income growth in the corporate sector has accrued to capital income (profits, interest, and dividend payments), an important factor in the rising participation of workers as investors in capital markets, in particular with ownership stakes in the firms that employ them" (Mishel et al. 2005). Equity stakes that workers purchase or are granted in the firms that employ them constitute an increasingly important portion of their compensation.

It is also true that investors and managers have become more willing to share the firm's equity and profits with workers (Pierce and Furo 1990). Employee stock ownership plans in the United States grew from 1,600 in 1975 to 11,400 in 1998 (National Center for Employee Ownership 2000). The percentage of large firms granting stock options to at least half of their employees increased from 17 percent in 1993 to 39 percent in 1999 (ACA News 1999). Broad-based ownership is associated with high firm performance (Blasi, Kruse, and Bernstein 2003) and also reinforces a sense of equity and fairness in firms where workers are interdependent, and thus their performance depends on shared goals and common understandings to achieve effective coordination.

This trend aligns with the concept of an ownership culture, where workers, managers, and financial investors have common interests. Investors may also obtain greater benefits from shares in those firms where workers themselves participate more directly in the benefits of ownership (e.g., Shperling, Rousseau, and Ferrante 2002). As we will see below, however, greater ownership shares can be a mixed blessing for workers, particularly when their pensions are involved.

Profit-sharing aligns worker interests with those of financial investors. Thus, profit-sharing is positively related to employee contributions to the firm (e.g., Brown, Fakhfakh, Sessions 1999), a finding consistent with instrumental theories of work motivation (e.g., Vroom 1964). Moreover, holding equity stakes in a firm in which one also shares in the profits can have a synergistic impact, enhancing the value derived from one's employment in and attachment to the organization as a whole. To this end, introducing profit-sharing has been found to have a more positive effect where workers already hold equity shares, but it is less effective when workers do not have equity (Brown et al. 1999).

### Fringe Benefits: From Benefits Coverage to Co-Pay or You Pay

The quality of pension and healthcare benefits has eroded considerably since the original *Work in America*. Two drivers of this erosion have been cost-containment and the differential treatment an employer gives its workers based on how critical they are to the firm's strategy. The essential purpose of fringe benefits has been to make jobs valuable to workers (who might otherwise quit to take a job elsewhere) by providing them with resources that contribute to their security both in the present and over the course of their lifetime. American workers place particular value on healthcare and pension benefits since neither of these are effectively provided by the government, in contrast to the governments of other industrialized countries such as France, Germany, Canada, or Scandinavia.

Fringe benefits are broadly awarded to workers independent of their or the firm's performance and have the advantage of reinforcing a sense of common interests across workers within a firm (Rousseau and Ho 2001). Indeed, so valued are fringe benefits as an entitlement that the families of 9/11 victims who were employed at Marsh and McLellan were livid upon learning that their deceased loved ones' employer had offered them (only) a three-year health coverage plan (Barstow and Henriques 2001). In a shift generating a similar response, oil services giant Halliburton reduced its pensions to some workers, despite large profits, by taking advantage of a legal loophole involved in its acquisition of the workers' former employer (Walsh 2004). Insofar as Americans depend on employers for healthcare and retirement benefits, corporate actions with regard to benefits such as these are likely to receive considerable scrutiny.

The erosion of pension quality has been observed since the 1980s, with the greatest decline being among high wage earners (Mischel et al. 2005, 140). As I write this in June 2005, United Airlines has just defaulted on its pension obligations to its workforce to the tune of $9.8 billion (McFeatters 2005). Such defaults are increasingly common, as American steel workers too can attest (Opdyke and Greene 2005).

Another aspect of the erosion of pension benefits among first-tier workers is the shift to defined contributions as opposed to defined benefits, which means that worker retirement income depends on his or her success in investing those contributions, with the risks borne by the employee rather than the employer (Mishel et al. 2005, 141). In an aptly titled *Time* article, "Don't Bet It All on Your Employer," the plunge of Enron stocks exemplified the risk employees take in having too much of their savings or pension invested where they work (Epperson 2001). In the private sector American workforce, pension coverage in the early years of the twenty-first century was at 45.5 percent, 5.1 percent lower than the coverage in 1979 (Mishel et al. 2005, 7). With less than half the workforce covered by employer-provided pensions, workers seek alternative provisions for their retirement. Thus, half of all Americans now participate in the stock market, one means of offsetting the limited support retirees receive from the government-maintained Social Security system (Nadler 1998).

Healthcare benefits have declined, too. In the private sector American workforce, employer-provided healthcare coverage is at 56.4 percent, 12.6 percent lower than the coverage in 1979 (Mishel et al. 2005, 138). Even where coverage exists, first-tier workers have picked up more of their own healthcare costs in the form of insurance premiums cost-sharing and co-pays for service. Between 20 and 30 percent of the top 40 percent of wage earners receive no healthcare benefits at all from their employers (Mishel et al. 2005, 138). Of course, the circumstances are far worse for the bottom 40 percent, of whom 50 to 75 percent receive no healthcare benefits, making them more dependent on public funds such as Medicaid. Shifts in healthcare coverage reflect attempts to contain healthcare costs, and in unionized environments these changes at times have been voluntarily agreed to as part of a broader effort to enhance firm competitiveness (e.g., Cutcher-Gershenfeld 2003).

Employees also hesitate even to use some of the benefits officially provided for them. Vacation is a traditional fringe benefit, yet American workers are often reluctant to take all their allotted vacation time. Reasons for taking less time off include both fear that they will be judged negatively if they are away too long and anxiety over the amount of work they would face upon their return (Kaminsky 2004; Rousseau 2005). Similar experiences are reported regarding family leave benefits, especially for males, who tend to be reluctant to use them (e.g., Shellenbarger 2002).

Reluctance to make use of benefits granting time off depends upon informal norms that affect the behavior of organizational members, such as pressure to minimize time away from the job and the anticipated negative impact on one's success in competing for promotion and raises—a state of affairs referred to as the "rat race redux" (Landers, Rebitzer, and Taylor 1996). Insofar as this reluctance is related to changing performance demands, diminished access to time off can have substantially adverse effects on an employee's life outside of work, the well-being of his/her family members, and the ability of the larger society to meet employee needs such as mental health and family services.

### How Do Employees Understand the New Risk?

The migration of risk to workers raises two questions: Do first-tier workers understand the new risk? And how do they interpret it? Surprisingly little attention has been given to what workers actually understand about the changes in their employment relations, with all of the implications for their careers and financial futures. Similarly, we know little regarding how employees have responded to their greater vulnerability to market forces and the escalating responsibility for managing their careers, healthcare costs, and pension benefits. But there are some hints.

One emerging concept relevant to employee awareness and understanding of risk is business literacy, the extent to which workers understand financial information relevant to their employers and how this affects their own personal finances (Ferrante and Rousseau 2001). Employers such as Eastman Chemical have made business literacy an important component in promoting more effective employee participation in decision making (Rousseau and Arthur 1999). The spillover effects of such efforts include having workers who identify more with their own financial portfolios, while they do recognize a link between employer business outcomes and their own future financial well-being (Nadler 1998). Some firms choose to engage in open-book management, sharing business information with their employees to develop their individual capabilities for understanding the information and making decisions accordingly (Case 1997; Ferrante and Rousseau 2001; Stack and Burlingham 2003).

Wherever they work, the understandings employees have of risk are likely to be closely tied to the autonomy they exercise with regard to business-related decisions in their workplace, the financial information provided and the metrics their employers share, and the level of personal and formal education they have with respect to economics and finance. Even educated professionals may lack the financial expertise to manage pension portfolios effectively. The 2003 landmark $1.4 billion dollar settlement with investment banks for providing misleading research to investors set aside $85 million dollars for investor education efforts. There is, however, dispute over how this money should be spent (Solomon 2005).

Moreover, while open-book management is promoted in many employee-owned firms, access to information regarding the financial health of one's employer is often limited to senior management in most other American firms (e.g., Shperling, Rousseau, and Ferrante 2002). Consequently, many workers are poorly prepared to understand, let alone manage, the new risks. Those who do often have accepted the notion that their careers are "boundaryless," incorporating relationships with differing kinds of work and firms over time (Rousseau and Arthur 1999).

### Implications

By migrating risks to employees, employers have expanded their own menu of choices in managing relations with employees. In particular, they can combine various arrangements to create new relationships with workers. The shift to variable pay provides workers an incentive when used in conjunction with escalating performance demands.

Combining benefit cuts with eroded seniority value motivates workers to look out for themselves. But by allocating these risks to workers, employers have departed from the broad array of resources they once guaranteed first-tier workers. In consequence, successful performance need not translate into sustained employment or steady financial rewards—at least not with the same employer. Instead, workers need to offset a risky future by managing more of their own careers, work life, and financial security.

Employees face greater uncertainty regarding their current conditions of employment, including the financial rewards and safeguards they can expect from it. As individuals, these workers are often ill-prepared to manage the risks they face or their consequences. So we must now look at the consequences of the shift in risk from employers to workers.

## Consequences

The practice of migrating risks from employers to first-tier workers is linked to increased disparity in wages among those with comparable education, experience, and positions. This rising within-group inequality is a fact largely ignored by contemporary scholars and public policy specialists (Mishel et al. 2005, 149). Interpretations for the disparity include suggestions that employers pay premiums for skills not captured by conventional human capital surveys and that these are simply changing wage norms. Firms using different human resource strategies such as buying talent, as opposed to developing it, also may account for some of the disparity.

There are, however, other factors that apply. For one, individual workers can bring about some of these differences themselves—for example, by accumulating human capital at varying rates due both to intra-firm opportunities and individual differences. Fast learners have the most career success, though fastest promotees also exit more often (Baker, Gibbs, and Homstrom 1994, 916). In contemporary firms, such high performing first-tier workers can have considerable bargaining power. Employee efforts to manage the new risks they face have led to greater mobility for many first-tier workers, greater interdependence in the employment arrangements that partners in working families make, and greater reliance on worker initiative to support the family, create career opportunity, and future security. The confluence of these coping strategies culminates in novel forms of employment relations that both worker and employer must learn to navigate.

### Mobility and Availability of Work Alternatives

Mobility is the extent to which workers have quality alternatives to remaining with their current employer. Mobile workers can decide when, how, and for whom to be productive while their less-mobile counterparts have limited choice. Mobility is itself a bargaining chit, in that a worker cannot make credible demands of an employer if he or she can be easily laid off, replaced, or forced into retirement. Alternative opportunities can mean not only a job offer elsewhere, but also going it alone as an independent contractor, or founding a firm of one's own. In a survey of high-technology employers in Pittsburgh, the vast majority indicated that at least some of their employees were capable of successfully founding their own businesses (Shperling, Rousseau, and Ferrante 2003).

Recent labor statistics indicated that contractors and the self-employed represented 7.3 percent of the female labor force and 10.6 percent of the male, while 69.1 percent of women and 77.1 percent of men are full-time employees. Regardless of gender, the self-employed and contractors had greater hourly wages than regular full-time workers (Mishel et al. 2005, 260). Growth of these employment alternatives has even sparked a whole new terminology, with labels such as permalancer, hired gun, guru, lone worker, and 1099er (Pink 2001). (Form 1099 is the the tax form received by self-employed American workers.) Mobile workers are preeminent self-managers and relate to their employers in ways radically different from the company men of the past (Arthur and Rousseau 1996; Sampson 1995). With alternatives to choose from, mobile workers benefit from distinctive competencies and supportive family circumstances that can ease the transition to another employer.

### The "Working Family"

How workers experience their employer's demands for higher performance or cuts in benefits needs to be calibrated in relation to impact on family. In the United States, the family unit often is as much party to new employment relationships as are individual workers, because the joint actions of two wage earners impact individual mobility, the family's current income and benefits, and its financial future. Failure to consider the family as a unit in employment confounds our understanding of the consequences of risk migration.

For example, it has been disputed whether workers work longer hours today than in years past. Between 1975 and 2002, average weekly hours show little upward movement. At their peak in 2000, average hours were only 3.1 percent above the 1975 level (Mishel et al. 2005). As Mishel and colleagues point out, however, that average is misleading because of the rise in the number of women in the workforce and their tendency to work part-time. Going by another index, the average hours worked by all family members, we see an 11 percent increase since 1975.

Flatter wages and declining benefits across all sectors of the American workforce often necessitate that both partners work. The middle-class family in particular manifests greater dependence on dual earners. Married couples with children in the middle-income range worked 500 hours more per year in 2000 than in 1979 (Mishel et al. 2005, 40). For married couples, wives' income has an equalizing effect, reducing the inequality across wage levels mentioned earlier (Mischel et al. 2004, 104). Healthcare coverage has declined twice as much among men as among women—down 15.7 percent versus 7.1 percent (Mishel et al. 2005, 137). One interpretation of this is that more women may be working in the kinds of jobs that provide the family healthcare while husbands pursue a larger income as an entrepreneur or independent contractor.

In the context of the working family, mobility may be constrained by the interdependence of each partner on the employment arrangements of the other. This pattern parallels the employment relationship synergy observed among middle-class Chinese workers, where one partner holds a state-owned enterprise job for the education, health, and housing benefits it offers while the other brings in the higher wages a multinational firm pays. Moreover, it suggests that an important unit of analysis for interpreting the impact of the migrating risk in employment is the family. It must also be noted that many families are single-parent households for whom the adverse consequences of risk migration are more difficult to offset.

Working parents are especially challenged by the demands knowledge workers and professionals face for ever-availability—that is, to respond immediately to the service demands of the firm, its clients, and customers. Family stresses extend to reservists fighting in Iraq, many of whom were unexpectedly called up from civilian life despite thinking that their time in the reserve had ended (Davey 2004). Cathy Kaus herself was a single parent with a son in college when she was called up to serve in Iraq. Working mothers find themselves making a difficult decision, figuring out the right way to answer the question, "Mommy, why do you have to work?" (Shellenbarger 2005). For working parents, even in the middle class, the choice is not whether to work, but how to manage the consequences for their families.

*Fewer Corporate Commitments Mean Individual*
*Workers must Bargain for Themselves*

With the stripping away of many traditional employment benefits they enjoyed as a group, first-tier workers more actively manage their own individual relationships with employers. One way to do so is by bargaining for preferred employment conditions that their employers would not otherwise provide. These individual negotiations, known as idiosyncratic deals, or "i-deals" for short (Rousseau 2005; Rousseau, Ho, and Greenberg 2006), occur when the combination of first-tier worker mobility and the value their employers place on them positions these employees to demand significantly greater compensation or perquisites than their less-advantaged coworkers receive. Strong overlaps in pay across levels within the same company (Shaw, Gupta, and Delery 2002) is evidence of an individual component in pay determination where the worker's mobility, market value, and bargaining behavior influence how much the company pays (Rousseau 2005). First-tier workers also bargain for flexibility to reduce the negative impact their high demands jobs have on families (Hochschild 1997).

Knowledge workers and others with scarce and highly valued skills who realize their power can bargain in ways not possible for those who see themselves as having less power. The notion of individual workers having power was to a great extent unimaginable at the turn of the twentieth century in the industrialized nations, with failed strikes characterizing the primary industries of the day, such as coal and steel (Guillen 1994). The dominant industries of the twenty-first century have a different balance of power. Insofar as their employer gains competitive advantage through its workforce, individual workers are more likely to assert their preferences and be accommodated by employers when they possess valued resources and can control how their resources are used, by either varying their levels of contribution or threatening to quit. Valued resources include worker skills, knowledge, and relationships (with coworkers, customers, or suppliers) that increase productivity (Coff and Rousseau 2000).

Negotiation strategies that workers use often leverage the i-deal's value for the employer, too, as a reward for a high performer or as a crucial source of innovation and adaptation to workforce and technology changes. Thus, a change to teleworking might be advantageous to both worker and employer (Rousseau 2005). But unjust and self-serving arrangements such as favoritism have clear negative consequences for the firm and are not even intended to benefit it directly, as in the case in which the nephew of a senior executive is automatically given fewer job demands and more flexible hours—in effect, lowering the quality of one worker's contributions to the firm (Rousseau 2004).

I-deals can aid both workers and employers by providing an effective means of attracting, motivating, or retaining the services of a valued contributor. The increasing use of I-deals highlights the changing nature of traditional paradigms for these necessary practices. I-deals represent an outgrowth of employer responses to market pressures and to workers' heightened expectations of having a say in what their experiences on the job ought to be like (Freeman and Rogers 1997). Together, these forces promote greater customization in aspects of employment, particularly for those workers whose performance or mobility gives them clout.

An implication of individual bargaining is that workers in the same firm can differ in the resources they garner from employment, from pay to advancement opportunities. Thus, i-deals provide one more explanation for the growth of wage inequality among workers with comparable education, experience, and positions (Mishel et al. 2005), where some are better able to capitalize upon their human capital than others. The idiosyncratic arrangements that in effect reward high performers are one reason why in a firm workers who have been stars for a long time are less likely to leave than are workers newly designated as stars (e.g., Groysberg, Nanda, and Norhia 2004). The long-time stars know that accumulated idiosyncrasies can be hard to replicate with a new employer.

### A New Hybrid Psychological Contract

First-tier American workers increasingly show signs of what have been termed hybrid psychological contracts (Rousseau and Schalk 2000). [The psychological contract refers to beliefs each party has regarding a reciprocal agreement between the worker and the employer (Rousseau 1995).] The modal first-tier psychological contract following World War II had been a relational one, offering workers job security and internal career opportunity with little risk exposure (Rousseau and Schalk 2000). Because workers with relational agreements demand less pay than their nonrelational counterparts, that wealth premium is effectively given to the firm and its investors (Garud and Shapira 1997).

Since the 1990s, however, hybrid psychological contracts have emerged, combining the relational factors of career development and mutual concern with terms contingent upon the performance of both worker and firm (Rousseau and Schalk 2000). Moreover, the meaning of "career development" has shifted from internal to external as the contract migrated from relational to hybrid, since the worker may ultimately have more opportunity for advancement by changing employers.

The existence of hybrid psychological contracts is evidence that risk is an accepted condition of employment, at least for some employees. This is a form of employment arrangement likely to be closely tied to employee understanding of market forces and business processes. Employers who create mutual expectations with employees regarding risk-sharing are characterized by human resource practices that promote business literacy and widespread business knowledge among their workers so that they can better support employee participation in a hybrid relationship (Rousseau and Arthur 1999; Rousseau 2003). They also encourage workers to establish a reputation for competence in both internal and external social networks as a means of creating future employability.

These supports offer workers ways to actively participate in the organization while managing their own careers. Because of supports, workers have the potential to benefit financially from the firm's success and still create alternative opportunities for themselves in the event of its failure. This supportive approach is characteristic of firms such as GE or McKinsey, where former employees are in effect alumni, whose time with the company credentials them for employment elsewhere. Thus, workers share with managers and investors, not only in the returns and the risk, but also in the controls exerted to manage risk. Hybrid psychological contracts promote positive attitudes toward risks, making them more acceptable when workers look forward to managing both their careers and their own financial assets, such as retirement funds (Rousseau and Arthur 1999).

Sharing ownership and related privileges promotes an array of mutual interests (Pierce et al. 1991) and increases the likelihood that investors, managers, and workers hold a common frame of reference (Case 1995). The alignment of worker interests with those of the firm requires a shared understanding regarding the psychological contract that underlies the employment relationship. That is, mutuality influences how well workers and employers fulfill each other's psychological contract. People typically are motivated to keep their commitments *as they understand them* (Shanteau and Harrison 1991; Rousseau 1995). Congruence or mutuality in the psychological contracts of employee and employer has been found to be positively related to objective and subjective measures of individual job performance (Dabos and Rousseau 2004). At issue is how congruent are the two parties' understandings.

Combining several privileges of ownership can enhance employer and worker agreement regarding the terms of the psychological contract (Rousseau and Shperling 2003). In high involvement work systems, bundling mutually reinforcing practices has been found to surpass the impact of involvement alone by increasing worker competence and motivation to perform the complex behaviors such systems entail (MacDuffie 1995; Ichniowski, Kochan, Levine, Olson, and Strauss 1996). Worker rights to stock ownership and/or profit-sharing are, like other human resource practices, more likely to give rise to coherent, mutually reinforcing messages and shared understanding when bundled with the support practices of participative decision making and dissemination of financial information.

A growing segment of the workforce in industrialized countries can be construed to have interorganizational or "boundaryless" careers (Arthur and Rousseau 1996; Arthur, Inkson, and Pringle 1999). Such individuals often are self-employed for significant periods of time and combine the perspectives of worker and owner through a market-related view of both employment and firms (Rousseau and Arthur 1999). Indeed, having an equity share in one's employer/company may be a required condition for retaining workers pursuing boundaryless careers. Sharing in the employer's equity and profits, where the worker has business information and exercises some control over how the firm's assets are used, creates conditions another employer may find tough to counter.

## Implications

Workers need to manage the risks now allocated to them. One way to do that is by crafting employment relationships that diversify the resources available to working families. Another is for workers to self-manage both their own careers and their financial futures. Doing either is easier where the individual can bargain advanta-geously for those valued resources no longer automatically provided as a condition of employment. Effective bargaining necessitates that the worker needs to be in a pow-erful position, which means having three things: control over the exercise of his or her labor, possession of market knowledge regarding the value of his or her labor to the employer, and some skill in negotiating.

The consequences of the shift in risk entail a mix of roles for first-tier workers that blur the long-established boundaries between the notions of the individual as a worker, self-manager, and entrepreneur/owner or financial investor. Mobile high performers are the big winners among first-tier workers when more conditions of employment are left up to individual bargaining. The average performer receives fewer resources and is less able to bargain for the opportunity and flexibility that might aid in managing both career and family concerns. The gaps between the risks workers face and the resources needed to neutralize, manage, or offset them are the challenges to which we now turn.

## Challenges, Gaps, and Dilemmas

Gaps exist between the risks now allocated to workers and how effectively workers, their families, their employers, and the larger society have responded to them. Just as in the changed conditions of fighting a war with civilian contractors and reservists, the infrastructure required to capitalize on these new employment relationships may require changes not only on the part of workers, but also on the part of the employer, and possibly society as well. I believe that we are in a time of transition, where the infrastructure is not in place to effectively both reap the benefits and manage the downsides of the shift in risks to workers. The challenges we face are apparent in the following dilemmas.

### Do People Take Risks Effectively when Everything is at Risk? Safety Nets for Common Needs

American workers at all levels have limited institutional or collective support to aid them and their families in coping with the new risks. Medical care for workers without health insurance, for example, is recognized as a societal problem, though effective policy has not yet emerged (Pear 2005). Uninsured workers risk destitution for them-selves and their families, should injury or illness strike. American life provides few safety nets, the collective supports for those needs that people hold in common, from healthcare and retirement benefits on the economic side to opportunities for retooling and adjusting when radical shifts occur in labor markets.

Having all one's financial assets at risk may not be good for either worker or employer. Bill Gates recognized this in the early years of Microsoft, when he insisted that the founding members of the firm take some of their assets out of the organization, so that their decisions about its future would not be compromised by fears of losses. Typical employees, many in the first tier and the vast majority of those in the second, have few resources apart from their job. When a worker in a start-up firm accepts stock options rather than a salary based on his or her market value, a substantial portion of that worker's financial future can be tied up in the firm (Shperling and Rousseau 2001). The same is the case for workers whose pensions are funded by employer stock.

Although many financial investors can diversify risks, workers/owners whose primary assets are attached to their jobs cannot. Rajan and Zingales (2003, 232) in their constructive critique (and defense) of the American economic system argue, "There is no theoretical reason to entrust responsibility for worker retirement benefits to firms employing them." But the downside risks are too great for pensions to depend upon workers alone. A more effective approach might be for firms to pay an appropriate amount into a private or public trust fund. Diversified and portable pensions are a way forward similar to the TIAA-CREF system that Andrew Carnegie created to allow teachers to accumulate pensions independent of their employers. On the other hand, employee owners may provide the patient capital that is often required to promote company growth (Smith, Pfeffer, and Rousseau 2001). We need research on the risks and benefits of varying degrees of employee investment in the firms that employ them to inform both policy and practice.

### Do Big Wins always Mean Tremendous Losses? Justice Pays

Justice issues are always important in the workplace, and even more so under conditions of rising wage inequality. Conditions whereby both employer and worker prosper by encouraging individual bargaining may depend not only on the kind of thing bargained for (career opportunity is an individual interest while healthcare benefits are broadly important) but also on the work being done. Expecting workers to self-manage where they are highly interdependent with others can lead to backlash, with resentment of a too-demanding peer or of the inequality in the outcomes enjoyed by people with whom they must cooperate to get work done.

Pay compression promotes better performance when workers are interdependent, while pay dispersion yields higher performance when work is independent, and the pay system as incentive system is formally administered (Shaw, Gupta, and Delery 2002). Employers need to become savvier regarding how to bargain with workers individually without jeopardizing the degree of cooperation and trust required among coworkers. The knowledge required here is how to implement flexibility with fairness.

The contemporary outrage generated by enormous CEO pay increases, with spillover effects upon other senior managers, is another facet of workplace justice that challenges the new employment relationship. The divergence of CEO pay from the average worker's has increased from 24 times in 1965 for U.S. CEOs in major firms to 300 times by the end of the 2000 recovery, falling to 185 in 2003 (Mishel et al. 2005, 214). Waging a war for talent based on the notion that a single individual makes the critical difference to a company's success ignores the strategic value of a firm's asset mix of human and intellectual capital. It reduces the overall performance of the firm, as employees with flattened wages react with a sense of outrage to lavish CEO salaries (Cowherd and Levine 1992). Basically, justice pays—and it cannot be achieved by viewing each individual worker (whether rank and file employee or CEO) in isolation from others in the organization.

### What if the Metrics that Employers Use Are Wrong? Making Effective Performance Demands

Much of the ultimate benefit employers get from demanding more from workers depends upon whether the employer is making the right demands. Effective performance demands and the metrics that communicate them require the organization to identify the critical factors underlying organizational performance in the first place (Goodman 2001). Unless the linkages to important organizational outcomes are well understood, the efforts of work groups to realize their local objectives can be at odds with those that produce strategically important organizational outcomes (Goodman and Rousseau 2004) and the actions their members take as individuals (Langred 2000). In managed healthcare, for example, the common metrics that once monitored group practices are increasingly applied to individual doctors, and this in consequence can diminish physician attention to clinical care quality (Terry 2005).

Moreover, when measures are too locally focused, emphasizing only individual or local group performance, employees can come to identify not with the firm as a whole, but with their team, resulting in less willingness to cooperate with others outside it (Kreiner and Ashforth 2004). For team goals to be effective, they need to shift attention away from individual productivity to the broader competencies that enhance the team and its impact on the overall firm (Grote 1999). Unfortunately, little collective understanding exists regarding how to most effectively manage individual, group, and organizational performance simultaneously.

Improving performance even on a single indicator can be difficult. Worker performance tends to remain fairly consistent under stable conditions (Rambo, Chomiak, and Price 1983) without substantial interventions to increase it. Moreover, group incentives can have unexpected effects on individual performance: Workers who are initially the least productive improve, whereas the most productive workers do not change. Efforts to improve group level performance often improve only the performance of the weakest individuals, leading group performance to converge on a standard level (Hansen 1997). So unless a set of interventions is applied, such as coupling training with sustained process innovation over time, it may be easier to elicit new kinds of worker contributions, such as joining an ongoing demand for efficiency with an additional goal of improved quality, than it is to improve on current performance.

These problems indicate that the practical knowledge that promotes performance improvement in the face of changing demands is not readily available or consistently acted upon across firms in the United States. In effect, as in the case of Cathy Kaus's unit in Iraq, there is a gap between the support the infrastructure provides and the demands workers face. Times of transition are often characterized by the need for lagging parts of an organization or society to "catch-up" with those more accelerated. It is for this reason that people caught in transitions often shoulder substantial burdens on their own.

### Is Employee Ownership a Pay Scheme or a Culture?
### Not by Financial Incentives Alone

Many firms depend on variable pay to align worker efforts with the broader firm. But variable pay in itself is not enough to effectively motivate workers when the desired contributions are complex or dependent upon cooperation among workers. Unless employees can participate in decisions that affect corporate growth, profits, or other such goals, variable pay may contribute little to enhanced performance (Pfeffer 2003; Lawler 2003). The problem is that financial incentives in themselves do not promote the kind of high individual and group performance and collaboration that business success often requires. An ownership culture does.

Shifting risks to workers effectively requires more than appropriate incentive contracts. According to Garud and Shapira (1997), "dealing with the issue of residual risks in market transactions goes beyond the domain of a formal contract to the domain of *trust*" (p. 248). The building blocks of trust are shared understanding and convergent expectations among company stakeholders, including workers, managers, and investors, where risks, returns, and controls are aligned. What is needed is an ownership culture, where employees are supported to exercise ownership's privileges by promoting informed participation, and they are compensated with shareholding and profit-sharing. Informed participation requires not only the sharing of financial and business-related information, but also the skills required to use it effectively. Sharing in ownership's multiple privileges strengthens agreement through congruent frames of reference, shared interests, and common information.

An ownership culture provides consistent cues regarding the role of workers as co-owners through structures and management practices that utilize worker owner-ship arrangements to best advantage (Pierce and Furo 1990). In the words of Corey Rosen (2005), president of the National Council on Employee Ownership,

> I have come to see ownership . . . as the reward for ownership behaviors, not their cause. Ownership culture is what structures ownership behaviors by providing the rights and the responsibilities for people to act that way; actual ownership provides legitimacy and glue to maintain these programs . . . A "sense of ownership," beloved by organizational consultants, doesn't cut it—it's like giving people a sense of lunch. Enticing, but ulti-mately unsatisfying.

## Implications

The shift in risks demands that first-tier workers become managers of themselves, their money, and their careers—and turn into owners and investors, too. In doing so it offers opportunities for choices that workers seldom enjoyed previously. This is a blessing and a burden. Some choices as a means of self-expression and autonomy are advantageous, but having too many decisions to make can be overwhelming, creating a reluctance to make choices for fear of adverse outcomes (Iyengar and Lepper 2000). For workers who are less successful in navigating the new risks, we need arrange-ments that aid the development of their resilience and protect them against the extreme downsides of risks.

Responsibility for these arrangements is societal, organizational, and personal. While individual bargaining is empowering and a source of rewards to high contrib-utors, the kinds of collective interests people have in the present and future well-being of families may be better handled by common or pooled arrangements. In recent years, national efforts to providing an infrastructure to support more effective worker strategies for coping with risks have bogged down in disputes regarding the proper role of government in American society. Nonetheless, recognition of the need for governmental support is increasingly shared across ideologically distinct communi-ties, from the healthcare industry to unions, and from liberals to conservatives (e.g., Pear 2005). As workers, firms, and society adjust to the migration of risks, new competencies need to be developed across all levels to gain the benefits and manage the losses this shift in risks brings.

## Conclusion

This chapter maps the shift in risk from employers to first-tier workers, its consequences, and the resulting dilemmas for workers, firms, and society. While both
employers and workers face increased uncertainty, no one faces more potential
distress from this uncertainty than workers who are *not* in the first-tier. Although risk
brings potential benefits to mobile, high performing, first-tier workers, it brings
largely losses to the less-advantaged second tier. In revisiting *Work in America*, it is
important to keep in mind the challenges brought on by the new employment contract:
the absence of safety nets, threats to fundamental fairness, and limited organizational
understanding of how to effectively motivate workers to contribute toward firm
success. In their spillover effects, these dilemmas are consequential for all American
workers.

*Postscript*   In June 2005, after serving six months in a military prison and paying a
$5000 fine, Major Cathy Kaus was granted partial clemency, allowing her to stay in
the military. She says she has no regrets (*The Akron Beacon Journal* 2005).

# 10

# Itinerant Professionals: Technical Contractors in a Knowledge Economy

*Stephen R. Barley and Gideon Kunda*

After World War II, bureaucratic employment relations, rooted in the ethos and institutions of the New Deal, dominated cultures of work for nearly three decades.[1] The bureaucratic bargain was simple: As long as firms remained profitable and the economy strong, employers would provide employees with secure jobs in return for effort and loyalty. Since the mid-1980s, three developments have progressively undermined the bargain. First, in the name of efficiency and global competitiveness, firms in the economy's core have repeatedly laid off large numbers of employees independent of economic cycles. Moreover, for the first time in history, layoffs have targeted significant numbers of managers and professionals (Heckscher 1995; Osterman 1996; Cappelli 1999). Second, job tenure for men has become shorter and labor markets have become more volatile (Bureau of Labor Statistics 1998). The third and perhaps most radical break with the culture of bureaucratic employment has been the expansion of the contingent labor force (Barker and Christensen 1998).

The term "contingent labor" has been applied to a number of short-term employment arrangements, including part-time work, temporary employment, self-employment, contracting, outsourcing, and home-based work. Accordingly, estimates of the size of the contingent labor force vary widely. The most conservative come from the Bureau of Labor Statistics (BLS). Under the most liberal of its restricted definitions, the BLS estimates that 13.3 percent of Americans were contingently employed in 1995 (Polivka 1996a, 1996b; Cohany 1996; Cohany et al. 1998).[2] Estimates for 1997 and 1999 were nearly identical (Bureau of Labor Statistics 1997, 2001). More liberal estimates suggest that the number may be as high as 30 percent (Dillon 1987; Belous 1989; Kalleberg et al. 1997).

It is nearly impossible to assess the rate at which contingent work has spread across the economy because the Bureau of Labor Statistics did not begin collecting data on contingent labor until 1995. However, data on the temporary service industry, which is composed of the staffing agencies that place contingent workers, suggest two significant trends (U.S. Department of Commerce 1997). First, between 1986 and 1996 there was spectacular growth in the relative size of the temporary service industry: Employment in temporary services grew 10.3 percent, while total employment in the United States grew by only 1.7 percent. Second, there has been a change in the distribution of contingent jobs. Since 1991 the percentage of the temporary service industry's payroll represented by office, clerical, and medical work declined, while the technical and professional (which includes the managerial) segments became more important (Staffing Industry Report 1997). By 2001, 37 percent of all placements by the staffing industry were in technical and professional occupations, and the percentage is still increasing (Berchem 2005).[3] For example, in the Silicon Valley, contractors often represent between 15 and 30 percent of a firm's workforce. Thus, three conclusions seem reasonable on the basis of available data: (a) a significant proportion of Americans are contingently employed, (b) this proportion has increased over the last decade, and (c) technicians, professionals, and managers represent a larger portion of the contingent workforce than they did in the past.

With few exceptions (Barker and Christensen 1998; Jurik 1998), researchers who have studied contingent work have either focused on temporary clerical and industrial jobs (McAlester 1998; Parker, 1994; Henson 1996; Rogers 1995; Smith 1996, 1998) or have relied on aggregate data heavily weighted toward members of these occupations (Cappelli 1999; Kalleberg et al. 1997; Spalter-Roth et al. 1997). As a result, commentators often portray contingent work as a form of exploitation marked by low wages, insecurity, uncertainty, and substandard working conditions. This assessment surely describes the lives of many temporary clerical and industrial workers, but it would be a mistake to generalize from this sector of the contingent workforce to others, especially to technical contractors. Just as conditions of permanent work vary significantly by occupation, so conditions of contingent employment vary by occupation. As we shall see, technical and professional contracting poses important social and economic issues, but the world of a technical contractor is as different from the world of a temporary clerk as the world of a permanently employed software developer is from that of a permanently employed administrative assistant.

In industry, "contractor" has a number of meanings. We shall use it exclusively in the sense of a person who is hired as an individual for a specified period of time to complete a particular task and who is usually paid an hourly wage for his or her services. Contractors sometimes call themselves freelancers or consultants, but most often they refer to themselves simply by occupation; for example, systems administrator, java developer, technical writer, chip designer, or electrical engineer. Although contractors can be found in most professional and managerial occupations, from physicians to CEOs, our comments pertain exclusively to technical professionals: engineers, programmers, technical writers, and others who work with information technologies. Our discussion draws on two and a half years of ethnographic research on technical contracting with data from three sources: (1) a year of observation in three staffing agencies that specialized in placing engineers, software developers, and IT professionals; (2) career histories with 71 contractors; and (3) interviews in 10 firms with permanent employees who worked with contractors and managers who hired them.[4]

Our purpose in this chapter is to sketch the main parameters of the world of technical contracting and to suggest what this form of employment may mean. We turn first to the basic structure of contract employment and then to the reasons why technical professionals become contractors and the reasons why firms hire them. Next we explore the roles that technical contractors play in the firms where they work and the social dynamics that their presence in the workplace elicits. With this information as background, we then explore contractors' identities and the nature and implications of a form of practice that we call "itinerant professionalism."

## The Structure of Contract Employment

Clients acquire contractors by two paths. They may deal directly with an individual, or they may procure the contractor through a staffing agency that serves as the contractor's "employer-of-record." In either case, the arrangement is executed by purchase order rather than a personnel process, thereby signaling to state and federal labor authorities that the contractor is a resource or commodity, rather than an employee.

Individuals who contract directly with clients are known as independents, while contractors placed through staffing agencies are known as "W2s," after the tax form that contractors sign so that an agency (as the employer-of-record) can withhold employment taxes from the contractor's pay check. If an independent contractor is incorporated, the client pays the contractor's company for the contractor's services. Clients pay unincorporated independent contractors as "1099s," after the form filed with the Internal Revenue Service to document "miscellaneous income." In contrast, for W2s, clients pay the contractor's staffing agency and, in turn, the agency pays the contractor. The bill rate that agencies charge clients includes a margin or markup over the contractor's hourly wage rate. Margins average around 35 to 40 percent, but may run as high as 100 percent or more.

Until the late-1980s, most technical contractors worked as independents, and usually as 1099s. During the 1980s, however, employing technical contractors became popular, as firms discovered that they could avoid paying benefits, payroll taxes, and the costs of training by substituting contractors for employees. In some cases, firms actually dismissed former employees and then rehired them as independent contractors, while continuing to treat them as employees. For instance, a firm might demand as a condition of employment that the contractor work extra hours or work exclusively for the firm. Microsoft became legendary in the late 1980s for firing permanent employees, rehiring them as contractors and then renewing their contracts year after year. Although substituting contractors for employees was common among high-technology firms, by prosecuting Microsoft, the IRS chose to take its stand against firms using "permatemps" to avoid taxes.

In 1987 the IRS announced a new test for determining whether a worker qualified as an independent contractor (Muhl 2002). Two years later, it used the new criteria to prosecute Microsoft for tax evasion. In a highly publicized ruling, the IRS found that Microsoft had illegally misclassified workers as independent contractors. Microsoft accepted the IRS's ruling, paid a stiff penalty, dismissed some of its contractors, and converted others to employees, which involved paying back taxes and benefits.

The IRS's decision to prosecute Microsoft, as well as a subsequent ruling by the Ninth Circuit Court in favor of a group of dismissed contractors who had sued Microsoft for denying them pension contributions and stock options, sent shock waves throughout industry. Firms suddenly became wary of hiring independent contractors. To avoid finding themselves in conflict with the IRS or in violation of employment law, lawyers advised executives to insist that even incorporated contractors work through staffing agencies. This change in how firms approached acquiring contractors benefited the staffing industry, which grew by leaps and bounds. Today, agencies are involved in placing most technical contractors.

## Why Contractors Contract

The technical contractors whom we interviewed told us they had turned to contracting with the hope of making more money. Most succeeded. By our calculations, even after accounting for the cost of benefits, technical contractors made between one and a half and three times the hourly wage of a permanent employee doing the same job. The experience of a numerical control programmer was typical:

> A little less than a year ago, my family and I were living in Seattle, and we were getting a little tight on money—getting behind, getting in debt too—because Boeing did not pay enough for me to support my family without my wife working. She doesn't work and I don't believe she should have to. We have four children. I actually worked two or three jobs at one time for about a year. I was even delivering newspapers and doing other odd jobs. At Boeing I was making about $40,000 to $44,000 a year plus overtime, which maybe averaged out to be another $5,000 a year. Here, in eight months I've made about $115,000.

Other technical professionals turned to contracting in search of greater autonomy over their work, opportunities to learn new skills, or more control over their time. A few simply liked the excitement of stringing together a series of new challenges and the variety of jobs and places that contracting inevitably brought. But to focus entirely on contracting's incentives would be to miss the underlying motive that united the vast majority of our informants. Contractors were not only pulled into contracting by the lure of money and freedom, but they were also pushed by their growing dissatisfaction with the way organizations were managed.

Woven throughout contractors' tales of why they became contractors were three motifs: politics, incompetence, and inequity. Of the three, politics was the most common. Politics, as contractors used the word, is best understood as a cover term for the many ways that managerial agendas and personal interests undermine technical rationality as a criterion for action. The perception that managers act primarily to further their own interests was so widespread that contractors frequently portrayed technical professionals and projects as pawns in management's political games. An electrical engineer who once worked for Motorola as a permanent employee put it this way:

> I worked a lot of long hours. It was for politics. It wasn't for getting the project done. It was like I was doing this for somebody else's ego, or somebody else's personal or career goals. They could check off, they got this or that done based on my work. I was getting the project done not for the goals of the project but for the goals of the people above.

Contractors also leveled charges of political gamesmanship against their former peers. They viewed organizational life as rife with conflicting agendas that they saw as a waste of time and a source of tension. They portrayed meetings, in particular, as opportunities for political grandstanding.

When complaining about politics, contractors were indicting organizational life in general. Stories of incompetence, on the other hand, were reserved for specific individuals. Contractors' charges of incompetence typically targeted middle managers, especially project managers. Often underlying such charges was the contractors' belief that they were *more* capable than the managers for whom they had worked. A database administrator who had returned briefly to permanent employment before becoming a confirmed contractor was particularly articulate on this point:

> I think I am a little bit smarter than a lot of people out there. If there were really good project managers, there wouldn't be any contractors. The reason contractors are hired is because they [*organizations*] are in deep shit. And the reason they are in so deep is because they have been poorly managed or poorly planned. Like when I was working at Astrotech. The project manager was bordering on schizophrenic. Things changed every day: the project plan, the features of the software product. When that happens, people cannot get work done. And then the team would be berated for not getting enough work done. They hire people as project managers who have not done the work that the people they are managing are doing. They have no clue as to what is required to get things done. They don't know what is reasonable and what is not.

The inequities of permanent employment, the third motif in contractors' stories, revolved around their perceptions that employers exploit technical experts by demanding long hours without commensurate pay. "There's no compensation for engineers," one contractor said, comparing contracting to his experience of permanent employment. "I had to take a lower salary, I didn't get to take any vacation, and I worked a lot longer hours. When I worked the last time as a permanent employee, I was required to work 12-hour shifts with no extra pay for months and months and months."

Ultimately, then, the decision to become a contractor reflected an ideology of work relations as well as a calculus of incentives. Contractors viewed themselves as professionals. Like many engineers and scientists, they believed that decisions about work should be governed primarily by an ethic of technical rationality based on logic, reason, and practicality. But they rapidly discovered that organizational life deviated from the way they believed the world should operate. Moreover, contractors thought that as permanent employees they had not received the respect that technical professionals deserved. Contractors saw contracting as a way to escape the burdens of organizational life while securing the pay and respect befitting a professional.

### Why Firms Hire Contractors

Firms hire contractors for a number of reasons. The business press and managerial research have stressed lower labor costs and the ability to respond quickly to changing markets (Handy 1989; Mangum, Mayall, and Nelson 1985; Abraham 1988; Abraham and Taylor 1996; Pfeffer and Baron 1988; Harrison and Kelley 1993; Davis-Blake and Uzzi 1993; Matusik and Hill 1998). By using contractors, firms avoid paying benefits, payroll taxes, and hiring and training costs, all of which are borne either by the contractor or an agency. Although firms usually pay more per hour for contractors than they do for permanent employees, they still save money, because firms usually have much shorter commitments to contractors than they do to employees. Firms also turn to contractors to achieve numerical flexibility, meaning the ability to expand and contract their workforce in response to economic cycles, and functional flexibility, meaning the capacity to shift their mix of skills in response to changes in technology and strategy.

Our conversations with managers and permanent employees in client firms suggested that the managerial literature offers only a partial explanation for firms' use of contractors. To be sure, managers and permanent employees told us that they used contractors for the reasons already discussed, but they often put a spin on these reasons that sounded different from the spin one finds in the business press or in academic journals. Among the firms that we studied, acquiring skills was the most important reason for hiring contractors. Every manager mentioned this motive first, as did half of the permanent employees.

There were two important variants of this motive, which, in turn, implied different roles for contractors. The first portrayed contractors as purveyors of "just-in-time" expertise—skills and knowledge that were needed immediately, but only for a limited time. The second variant was that firms turned to contractors to acquire skills that permanent employees lacked. In this case contractors were hired as experts with the hope that they would promote "knowledge transfer." While the first perspective was articulated at all levels of the organization, only managers voiced the second.

A second important but rarely discussed reason for hiring contractors is to "manage headcount" and "hide personnel costs." Many firms set hard limits on the number of permanent employees that they would carry during a fiscal year. When commissioning projects, upper management typically set two constraints within which they expected hiring managers to work. The first was the number of full-time employees who would be allocated to a project or area, commonly known as headcount. Most firms set the headcount ceiling lower than the full compliment of people needed to do the work. The second was budget, the total number of dollars allotted to the project. Because upper management knew headcount would be inadequate for completing the project, they expected project managers to assemble additional human resources by spending a portion of their budget on contractors. In fact, the practice was so common that in the negotiations that we observed, hiring managers and staffing agents used the term "budget" to refer specifically to funds available to hire contractors. Moreover, in managerial circles it was well known that contractors do not figure in productivity calculations. Thus, using contractors was a way to inflate assessments of a firm's productivity, which improved analysts' valuations of the firm and, hence, its stock price.

Start-ups also had financial incentives to use contractors rather than employees: Using contractors slowed the rate at which a start-up burned venture capital, because contractors could be jettisoned once a project was complete. Finally, some firms routinely hired contractors as a way of screening potential employees. U.S. employment law grants employers an initial 90-day period during which they can evaluate and dismiss a new hire without building a case for termination. Because firms could repeatedly renew a contractor's contract and could also sever it on short notice, by using a "temp-to-perm" hiring strategy a firm could de facto create a probationary period of 18 months or more.

## The Roles Contractors Play

The client's needs and the contractor's expertise jointly shape the relationships that contractors have with managers and employees while on contract. An Oracle database programmer summarized the range of possibilities: "There are two kinds of environments that I have worked in. In one, contractors are running the show. In the other, contractors are brought in more or less as technical janitors to clean up or do the extra work." Most contractors, and the managers who hired them, concurred. Three broad roles, each associated with its own vernacular, characterized our informants' descriptions of how contractors fit into client firms.

### Gurus

"Gurus" were contractors widely known in technical communities as master practitioners, the ones to whom clients turned for their technical virtuosity. Gurus typically established one of two relationships with firms. As developer-consultants, they were hired to design, develop, implement, modify, or maintain an entire component of a firm's information system or were responsible for other significant, but bounded, tasks. For example, they might configure a network, develop an application or database for managing business transactions, conceptualize a firm's Web presence, or develop protocols for testing software. Developer-consultants were typically independent contractors who worked with small firms and served as experts on a range of tasks. They enjoyed considerable autonomy and opportunities to develop an array of skills. Many had ongoing relationships with their clients, which meant repeat business and possibilities for retainers. A typical developer-consultant described his experience:

> I have built inventory systems, customer-tracking systems. I've done the database for Top-5. Now, I'm getting into Web sites and Web site design and databases for Web sites. With some exceptions, I don't think any two customers have been the same thing. Rather than focus on a particular industry, I just say, "Hey, whatever needs to be done, give me a phone call and we'll see if we can work something out." And so, the jobs have been kind of scatterbrained, but on the other hand, I've had a lot of fun. You know, I've built multimedia CD-ROMs, and all the issues that go along with that. Mac and PC. Take the same CD-ROM and put it on a Mac or on a PC and it'll run. That was a neat trick.

Like developer-consultants, contractors known as experienced experts tended to be older, had contracted for significant periods of time, had reputations for expertise, and were granted considerable autonomy. But unlike developer-consultants, experienced experts typically worked for larger firms and played less of an advisory role. They had deep knowledge of an area of technology and were gifted at their craft, whether it was writing C++ or designing interfaces. Some worked with legacy systems and, hence, possessed scarce skills (such as the ability to write COBOL) that were critical to a class of clients who were willing to pay handsomely for the use of this knowledge. Others were considered gurus because they understood technologies in ways that young engineers were no longer trained to understand. Experienced experts typically called themselves "troubleshooters," "problem-solvers," or "analysts." By these terms they conveyed their preference for working on problems that permanent employees were having difficulty resolving. An experienced technical writer illustrated the relationship that experienced experts had with their clients:

> Here is what I do. It depends on the level. It depends on if someone wants a high level description of how something works. For example, Toshiba MRI needed me to do just

that. They did not want me to go into the bits and bytes of the computer. They just wanted to know how the system worked and what that system did. That is called high level. High level does not mean, "better than low level," it just means that it is more of a bird's eye view. They say, "Well, we have a problem." One of my assignments right now is to find out what the problem is. I will be specific. They have a simulator that simulates one of these expensive machines. The software people use the simulator to test their software. By doing it on a simulator instead of a real machine, the company saves the cost of owning and maintaining an expensive machine. It seems as if no one is keeping the simulators. One is broken, another got burned up in a truck fire, another seems to be over in another building, and the two that the software engineers are using are out of order half the time. There are no technicians assigned specifically to those machines. So the boss usually begs the other department to lend him technicians for a short while. Get the idea? Now he says, "Is there anything you can do about this? Can you pull together some documentation on how this machine works and how we can fix it?"

Hiring managers routinely distinguished between gurus and other contractors. They gave developer-consultants and experienced experts more autonomy, and they usually relied on them to educate permanent employees.

### Hired Guns

What clients expected from most contractors, however, was an extra hand, a role known among contractors as the "hired gun." Thus, most contracts entailed assuming a role very much like that of a permanent employee. From the perspective of the work itself, there were no significant differences between what contractors and full-timers did. Clients turned to hired guns because a project team needed additional bodies, but upper management would not authorize the project manager to increase the project's headcount. Managers might turn to hired guns because the project was behind schedule or because the project had reached a stage where special skills were needed in, for example, quality assurance or technical writing. Because these situations were commonplace, contractors rarely discussed such experiences in depth. Instead, they would simply remark, "I was treated like an employee." Contractors did note, however, that in such jobs there was an initial period of adjustment and that it took time before they were fully integrated into the work process.

### Warm Bodies

As previously noted, clients sometimes hired contractors to do mundane work that full-timers did not want to do. What that work entailed varied from occupation to occupation and firm to firm, but it usually contributed to the maintenance of a technical infrastructure. On such contracts the contractor became a kind of support technician, called a "warm body." Contractors generally had two responses to playing the role of a warm body. The first was to complain that the work was not challenging, that it offered no opportunities to learn new skills and, hence, that it provided no leverage on the future. The second was to offer caveats. Although working on mundane tasks lacked challenge, the work was easy and the level of compensation was usually so high that it did not matter.

This attitude was especially common among contractors who had an instrumental orientation to work, like a 61-year-old database programmer who specialized in data conversions: "I'm pretty much following a plan that has already been set up. I'm just dealing with quirks of the data, idiosyncrasies—you know, data problems, that sort of thing. It's not a very creative job. It can get to be very tedious. The only reason for doing it is it's reasonably straightforward, it's easy to do and it pays well."

It would be a mistake, however, to conclude that warm bodies were contractors who did low-skilled work. In technical fields, routine work was not thought of as unskilled, it was simply considered uninteresting. An IT manager at a chip company explained,

> These contractors have Oracle tool experience, with the Oracle SQL language. We assign them to projects. Like when we went through an upgrade, all the reports needed dates changed or they needed certain changes made over and over and over again through all the reports. And we had to test the reports to make sure they worked right. We used them for that, to make those kinds of changes. It's routine and it's specific too. But nobody here really knows Oracle tools very well. It's complicated. It's hard to learn. And it doesn't always work the way you think it's going to. [So] the routine change wasn't all that easy. But it had to be done. It had to be done over and over and over again. It may be complicated, but it is repetitive. That's the type of thing that contractors can be very effective on.

Although the roles that contractors played varied from contract to contract, most seemed to accept contracts that entailed similar relationships with clients. Those who worked regularly as warm bodies were a minority among the contractors we interviewed. Although most contractors had certainly done mundane work from time to time, only 17 percent (12 of 71) routinely took contracts that involved doing tasks that permanent employees thought undesirable. With a few notable exceptions, these contractors were younger, had fewer years of experience, and specialized in information technology, quality assurance, or technical writing. Nearly 40 percent of our informants described careers in which they now functioned as developer-consultants or technical experts. These were typically older and more experienced contractors. The remainder (43 percent) typically worked as hired guns.

## Organizational Dynamics Created by Hiring Contractors

### *Dependence*

Regardless of role, all technical contractors took responsibility for tasks on the successful completion of which the work of others hinged. Technical work often consists of sub-projects, such as writing a module of code, that are done individually and that have their own logic and history of development. Consequently, it is difficult for one technical worker to take over a partially completed task from another. No matter how routine it may be, technical work also involves a significant amount of contextual knowledge. Writing a subroutine, altering the structure of a database, and even testing a software application requires familiarity with the larger system to which the work contributes. Developing this kind of contextual knowledge takes time. Thus, the departure of a contractor before a project ends usually means, at minimum, an unanticipated delay and extra work for employees. In many cases, losing a contractor also means losing knowledge for which there was no ready exact substitute. For this reason clients tended to become reliant even on contractors whom they hired as warm bodies, at least for the duration of a project.

A lead engineer at a computer manufacturer whose team included several hired guns who were consolidating data from legacy databases, remarked, "If our contractors left, it would be devastating. They have so much knowledge! I try to put some of the tasks onto permanent employees. But they have lots to do already. So, if they leave, they leave big holes." When firms hired a developer-consultant or an experienced expert, the odds of dependency increased. Clients could not easily dismiss or replace highly skilled contractors who provided knowledge that permanent employees lacked. Losing a contractor with crucial expertise could bring work to a standstill.

An IT manager at a large telecommunications company spoke of losing highly skilled experts. He confided,

> Frankly in many ways contractors are sometimes better than permanent employees, just because you have the right skill set. They're better trained. They are focused on the job because they do not have to worry about anything else. But there's a downside. We're getting in the mode of having them come in and build new things and when the contract is up and they walk out the door, the people who have to maintain it have no idea what the code looks like.

To guard against becoming too dependent, one might think that firms would limit contractors' engagements. But most firms that we encountered responded to the question of dependency with the opposite strategy: Rather than dismiss valuable contractors, they extended contracts. The contractors whom we interviewed told us that it was commonplace to have contracts renewed several times. Although contracts were initially written for periods of three months, in practice, most contract jobs ended up lasting anywhere from 6 to 18 months. If the contractor was an incorporated independent, contracts could last for years. Many highly skilled contractors had been in situations where they continued to work while employees were being laid off in significant numbers.

Extremely long periods of service were particularly common among independent developer-consultants and experienced experts. Some became fixtures in the firms where they worked, as had the programmer who told us the following.

> At Seamax the original contract was for 10 days. They were a very small company—had 30 employees. They told me they only had enough money to pay me for 10 days. Presidents of that company have come and gone. Department heads have come and gone. The ownership of the company has come and gone. Even the company's name has changed. I'm like the guy at the post office. No matter who gets elected to Congress, I still deliver your mail. In fact, the guy that hired me was VP of their internal operations. He brought me in and told me, "We don't have a lot of money. If you can't do it in 10 days, tell me now." A year later he left the company. I was still there. A year after he left, he stopped by, he walked in the door, and when he saw me he said, "What the hell are you doing here?" "Same thing." He's been back twice in the last two years, and I've been there both times. They now have 800 employees. There're only 24 that have been there longer than I have.

The interplay between expertise and dependency engendered ambivalence. On one hand, managers and employees spoke of contractors with respect. Yet, at the same time, they resented the contractors' presence. Respect was most clearly expressed by managers and resentment was especially common among employees.

## Respect

Although contractors were officially hired to perform specific and sometimes narrow jobs, they frequently found their roles expanding, especially in their interactions with hiring managers. Because contractors eschewed organizational politics and because all parties expected them to be highly mobile, contractors claimed that they were able to establish what they called "more honest" relationships with their clients. As a contractor who managed IT projects for government agencies explained, "One thing I can do as a contract employee that I couldn't do as a full-timer is be honest, straight-forward, and upfront. I can say, 'Here are the facts.' I don't have to worry about politics. On the way in, I say, 'I am going to tell you exactly the way I feel about everything. You can take it or leave it. That's why you hired me, to give you my opinion.' "

Many hiring managers concurred that contractors were valuable because they spoke their minds. Like contractors, managers attributed this frankness to the fact that contractors stood outside the world of corporate politics and organizational careers. Some managers even suggested that contractors' status as outsiders made them easier to work with than full-timers. A manager in the IT department of a high-tech firm remarked, "Some of the problems we usually have between people disappear when you hire contractors. Contractors know they're only here for a limited time, and the full-time people know that too. So there's not that much competition or friction between them. Contractors tend to be more professional and they don't take personal sides. Full-time people are always interested in promotions and reviews, and so there is competition, friction, which doesn't happen with contractors."

Managers sometimes reciprocated this frankness and openness. Developer-consultants and experienced experts often said that managers not only sought their opinions, but they also treated them as confidants. For instance, contractors reported that managers used them as sounding boards for troubling organizational issues that they could not share with employees. A software developer, well known in the UNIX community, reported,

> I actually have had managers tell me things about politics that they didn't want the employees to know. Like, "This product is dead. There is no future in this thing you're working on. Don't tell any of the employees. Don't destroy morale here. We don't want to bum them out. But this is the way it's going to be." They know we're not likely to leave just because the product is dead. We're not thinking of a career, because we don't have a career path. They tell you to get your opinion, to inform you, to keep you abreast of the fact that you may need to look for another job.

One of the strongest signals of appreciation and respect was receiving an offer to join a firm as a full-time employee. Most informants who had worked as contractors for any significant period of time had fielded such offers. Although contractors found the offers flattering, few accepted. Of the 71 contractors we interviewed, 21 percent (15) had at one time or another accepted an offer to "go perm" after trying their hand at contracting. Those who had "gone perm" usually did so because they liked the firm and its people, because they hoped to get stock options, or because a spouse was uncomfortable with contracting's risks. It is telling that all but one of these individuals returned to contracting because they rediscovered why they disliked working for firms or because they missed contracting's freedom and higher wages.

Another sign of respect was being asked to be the technical lead of a project. A little over a fifth (22 percent) of the contractors we interviewed had been asked at least once to assume the duties of a lead during the course of a contract. In engineering environments, being a lead means coordinating and integrating the technical efforts of a group of engineers, as well as making decisions about the technical direction of the team's work. Thus, when contractors became leads, they acquired authority over permanent employees as well as other contractors.

### Resentment

If respect was the yin of the contractor's experience on the job, resentment was its yang. Resentment was manifested in two kinds of complaints about contractors. The first, shared by managers and employees, focused on contractors' "lack of commitment" and the performance problems that resulted from it. The second complaint ran deeper and was usually expressed by employees rather than managers: the perceived inequities between contractors and employees.

#### Lack of Commitment

Even in an era of downsizing, firms are a primary source of identity and an object of emotional attachment for many white-collar workers. In such a world, there are few criticisms more biting than having your colleagues say that you are undependable, disloyal, or lack commitment. Most managers and employees we interviewed still felt it was proper to be committed and loyal to their firms, though their belief system had been strained by the realities of the new economic order. Contractors represented a visible, daily challenge to the continued belief in an employment regime based on reciprocal trust and commitment. It is, therefore, perhaps unsurprising that full-timers articulated an imagery of contracting that portrayed contractors, however experienced they might be, as self-interested mercenaries who, in a pinch, could not be trusted. A project manager in a computer firm expressed the opinion held by many employees:

> I don't think of contractors as being very emotionally invested in what they are doing. That's completely unappealing to me. I feel a part of this company. I don't like to say that it defines me, but it is part of who I am. I would like for this company to do well. I'm disappointed when it doesn't. More than one contractor has said that to me: "Look, I just want to make it clear. I will do whatever you tell me. I don't need to be happy. I don't really care." Sometimes we've had philosophical conversations about the direction of the company, and the conversation with them will generally end with, "Yeah, I don't really care. I don't care how the company is doing. I'm just hired to do this piece of work and that's all I really want to worry about, and then I'm going home."

Managers and permanent employees supported their claim that contractors, as a group, were undependable and uncommitted by pointing to a constellation of sins that they felt were common among contractors. One widespread complaint was that contractors did "shoddy work." The essence of the complaint was not that contractors' lacked skills. Instead, the issue was how contractors' attitudes shaped the way they applied their skills. Permanent employees seemed to believe that superior technical work demanded an attitude of persistence and long-term responsibility that the structure of contracting did not permit. Permanent employees argued that because contractors had short time horizons and cared only for their own welfare, they cut corners, put in minimum effort, and sometimes even sacrificed quality. By the time any mistakes were discovered, the offending contractors were long gone, and employees were left to rectify the situation.

Closely related to the claim that contractors' lack commitment was the widespread complaint that contractors often left without even finishing the job they were assigned. In such cases, either another contractor had to be hired or a permanent employee had to complete the task. Permanent employees and managers almost always illustrated this complaint with some variant of the story of a contractor who mysteriously disappeared one day without prior notice. A manager at a small start-up recounted the story as follows: "One guy was in the middle of a project. We thought everything was going fine. One day his coat is over the back of his chair, his coffee is there warm and his monitor is on, but he was gone. He just left everything. He just walked out." The moral of such stories seemed to be that contractors are so self-interested that one cannot count on them to fulfill the terms of even the short-term bargains they strike.

A third observation by which managers and employees bolstered the claim that contractors lacked commitment was that they were less willing than full-timers to shoulder extra responsibilities. Permanent employees accepted open-ended job descriptions because they were invested in the firm's well-being, because they were evaluated on their willingness to do anything asked of them, and because failing to do so brought peer pressure. Firms relied on the employee's spirit of voluntarism to cover unforeseen circumstances. Contractors, in contrast, felt bound only to perform the tasks for which they were hired. Furthermore, employees complained, contractors did not seem to share their anxiety about deadlines. One full-time software developer said,

> In the New Jersey start-up there were a lot of contractors. I worked with one, a voice specialist. He was very sharp, very bright. But he would just do as little as was necessary and not work as much as we were working. In fact there was another contractor. He was like cranking out computer screens. He had a specific rate in mind, one screen every two days. And since only he knew how to do that stuff, he could pretty much do it at his own pace. He was taking his time about it, and the director asked him during a meeting, "Can you do it any faster? We have this deadline coming up, we're behind." And he did not and just kept on. They have no commitment to the company, especially in a start-up.

*Inequity*
Complaints about inequity focused on two issues that troubled employees: the contractors' higher pay and the fact that contractors were often given more interesting work. In the world of permanent employment, higher wages have long signaled seniority, greater skill, or greater authority. The association of money and merit lies at the heart of the incentive system that employers have used for decades to motivate employees. In fact, the system has become part of our culture—an unwritten psychological contract that we expect employers to honor, an expectation that is particularly strong among white-collar, professional employees. Workers rarely openly resent

another person's salary, as long as it seems commensurate with their service, status, or contributions. The problem was that contractors generally had less seniority than all but the most recently hired employees. Many had no more expertise than the full-timers with whom they worked, and most had no formal authority. By all rights, employees reasoned, contractors should be paid the same as, and perhaps even less than, employees with similar skills.

Hiring managers also spoke of the troubles that wage inequities created. In fact, jealousy over wages was the most frequent problem that managers cited when asked about the challenges of managing project teams composed of contractors and employees. A number of managers we interviewed admitted that some employees had left their firm over the issue. When confronted by an employee disgruntled over discrepancies in pay, the manager's only recourse was to point out that contractors paid their own benefits, had less job security, and did not enjoy the perquisites of membership. If the employee remained unconvinced, the managers could say little else except to suggest that the employee try contracting for himself or herself. That more employees do not try contracting most likely reflects their perception that contracting is economically risky and that full-time employment offers greater security

Technical employees also disliked the fact that contractors were often hired to do technically more challenging and exciting tasks. Employees felt that the technical challenges should be theirs, and that contractors, if used at all, should be assigned more routine jobs. They believed that assigning "sexy" work to contractors indicated that their managers did not believe they were sufficiently skilled, which, in many cases, was what the managers did think.

Contractors reported that employees made their feelings known in subtle ways, typically by either ignoring the contractor or by making jokes that revealed underlying tensions. Occasionally, however, resentment led employees to behave in ways that intentionally complicated the contractor's job. In some cases, resentment, and the resistance it spawned, actually erupted in open hostility, as a contractor who specialized in quality assurance testified:

> When I worked at HP last year, [I was part of] an integration group, so it all came down through us. There was a guy that I worked with; he was nice to me the first month. I was working through Volt (a staffing firm) at the time. I told them to take me off of per diem because I had moved there after a month. So they said, "Okay, we'll send you a new contract." What do they do? They faxed it to HP! All this stuff is supposed to be real confidential, the rates you're making. So who picks up the thing off the fax machine but the guy that's sitting across from me! So from that point on, he literally won't talk to me. I had to go to the boss and ask him, "Can you please get this guy to talk to me?" So it turns out [the guy gives me] a 15-minute slot in the morning and a 15-minute slot in the afternoon. I was talking with him every day up to this point. The animosity starts when they see the differential in pay.

In short, contractors experienced life on the job as a never ending series of mixed messages. On one hand, clients needed their expertise and respected, sometimes even celebrated, their contributions. On the other hand, their presence, regardless of their performance, inevitably engendered suspicion and resentment. These conflicting messages created a kind of Catch-22. If contractors took responsibility and initiative, then full-timers who worried about job security perceived them as a threat and an object of envy. If they worked by the book, they were condemned for lack of commitment and shoddy work. It was partially around resolving such dilemmas that contractors forged a professional identity compatible with the way they needed to work to get the job done.

## Resolving the Dilemmas of Contracting

Contractors understood that adapting to the double bind required resolving three issues. First, they had to decide how they would approach work in environments where they would never be seen as members. Some chose to take the initiative and go beyond the letter of the contract. They adopted the distanced, impartial stance of an expert, ignored the organization's politics, and championed, without compromise, a technical perspective on their work. These contractors understood that such a stance might ultimately threaten employees. They also understood that taking a strong technical stance could sometimes threaten managers, thereby risking dismissal. This strategy's payoff was that they were more likely to be perceived as competent practitioners and sometimes even gurus.

Other contractors chose to work by the book. They stuck to the terms of their contracts and focused on the specifics of the task. Regardless of the quality of their performance, these contractors risked being viewed as mercenaries. Employees often ignored their presence, viewed them as servants, and sometimes used them as scapegoats. Still others took a middle position depending on the exigencies of the situation, the specifics of the task, and their own preferences and skills.

Whichever stance contractors took, their outsider status forced them to resolve a second issue: how to present themselves to managers and employees. Some contractors did not care what others thought and staked their reputations entirely on their technical accomplishments. They accepted that they would simply move on when their work was done, possessing both a fatter wallet and more experience, which they hoped to use in landing their next contract. Thus, they kept their distance and focused on their work. Many others, however, recognized that it was to their benefit to build relationships that would allow them to navigate between respect and resentment.

Contractors did this by sending messages that assured managers and employees that they were persons who would work diligently in the client's best interest. For example, several informants told us that the first weeks of a contract were crucial for framing the client's perceptions. These contractors made a point of initially working longer hours than the contract required and making those hours visible for all to see. They also agreed to participate in meetings that they could have easily avoided and did not charge the client for the time. Once expectations were set, these contractors returned to more normal hours. Contractors also knew that they could curry favor with employees by willingly sharing what they knew, by helping employees anticipate and resolve problems, and by socializing with employees after hours. Ironically, contractors who had chosen contracting, in part, to remove themselves from corporate gamesmanship found themselves back in the impression management business.

The third and perhaps most fundamental issue that contractors had to resolve was developing a coherent identity that could account for their experience and guide their actions. The terms that contractors used as they struggled to describe their roles provided clues to the identities they constructed for themselves. These ranged from "guest" and "resident alien" to "troubleshooter," "problem solver," and "consultant." Although these terms differed in their various connotations, all pointed to an identity that was widely shared among our informants, an identity that turned outsider status and social distance into a professional tool. The imagery of the coolly detached expert created a buffer that allowed contractors to disassociate their sense of self-worth from the cues they received from clients.

In fact, by coming to view themselves as detached specialists, contractors were often able to empathize with and even feel superior to employees. They could see that their presence in the workplace violated the promise of traditional employment on which employees based their sense of security and self-worth and reasoned that one could hardly blame employees for being resentful.

Unlike full-timers doing similar work, contractors learned to disassociate their definition of self from the immediate context of their technical practice. Instead, they came to orient themselves to the larger world of contracting and to reference groups that lay beyond the boundaries of the firms for which they worked. They became, in their own eyes, itinerant professionals whose expertise consisted not only of their technical skills but also of their ability to construct honorable and meaningful careers by moving between clients.

## Itinerant Professionals

Historically, professions have been organized in three ways: what occupational sociologists call free professions, professional firms, and corporate professions (Scott 1965, 1981; Whalley 1986; Whalley and Barley 1997). Each form of organizing provides solutions to three practical problems: how to secure clients, how to maintain expertise, and how to ensure economic security. Historically, the occupations that our informants practiced were organized as corporate professions: Practitioners worked as salaried employees of firms staffed by a variety of occupations and ultimately answered to managers who were not members of their profession.

Becoming a contractor meant setting aside traditional models of professionalism and, hence, readymade solutions for resolving the practical problems of a professional. As a result, contractors had to invent their own solutions or adopt solutions widely practiced by other contractors. As they did so, they collectively and perhaps unwittingly began to forge a new form of professional practice.

Like free professionals, technical contractors worked as solo practitioners and, in most cases, arranged for their own benefits. They drew on their professional networks for referrals and took responsibility for their own professional development. Like members of professional firms, contractors frequently worked for one organization, a staffing agency, but offered their services to another. Like corporate professionals, they practiced inside organizations, often as members of a team that is subject to management's direction. But unlike free professionals and members of professional firms, technical contractors rarely had ongoing relationships with clients and were not paid on a fee-for-service basis, nor were they salaried like corporate professionals or members of professional service firms.

Itinerant professionalism led contractors to different solutions to the problems of finding clients, maintaining expertise, and ensuring long-term security. Unlike other professionals, they found clients by augmenting their networks with the services of staffing agencies. In fact, some relied exclusively on agencies. These contractors were well aware that using an agency conflicted with traditional images of professionalism. They resented submitting themselves to members of a sales culture and allowing nonprofessionals to make a substantial profit on their services. But since using a staffing agency was often a necessity, contractors resolved their dissonance by incorporating agencies into their model of professional practice: Being savvy in one's dealings with agents was a form of expertise.

Contractors generally developed and maintained their technical expertise much like any other professionals: They took classes, joined professional associations, consulted other professionals, and educated themselves. But compared to professionals who practiced in other contexts, the contractors found that their skills were subject to more frequent evaluation in the marketplace, and that they enjoyed fewer protections against obsolescence. Contractors' efforts to stay up-to-date were consequently sustained, intense, and ongoing. Moreover, unlike most other professionals who distinguish between apprentices and full-fledged practitioners, contractors blurred the distinction between newcomers and veterans.[5] Regardless of experience, they thought of—and presented—themselves as continual learners. They saw jobs as opportunities for learning and sought to arrange contracts into sequences that enabled them to acquire and practice new skills. Thus, under itinerant professionalism, work itself became a credentialing process.

Itinerant professionalism also hinged on a radically different solution to the problem of security. Security always entails guaranteeing one's continued employability, which, in turn, can rest on a variety of foundations. Although all professionals must rely on the enduring value of their expertise, traditional models of professionalism bolster security in other ways. The free professional's security rests partly on his or her reputation in a community and partly on the fact that clients have recurring needs in which they have little or no expertise. For security, corporate professionals and members of professional firms rely on their continued affiliation with, and the goodwill of, their employers. Contractors had recourse to neither safety net because of their transitory relationships with clients and agencies. Their security as itinerant professionals rested entirely on their ability to network and to maintain skills that others would buy.

In short, our informants' mode of practice had the trappings of a distinct form of professionalism, and contractors themselves seemed to experience their practice as unique and coherent. Setting aside technical specialty, contractors believed that they had more in common with each other than they did with professionals who did similar work under other models of professionalism. Informants repeatedly told us that their permanently employed counterparts had little understanding of their brand of practice or of the problems and opportunities they faced. More importantly, even though clients occasionally tried to tempt contractors back into corporate professionalism, most were unwilling to return. Thus, despite itinerant professionalism's problems and challenges, our informants overwhelmingly preferred it to corporate professionalism.

Nevertheless, itinerant professionalism had a significant Achilles' heel, especially for members of technical occupations. Historically, technical occupations have lacked strong institutional supports to underwrite their professionalism. By institutional supports we mean organized systems and communities that foster occupational identities and that assist in creating, storing, and disseminating substantive knowledge. Most professions have occupational associations, training programs, conferences, journals, and accreditation procedures that support all members of the occupation regardless of their mode of practice. But, when compared to medicine, law, and accounting, the institutions of technical occupations have long been weak (Perrucci and Gertzl 1969; Whalley 1986; Barley 2005).

For this reason, technical occupations have long relied on corporate employers for institutional support. Firms have been particularly important in funding technical schools and have played active roles in technical societies. They have also served as important repositories of expertise, largely because technical knowledge is often proprietary and application-specific. Beyond the initial degree required for practice, most advanced technical training occurs on the job within firms. Gouldner (1957–1958) would have called engineers and technicians "local" professionals. Unlike "cosmopolitan" professionals, who are involved in national and international networks of practice, local professionals orient primarily to their employers, and their occupational networks are composed primarily of fellow employees (Goldner and Ritti 1967; Kronus 1976; Goldberg 1976).

Consequently, even though technical professionals may gain independence when they become contractors, they lose access to corporate professionalism's supports. This loss is crucial. Practitioners require contact with other members of their occupational community to function as technical professionals, because technical knowledge typically emerges unevenly across a community of practitioners as different members encounter problems and devise solutions (Van Maanen and Barley 1984; Orr 1997). Without involvement in an occupational community, practitioners lack access to these developments. Nontechnical issues of practice, such as finding work, also usually require collective solutions. To fill the institutional vacuum, our contractors had begun to build occupational communities conducive to itinerant professionalism, often with the help of sophisticated communication technologies.

Community building was usually spontaneous and informal, driven largely by contractors' efforts to solve immediate problems. We observed contractors forming and participating in networks that offered both technical and nontechnical support. Some of these communities involved face-to-face interaction, but many others were virtual: They existed primarily on the Internet and were organized around bulletin boards, chat rooms, and Usenet groups. These forms of communication were important channels for exchanging market information and technical tips.

We also observed formal efforts to organize contractors along occupational lines. Some of our informants had taken responsibility for founding and managing user groups. Others had founded partnerships and occupational collectives that enabled group practice. Entrepreneurs had begun to cater to the contractors' need for occupational community by publishing journals and magazines, such as *Contract Professional*, which addressed issues that contractors repeatedly faced. Other entrepreneurs had founded Web-based employment services, such as DICE (http://www.dice.com) and *Contract Employment Weekly* (http://www.ceweekly.com), and affinity groups, such as Working Today and the Professional Association of Contract Employees, which provided contractors with group insurance plans and discounts on the tools of the trade.[6]

These proto-institutions were embryonic. By comparison to the more entrenched institutions of more traditional modes of professionalism, they were incipient, loose, and decentralized. They lacked a well-developed professional ideology, an accepted theory of practice, and a formal mandate to legitimize their status as institutions. Nevertheless, these arrangements, however weak, represent important steps toward institutionalizing itinerant professionalism as a stable and coherent mode of practice. Thus, the emergence of itinerant professionalism as an identifiable trend provides a vantage point not only for conceptualizing the structure of postindustrial labor markets, but also for formulating policies that would shape these developments in useful directions.

Because our research focused exclusively on technical contractors, parts of our analysis may reflect idiosyncrasies of the worlds of high technology and information systems. Nevertheless, it would be a mistake to conclude that contracting is somehow confined to high-tech firms and occupations. First, most of our informants had contracted in an incredible array of firms and industries outside high-tech, such as banks, government agencies, retailers, hospitals, manufacturers of durable goods, defense firms, railroads, and schools.

Moreover, contracting is spreading to other professional occupations. Contracting is particularly common in healthcare. Not only is it common today for hospitals to use contract nurses, medical technicians, and radiological technologists, but staffing agencies are also beginning to offer contract physicians. Contracting is prevalent in accounting, and it has recently made a beachhead in law. Firms can even contract for temporary CEOs, CFOs, and other top management positions through specialized staffing agencies.

Thus, contracting or contingent work is a form of employment that is spreading across the entire occupational spectrum. It is every bit as important as offshoring, and, at least for the moment, it is far more common, though offshoring has recently garnered much attention. Over the next several decades it may well come to pass that permanent and contract employment will be viewed by firms and individuals as alternative, if not competing, labor markets. Right now we have only an inkling of what such a change will mean for employers and even less of an understanding of its implications for people's lives and careers. Our intent has been to open the topic for further research and debate among those who are interested in how work in America and most other industrial societies is evolving.

# The Changing Employment Circumstances of Managers

*Paul Osterman*

In 2003, just under 6.5 million Americans worked as managers, and they earned an average annual salary of $83,400, while the average for all workers was $36,520.[1] The unemployment rate for managers that year was 2.9 percent, less than half the overall unemployment rate of 6 percent. Clearly, managers are a privileged group. But perhaps surprisingly, they are often seen as victims.

Middle managers, their travails, and their moral dilemmas have long figured prominently in American literature. From *The Man in the Grey Flannel Suit* to Joseph Heller's *Something Happened*, novelists have mined the challenges of working and advancing in corporate America. But for the managers in today's labor force, the challenges are more than fictional. The restructuring of the past two decades has remade their work world, or at least so it is alleged by many observers. The goal of this chapter is to understand just what, if anything, has changed in the nature of work and careers for the people who make the modern corporation function.

The concerns of novelists have been mirrored in the writings of social scientists. More than 50 years ago, sociologist C. Wright Mills (1953, 87, 107) characterized the world of middle management thusly:

> As with any "middle" group, what happens to the middle managers is largely dependent on what happens to those above and below them—to top management and to foremen. The pace and character of work in the middle management are coming increasingly to resemble those in the lower ranks of the management hierarchy . . . middle managers become the routinized general staff without final responsibility and decision.

The views of Mills mirror one side of a debate that has taken on renewed vigor in the face of widespread corporate layoffs and restructuring. Many, perhaps most, observers believe that world of middle managers has been radically transformed. Kunda and Ailon-Souday (2004, 210) wrote, "often the target of downsizing, managers went from one of the most secure occupations to one of the least," and their perspective is mirrored in the comment of corporate raider Carl Icahn, who described his objective as eliminating "layers of bureaucrats reporting to bureaucrats" (Smith 1990, 14).

These views reflect two distinct perspectives that, nonetheless, lead to the same result. In one view, managers over the years succeeded in building and protecting wasteful bureaucratic empires that were, in effect, the white-collar analog to featherbedding. Protected both by weak corporate governance and by the widespread acceptance of norms that hold that white-collar employees were a fixed factor of production, managerial ranks grew and prospered without reference to need or to productivity. The revolution in corporate governance and the rise of aggressive stockholders and takeover artists have put an end to this.

The second perspective points to the emergence of new ideas about management itself. The bible of this view, Champy and Hammer's *Reengineering the Corporation*, introduced the idea of process reengineering, or what General Electric calls its "workout" process. The spread of information technology permitted firms to get their work done with fewer intermediate layers and, to the extent that the role of middle management was to process information for high levels, to dispense with many of the human information processors. The spread of new organizational ideas, such as outsourcing and contract work, contributed to this trend.

Regardless of whether the impetus was tougher governance or organizational innovation, at a first approximation the results were the same for many middle managers: They lost their jobs or, at the minimum, came to live with much higher levels of insecurity than they had ever experienced in the past. There is, however, another perspective. Some observers argued that the new organizational architecture fundamentally changed the nature of middle management for the better. Instead of being the automatons portrayed in the novels and by C. Wright Mills, modern organizations invite middle managers to become "intrapreneurs," to take charge of their careers and to express their creativity.

Speaking of intrapreneurship, Rosabeth Moss Kanter (1989, 384) wrote, "One offshoot of many of these programs is the weakening of hierarchy and the reduction of levels of organizations as employees are given more opportunities to influence decisions and to exercise control." In this perspective, the organizational redesign that seems at first glance to undermine job security is really an opening for middle managers to find new roles and to manage their own growth and careers in ways that had never before been permitted.

It is clear that there are very different views about what has happened to managers. To sort them out, I begin this chapter with a discussion of the forces that have led firms to reorganize work. I will then turn to a discussion of what the evidence shows regarding the impact of these shifts upon middle management. I examine available data on the employment patterns of managers and then review the findings of field-based research on changes within firms and industries. In the final section of the chapter I will discuss what policies may be appropriate to deal with the new employment situation of middle managers.

## Why the World Changed

There are several conceptually distinct explanations for why the employment circumstances of middle managers may have shifted. These explanations are often conflated in the popular discussion, but it is worth attempting to make the distinctions clearer.

*Times Are Tougher, Competition Has Increased*

For a variety of reasons, many firms are operating in a tougher environment than before. In some industries, such as telecommunications, deregulation and the emergence of new competitors have radically changed the game. Changes in interstate banking laws have triggered fierce competition, mergers, and layoffs in many large financial institutions.

Deregulation is not the only source of more difficult times. The insurance industry, for example, faces numerous challenges. Large firms are increasingly self-insuring, banks are going after easy business, such as workers compensation, and nimble smaller firms are offering new products that old multiline insurers find hard to match. The consequence in firms such as Prudential, Travelers, and Aetna has been restructuring.

The foregoing examples are driven by largely domestic considerations. It is important to see this because so much attention has been devoted to issues of trade. Nonetheless, while not the whole story, trade clearly adds to the list of reasons why life is tougher—as the auto, steel, and textile industries can attest.

Evidence of tougher competition is real and could be multiplied many times. In some sense, however, the point is too facile. Firms have always faced competition and have responded by cutting prices, laying off employees (historically blue-collar ones), and innovating new products. Nevertheless, only recently have fundamental organizational structures been called into question. If firms had been optimally organized before, then the presence of competition today should stimulate the traditional responses, but not necessarily lead to radical rethinking of the organization itself. Something else must be at play, something that enables a more far-reaching response than was possible in the past or that overcomes past political and social obstacles to such a response. This is a crucial point, because it gets us beyond overly simple appeals to tough competition as an explanation for changes in employer organization and strategy.

*Technology, Hard and Soft*

Alfred Chandler, the dean of business historians and chronicler of the traditional American bureaucratic firm, likens the spread of microcomputers and chips to the extension of the railroad. The railroad created the modern corporation by enabling mass markets, and analogously the microchip enables new forms of management and control. With more than 40 percent of new capital investment spent on information technology, and with a 6000 percent quality adjusted price decline in computers over the past 30 years, this argument is more than plausible (Brynjolfsson 1993).

At a crude level, computers can substitute for labor, enabling more to be produced with less. However, the more interesting impact is deeper, because computers enable new systems of management and control. Much energy inside firms and business schools is spent thinking about how to use computers to radically change business processes. Classic examples include combining steps in customer service and order entry, or streamlining backroom processing of financial records in banking and insurance.

As impressive as is the impact of microprocessors, it is crucial not to overlook the importance of a "soft" technological innovation: new ideas about organizational design. These new ideas, which have become broadly accessible to the managerial community in recent years, have implications that may well equal or exceed more traditional technological change. Although perhaps arbitrary, I would list the central organizational ideas as follows: (a) A new approach toward quality that shifted it from being the province of a separate unit and instead diffused accountability throughout the production process; (b) devolution of increased responsibility to ordinary workers (white- and blue-collar) to come up with new ideas and processes and the devolution of related organization of the workforce into teams with substantial training and job rotation; (c) the notion that some workers are core to the organization while others are peripheral and can be managed with quite different sets of rules and expectations; (d) production process innovations, notably just-in-time systems of inventory; and (e) long-term and intimate relationships with suppliers and hence a considerable interpenetration between what others might perceive as distinct organizational units.

While these organizational innovations quickly became part of American business vocabulary, it is important to understand that they played out in different ways in different settings. Furthermore, in many firms it is doubtlessly the case that the vocabulary has been adopted with little real change in practices. Nonetheless, the diffusion of these ideas has been substantial (Osterman 1994, 2000).

Even with these qualifications in mind, however, it is clear that the new organizational ideas present firms with opportunities similar to those offered by information technology as they seek ways to respond to competitive stress. There is perhaps even more scope for values, external constraints, and internal power-politics to shape just how these opportunities are used, but their far-reaching implications seem undeniable. The very boundaries of the firm are placed into question, the flow of work is again open to reconsideration, and fundamental issues arise regarding which set of workers the firm is willing to make any degree of commitment to.

### Capital Markets Are Calling the Tune

Informational and organizational technology are tools offering firms new ways to respond to competitive stress. The capital market explanation is different, in that it looks outside the organization and calls attention to the role of the financial community in influencing the motivation and objectives of firms. There are basically three lines of argument. The first is that the institutional investors currently place much greater pressure on firms to perform than they did in the past. The second is that, in general, the stock market undervalues "soft" investments in people. This might happen because these investments are hard to observe and hence are subject to the suspicion that they really represent managerial featherbedding. Another possibility is that analysts simply do not believe that such investments pay off. The third argument is that the stock market places unreasonably short time horizons on firms, who must then manage for quarterly performance and not long-term growth.

The stories summarized above suggest two related but distinct hypotheses. The first is that capital markets are making firms more performance oriented than in the past. This might help explain the rapid adoption of the new organizational and IT technologies. The second argument is that capital markets bias firms away from investments in people and that this bias is increasing. Here, it is worth making a few points. First, for capital market explanations to hold water, it must be the case that firms are either sub-optimally structured in the past or else, absent capital market pressures, would be too slow to take up the opportunities offered by the "hard" and "soft" technologies described above. If firms were doing their best in tough circumstances, then capital market participants would have no incentives to pressure managers.

From the viewpoint of capital markets, this sub-optimality can take two forms: Either managers are simply making bad decisions and need to be set back on course, or managers are doing fine on their own terms but are pursuing somewhat different objectives than simply maximizing stockholders returns. For example, if managers placed a positive value on loyalty to long-standing employees, this might be seen by the investment community as wasteful spending. The trick in assessing claims regarding the impact of capital markets lies in distinguishing between firms that really need a wake-up call from those wherein capital markets are simply struggling for a higher share of profits at the expense of employment and wages.

These qualifications and amendments aside, the interaction between heightened competition and shifting capital market constraints are most likely an additional source of pressure on firms. Although the complaints of incumbent management probably have a strongly self-serving element (attacks on "impatient" investors may be simply pleas by management to retain their unchecked and poorly utilized discretion), observation of managerial behavior does suggest that, for good or bad reasons, concerns about capital markets are shaping behavior in ways that were not true in the past.

In his study of the impact of institutional investors, Michael Useem (1996, 138) concluded,

> Management has been responding. In reviewing executive compensation plans . . . general counsels often review the plans privately with activist pension funds. When considering . . . an acquisition chief executives turn to investor specialists for a prediction of how the markets will react. Whether in setting strategy or selling divisions, investor preferences now unite with regulatory constraints and legal risks as part of the operating environment that executives no longer ignore.

## What Has Happened to Middle Managers

A casual reading of the business press would lead to the conclusion that managers are an endangered species. Certainly, the journalistic drumbeat of layoffs implies that managerial ranks are shrinking. If this were true, it would be a remarkable reversal from a long-term trend of increased administrative intensity in American firms. The story of the rise of large corporations in the economic landscape is the story of the need for more managers. The emergence of the "visible hand," to use Alfred Chandler's image, is the story of managers substituting for impersonal market forces in guiding the paths of production and distribution. As the scope of corporations expanded, one would expect the need for managers and the relative importance of managers in production to have also grown. The data do in fact support this expectation. Guillen (1994, 36) reported that in manufacturing, the ratio of administrative employees to production employees grew from 8 in every 100 in 1900 to 16 in 1920 and 18 in 1929.

But, one might reasonably ask, has restructuring reversed this trend? The answer appears to be "no." David Gordon (1996, 46) reported that the percent of nonproduction and supervisory employees in total private sector employment grew from 6.6 percent in 1960 to 11.4 percent in 1980 and 13.0 percent in 1989. Gordon used

Bureau of Labor Statistics (BLS) establishment surveys to arrive at this estimate, but a similar tale is told by the household based Current Population Survey. These data show that between 1969 and 1999 managers and administrators increased from 8 percent to 14 percent of total employment (Levy and Murnane 2005, 42).

The data cited above are broad-brushed and do not finely distinguish among types of managers nor do they focus uniquely upon the large corporations that are at the center of the restructuring debate. Nonetheless, they are strongly suggestive that what has changed is not the overall importance of managers in the economy. Restructuring has not eliminated the need for managers. What it has done is to change the conditions and nature of managerial work.

To sort out the different perspectives on the fate of middle managers, it makes sense to begin with what can be discerned in labor market data. The limitation of these data, of course, is that they can tell us little about what managers actually do. To attempt to answer that question I will turn later in the chapter to reports from a number of observers as well as interviews I conducted with a range of middle managers. However, the data are useful in understanding the broad outlines of recent events.

One angle on the question is to ask what has happened to job tenure for managers over the decades of restructuring. Information on job tenure, the number of years employees have spent with their firm, has been collected by the Census Bureau from the household survey every two years since 1983. There are a series of complicated technical issues involved in analyzing these data. In addition, it is important to understand that job tenure is a function of both quits and layoffs, and these tend to be offsetting behaviors. That is, in a period of high layoffs, quits are likely to fall as employees become risk adverse. Hence tenure data do not speak directly to the question of whether work has become less secure. Nonetheless, they do help us understand if it has become less stable.

Table 11.1 below provides the basic facts on job tenure. Because of changes in occupational classifications, the data are shown in two parts, but both tell the same story. Managers enjoy more years of job tenure than does the labor force in general and the blue-collar worker in particular. Furthermore, there is little evidence of a decline in recent years.

There are two important qualifications to this optimistic picture. First, the data represent the entire American workforce, whereas much of the discussion about the reduction of managerial employment has been centered in large firms. Second, these

**Table 11.1**   Job Tenure (in years)

|  | 1983 | 1987 | 1991 | 1996 | 1998 |
|---|---|---|---|---|---|
| All, 16 plus in age | 3.5 | 3.4 | 3.6 | 3.8 | 3.6 |
| Executive, Administrative, and Managerial | 5.3 | 5.1 | 5.5 | 5.5 | 5.3 |
| Precision Craft, Repair, and Production | 4.8 | 4.7 | 4.8 | 4.9 | 4.6 |

|  | 2000 | 2002 | 2004 |
|---|---|---|---|
| All, 16 plus in age | 3.5 | 3.7 | 4.0 |
| Management Occupations | 4.9 | 5.2 | 5.5 |

*Source*: United States Bureau of Labor Statistics.

data are for both men and women, whereas the tenure data suggest that the experience of the two genders has been quite different. For example, between 1983 and 2000 the median job tenure of 45- to 54-year-old men declined from 12.8 years to 9.5 years, while for women of the same age group tenure increased from 6.3 years to 7.3 years.

Another source of national data comes from surveys of worker displacement that are conducted by the Census Bureau. Employees are defined as "displaced" if they have three or more years of tenure on their job and have lost that job due to plant or company closing, insufficient work, or abolition of their position or shift. In the latest survey of all those who were displaced between January 2001 and December 2003, 17 percent were classified in the occupation "management, business, or financial operations." This displacement rate should be compared to the overall occupational distribution. Employees in this grouping accounted for 9 percent of overall employment.[2] Thus it does appear from these data that managers are disproportionately at risk.

### The Changing Shape of the Managerial Ladder

One implication of both the popular discussion and the data reviewed above is that the structure of organizations has shifted in ways that impact managerial careers. The quantitative data that we have on this question is thin, but it is supportive of the view that the world is quite different for middle managers today than in the past.

An important issue is whether the shape of the managerial hierarchy is in fact shifting in ways implied by the popular discussion. That is, is the firm getting flatter with fewer rungs on the ladder? Recent research by Raghuram Rajan and Julie Wulf (2003) suggested that this is indeed happening. Working with an original database that includes the job descriptions and reporting relationships of senior managers in 300 large American corporations, Rajan and Wulf found that the number of managers reporting to the CEO has increased substantially in recent years, from an average of 4.4 in 1986 to 7.2 in 1999. This implies a substantial flattening in the hierarchy of organizations and the reduction of managerial levels.

Rajan and Wulf explored several possible explanations of this trend. The candidates they examined include strengthening corporate governance (which might lead to reduction in empire building), CEO entrenchment (which might lead to reduction in the number of potential competitors to the CEO for power), and the increased importance of human capital and intangible assets (which leads firms to look more like partnerships that are unwilling to permit lower-level managers to have significant power or access to clients). The evidence on each of these is fairly weak, but Rajan and Wulf favored the last explanation. However, regardless of what lies behind the trend, the development itself—the flattening of corporate hierarchies—seems not to be in doubt.

A second important organizational trend within firms for which we have data is the spread of self-managed work teams and quality programs, which together are often called High Performance Work Organizations (HPWO). These systems have spread substantially in American firms (Osterman 1994, 2000). HPWO systems tend to devolve substantial authority to frontline workers and as such have important potential implications for the responsibilities, employment levels, and wages of managers.

Analysis of the surveys cited above did in fact find that these systems impacted the employment circumstances of managers. First, as the use of HPWO systems increased, the employment levels of managers fell (Osterman 2000). Second, establishments with greater usage of HPWO systems tended to pay their managers more than establishments with less utilization (Osterman 2006). Taken together, these patterns suggest that new work systems require fewer managers (as responsibility is devolved to frontline employees) but that the required skill for managers does in fact increase.

### The Changing Basis of Compensation

The compensation of managers at the top of firms is widely publicized and has been the source of much public discussion and debate. For example, in 1965 CEOs in major companies earned 26 times the average workers' pay, while in 2000 they earned 310 times the average pay.[3]

Stunning as these numbers are, of greater interest for this chapter are compensation developments for the millions of managers lower in the hierarchy. One of the most noted trends in the U.S. labor market in the 1980s and 1990s was a rise in wage inequality. The compensation trajectory of managers has followed the same trend. Using a national data-set of managerial salaries maintained by the Hay company (the firm that devised the widely used Hay points system of compensation), O'Shaughnessy, Levine, and Cappelli found that between 1986 and 1992 the standard deviation of managerial wages rose from 31.6 percent to 34.3 percent, a 9 percent increase in inequality (O'Shaughnessy, Levine, and Cappelli 1998).

One of the major consequences of restructuring has been a shift in the basis of compensation. In the past, most compensation regimes were based on systems that emphasized internal equity. A large fraction of pay increases took the form of across-the-board raises that applied equally to everyone. With supervisors asked to rate their employees on a simple scale, and with these supervisors having a tendency to emphasize equity rather than performance in making these ratings, merit pay systems were relatively mild .

All of this has changed. Firms today put much greater emphasis on distinguishing among levels of performance and rewarding and punishing accordingly. This can be interpreted as an extension of the compensation of the same "at risk" attitude that has been applied to employment itself. For example, the BLS Employee Benefits Survey finds that the percentage of employees eligible for bonuses grew from 29 percent in 1989 to 39 percent by the late 1990s (cited in Cappelli 1999, 158).

A sense of the extent of this trend, and also of the fact that it applies more severely to managers than to other employees, can be gained from my 1997 survey of American establishments (Osterman 2006). The survey asked what percentage of an employee's wage increase was due to an across-the-board increase related to firm or group performance and what percentage was due to individual merit. For blue-collar core employees, the former accounted for 62 percent of wage increases, while individual performance or merit accounted for 38 percent. By contrast, for managers the relative importance is reversed: Across-the-board increases accounted for 33 percent and individual performance factors 67 percent.

### How Managerial Work Has Changed

The data presented above are aggregate, frequently taken from surveys of individuals, but in any case with very little grounding in the firm itself. However, there are both ethnographic and statistical studies of managers that draw on the actual experience within firms.

Perhaps the classic ethnographic study of managerial careers in the "old economy" is Rosabeth Moss Kanter's (1977) description of "Indesco" in *Men and Women of the_Corporation*. Kanter portrays a world of hierarchies and job ladders in which upward mobility is the sine qua non of success. At the time of her writing, many managers did, in fact, have reasonable expectations of climbing these ladders. What has changed since?

Studies of managerial work in a range of industries have, in fact, documented substantial changes in these traditional patterns. I begin by reviewing findings from three quite distinct industries: automobiles, high technology, and insurance.

In his examination of how restructuring has affected managers in the automobile industry, John-Paul MacDuffie (1996) summarized as follows (81–82):

> The middle managers, corporate and divisional staff, engineers, clerical employees and first line supervisors at General Motors, Ford, and Chrysler now find themselves affected by all the woes commonly associated with blue collar production workers— layoffs, outsourcing of work, concessions in pay and benefits, and redundancies due to the reorganization of work for greater efficiency . . . Besides the erosion of status that this implies, white collar employees also face many new demands in their jobs, including more work, more decision-making responsibility, more cross-functional interaction, and more of a support role vis-à-vis blue collar workers.

The starting point of these changes is the recognition that in many respects the auto firms represented the classic bureaucratic form. In fact, it was at General Motors that the multidivision corporate form, organized in silos with a central headquarters performing the coordination function, was invented. Yet over time this style of management came to be dysfunctional. In the words of one employee (quoted by MacDuffie 97), "Unless you're working on the Fourteenth Floor, you have about a zillion bosses. Every small thing requires approval up the line. They have thirteen thousand checkers in this company to make sure things are done right. Hell, they have checkers to check the checkers. It's madness."

In response to this, the firms in the early 1990s began to make structural changes. Jack Smith, the CEO of General Motors, moved his office out of the Fourteenth Floor and reduced central staff from 13,500 to 2,500. Ford, for its part, expanded cross-functional activities and set up teams that included representatives from engineering, manufacturing, finance, components, and suppliers.

However, the sources of pressure for change in managerial work were deeper than simple changes in the organization chart. Spurred by the example of their Japanese competitors, American automobile firms began to implement versions of lean-production systems. This production system, with its emphasis on reducing buffers, team production, continuous improvement, and quality, had deep implications for the nature of managerial work (MacDuffie 106).

Under lean production, there are a series of shifts in managerial work: First, managers are more exposed to the market and to customer pressures, yet the dynamics of lean production dampens the impact of market volatility. Second, managers have to broaden what they do. They cannot limit themselves anymore to just "conceptual" tasks. Because of the absence of buffers, they also have to worry about execution. However, from this they gain a broader knowledge of the production process and can play a more integrative role. Third, managers have to pay more attention to the process of decision making. They are less likely to simply make decisions by fiat. The decisions that do get made are less intuitive and more data driven than in the past. Fourth, managers have much more interdependence with managers from other functions and also from other companies (suppliers), yet they also experience lower coordination costs and faster decision making.

The "market-in" philosophy of lean production leads to lots of data being distributed to many more people in the organization. This reduces managers' role as "owners" of information. Instead, they work with large numbers of people in interpreting data, which requires important shifts in the nature of managerial skills (MacDuffie 09):

> With their specialized expertise either subsumed by subordinates or more open to challenge, managers must find ways to contribute that draw on their broad knowledge of the organization, its products, its suppliers, and its customers. With less ability to command based on positional authority, managers must instead persuade based on their skills in analyzing and interpreting what they have learned form their subordinates and from their interactions across functional and company boundaries. Knowing how to guide subordinates as they develop expertise, how to pull together the appropriate people and resources to address various problems, and what balance to strike between autonomy and direction when allowing subordinates to take on "thinking" tasks become important skills for managers under lean production . . .

The shifts in managerial work in high tech and insurance track the developments in automobiles remarkably closely. In her study of Hewlett-Packard, Sara Beckman (1996) described organizational shifts away from narrow silos and toward broader cross-functional structures. She commented (167),

> These three changes—consolidation, vertical disintegration, horizontal process management—have created a substantively different environment for manufacturing managers and white collar professionals. That environment is more networked externally, with more critical vendor relationships and tighter outbound partnerships, as well as internally, across both functional and divisional boundaries.

Her description of the new skills that managers need in this environment track closely MacDuffie's analysis of automobiles (Beckman 173):

> [M]any manufacturing managers in today's environment share the need to accomplish their objectives through influence rather than direct control. Forced to operate in teams, either with internal R&D and marketing partners or with external operators, they must learn to take others' perspectives and to think strategically in integrating other's needs with their own. Interpersonal, negotiation, and business skills are far more critical than technical skills . . .

Finally, in that most quintessential white-collar industry, insurance, the shifts in managerial work are remarkably similar. Scott, O'Shaughnessy, and Cappelli (1996) used a combination of field work and analysis of Hay data to map what had happened to managers. They described an "old world" that could have been General Motors (128):

> Managers had to be sure that each functional unit completed its tasks effectively in a timely fashion . . . Career ladders were defined hierarchically, and steep hierarchies were

needed to ensure coordination among various functional areas . . . The skills needed from managers were planning, delegation, motivation, evaluation, coordination, and control.

The "new world" also tracks the changes we have already seen (128):

[I]nsurance management jobs are more like those in lean-production manufacturing organizations, where teams of workers are responsible for production and the manager is responsible for leadership . . . Different skill sets are needed for managers to coordinate these independent teams . . . One manager said, "Managers' jobs are not as well defined as they were." Managers are having to demonstrate more "soft" skills.

Their analysis of the Hay data showed that the organizations have become much flatter, with wider spans of control. They also concluded that while the compensation of top management increased substantially over the period they examined (1986–1992), the pay of middle managers rose only modestly. In this they again match the automobile story, in which MacDuffie found that middle managers were hit badly in terms of pay. Top managers continued to get bonuses based on the profitability of nonproduction areas such as finance operations. Blue-collar employees were protected by the union. The middle management got pay freezes and an increased share of medical costs (MacDuffie 101).

### An Important Qualification

All of the foregoing discussion refers to the changing employment situation of managers in large bureaucratic firms. This focus has long seemed justified, despite the common understanding that many Americans work in small firms that operate under very different rules. The rationale has been that, while small firms are numerically important, the tendency in the American economy is toward the large, bureaucratic form. Furthermore, large firms were long seen as the desired outcome and the epitome of best practice.

These assumptions have been challenged in recent years, most particularly by the rise of new entrepreneurial firms in regions such as the Silicon Valley. While it is possible to exaggerate the differences between many of these firms and the traditional model—after all, companies such as Hewlett-Packard and Intel are certainly large and bureaucratic and have well-structured managerial career paths—there are, nonetheless, reasons to believe that important differences between the models do exist.

One key distinction lies in the higher rate of mobility that is said to characterize the Silicon Valley labor market. Most observers believe that a great deal more job changing goes on there than in other regions. A second difference lies in the fluidity of occupational roles. The nature of new start-ups is that the content of jobs is up for grabs, as founding teams work out their division of labor (Beckman and Burton 2005). Titles may seem traditional, but the actual nature of the work may vary substantially over time within a start-up and also across start-ups.

Although the emerging pattern in the Silicon Valley and other similar labor markets may represent a new model, as of now we lack enough data or description to accurately characterize it. Furthermore, the vast majority of American managers continue to work in more traditional settings, and it is from these settings that we have our best understanding of what has happened.

## How Managers Feel about the Changes

We have seen that managerial work has changed in a variety of ways. It is less secure, it requires new and in many cases more complex skills, and compensation is much more at risk today than in the past. Not all of these changes are for the worse, but it is certainly the case that pressures have ratcheted up. What are the reactions of managers to these developments?

Early in the process of restructuring, Viki Smith (1990) reported on the attitudes of managers in a large bank and found them to be confused and ambivalent about the changes. This pattern is consistent with the most extensive ethnographic study of the state of mind of managers in the current situation, a study of 14 firms conducted by Charles Heckscher (1995). Heckscher focused his attention on their attitudes toward the firm, on how their loyalties were shifting, and on how they viewed their careers.

Most of his managers were in a state of shock. Perhaps paradoxically, they remained loyal to the firm, but they had withdrawn and lost sight of the larger purpose. As Heckscher wrote (95),

> [T]he problem . . . is that this goodwill has not led to coordinated and effective organizations. Rather, it leads managers—after an initial phase of shock and rage—to dig into their own trenches, trying to do their narrow jobs as well as possible, but losing touch with the whole. Their reaction has all the earmarks of defensiveness: denial of reality, avoidance of difficult questions; they consistently underestimate their company's competitive problems and sidestep questions about their future careers. They remain inwardly focused and reactive, unable to grasp the full import of the changes they are facing and therefore unable to respond creatively to them.

This mixed set of attitudes of managers is reflected in the survey conducted for this study by the Society for the Study of Human Resource Management, the largest organization of human resource (HR) professionals. This survey of HR managers in private sector firms asked about their attitudes toward their employer. HR managers are probably among the most likely managers to remain loyal and committed to the firm, and this is reflected in the data. In response to the statement, "I feel little loyalty to my employer," 49 percent strongly disagreed and 22 percent disagreed.

On the other hand, the respondents are hard-eyed in their view of what the firm is about. In response to the question of whether the senior management made decisions in the best interest of the employees, only 59 percent were somewhat or very confident that this was the case. But when asked whether senior management made decisions in the best interests of stockholders or owners, 84 percent were somewhat or very confident.

To pursue these topics, I interviewed 75 middle managers in two large corporations. The corporations were chosen because together they represent the range of transformations that have shaken the work world of managers. One of the firms is a large financial institution that has gone through a number of mergers and whose managers I interviewed just as it was being acquired by another, larger competitor. The other is a large, high-technology firm operating in a highly volatile product market that has made considerable use of internal project teams and other flexible organizational designs.

The managers whom I interviewed were several levels removed from the top. They are the account managers, project leaders, IT supervisors, lenders, sales managers, customer support managers, HR managers, and other representatives of the army of managers who constitute the modern corporation. These people by and large are not candidates for the top positions in their organizations, and most of them have no interest in climbing that high. In any case, these are the people who make the firm function, and they are also the people who represent the largest group of potential victims of the new rules of corporate careers.

Four major themes emerged from these interviews: First, the managers I interviewed were committed to their work. They enjoyed their tasks. In this sense they were very much like craft workers. Second, the managers feel that over time the nature of their work has changed in negative ways. They face more controls, they have lost discretion, and in some instances their job has been disassembled in ways that resemble what happened to factory work. Third, while the managers feel committed to their work, to the tasks, they feel much less commitment, respect, and loyalty to their employer than they had in the past. Fourth, despite this latter point, the conclusions that they draw tend to either be very privatized or else broadly apolitical. They see the changes that have taken place as inevitable and, in some cases, desirable.

## Craft Work

Virtually all of the managers that I interviewed took what might be termed as an attitude of craft pride in their work. Regardless of their attitude toward the organization, when it came to the job itself, there was a high degree of enjoyment and commitment. Consider this comment by a bank manager:

> Love the people, love managing people . . . I have no associate turnover, everybody stays with the company, everybody goes to other opportunities within the company. I pride myself on that. In the past year I have probably trained four or five managers here.

The managers in the high-technology firm echoed these sentiments. When asked what they liked about the work, a typical comment was, "Building things and getting products out to a customer . . . To me that's the most exciting part of project, is getting the hardware and making it work and then getting out to the customer."

## Loss of Control

Many, although not all, of the managers whom I interviewed believe that in recent years they have been subject to more control, they have lost a degree of discretion, and their jobs have been narrowed or split apart.

Consider the case of the bank manager cited above who took a craft-like pride in his work. Nonetheless, his discretion over his time has been sharply reduced. The senior management of the bank has established a list of behaviors and goals that the bank manager must follow *on an hourly basis*. In his words:

> Our company has seven priorities, and those don't define everything they do, but instead of having a priority, it has seven priorities and then you have 50 goals and you can do 49 of them 120 percent but you know what, we are going to talk about that one. That happens so often, that you are just numb to it, you are frustrated by it . . . I have a goal every hour, I have to refer a product. Everyone that has walked through here today I know already, it is not going to happen. It is impossible.

A lender described her job as being "blasted apart" into pieces, and another manager commented,

> There is a huge thing of tracking . . . Everything gets tracked to a degree that I think is unreasonable but—you are trained, every time you do the—this month you might do your web base training, it gets tracked. So you do 15 hours you have got to do this quarter, it gets tracked. It gets recorded. I guess the demands for information sometimes—all of the company looking for similar things, data from you—it gets to be overbearing . . . .I think it is very hierarchical and it is very top down driven.

Ironically, what many of these managers described is very much the process that the Marxist economist Harry Braverman described for blue-collar workers. Employers, in a search of both more control and for lower costs, divide up the work and impose various forms of monitoring. There is a certain irony in this, since for blue-collar workers the spread of HPWO has led to a reversal of this process and a broadening of responsibility.

### Loyalty and Commitment

The turmoil of the past two decades has, not surprisingly, taken its toll on the loyalty and commitment of managers to their firms. There is certainly variation in this, and a nontrivial minority of the managers I interviewed expressed a strong, continuing commitment to their employer. Nonetheless, this group is a minority. The majority of managers expressed major doubts about their employer and their loyalty. The following comment by an engineering manager at the high-tech firm was typical:

> I think that it's really taken a big hit . . . I don't think that there's much loyalty between business and employees period nowadays. Within—you have people who have been here for a very long time and have a history of performance and I think are very loyal to the company because they know that they're in the culture, they know what to do to succeed, they feel comfortable. I think anyone who isn't in that group has to be somewhat concerned, you know, you're one cycle away from . . . one cycle and boss who doesn't think you're a major contributor to being job hunting, so it's difficult to be loyal in these situations.

Even successful employees feel this way. One of the managers I interviewed at the bank had survived the merger and, in fact, was in a better position than prior to the restructuring. Nonetheless, she had the following view:

> I think it has changed a lot in 18 years, I mean you look at it, so you have a lot more stats in terms of loyalty even in Japan where everyone is loyal, with the same company till the day they die, that will not happen anymore. That does not happen here in the states anymore. It is interesting I have been here for 18 years but I go around the table and a lot of folks that worked with the institution for 18 years, 20 years, 25 years, which is pretty mind boggling quite frankly and I wonder if I am stupid or I am just comfortable and I am pretty conservative, so I do not like to take certain risks and I have been the more constant work force within the two incomes of the household. I cannot say I am loyal.

## Conclusion

It is clear that managerial work has changed quite dramatically. Managers still retain their privileged positions compared to most other workers in the economy. They are paid more and they keep their jobs longer. At the same time, it is undeniable that managerial work is much less secure today than in the past, that pay is more at risk, and that the nature of the work itself has changed. Today's managers are expected to take on a much broader array of tasks than they were in the past and to be able to operate effectively across organizational boundaries. Furthermore, setting aside even the possibility of job loss, the career trajectory of managers is much more uncertain, as organizations have flattened their hierarchies and reduced opportunities for promotion. In some important sense, the situation of middle managers has come to resemble more closely that of frontline workers than that of the most members of senior management.

In thinking about how managers might respond to these developments, one theoretical possibility is the kind of collective response that characterized other labor force groups exposed to sudden economic dislocation. For example, one possible collective response might be efforts to limit the ability of firms to restructure and to lay people off. At least in the realm of managerial employment, there appears to be no support for this option. Although many of the managers I interviewed were angry, none of them thought of their plight in political terms. They all took the view that the changes in their circumstances were the inevitable result of economic changes. They saw specific examples of inequity (such as the high severance pay of top level managers compared to the support given to those lower down) but they drew no general conclusions from this.

A more hopeful path for collective action is for managers to establish professional associations that can provide assistance in skill acquisition and job search. Associations of this sort are increasingly common in professional fields. Examples include the Graphic Arts Guild and the Web Designers Guild. There is no reason why such a model should not apply also to managers.

These associations can be formal, as in the Forty Plus Club described by Katherine Newman (1999). This was a self-help group of unemployed managers who helped each other cope with their situation and to find new work. The groups can also be informal, as was the case with a group of laid-off managers who met regularly at a church in Dallas where I interviewed some of them. Organizations of this kind can also be sponsored by larger entities, and American unions are increasingly thinking about nontraditional alternatives that they might offer to people who need help but who are not ready to sign a union card.

One of the important functions of such an association is to help people find new jobs. This is the classic role of a labor market intermediary, and the importance of these intermediaries in today's economy can be seen in a variety of ways. At the highest level, the U.S. revenue of the four largest executive search firms rose from $214 million in 1993 to $738.3 million in 2000 (Khurana 2002, 123). More generally, in 2000 there were 3000 online job boards, with 7,000,000 unique resumes and 29,000,000 not-necessarily unique jobs posted (Autor 2001). Between 1972 and 2000 employment in temporary help firms grew five times more rapidly than average, accounting for 10 percent of all job growth (Autor 2004).

The private sector has clearly responded to the need for intermediaries, but there is also scope for public policy. In recent years the Department of Labor has sought to reform the Employment Service, the major public intermediary, by creating so-called one-stop centers that are intended to provide a broad range of services and to be customer friendly.

Another policy tool may be to reconsider issues of corporate governance. The central issue posed by governance discussions is, "In whose interest does the firm act?" The last several years have witnessed growing academic and political interest in this and other questions. What might be termed the "pro-employee voice" perspective on governance is motivated by takeovers and downsizing, which seem driven by quick stock market gains regardless of the cost to employees or communities. Actions of this sort are contrasted with what would presumably result if the firm had broader objectives than only enriching those who own its stock.

In thinking about whether reforming corporate governance may be a solution to the woes confronting managers, it is important to understand that most current interest in governance proceeds from a quite different angle. The debate is being driven by those who believe that stockholder interests are *insufficiently* valued by firms. The concern is that top managers have not been restrained by effective supervision and hence have followed poor policies for far too long or engaged in self-serving empire building and perk-expanding activities. A variety of solutions have been offered, but they all start from the proposition that the ultimate goal of the firm is and should be to maximize the wealth of people who own its stock. Employee interests are considered only to the extent that they benefit stockholders.

It seems clear that the pro-stockholder perspective is currently triumphant. In the academic literature the implicit assumption, deriving from microeconomics, has always been that economic efficiency is maximized when firms maximize profits and, since the owners of these profits are the owners of shares, firms should in this view maximize the wealth of their stockholders. This view has been given greater credibility and a more sophisticated defense by the emergence of the so-called finance view of the firm. From this perspective the firm is nothing more than a "nexus of contacts" or a collection of financial assets. The problem is how to maximize the return on these assets, and this requires a market for corporate control that permits the buying and selling of these assets and hence applies the discipline of market forces to those who manage them. This discipline is effective, because if the assets are mismanaged, the stock price will fall, inviting takeovers by those who will do a better management job and thus raise the stock price.

The finance view stands in contrast with the traditional conception of the American firm, in which the wide dispersion of ownership gave professional managers a great deal of leeway in how they ran their business. Although these managers, and their defenders, never overtly questioned the assumption that ultimately they were managing in the interest of stockholders, in fact there is some reason to doubt that this was the case. While from the perspective of finance theorists the managers may have engaged in empire building or even more wasteful activities (and they probably did buy too many corporate jets and hire too many friends), these managers also had an implicit stakeholder view of the firm and hence made decisions (increasing wages when profits were high, being reluctant to layoff except under duress) that were sometimes slanted toward the interests of employees and away from the immediate interests of stockholders.

Scholars and activists who view shifts in governance arrangements as a central strategy for improving outcomes experienced by employees make several different points, some of which are more threatening to the traditional conception of the role of the firm than others. The least threatening arguments focus upon the particular institutional framework within which governance is conducted. One version accepts the centrality of stockholders but argues that the institutional set-up of financial markets leads to an excessive focus on short-term stock gains rather than maximizing value in the long run. The emphasis on the short term makes it difficult for the firm to undertake investments, such as those in people, that have long time horizons.

A second line of thought is that owners, or their agents, are too distant from the operations of the firm to appropriately value hard-to-observe investments such as those in people. As a result, investments of this sort tend to be undervalued by the stock market and hence by managers. Neither of these points fundamentally challenges the primacy of the stockholders but rather each claims that their interests are being poorly served by the current system and that improvements would also make employees better off.

But a third perspective challenges the core belief that the only legitimate objective of the firm is to maximize stockholder value, arguing that other stakeholders have legitimate claims. When it comes to changing the fundamental purpose of the firm, the implication of the stakeholder argument is to initiate reforms that insure that representatives of interests other than stockholders sit on the board of directors and have a voice in decision-making. It is not clear, however, whether this approach will lead to any significant shifts in firm behavior. We have limited experience in this country with employee representatives on boards of directors, but what experience we do have is not particularly encouraging. Several of the examples that we do have, such as Eastern Airlines and United Airlines, have gone very badly for employees.

The real limitation of the corporate governance approach, from the perspective of this particular chapter, is that if employees do gain power (via, for example, the heft of union pension funds), this power is unlikely to be deployed to help managers. Managers will be seen as the beneficiaries of overly protective policies at the expense of employees lower down in the organization. Hence reforming corporate governance, although perhaps a very desirable objective from a global perspective, is of limited relevance in this particular case.

At the end of the day, the plight of managers is unlikely to elicit a great deal of sympathy or investment in public policy. After all, as noted at the beginning of the chapter, even in today's environment managers remain a privileged group. This does not mean, however, that they do not face significant challenges within their firms and within today's labor market. However, much as in the many fictional works that they have inspired, managers are probably going to have to face and solve these challenges on their own or in cooperation with small groups of colleagues in similar circumstances.

# Changing Career Paths and their Implications

*Peter Cappelli*

Important changes in the business and corporate world over the last two decades have led to important changes in the management of employees and their careers. More rapid restructurings and changes in business strategy, in response to fast-changing markets and the adaptations of increasingly global competitors, have weakened the bonds between employers and employees, especially in the managerial and executive ranks. Further, the paths that individuals take to get to the top of the organization have changed with much less reliance on internal, "grow your own" approaches to talent.

These developments raise interesting questions about the new approaches to talent, which rely to a much greater extent on the outside labor market. Do they change the attributes of the individuals who get to the top—are these arrangements more or less meritocratic, for example? The results suggest that the new model of careers provides greater access than the old model. The information used to make decisions arguably relies more on prior job related outcomes than on potential. But the depth and accuracy of information may be more limited than these were in the past. Careers are typically described as the succession of jobs that makes up one's working life. A typical assumption about careers is that, over time, an individual's jobs and circumstances tend to improve. As such, the notion of a career is deeply tied to questions of mobility—economic and social—as well as individual-level outcomes such as job satisfaction. Changes in career outcomes or in the criteria that shape careers therefore have important implications for society.

The focus of career research has been on white-collar work, especially managerial work. Such jobs were often organized in large hierarchies, which offered rich and interesting sequences of job opportunities over one's life. The arguments below examine what we know about changes in careers and consider the implications of those changes for broader outcomes.

### Historical Patterns in Management Careers

Research on careers has a long history in the United States, where notions of social mobility are central to national culture and values. Popular biographies of the "robber baron" generation and its leading figures, such as John D. Rockefeller and Andrew Carnegie, reinforced the notion that individuals became business leaders through hard work or, in the case of manufacturing leaders such as Henry Ford and Thomas Edison, inventive genius, typically overcoming hardships in the process. Arguably the first study to examine this meritocratic thesis was Pitirim Sorokin's (1925) study of millionaires in the United States. He compared an older generation of millionaires to the then current generation and found that while about half of the former had come from middle- or upper-class backgrounds, three quarters of the latter had done so. This suggested to him that society was becoming less meritocratic and that it had become more difficult to work one's way up economic and class levels.

Carl S. Joslyn and Frank W. Taussig (1932) aimed their study of social mobility precisely at business executives. They studied the backgrounds of 7,371 executives drawn from the ranks of corporate directors in the 1920s. While they found that the vast majority of these executives had fathers who were also businessmen and that this percentage actually had grown over time, they also found that 11 percent had fathers who were laborers. They focused on this finding and concluded that individuals with merit could work their way to the top of the business community. Differences in the probability of advancement by social class, they argued, were the result of differences in merit and ability—the upper class had more able people.

A number of studies followed the Joslyn and Taussig investigations in examining more closely the origins of the business leadership in the United States. William Miller (1949) looked into the backgrounds of 190 of the most elite executive—presidents and chairmen of boards of directors of the largest companies in the most important industries—at the beginning of the industrial age, from 1900–1910. What was interesting about this group, in contrast to business leaders from earlier generations, is that most were professional managers, not the founders or entrepreneurs who had started the businesses. Miller concluded that half had come from upper-class backgrounds and only 5 percent from working or lower-class families.

Frances Gregory and Irene Neu (1952) looked back even farther in time at the backgrounds of business leaders just before the beginnings of the modern corporation in the 1880s. They found that most of the business leaders before the turn of the last century had inherited money, which allowed them to invest in and then become leaders of companies. The meritocracy argument was no longer looking credible.

A generation later, the notion of a corporate career with entry-level jobs and promotion from within was more fully in place. Lloyd Warner and James Abbeglan (1995) attempted to replicate and extend the Joslyn and Taussig study. They looked at the background and careers of 8300 corporate executives in 1953 and found far fewer founders or entrepreneurs in the ranks and relatively fewer members of the rich or idle class than had the Joslyn and Taussig study. There was also a sharp decline since earlier studies in the percentage of executives who had inherited their positions or who were in the same firm as their fathers.

What Warner and Abbeglan saw instead was something that looked, at least relative to earlier periods, like an increase in more meritocratic arrangements. In an era when about half the men did not even finish high school, they found that roughly half of the executives of large companies they surveyed were college graduates (three-quarters had attended college), and 20 percent had gone on to graduate school. By far the most common route to the top was to begin either in sales or as a clerk in the company (34 percent of future executives). The next most common path began in production work (14 percent). The most striking statistics, however, concerned the stability of their career in the same company. The executives they surveyed averaged 54 years in age, they had been in their current executive job seven years, and had spent 24 years in their current firm, roughly half their life. Almost 50 percent had only worked at their current firm, and 26 percent had been an executive at only one other firm (Warner and Abbeglen 1995).

At roughly the same time, Mabel Newcomer (1955) undertook a systematic assessment of changes in executive careers over time, changes that focused on their experiences inside their corporations. She looked at the backgrounds and experiences of the very top executives—presidents and board chairmen—of the largest companies in 1900, 1925, and 1950, around 400 individuals in each period. In terms of the importance of the participants' positions in the organization and the importance of their organizations, this sample was more elite than the samples of earlier studies. Newcomer's results reinforced the conclusion that top executives were increasingly professional managers (as opposed to entrepreneurs or financiers) who were promoted to the top from within the company where they began their career. The extent to which these leaders held positions in companies where their fathers or close relatives worked declined from 26 percent in 1900 to 16 percent in 1925 and then to 11 percent in 1950. In 1925, 30 percent had begun their careers as entrepreneurs. By 1950, that figure was down to 10 percent.

More important for the study here is the fact that half of these leaders were hired from outside their corporations in 1900, but by 1950, only 20 percent were outside hires. Warner and Abbeglen estimated that half of all executives were promoted from within, so Newcomer's finding that 80 percent of top executives came from within suggests that this more elite executive population was more likely to have been developed internally than was a more typical executive. In 1950, 47 percent of Newcomer's sample retired in office, as opposed to only 11 percent in 1900. Of those who retired in office, 40 percent had been with their firm more than 40 years in 1950, in contrast to 21 percent in 1925 and only five percent in 1900.

In part as a result of the Newcomer study, ideas about what constituted a business career changed. The dominant notion now was that a business career was an organizational career—that is, it operated inside a corporation. William H. Whyte, an editor at *Fortune* magazine, became arguably the best-known commentator on the rise of the new organizational career with his famous book *The Organization Man* (1956). He cited a study by the Booz-Allen consulting firm that asked what was seen at the time as a novel question: Why would executives ever leave their corporation? The study of 422 executives who had left their first employer found that they did so only if their corporation could not deliver on its implicit promise of upward mobility (Whyte 1956).

Sociologists such as Theodore Caplow (1954) recognized that the internal arrangements for placing people into jobs, especially for white-collar work, resembled classical bureaucratic principles, and researchers began to describe the employment practices within firms in those terms. A series of studies throughout the 1960s and 1970s went on to map out the intricate details of how careers played out in practice, studies such as Rosabeth Kanter's famous account of in-breeding at the pseudonymous "Indisco" corporation (Kanter 1977). What linked these studies was an effort to map out what was, at least to outsiders, the hidden world of corporate career policies. As Jacoby (1983) documents, most employees since the 1930s have worked in organizations with bureaucratized employment practices.

The typical employee came in through a few entry ports or entry-level jobs, most often at the very bottom of the organizational hierarchy, and advanced along a predictable path that was described as a job ladder. The metaphor of a ladder emphasizes that movement up was discrete (that is, typically one promotion at a time) and extremely predictable (there was only one path, and it was extremely difficult to skip a "rung" of the ladder). Some advancements were simply seniority-related ("time in grade") and reflected managers' presumed greater expertise in their current job, as opposed to promotion to a new and more challenging position.

But there were also real advancements, typically through positions in "job clusters," a set of jobs that required additional but related skills that could be learned through on-the-job experience and training. Promotion ladders for the managerial ranks stayed within functional areas, or "silos," until one got near the top of the ladder. Sometimes the moves across jobs were not necessarily promotions in the strict sense of a higher job title but may have been promotions to jobs that were seen as development opportunities that prepared employees for future advancement. At some point in their advancement, skills associated with general management became relevant— the ability to manage workers in one's functional area was a general skill that translated to managing other areas. Once managers had those skills, they were eligible for "general manager" jobs that gave them operating responsibility and eligibility for executive development.

The model for organizing the personnel systems that managed career advancement was engineering—predict future demand for skilled employees, estimate the flow of workers up career ladders, and optimize along the way by adjusting hiring, development, redeployment, and so on, to match long-term supply to future demand (Galbraith 1967). An important point about those systems, related to their bureaucratic origins, was that the organization was deciding who would move to what jobs in order to best serve the goals of the organization. The individuals had no choice in the matter. Indeed, in the American version of these arrangements, the individual employee's status, tasks, and prospects were entirely defined by his position in the bureaucracy, by his job title.[1]

Career advancement looked somewhat different for production and hourly workers, in that while there were job ladders, there were typically far fewer steps and advancement possibilities. The craft union model existed for craft workers in many manufacturing plants, where advancement from apprentice to journeyman to master was at least influenced by union standards and objective criteria such as work sample tests. Otherwise, the most important advancement was from the production workforce to foreman or supervisor, the first level of management.

How real the likelihood of such advancement was is an empirical matter. Chinoy's (1955) study of workers in the auto industry, for example, found that there was one foreman job for every 120 workers and only about 10 such openings per year for in a 6000-worker plant. The chances of a promotion were incredibly small, even for the most able workers. Other industries had different paths to the top, however, including development programs that pulled hourly workers directly into managerial tracks. For example, I examined the biographies of the top 12 executives of the U.S. Steel Corporation in 1980, every one of whom began his career with the company. Most importantly, however, virtually all began in hourly jobs and were sent to college by the company, and then into management trainee positions. And as Warner and Abbeglen (1995) found, 14 percent of executives actually began their careers doing production work. The possibility of advancing into the executive suite remained at the very least a powerful normative idea.

## Meritocracy and the Corporation

The job ladders and other arrangements for advancement inside business enterprises were clearly the paths to upward mobility. And compared to earlier periods in U.S. history, there was little doubt that the leaders of industry were no longer simply the sons of the rich and business elite (there were no daughters in top executive jobs). The 1950s research mentioned above suggested that the arrangements for advancement inside companies rewarded the most able and were therefore more meritocratic than earlier systems.

Perhaps the strongest evidence for this view was the disproportionate rise of college education and specialist degrees among business leaders. Management job ladders in many, perhaps most major corporations, now began with college graduation, and getting into and graduating from college were seen as an important measure of merit. The most important factors in creating opportunity for capable individuals to gain access to leadership positions in business, therefore, was the enactment of the GI Bill and other programs that expanded access to higher education.

Most of the interest concerning career advancement and business, however, focused on what happened inside those organizations. Whether or not corporate career development arrangements allowed merit to rise to the top may depend on how one defines merit. Sophisticated selection tests—such as personality tests, interviews with psychiatrists, "in-basket" tests, and other work samples—rose in popularity and were used not only in hiring, but also in promoting. The stated goal of these tests, indeed of the entire selection process, was to identify merit. But the studies of corporate arrangements in this period, from Mills (1951) to Whyte (1956) to Kanter (1977), uniformly took the view that advancement criteria were dominated by factors other than individual merit, at least as defined by one's ability to perform a job. One's ability to fit in and conform to the dominant culture within each organization was arguably the central criterion.

To some extent, "fitting in" rising to the top of the list of criteria was an inevitable consequence of the epistemological problems associated with prediction that are known as "justification principles": How can one tell whether individuals will be able to succeed in tasks that they have never done before, doing activities that we cannot observe until they happen? One way is to choose an individual who seems to have the attributes of those who have succeeded before; hence, the pressures to conform in order to look like those who have been successful previously. Indeed, the mechanisms of internal selection may well have been the most important factor creating the conformity environment.

## Careers in the Present

There were some hints in the late 1970s that perhaps things were changing for executive careers.[2] But a number of studies suggest that the early 1980s represented a watershed moment for the U.S. economy, for corporations in particular, and for individual careers. In 1981, the worst recession since the Great Depression unleashed a massive wave of corporate restructuring. The rise of deregulation and global competition, especially in manufacturing (most prominently from Japan), greatly increased the pressure to improve quality and productivity while the growing power of institutional investors and the shareholder value movement increased the demands to improve financial performance. Together these forces contributed to a wave of corporate restructuring, and terms like "downsizing" and "reengineering" as well as record levels of mergers and acquisitions became a continuous part of the business landscape.[3]

By the 1990s, career paths became a topic of special interest because of concerns that downsizing was disrupting traditional patterns of advancement. Specifically, the apparent willingness to lay off white-collar workers and managers broke the old notions of lifetime job security in return for employee loyalty. Growing problems with employee retention in the 1990s suggested that employees had as little loyalty to their employers as the employers had shown them in the downsizing waves. The notion that careers should be thought of as spanning more than one organization, a concept called the boundaryless career Arthur and Rousseau 1996 is it Arthur and Rousseau [Let's keep it with them.], became popular in organizational psychology, although there was little evidence as to the extent to which this was actually happening and even less evidence that it was directed by the employees. A flurry of articles debated the issue of whether employee tenure was falling across the workforce as a whole (e.g., Neumark 2000), and there was some evidence that white-collar and managerial job tenure was declining faster than the overall tenure for the workforce. The extent to which internal development practices and associated career paths were eroding was also a topic for debate (e.g., see the exchange between Sanford Jacoby and Peter Cappelli in *California Management Review* 1999).

Partly because there is no single measure that can capture internal promotion and development practices, especially for the executive ranks, there is no simple measure with which to examine how individuals progress through organizational careers or to get at the more complex question of whether current arrangements are more or less meritocratic than these were in the past. Overall, we do have reasonably systematic studies of economic mobility in the United States. These studies suggest that inter-generational mobility—the extent to which our economic position in society differs from that of our parents—has declined relative to other countries and also relative to earlier periods in U.S. history, before World War II.

The recent research on mobility and career paths seems to have concentrated on lower-wage workers, perhaps because of the findings that labor market outcomes for lower-wage workers have worsened, especially relative to higher-income groups. Among the most important of these findings is that workers in the 1960s and 1970s had an easier time advancing economically than did those in more recent decades when job instability and insecurity became bigger problems (Bernhardt, Morris, Handcock, and Scott 2001). Even more telling is the finding about the paths that offered the greatest opportunity for low-wage workers to advance. They did better when they changed employers than when they stayed and tried to advance from within the same organization (Andersson, Holzer, and Lane 2005). Unfortunately, similar studies have not yet been conducted for middle- and upper-income workers. But we can look at several separate measures to get a sense of the extent to which their career paths have changed.

### Employee Tenure

The first of these measures, and one favored by labor economists, is employee tenure, the number of years an employee remains with the same employer. The debates in the 1990s about whether tenure has fallen appear to have faded, now that more recent

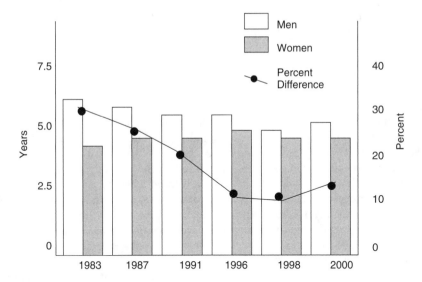

**Figure 12.1**    Median Tenure for Employed Men and Women 25 and Older, Selected Years, 1983–2000

*Source*:  Bureau of Labor Statistics.

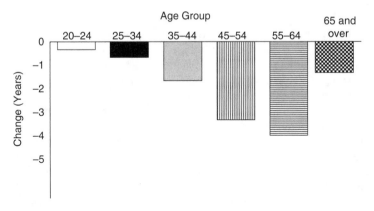

**Figure 12.2**    Change in Median Years of Tenure, 1983 to 1998, Adult Men by Age

*Source*:  Bureau of Labor Statistics.

data are available. Figure 12.1, drawn from the Current Population Survey of the Bureau of the Census, shows tenure dropping reasonably sharply for men. Tenure for women has not declined, however, possibly reflecting changes in legislation that make it easier for women to stay in their jobs when family responsibilities change as well as when there is greater economic necessity to do so.

Changes in tenure for men appear sharper when one examines the changes within age groups (see figure 12.2). Because older men quit jobs less frequently, the aging of the workforce over the past decade or so worked to *increase* tenure. Estimates for separate age groups controls for that fact. The striking point is that tenure is falling precisely among those older age groups that have historically had the highest attachment to their employers, especially the cohort just before retirement. Tenure is driven by both dismissals/layoffs and quits, so changes in tenure capture changes in the behavior of both employers and employees.

## Hiring Trends

Another aspect of career to examine is changes in hiring practices. In the period from *The Organization Man* through the 1970s, companies would hire trainees fresh out of college and provide them with education and development experiences to prepare them for managerial careers. One measure of change in these practices is the extent to which companies are willing to hire experienced workers, as opposed to new hires who are then developed internally for more advanced jobs. Tracking changes in the proportion of experienced workers hired is not easy to do. One measure is the rise of search and staffing firms, which tripled in revenue from 1993 to 1998; in the executive ranks, 53 percent of all vice-president level executive vacancies in the United States during 2004 had a retained executive search firm engaged to find an outsider to fill them (Cappelli and Hamori 2005a). Though not all these vacancies will ultimately be filled from the outside, before the 1980s, *any* outside hiring in the executive ranks was almost unheard of in large corporations.

The trend toward outside hiring is arguably most notable at the CEO level, in part because when CEOs turn over, other parts of the organization often change as well. In 2001, annual CEO turnover amounted to 9.2 percent, a 53 percent increase from 1995, while the average CEO tenure declined from 9.5 years to 7.3 years (Lucier, Spiegel, and Schuyt 2002). And more firms are going outside to find replacements. In a sample of 120 U.S. industrial corporations that are reasonably representative of publicly held companies (Ocasio 1999), the prevalence of outsider selection for CEO was approximately 25 percent. Murphy and Zabojnik (2004) reported that outsider CEOs represented 30 percent of all CEOs in the late 1990s.

An important development accelerating this development in outside hiring for lower-level and more traditional positions has been the rise of non-degree credentials that certify skills and proficiency in various technical areas. These credentials are typically issued by independent organizations outside the educational community and are most closely associated with information technology, where companies such as Microsoft and Cisco issue certifications for individuals who have completed training and demonstrated proficiency in the use of those systems. Literally millions of these credentials have now been issued, and unlike academic degrees, they are highly focused on actual job tasks (Adelman 1997).

Outside of the context of skilled trades, such credentials were essentially unheard of before the 1980s. The idea behind these credentials is to increase the ease with which individuals can move across organizations by certifying that the certified can perform with a high level of proficiency tasks that are central to all reasonably standard jobs. They have accelerated the movement toward something like professional labor markets for jobs that were previously seen as internal, technical functions.

Has anything changed since the 1950s with respect to the pressure to conform? It is of course difficult to say, but the National Survey in 1997 asked a nationally representative sample of employers about the criteria they used when selecting employees. Interestingly, information on a candidate's "attitude," a proxy for issues associated with personality and "fit," comes out at the top of the list (table 12.1).

**Table 12.1**   Selectivity Questions

After you have established your applicant pool and obtained information about potential [production or front-line job title] employees, what characteristics or attributes are most critical in making your hiring decision?

Please rank each method (5 = essential, 3 = important, 1 = no value).

| Item | Mean | Std. Dev. |
|------|------|-----------|
| Attitude | 4.40 | 0.78 |
| Full-Time Work Experience | 3.83 | 0.93 |
| After-School or Summer Work | 2.55 | 1.03 |
| Previous Job Performance | 3.99 | 0.96 |
| Industry Based Credentials | 3.33 | 1.23 |
| Communication skills | 3.80 | 1.03 |
| Education Level (Yrs. Completed) | 3.05 | 1.00 |
| School Reputation | 2.04 | 0.98 |
| Academic Performance | 2.52 | 1.06 |
| Technical Course Work | 2.79 | 1.14 |
| General Course Work | 2.38 | 0.95 |
| Extracurricular Activities | 2.11 | 0.97 |

*Source*: National Employer Survey, 1997.

### Forune 100 Executives

To examine the issue of how career paths have changed for executives, we collected information on the ten top executives from each of the *Fortune* 100 companies in 1980 and then again in 2001 (see Cappelli and Hamori 2005b for more details). We focused on these 100 corporations precisely because they are the largest and most stable corporations with the scale to manage internal employee development and career programs. This sampling frame stacks the deck against finding change, given that these are the companies most likely to be able to persist in the traditional, organizational career model. The companies in 2001 are significantly older, despite the apparent turmoil, restructuring, and business failures in the economy since 1980. They are also significantly bigger in financial terms. Total sales, for example, were more than four times greater. The differences in financial size cannot be accounted for by inflation over this period, which totaled only 115 percent. The average number of employees is greater only by about 34 percent.

The results shown in table 12.2 suggest some striking differences between the characteristics of executives in 1980 and 2001. (Significance levels for difference of means tests between the two periods are reported in column three.) First, there are more women in these executive positions in 2001—not a difficult achievement given that the number was zero in 1980. Eleven percent of the incumbents in these positions in 2001 are women who differ from their male counterparts in important ways (examined below). A more surprising change is that the average top executive is considerably younger in 2001—more than four years younger than in 1980. It is not immediately obvious why this should be the case.[4] Economic growth that might have pulled younger executives into the top ranks, for example, was not noticeably

**Table 12.2**  Human Capital Comparisons in 1980 and 2001 Samples

| | Year | N | Mean | Sign |
|---|---|---|---|---|
| Gender of Executive | 1980 | 801 | 1.00 | 0.000 |
| (1 = male) | 2001 | 1159 | 0.89 | |
| Age of Executive | 1980 | 704 | 56.04 | 0.000 |
| | 2001 | 705 | 51.90 | |
| Years of Schooling | 1980 | 726 | 17.02 | 0.000 |
| | 2001 | 802 | 17.26 | |
| *1st Degree Institution* | | | | |
| Public ( = 1) | 1980 | 728 | 0.32 | 0.000 |
| | 2001 | 778 | 0.48 | |
| Ivy League ( = 1) | 1980 | 728 | 0.14 | 0.017 |
| | 2001 | 778 | 0.10 | |
| *2nd Degree Institution* | | | | |
| Public | 1980 | 345 | 0.26 | 0.021 |
| | 2001 | 496 | 0.34 | |
| Ivy League | 1980 | 345 | 0.35 | 0.000 |
| | 2001 | 496 | 0.21 | |
| *3rd Degree Institution* | | | | |
| Public | 1980 | 38 | 0.29 | 0.832 |
| | 2001 | 74 | 0.27 | |
| Ivy League | 1980 | 38 | 0.21 | 0.592 |
| | 2001 | 74 | 0.26 | |

stronger during the careers of the 2001 executives (from roughly 1970 to 2000) than during the careers of the 1980 executives (1950 to 1980).

Average years of education for top executives are significantly higher in 2001, roughly in line with higher levels of education for the population as a whole over this period. (Median years of education are not significantly different, however.) But the nature of the schools that executives attended changed. In 1980, a full 14 percent of top executives in the *Fortune* 100 companies attended one of eight Ivy League institutions for their undergraduate education. Only 32 percent attended public or state-sponsored schools. Michael Useem and Jerome Karabel (1986) examined the educational background of 3105 *Fortune* 500 executives in 1977 and found some roughly similar results—11 percent had a first degree from one of top ten elite, private institutions, and about 22 percent had a second, professional degree (MBA or law degree) from one of these institutions. They found that holding a bachelor's degree from an elite institution increased the odds of becoming CEO by 42 percent.

In 2001, in contrast, only 10 percent of the equivalent executives received undergraduate degrees from Ivy League schools, and 48 percent attended public institutions. The percentage of executives who attended private, non–Ivy League institutions (that is, non-public and non-Ivy) fell sharply across the two periods, from 54 percent in 1980 to 42 percent in 2001. The rise in the number of public post-secondary graduates was not the result of an overall shift in graduates toward such schools.[5]

The results for second degrees suggest an even greater change. There is something of an increase in the proportion of second degrees among these executives by 2001, and the decline in the percentage of second degrees that came from Ivy League

**Table 12.3** Descriptive Statistics for Top Executives, 1980–2001 Full Sample

|  | Year | N | Mean | Std. Dev. | Sign |
|---|---|---|---|---|---|
| Lifetime Employees | 1980 | 749 | .53 | .499 | .001 |
|  | 2001 | 1099 | .45 | .498 |  |
| Time to the Top | 1980 | 735 | 28.38 | 6.52 | .000 |
|  | 2001 | 778 | 24.11 | 8.93 |  |
| Average Job Tenure | 1980 | 740 | 4.32 | 2.44 | .012 |
|  | 2001 | 771 | 3.99 | 2.62 |  |
| Average Promotion Size | 1980 | 802 | 1.10 | .91 | .004 |
|  | 2001 | 1160 | 1.25 | 1.21 |  |
| Number of Positions Held | 1980 | 761 | 5.76 | 2.27 | .000 |
|  | 2001 | 1104 | 5.04 | 2.60 |  |
| Organizational Tenure | 1980 | 742 | 20.63 | 10.94 | .000 |
|  | 2001 | 916 | 15.15 | 11.80 |  |

institutions was much greater than for first degrees. (Most of these degrees are MBA or law degrees, and there are only five Ivy League law schools and six MBA programs.[6])

Do these results suggest that corporations became less elitist and more open to students from all levels of society in this period? By 2001, graduates from public institutions had greater access to executive positions, especially individuals with advanced degrees. It is true that the Ivy League represented a smaller share of the population of graduates over time, especially in the exploding arena of professional degrees where the scale of Ivy League programs was particularly small, but that is not the case for all private colleges and universities. It is also true that the growing popularity of the MBA degree itself may allow for a different path into the corporation and its top ranks, this is quite contrary to how the degree was seen in earlier decades, when such degrees were relatively unknown. To the extent that top employers focus their recruiting of MBAs on the more elite schools, perhaps the system of recruitment is actually less open than otherwise.

Table 12.3 presents analyses concerning the employment history of these executives. There was a large and significant decline over this period in the percentage of top executives who spent their entire career at the same company—12 percentage points in the sample with complete career data, falling somewhat to eight points in the full sample. Average tenure for these executives in their current company, a related statistic, dropped between 1980 and 2001 by almost a full five years. Differences in median tenure are even sharper, dropping by seven and a half years.

Arguably the most important development above concerns the nature of the path to the executive suite. Average time taken to the top is significantly less in 2001 than in 1980, a result that is consistent with the younger age reported for executives in 2001. The reductions in time to the top do not necessarily lead to reductions in organizational tenure, however. The declines in organizational tenure appear to be larger than the declines in time taken to the top. The average amount of time these executives spent in each position was not that different in 2001 than it was in 1980—a little over four years. So the explanation for the more rapid promotion path of executives in 2001 is that they held fewer jobs on their climb up the corporate ladder. There were fewer stops along the way. And, as the data above indicate, the average size of a promotion was therefore bigger. These results are consistent with the perception that corporate hierarchies are flatter now with the result that the differences between positions in terms of responsibilities at each level are greater (e.g., Rajan and Wulf 2003). Moving at the same speed up a ladder with fewer steps means one gets to the top faster.

Because there were no women in the sample in 1980, it is possible to examine gender issues only within the 2001 sample. The manufacturing/service distinction is the only significant predictor of gender differences in the above analyses, with women being significantly more represented in the service sector. In additional analyses available on request, we explored how the experiences of executive women in 2001 were different from those of their male counterparts. They were significantly younger (47 years old vs. 52 for men), less likely to have been a lifetime employee (32 percent vs. 47 percent), they spent less time on average in each of their jobs (3.4 years vs. 4.0 years), and got to the executive ranks much more quickly (21 years vs. 25 years) than did their male counterparts. The corporations in which they are employed are not significantly different than average in terms of age or size. Nor can this result be attributed to differences in the level of jobs held by women executives.[7]

Because executives vary in the number of jobs they held, and there are considerable differences in the titles of jobs that each executive held, it is next to impossible to draw comparisons by job title. We can, however, compare the amount of time executives in 1980 spent in their first job—whatever its title—with the amount of time executives in 2001 spent in their first job, and so on over the course of their careers. The differences shown in figure 12.3 are statistically significant only for jobs 1 through 4 and job 12, but these results suggest that the 2001 pool of executives spent slightly more time in their initial jobs, then sharply less time in their fourth position (the modal title of which was "general manager") before moving on.

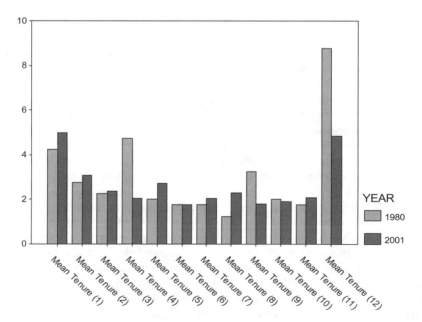

**Figure 12.3**    Tenure by Previous Job Title, 1980 and 2001

The Warner and Abbeglen figure of 50 percent, noted earlier for the proportion of executives who were lifetime employees in the 1950s, included lower-level executives from smaller companies, but it is only slightly less than the figure presented here for 1980. The average age of the executives in 1980 was 56, quite close to the Warner and Abbeglen estimate of 54, though again, the *Fortune* 100 executives were on average more senior in level, and that may explain the small difference. More important, average organizational tenure was very similar in the 1950s (24 years) to our estimate in 1980 (23.7 years in the restricted sample). These results suggest that career patterns may have been reasonably similar from the 1950s through 1980, suggesting that the post-1980 period may well represent an important breaking point in corporate careers. A contemporary study by Murphy and Zabonjnik (2003) of CEO turnover during this period found a pattern similar to our results. They found that the proportion of CEOs having been at their firm less than one year grew only slightly from 15 percent in 1970 to 17 percent in 1980 but then rose sharply to 25 percent by the 1990s.

### Summarizing the Changes

There is little doubt that careers and career paths have changed over time and that the "organization man" model of entry-level hiring of inexperienced workers followed by internal development and promotion from within has changed. Describing exactly how it has changed is more difficult, however, because there are few measures and little data that track the internal practices of employers with respect to career paths. There is little doubt, however, that attachment between employers and employees as measured by job tenure has declined. There is also little doubt that there is more outside hiring of experienced workers, the factor driving reductions in tenure. For executive jobs, we know that there is some increased openness in terms of educational credentials.

The biggest changes, however, seem to be associated with the climb to the top. Individuals get to the executive suite considerably faster and younger than in the past. They hold fewer jobs along the way up, and their careers seem to accelerate once they get through lower-level management. But they may not necessarily stay in those top jobs very long.

What do these results suggest overall about modern careers? For example, do careers now offer more freedom, do they allow individuals with more merit to get to the top more easily and more quickly? These are provocative and important questions that are difficult to answer with certainty. What we can conclude about modern careers is as follows.

First, modern careers have broken the attachment between employer and employee that we saw in previous generations. The decline of internal development and the sharp increase in outside hiring implies an important shift in the mechanisms that govern careers—away from bureaucracies and their internal rules and toward markets and competitive principles. In this context, labor markets are much better at giving more people greater access to opportunities than are bureaucracies, because the employment bureaucracies are limited to individual companies and, in many cases, restricted to functions or sub-areas. Individuals who are blocked from advancement in their own firms may nevertheless have the opportunity to advance somewhere else. Although markets potentially open opportunity to more individuals and more jobs, they require information to operate effectively. It is not clear whether helpful information is truly available about job openings and about the interests and abilities of individual job seekers in order to make better matches. Khurana's (2002) work on outside hiring for top-level executives, for example, suggests that the process is far from objective and efficient and that the players involved are subject to all kinds of biases. The bureaucratic practices of internal development created much more detailed information about potential candidates for promotion, although how well it actually predicted performance remains a subject of some debate.

The bureaucratic models used in employment in earlier periods were based at least in part on the ability to predict an individual's potential to do different jobs. The idea was to identify who could perform jobs before they were actually promoted into them. The outside hiring and market-based models are much less interested in predicting who can perform a new job. They focus very strongly on making matches between skills a candidate has already proved and jobs having requirements similar to these skills. The greater the overlap, the more likely from an employer's perspective that the match will be made.

Managers who aspire to top-level jobs no longer have to pass aptitude tests or fit into the culture of their current organization. But they somehow have to get the opportunity to shine through actual job performance. In summary, the outside hiring approach gives more people opportunity for more jobs that are reasonably similar to the ones they already have held; the internal bureaucratic models gave a few people opportunity to do a small number of jobs that represented significant advances in careers.

What we can say about opportunities inside organizations is less clear. The fact that more women get to the top and get there faster, for example, does seem to reflect greater openness of the corporate system, as does the fact that more public college and university graduates make it to top executive ranks. We cannot be sure why top executives get through the ranks faster now than in the past. It could be that those with more ability are pulled up more quickly. The fact that careers now seem to take off faster after about the fourth job may be consistent with that view. The fact that there is more turnover in the top ranks would seem to create more opportunity for replacements to be promoted. But because vacancies are filled increasingly from the outside, it is not clear whether those replacements have to come from the ranks of more junior workers. At the very least, putting in one's time no longer seems to be a necessary condition for advancement.

From the perspective of employers, it is worth speculating whether firms that "poach" talent away from competitors who do invest in developing employees will eventually force those competitors to give up on development or, at least, find a cheaper, alternative way to make those investments.

Part 3

# Organizational Effectiveness

# 13

# The Value of Innovative Human Resource Management Practices

## *Kathryn Shaw*

I n the last 30 years, there has been a dramatic change in firms' choices of human resource management (HRM) practices in that firms have moved toward what are often labeled "innovative" or "high-performance" practices. These new practices often include greater teamwork, greater participation by employees in decision making, more information sharing among employees, greater training and education, and, often, new forms of incentive pay to complement these changes. In fact, these new practices represent a "technology shock" that is similar to the "technology shock" of new information technologies.

In the case of information technology, firms have purchased new information technologies because new discoveries in computing technologies have lowered the price of computing and increased its uses. Similarly, firms have discovered the value of innovative HRM practices—they have discovered new ways of including teamwork and related practices that raise the performance of employees with the implementation of new HRM technologies. There is also a link between the new information technologies and HRM practices: The new information technologies are likely to facilitate investments in human resource practices that build teamwork and decision making.

The result of these new HRM technologies is that workers' performance levels have risen. Since 1995, labor productivity has risen dramatically in the United States: Previously (from 1973 to 1994) the rate of labor productivity grew at about 1.5 percent a year; since 1995 it has grown at about 2.5 percent a year. Using fairly aggregate data, researchers have shown that information technologies contributed to these productivity gains, but in addition they have suggested that a significant part of the productivity gains has been a result of the long-term introduction of new HRM practices (Jorgenson, Ho, and Stiroh 2002; Olinor and Sichel 2002). There is no time series data that might link HRM to other economic productivity gains.

In this chapter, we examine the possible increase in labor performance due to innovative HRM practices. To examine the effects of HRM performance, researchers must go inside firms and gather evidence from the firms on the organizational changes and performance outcomes. We show that some firms have certainly gained from new HRM practices. We also ask which firms gain the most from the adoption of new work practices, and why. Increased labor productivity translates into higher wage rates, and rising gross domestic product—or greater productivity—creates greater economic wellbeing in the United States. Thus, we ask what role government policies might play in facilitating firms' adoption of innovative HRM practices. We highlight two issues: first, that investment in education is crucial, and second, that we should begin to build new institutions within firms for valuing the investments in human capital or human resource practices.

## Technology Shocks

The evidence I present shows that firms began utilizing "innovative" HRM practices in the 1970s and that the trend continues. Here, the question that naturally arises is that if firms knew of the value of innovative HRM practices, why were these practices not adopted earlier? I argue that the value of these innovative practices was gradually discovered in the United States beginning in the 1970s.

### The Information Technology Shock

The IT "shock" is evident in the falling prices of computer products, a fall that led to higher investments in IT. Since 1980, the speed of microprocessors used in PCs has increased more than hundred-fold, so that the cost of performing one million instructions per second has fallen from $100 to less than 20 cents. The cost of a megabyte of hard disk storage has fallen from $100 in 1980 to less than 1 cent today. Data transmission has also skyrocketed, as fiber optics lowered the costs of sending one trillion bits of information from $120,000 to 12 cents from 1980 to 1999 (Council of Economic Advisers 2001).

The next effect of these performance gains per dollar of expenditure is that prices of computers and equipment fell constantly over time, and just recently fell by 71 percent between 1995 and 2000. Increased investments by firms followed. Use of the personal computer began in the early 1980s, with extensive power and very wide-spread use of developments coming in the 1990s, and computer investment acceler-ated to a 28 percent annual rate after 1995. Complementary investment in software also doubled in those years (rising from $10 billion in 1980, to $50 billion in 1990, to $225 billion in 1999), though the price of software fell by only 2 percent a year. While the huge investments in computing of the late 1990s were not sustained after the technology bubble burst, observers believe that strong investments will resume shortly.

### The HRM Technology Shock

Like IT, innovations in HRM practices over the last 30 years can be considered a "technology shock," though it is difficult to measure the size of the shock. Robert Cole (2000) described potential innovations in HRM practices as a shock to managers: Thirty years ago, the traditional U.S. system of HRM practices gave production work-ers very little problem-solving responsibility—but then the Japanese demonstrated that participatory practices could raise performance. Cole documented the huge gap in product quality in the United States relative to the Japanese in the 1970s and early 1980s and U.S. managers' eventual discovery that the technology of production had changed. Even though the need for innovative work practices was identified more than 30 years ago (O'Toole et al. 1973), some innovative firms took up the challenge immediately and adopted innovative HRM, but most moved slowly.

While firms choose slightly different sets of innovative HRM practices to suit their environment, the overall adoption of these innovative practices has increased over the last 30 years. Lawler, Mohrman, and Benson (2001) showed that very large *Fortune* 500 firms substantially increased their use of teams (or work groups) and of self-managed work teams—see figure 13.1. In these firms, these practices became more pervasive: From 1987 to 1999, the percent of large firms having more than 20 percent of workers participating in work groups rose from 37 percent to more than 60 percent, and the percent of firms having some workers participating in self-managed teams rose from 27 percent to more than 70 percent. While the survey does not go back to the early 1980s, earlier questions in other surveys on total quality management (which is the precursor to teams) suggest that these practices began to be adopted in the 1970s. Also note that over time these firms began training more for team skills as well (figure 13.1).

Firms also increased their use of incentive pay. Team-based incentive pay rose from 27 percent to 53 percent from 1987 to 1999 (figure 13.2, "Gainsharing"). The use of individual-based incentive pay became much more pervasive, as the percent of firms with more than 20 percent of the workforce having individual incentives rose from 38 percent to 68 percent. Increases also were widespread in the use of skill-based pay.

In the 1990s, across all types of establishments, including nonmanufacturing, there has been significant increase in the use of multiple innovative HRM practices. Using survey data of all types of establishments, Osterman (2000) found that from 1992 to 1997, the percent of establishments wherein at least half of the workforce utilizes two or more practices rose from 25 percent to 38 percent when he followed the same establishments.

In sum, a conservative assessment suggests that, prior to the 1970s, very few firms in the United States had HRM practices emphasizing employee involvement and incentive pay, but their use grew fairly steadily over the 1980s and into the 1990s. The

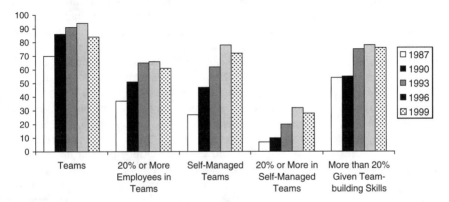

**Figure 13.1**    HRM Practices in Large Firms, Teams

*Sources*: Lawler, Mohrman, and Ledford 1995; Lawler, Mohrman, and Benson 2001.

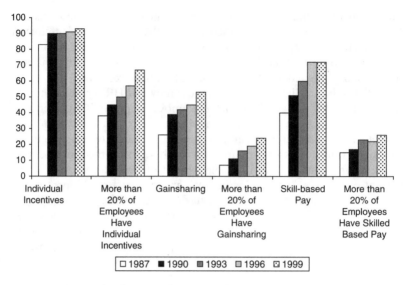

**Figure 13.2**   HRM Practices in Large Firms, Incentive Pay

*Sources*:  Lawler, Mohrman, and Ledford 1995; Lawler, Mohrman, and Benson 2001.

more widespread introduction of participation practices began in the early 1980s. By 1990 approximately half of all firms had some innovations, and since 1990 there has been variable, but continued, progress. Thus, to the extent that participatory or incentive-based HRM represents a technology innovation to managers, that shock began about 30 years ago and adjustments have occurred since then in the 1980s and into the 1990s.

*The Effects of Innovative HRM Practices: Improvements in Performance*

The typical firm that is utilizing innovative HRM practices is making an investment—an investment in changing HRM and in ongoing costs of maintaining practices. These investments should be rewarded, through greater productivity and higher stock-market valuations. To the casual observer, it is clear that stock-market value of firms is increasingly very different from their measured book values (or value of physical capital), and the evidence confirms this (Chan, Lakonishok, and Sougiannis 1999). The difference is likely to be the value of intangible capital that firms possess. As pointed out by Brynjolfsson, Hitt, and Yang (2002), Bresnahan, Brynjolfsson, and Hitt (2001), and Bresnahan and Greenstein (1996), when firms purchase new computers, the cost of the reorganization, redesigned monitoring, and worker incentive systems required to utilize the computers can be many times greater than the cost of the original capital. Many of these firms that invest in this organizational capital, such as innovative HRM practices, should and do earn market returns on their investments. Looking across firms, Brynjolfsson, Hitt, and Yang (2001) showed that the firms that adopt organizational changes have higher stock-market valuations, especially when these organizational changes are combined with information technology investments.

Thus, we have evidence that the market values of firms rise from organizational investments, but we would like to much better understand the causal link between HRM and firm performance and to understand which firms are likely to gain the most. To provide evidence on the extent and nature of the gains from innovative HRM practices, researchers must go deep within firms and over time gather data from the firms (called "insider econometrics" by Ichniowski and Shaw 2003). There are two sources of research evidence: industry-specific studies and data-based case studies of particular firms.

### Has Increased Use of New Human Resource Management Practices Improved Business Performance?

Research based on data from inside companies shows that adopting innovative HRM practices raises the production of high quality output and raises the productivity of workers in many firms. Consider the results from a series of studies of steel rolling mills and steel minimills. One study showed that quality output rose very significantly when innovative HRM practices were adopted. Using data from 36 steel rolling mills that produce flat-rolled steel, researchers showed that productivity rose when mills introduced a set of innovative HRM practices (Ichniowski, Shaw, and Prennushi 1997). Productivity is defined here as the percent of time the line is up and running or the "uptime" of the mill. When there was a move from traditional HRM practices to a set innovative practices, the uptime rose from about 88 percent to about 95 percent. Moreover, the amount of output that was of high quality rose.

When minimills introduced team-based problem solving, their production yield rose. Yield is defined as the percent of the output that is salable to the intended customer, with the average value 94 percent. The remaining 6 percent of output is scrap. A study of minimills followed 34 minimills over about five years (Boning, Ichniowski, and Shaw 2001). When minimills introduced teams (after incentive pay), their scrap rate fell by up to 20 percent.

One of the primary conclusions of these studies is that firms gain the most from innovative HRM practices when they adopt sets of complementary HRM practices. That is, in steel mills, for example, the mills with the largest gains in productivity simultaneously adopted problem-solving teams, incentive pay, increased training, information sharing, and job rotation. These practices are complements, because if teams are adopted, for example, then incentive pay is needed to reward their teamwork, and training and job rotation are necessary to facilitate it.

As shown in figure 13.2, firms have also increased their use of different forms of incentive pay. The introduction of incentive pay plans is likely to be aimed at performance gains. Productivity gains from incentive pay were shown to be very sizable in Lazear (1999). The gains come in part from workers' self-selection—those workers who would benefit the most from the incentive pay, because they are rewarded when they are most productive, are those who are attracted to firms that offer incentive pay plans.

Performance gains from teamwork go beyond productivity to include more responsive just-in-time production to meet customer demands. This is particularly evident in the apparel industry. Though the United States has lost much of its apparel production, firms that develop more team-based module production have raised the firm's performance by increasing its responsiveness to demand changes (Dunlop and Weil 1996; Appelbaum, Bailey, Berg, and Kelleberg 2000). Other industries that have seen a mixture of these gains are auto, machine tool industries, and those with call centers (MacDuffie 1995; Kelley 1994; Batt 1999). Thus, there is evidence within and across plants that innovative HRM practices raise performance.

Researchers in a number of European countries have had access to firm- or establishment- level data concerning HRM practices and performance. As in the U.S. studies, two main themes documented in intra-industry studies continue to gain support in these nationwide, cross-industry analyses of HRM practices and economic performance. First, firms tend to use multiple human resource management innovations. Second, new work practices, and more specifically interactions among new work practices, are associated with higher business performance. Overall, these conclusions apply based on research for Denmark (Eriksson 2001), Italy (Leoni, Cristini, Labory, and Gaj 2001), Great Britain (Fernie and Metcalf 1995; Michie and Sheehan 1999; Millward, Bryson, and Forth 2000), and France (Ballot, Fakhfaky, and Taymaz 2002; Greenan and Guellec 1998; Greenan and Mairesse 1999).

### The Effects of HRM Technology Shocks: Building Problem-Solving Capacity

One typical goal of innovative HRM practices is to move decision-making rights from managers to workers at lower levels in the organization. For example, Jensen and Mechling (1992) posited that firms should "co-locate" decision-making authority with employees who have the most relevant information.

The movement toward greater degrees of worker participation in decision making is likely to have grown over the last 30 years across all types of firms as a result of three changes. First, firms began to recognize that workers possess valuable information and skills at every level of the organization. For example, production workers possess information that engineers and supervisors themselves often lack. Second, the IT revolution resulted in two changes: All individuals now have more and equal information available to them at all levels, and communications are much more rapid and information intensive. These communications links and the availability of decentralized information have increased progressively over time, with the latest improvements arising from networking and extensive developments in within-firm intranets and the Internet for B2B and B2C communications. And third, in today's competitive environment, the competitive advantage of U.S. firms is often in the domain of producing niche products, or products that are R&D- or knowledge-intensive. In this environment, employees at all levels are required to undertake problem-solving activities: The days of producing commodities with cheap labor are gone, and the need for new innovations is greatly accelerated.

As a result of these changes, firms are making new investments in practices to enhance workers' performance—firms are building their internal "problem-solving capacity" (Gant, Ichniowski, and Shaw 2002; Ichniowski and Shaw 2005). An example would help us clarify the concept of problem-solving capacity. In the traditional steel mill, if a production worker recognizes a quality problem on the line, such as a surface defect in the new steel, he will call the foreman and report the problem. However, if the mill introduces innovative HRM practices, the production worker will have more knowledge of options for correcting the problem (due to his higher training level), and he will have up-to-date information as to whether the current customer would reject such steel. And he will have easy access to other production workers and staff so that he can gather the necessary knowledge to solve the problem.

Thus, problem-solving capacity is the capacity each individual worker has to solve problems by tapping into his coworkers' knowledge base (or into his social network). Firms build problem-solving capacity by encouraging their employees to build social networks or networks of experts to tap into.

Data from the steel industry provides quantitative evidence of these social networks, though such networks are widespread across industries. To look for differences in communications patterns in mills, a survey was conducted to measure each worker's communication links with all other workers as they work on the job (Gant, Ichniowski, and Shaw 2002). On those steelmaking lines with innovative human resource management systems, workers interacted with a majority of other line workers, both within shifts and across shifts. On steelmaking lines with traditional human resource management practices, workers interacted with a much smaller number of their peers or managers. Data on the individual communications patterns from within firms in the steel industry suggests that plants with more innovative HRM practices are raising their problem-solving capacity by increasing the communications network of their production employees.

### Investing in Innovative HRM Practices—Should All Firms Invest?

We have provided evidence that innovative HRM practices in some firms and industries raise workers' performance levels significantly. However, like all investments, the investments in innovative HRM practices certainly have different rates of return across firms and not all firms should invest equally in them.

#### *Who Should Invest in HRM?*

The average firm should find it increasingly advantageous to make investments in innovative HRM practices, for several reasons: On average, product quality and product customization have gone up over time in the United States, and innovative HRM practices are aimed at producing higher-quality or more complex products; greater information technology is complementary with problem-solving capacity, or HRM practices are likely to be complements; and as firms continue to discover the value of new HRM practices, they should raise investments in these practices independent of changes in product quality or IT.

Studies suggest that the value of innovative HRM is greater in environments that produce more complex products or more customized products. The minimills that gain the most from teams, and that adopt teams the most, are those that produce bar products that are the most complicated to make and that are higher priced (Boning, Ichniowski, and Shaw 2001). This result is intuitively appealing: Problem-solving is more valuable when the production environment faces greater problems due to its greater complexity or when output must be of the highest quality. Going across industries, Osterman (1994) in his establishment survey concluded that plants that are more likely to adopt innovative team practices follow a strategy that emphasizes product quality and service rather than low costs.

Many researchers have now emphasized the value of new HRM practices to complement firms' investments in IT. As Brynjolfsson, Hitt, and Yang (2002) stated, "A computer that is integrated with complementary organizational assets should be significantly more valuable to a business than a computer in a box on the loading dock." Using data on 1,216 firms from 1987 to 1997, they found that organizational practices are more likely to be adopted when new investments are made in computers, and that the combination raises productivity (Breshahan, Brynjolfsson, and Hitt 2001). Thus, if

IT raises the returns on HRM practices, then the greater investments in IT over the last 25 years could contribute to the greater adoption of innovative HRM practices. Overall, these studies suggest that the use of IT and HRM may be complements because IT raises the returns on HRM by providing the technology to facilitate decision making and that HRM changes enable workers to make the best use of the investments in IT.

### Why Do not More Firms Invest in HRM?

Differences across firms or plants in the long-run value of innovative HRM practices may explain why some firms adopt new practices and some do not, there may, however, also be transition costs that limit adoption. While 93 percent of large firms have some form of teamwork (Lawler, Morman, and Ledford 1999), only about 40 percent of all establishments use teams extensively for more than half of the workforce (Osterman 2000).

There are two forms of transition costs associated with new HRM adoption. First, workers and managers must invest in entirely new skills—workers invest in decision-making skills and managers invest in "coaching" or advisory skills. Workers and firms may be slow to undertake these investments. Second, complementarities between HRM practices or between IT and HRM practices can raise transition costs. The evidence suggests that systems of multiple innovative human resource practices should be utilized simultaneously to raise performance, and these HRM practices are often coupled with other management policies or with changes in IT to improve performance, such as the use of inventory management software and policies in auto assembly plants (MacDuffie 1995). The need to adopt systems of multiple practices, rather than individual practices, makes the up-front costs more sizable, and perhaps insurmountable, for some firms. For these reasons, new firms are far more likely to adopt innovative practices than old firms (Osterman 2000). As in the case of investing in equipment for plants, major changes in HRM must often be undertaken in new organizations.

## Changes in Labor Demand: Building
## Problem-Solving Capacity

The greater use of information technologies and of innovative human resource practices have resulted in continuous changes in the skills that firms want in workers. As recently as 30 years ago, the typical manufacturing job was one of largely manual labor, with little problem-solving discretion on the job. While there certainly are jobs in the United States that continue to be relatively unskilled, or that have de-skilled as a result of changes over time (such as cashier checkout jobs), many jobs have increased their skill demands.

Given the innovative HRM practices described above, employees are often expected to work in a team environment, to work smarter and to work harder, and to take greater responsibility in their day-to-day decision-making. To achieve these goals, the personal strengths that firms seek in hiring workers are "team skills" to cooperate and communicate well with others in a team setting, personal motivation and drive to respond to reward incentives such as pay and recognition; and desire to take on additional responsibility (perhaps in response to better rewards). Overall, firms want employees with a "can-do" attitude or the desire to make a difference. These features show up in the personal traits that firms look for in new employees.

If we look to the midpoint of the last three decades, back to the early 1990s, we see that problem-solving skills and attitudes were ranked more important than education when the typical firm stated its hiring criteria. Black and Lynch (1996, 266) asked establishments to rank on a scale of one to five (five most valuable) each of their criteria in hiring.

As the applicant's attitude, communications skills, and experience are considerably more important than education. Of course, in highly skilled occupations, meeting the education standard is a basic requirement before the person is considered even for an interview.

New research shows that in the United States, job growth over the last 30 years has been in occupations that require nonroutine cognitive skills. Using CPS data and information on required skills from the Dictionary of Occupational Titles, Autor, Levy, and Murnane (2002) measure the demand for different skill types, showing that the demand for nonroutine cognitive skills has risen over time. Jobs that require routine behavior, such as processing checks, or checking a car's electrical system, or checking the surface quality in flat-rolled steel, or inspecting a final valve produced, can all be accomplished by computers. Moreover, even quite sophisticated jobs can be done by computers, take for example computer tools used to check for bugs in a newly written computer program. Thus, there is less demand for jobs that are routine, because routine jobs can be computerized.

However, there is greater demand for skills that are nonroutine cognitive skills. On the production line, if one operator discovers poor surface quality in the steel production, a team of operators and engineers will get together to solve the problem. Or similarly, after a software development "tool" discovers a programming problem, the programmer or a group of programmers solve the problem. Thus, there has been an increase in the demand for nonroutine problem solving (or cognitive) skills, at all levels of the educational spectrum.

Even though running a steel mill requires a high school degree and software development requires a college degree, both jobs require problem-solving skills. And problem-solving skills reflect a set of personal traits: basic math and English skills, a good attitude toward wanting to solve problems, the ability to communicate with others and work together. Moreover, this increase in demand for cognitive skills is correlated with the use of new technologies. In a different study, one that identifies the underlying skill distribution of workers, Abowd, Haltiwanger, Lane, and Sandusky (2001) also showed that demand for cognitive skills has risen. And finally, industry studies containing detailed descriptions of hiring changes in workplaces that adopt new technologies add corroborating evidence of a connection between new work practices and an increased demand for problem-solving skills (Bartel, Ichniowski, and Shaw 2001; Autor, Levy, and Murnane 2001; Appelbaum, Bailey, Berg, and Kalleberg 2000; Holzer 1996).

## Policy Implications

The results above suggest that what employers look for most in employees today is the ability to solve problems, to work cooperatively, and to have a positive "can-do" attitude toward work. Today these are the basic hiring traits needed for jobs ranging from steel mill operators to software programmers. These characteristics reflect the changes that have taken place in our economy—the movement toward innovative HRM practices to raise performance, the higher performance standards to produce customized and quality products that are now the key to U.S. economic growth, and the greater use of information technologies on the job.

The question is, should government policy be involved in facilitating companies' move toward innovative HRM practices? Levy and Murane (2004) offer an extensive policy discussion. We address two topics—education and company valuation. Where should the government focus its tax dollars for education? For numerous reasons, the government subsidizes education because education is a clear public good that would have too low an investment rate if left to individuals, so in order to see where the government should be focusing their subsidies, we look to see where the returns on education are highest.

### The Investment in Human Resources: Investing in Basic Education

The highest return on education expenditures is in spending on early education. As described in Carneiro and Heckman (2002), the rate of return on education, as measured by income gains from education, tends to fall with increases in education—the return on education is highest for preschool or early elementary and falls over time. This means, for example, that programs to improve the skills of high school dropouts are rarely successful from a cost-benefit angle. High school dropouts may choose to complete high school by passing a series of tests to receive a GED, a degree equivalent to high-school. Though about 15 percent of all high school degrees granted today are GED degrees, the research shows that those achieving a GED do not earn higher wages than high school dropouts who have the same basic ability. Similarly, the income gains from postschool training, such as job training programs, are lower than the gains per dollar invested from preschool educational investments. Therefore, when compared with the opportunity cost of investing, it is clear that optimal investment levels are very high for early education and fall from there on.

The greater use of innovative HRM practices and problem-solving skills increases the return on early education that Carneiro and Heckman described. The skills that tend to be taught in the early years, such as reading, math, communications, and interpersonal relations, are those skills that are particularly valuable in firms with innovative HRM practices. Moreover, studies in child development emphasize that there are lifecycle patterns to effective learning, and that cognitive skills are best taught early in the educational lifecycle (Carneiro and Heckman 2002, 27). These are the general skills that are very valuable and that are very difficult to teach later in life. Note also that the often stated quote "good families produce good children" implies that programs aimed at family or parental support frequently have indirect benefits in raising the standard of the children and the quality of their educational outcomes.

Furthermore, note that the data show that some noncognitive traits, such as motivation, can be instilled later in the high school years through, for example, mentoring programs for teenagers. But most training programs for adults or teens inadequately address the need for these noncognitive skills or traits.

In the United States, there is rising investment in higher education and less in elementary education. The investments in "basic skills" have been declining over time in the United States, and overall there is increasingly a bimodal distribution to investments in human capital.[1]

The data show that once GED degrees are subtracted from the measure of annual high school graduation rates, the numbers of high school graduates is trending down over time. The United States is now producing a greater fraction of low-skill dropout youth than it was 30 years ago, even though it is these basic skills that are necessary to obtain the higher-wage, higher-performing jobs at all education levels.

Finally, firms are unlikely to teach basic skills to their employees for several reasons. When we look at data on training done within firms, we see first that the majority of training is of an informal nature, and thus it would not produce basic skills training (Lowenstein and Spletzer 1999). Second, most of the training dollars go to the better-educated workers, who are learning how to do very specific jobs. Even among newly hired workers, most of the formal and informal training goes to those who have higher levels of education (above high school). Thus, workers with more sophisticated tasks get more training, and these are workers who are already likely to have the necessary basic skills, such as math, reading, and verbal skills. Third, these basic skills are very "general" skills, ones that are not specific to the firm, and firms have no incentive to invest in skills that workers can take with them when they quit for higher pay elsewhere. When firms do train in skills that are valuable to other firms [and 70 percent of all firms believe that most of their training is in largely general skills (Barron, Berger, and Black 1999, 282)], the skills tend to be very specific to the occupation, and not "basic" in nature.[2]

In sum, the basic skills, those that are likely to have the biggest returns in the labor market, must be taught in school. The estimated return-on-investment is in the range of 17–20 percent (Carniero and Hechan 1999, 23). The evidence on hiring and screening patterns corroborates this conclusion: Firms increasingly search for workers who have the basic skills; firms do not hire less-skilled workers and then train them. To prosper and compete, firms need well-educated workers at every level.

### The Investment in Human Resources:
### Investing in Higher Education

Given the adequate funding for basic education, the next priority is higher education. In the last 30 years, the returns that an individual earns by investing in college have increased dramatically. There is a very extensive literature documenting the rising incomes of the college-educated relative to the less educated and the possible reasons for it over the last 30 years (Autor and Katz 1999).

The question is, how much should government subsidize higher education? Note that individuals have their own rewards for attending college—students take out college loans because they see that they will earn a huge return on that investment. Thus, to some degree, the government can stay out of the market for higher education. However, individuals are liquidity constrained, especially lower income individuals: Banks are reluctant to offer loans to people for their investment in human capital because there is no collateral backing their loans. To counter this problem, the federal loan programs provide the needed collateral by offering loan guarantees to banks that offer student loans. The rising pay premium for college over the last 30 years suggests that tax dollars spent on loan guarantees are offering increasingly higher rates of return. Thus, we return to our original point: Innovative HRM practices require more problem-solving at all occupational levels.

College degrees are valued today because they do two things: They offer concrete skills (in highly skilled occupations such as scientific research and marketing to produce new innovative products), and they increase the amount of problem-solving that workers can do at the highest level. Both are highly valued today. Moreover, studies show that the demographic groups that have increased their educational levels in recent years in response to higher wage returns on education are predominately white and middle-income—youths coming from lower-income households have been responding more slowly to the wage returns on education, and thus the income gap between households is growing. There is a need for continued government subsidies to higher education in the form of loans and grants to students, particularly low-income students.

### The Investment in Human Resources: Valuing the Investment

Due to the intangible and unmeasurable nature of investments in HRM practices, it is possible that firms are underinvesting in these practices relative to more tangible investments, such as physical capital or research and development (R&D). As was described above, firms that invest in greater organizational practices, such as innovative HRM practices, earn higher stock-market returns. When firms adopt innovative HRM practices, we describe it as an investment that should earn a return over the long run. However, unlike the investments in physical capital or R&D, firms typically do not measure their investments in human resources.

Most firms do not know how much they spend on training programs—formal as well as informal—and certainly do not measure what they spend on other HRM practices. However, firms are constantly trying to signal to the stock market that the firm is making these HRM investments—they advertise their reorganizations or new practices so the market will decide how to value them. In the case of physical investments, the cost of the investment is measured, and then the market decides how to value the expected returns. With HRM practices, the costs are not measured and are hard to display. Thus, firms may well underinvest.

Moreover, a second reason for underinvestment is that internal resource allocation undervalues HRM investments. There is a well-known statement: What gets measured gets managed. When firms do not measure their HRM investment expenses or returns, they are more prone to misallocating resources in one area relative to another.

Since most agree that knowledge capital is critical to the U.S. competitive advantage, firms are seeking ways of valuing their intangible investments. For example, the Balanced Scorecard has that aim (Kaplan 1992) for internal valuation. Another accounting development is that of "structural capital," in which the value of intangible capital is imputed from sales and expenditures data (Lev 2002) with the goal of measuring organizational capital such as managerial processes.

Thus, firms are seeking ways of measuring their investments in HRM practices and earning returns to these investments. Firms have an incentive to invest in the measurement of intangibles—to allocate internal resources more wisely and to signal to investors—but no one firm earns the full returns to developing new systems of reporting intangible investments. In the short run, consulting firms and academics have been developing ways of valuing intangibles that firms use and value. In the long run, the government regulations may play a role in the structuring of new accounting methods for intangibles.

## Conclusion

There is now an increasing body of evidence, based on research using data from within firms, that investments in innovative HRM practices raise workers' performance levels. These HRM practices—practices such as teamwork, new forms of incentive pay, information sharing, training, careful screening and hiring, and job rotation—are often adopted simultaneously within firms to form complementary systems of HRM practices that enhance performance.

Of course, some investments are best left to individuals, not firms. As described above, investment in general skills, such as basic education that is valued across employers, should be undertaken by individuals (with some government subsidies). There are many firm-specific skills, including the investments in new technologies (such as new programming tools) that firms are undertaking. When these are for specific skills, firms are constantly seeking ways of verifying and displaying their returns on investment.

Given the evidence of the value of innovative practices for some firms, two questions remain: Which are the firms that gain from innovative practices, and why do they gain? The evidence suggests that firms benefit from innovative HRM practices for two reasons: The practices raise the opportunity for problem-solving, and they raise the value of problem-solving with new forms of incentive pay. Thus, the empirical evidence suggests that the firms most likely to gain from innovative HRM practices are either those that produce high-quality or highly complex products, or those that are also making investments in new information technologies. Both environments are likely to benefit from the greater problem-solving skills and incentives that innovative HRM practices generate.

There are two sets of potential government educational policies that support the firms' use of innovative HRM practices. First, the investment in basic education—in reading, math, and problem solving at the elementary and secondary level—is a public good that earns long-term returns and enables firms to utilize innovative HRM practices requiring workers with these basic skills. Second, firms and markets are now placing greater value on highly skilled knowledge workers, and government support for higher education—particularly loans for lower-income families—will continue to earn a high return.

# 14

# The Economic Impact
# of Employee Behaviors on
# Organizational Performance

*Wayne F. Cascio*

Consider a recent quote from the *Wall Street Journal* (July 14, 2003): "It's no longer about what you own or build; success is hinged to the resources and talent you can access." Unfortunately, recent statistics indicate that American workplaces are not doing a very good job of managing the talent they currently have. Thus

- Only 14 percent of American workers say they are very satisfied with their jobs.
- Twenty-five percent say they "are just showing up to collect a paycheck" (The Stat 2005).
- From January 2004, to January 2005, 24 percent of American workers voluntarily quit their jobs, a 13 percent rise since the previous year. That figure varies widely by industry, though, with relatively low rates in manufacturing and transportation (roughly 15 percent), and relatively high rates in leisure and hospitality, retail, and construction industries (ranging from about 25–45 percent) (Employment Policy Foundation 2005). To appreciate what that means for an individual firm, consider the number of people Wal-Mart employed at the end of 2004—1,600,000 people (*Fortune* 500, 2005). Its annual employee turnover rate is 44 percent—close to the retail industry average (Frontline 2005). *Each year*, therefore, Wal-Mart must recruit, hire, and train more than 700,000 new employees just to replace those who left.
- Women now outnumber men in managerial and professional jobs, yet many leave even blue-chip employers because they do not feel valued, their companies do not offer flexible-employment policies, or their work is not intellectually challenging. Rather than leave the workforce, most resurface at companies that offer more progressive policies (Deutsch 2005).
- The fully loaded cost of replacing a worker who leaves (separation, replacement, and training costs), depending on the level of the job, varies from 1.5 to 2.5 times the annual salary paid for that job (Cascio 2000). Historically, for example,

in 1914, when the prevailing wage was $2.34 per day, Henry Ford offered his assembly-line workers $5 per day. Why? Because employee turnover of 370 percent meant hiring almost 50,000 people a year just to maintain a workforce of 14,000 (Useem 2005)!

In fact, the behavior of employees has important effects on the operating expenses of organizations in both the private and public sectors of our economy. These effects are not widely known, or even, in some cases, appreciated by employers, but they are, nonetheless, very real. In this chapter we consider some key areas where the behavior of employees has a meaningful financial impact on their organizations. The areas we will examine—the effects of high- versus low-wage employment strategies on employee turnover and productivity; employee retention; absenteeism and presenteeism; healthcare costs associated with unhealthy lifestyles; employee attitudes; payoffs from training through development programs; and payoffs from the use of valid staffing procedures—are by no means exhaustive. Rather they are representative of those that most employers encounter. Thereafter we consider some policy implications for employers, as they seek to reduce costs or increase the payoffs associated with managing people wisely. Let us begin by considering the competitive employment strategies of two well-known retailers, Costco and Wal-Mart's Sam's Club.

## Financial Impacts of Employee Behavior

### Costco Versus Sam's Club: A Tale of Two Employment Strategies

Material in this section comes from an in-depth investigation by *Business Week* (Holmes and Zellner 2004).

In 2004, Costco employed 68,000 workers, one-fifth of whom are unionized, while Sam's Club employed 102,000. In terms of wages alone, a Costco employee earned, on average, $33,218 ($15.97 per hour). The average Sam's Club employee earned $23,962 ($11.52 per hour). If a Costco employee quits voluntarily, the fully loaded cost to replace him or her is about $49,827 (1.5 times annual salary). If a Sam's Club employee leaves, the cost is $35,943.

At first glance it may look as if the low-wage strategy at Sam's Club yields greater savings in turnover. But wait! Employee turnover at the end of the first year of employment is only 6 percent per year at Costco (4,080 employees), while it is 21 percent a year at Sam's Club (21,420 employees). The total cost to Costco is therefore $49,827 × 4,080 = $203,290,000, while the total cost to Sam's Club is $35,943 × 21,420 = $769,900,000. Costco's opportunity savings (costs not incurred) thus exceed $566 million *per year*! Of course, the overall costs and numbers of employees who leave at Sam's Club is higher, because it employs more people to begin with. Averaged over the total number of employees at each firm, however, the per-employee cost at Costco is about $300, while that at Sam's Club is about $755. High employee-turnover rates are expensive any way you look at it.

Wages are not the only distinguishing characteristic between the two retailers. At Costco, 82 percent of employees are covered by the company's healthcare insurance plan, with the company paying an average of $5,735 per worker. Sam's Club covers 47 percent of its workers, at an average annual outlay of $3,500. Fully 91 percent of Costco's employees are covered by retirement plans, with the company contributing an average of $1,330 per employee, versus 64 percent of employees at Sam's Club, with the company contributing an average of $747 per employee.

In return for all of its generosity, Costco gets one of the most loyal and productive workforces in all of retailing. While Sam's Club's 102,000 employees generated some $35 billion in sales in 2003, Costco generated $34 billion with one-third fewer employees. As a result, Costco generated $13,647 in its United States operating profit per hourly employee, compared to $11,039 at Sam's Club. Labor and overhead costs at Costco were 9.8 percent of sales, versus an estimated 17 percent of sales at Sam's Club. By comparison, it was 24 percent at Target Stores. Costco's motivated employees also sell more: $795 of sales per square foot, versus only $516 at Sam's Club, and $411 at BJ's Wholesale Club, its other primary club rival.

These figures illustrate nicely the common fallacy that labor rates equal labor costs. Costco's hourly labor rates are almost 40 percent higher than those at Sam's Club ($15.97 versus $11.52), but when employee productivity is considered (sales per employee), Costco's labor costs are significantly lower (9.8 percent vs. 17 percent). As Costco CEO James Sinegal put it: "Paying your employees well is not only the right thing to do, but it makes for good business."

To make its high-wage strategy pay off, however, Costco is constantly looking for ways to increase efficiency, such as by repackaging goods into bulk items to reduce labor, speed up Costco's just-in-time inventory and distribution system, and boost sales per square foot. Nor have rivals been able to match Costco's innovative packaging or merchandising mix. Costco was the first wholesale club to offer fresh meat, pharmacies, and photo labs.

Defenders of Wal-Mart's low-wage strategy focus on the undeniable benefits its low prices bring to consumers. But the broader question is this: Which model of competition will predominate in the United States? While shareholders may do just as well with either strategy over the long run, it is important to note that the cheap-labor model is costly in many ways. It can lead to poverty and related social problems and transfer costs to other companies and taxpayers, who indirectly pay the healthcare costs of all the workers not insured by their frugal employers.

If a large number of employers adopted the same low-wage strategy, their policies would certainly reduce the wages of U.S. workers, along with their standards of living. Such a low-wage strategy also would crimp consumer spending and constrict economic growth. Costco's strategy, in contrast, shows that with innovative ideas and a productive workforce, consumers, workers, and shareholders all can benefit.

*Financial Payoffs from Employee Retention*

The flip side of employee turnover is employee retention. It is a major issue for employers as varied as Farmers Insurance Group, S. C. Johnson, and Walt Disney World, especially as labor markets tighten. To illustrate the effect of improved employee retention on the bottom line, and on a company's stock price, let us consider SYSCO Corporation of Houston, Texas. SYSCO is the number one food service marketer and distributor in North America. In 2004, its revenues exceeded $29 billion, it employed almost 48,000 people, and it served 420,000 customers with approximately 300,000 different products. SYSCO is composed of 147 operating companies, each of which serves a geographic area.

Approximately 75 percent of SYSCO's operating costs are people-related, at an annual cost of roughly $3 billion. Its marketing associates alone number about

10,000. Imagine the financial impact on the company if it improved its retention rate among marketing associates from 70 percent to 80 percent. Using a conservative estimate of the cost of employee turnover of $50,000 per marketing associate, SYSCO found that a 10 percent improvement in retention resulted in more than $70 million of savings *per year*. Since 1998, SYSCO has increased its marketing associates' retention rate from 70 percent to 82 percent.

Next consider delivery associates, who are very critical to SYSCO's success because they know the customers and are the people whom the customers rely on to get their groceries to them on time and in good condition. To do that, the company needs to have the same person delivering groceries to the same customer on a regular basis. SYSCO was able to increase the retention rate of its delivery associates from about 65 percent in 1998 to 85 percent in 2004 (a 31 percent improvement). Human resource (HR) professionals found the training and hiring loss for a delivery associate to be about $35,000. That 20 percent improvement represents almost another $50 million in annual savings. For SYSCO investors, every $5 million represents a penny per share, so the improved retention of delivery associates alone represents about 10 cents per share (Carrig, 2004). In 2004, SYSCO reported a 39 percent return on the average shareholders' equity (http://www.SYSCO.com/annual report).

How did SYSCO produce such impressive results in employee retention? Among other things, it began to measure characteristics of the work environment on a regular basis, and then it helped operating companies with low ratings to improve. More specifically, employees of each operating company periodically complete a "work climate survey" that assesses seven dimensions related to employee satisfaction. These are leadership support, front-line supervisor, rewards, quality of work life, engagement, diversity, and customer focus.

Through statistical analysis, the company was able to demonstrate that operating companies with highly satisfied employees delivered systematically better results in terms of improved customer loyalty, higher pretax operating income, lower operating costs, and improved retention of drivers, marketing associates, and night-warehouse employees. Then it developed a "best-practices" database, so, for example, an operating company in Atlanta that might be experiencing high turnover among marketing associates could learn from an operating company in Dallas that might be a leader in retaining marketing associates.

SYSCO's experience is typical of many contemporary organizations, in that more and more of its asset value rests in its human capital. To prosper and grow, organizations need to be able to retain current employees and to attract a steady supply of new ones. To accomplish both of those objectives, they need to develop an employer brand that attracts the right kind of applicants.

So we have shown that the financial impact of employee retention is significant. At a broader level, however, at least some employers might ask, "Why should we worry about retention?" One reason is that supply/demand imbalances in many types of jobs are building. A recent report from the Society for Human Resource Management estimates that by 2012, the U.S. economy will experience a 33 percent shortfall of degreed candidates—approximately six million graduates fewer than expected to fill new jobs and to replace retirees. Beyond that, consider these survey results (Collison 2005):

- Only 9 percent of organizations rate their retention efforts as highly successful.
- Despite company rhetoric to the contrary, only 35 percent of U.S. workers truly believe that their performance has a significant impact on their pay increases.
- Fully 55 percent of employees think of quitting or plan to quit within a year.

As if these results were not alarming enough, consider the impending exodus from the full-time workforce of baby boomers, along with their experience and know-how. To be sure, the majority of baby boomers say they want to continue to work, at least part-time (Coy and Brady, 2005), yet there are solid reasons why every employer should be looking for ways to increase retention now. At the conclusion of this chapter we examine what some of those ways might be.

In the meantime, let us consider several other areas where the behavior of employees has an important, economically significant effect on financial outcomes. The first of these is employee absenteeism and presenteeism.

### The Financial Impact of Employee Absenteeism and Presenteeism

From a business standpoint, absenteeism is "any failure of an employee to report for or to remain at work as scheduled, regardless of reason" (Cascio 2000). The term "as scheduled" is very significant, for it automatically excludes vacations, holidays, jury duty, and the like. It also eliminates the problem of determining whether an absence is "excusable" or not. Medically verified illness is a good example. From a business perspective, the employee is absent and is simply not available to perform his or her job; that absence will cost money. How much money? In 2003, the cost of unscheduled absences in U.S. workplaces was about $800 *per employee per year* (Demby 2004). For every 100 employees, that is $80,000.

Surprisingly, the leading causes of absenteeism are family-related issues (e.g., lack of childcare alternatives, eldercare responsibilities) (Onsite childcare 2003; Parkes 1987). Personal illness, the reason one might expect to be the main justification for calling in sick, is actually true only in about one in five cases. Other causes are personal needs (about one in five cases), stress (about one in six cases), and entitlement mentality (about one in six cases).

It is also important to note that for some organizations, or business units, absenteeism may be a nonissue. Specifically, if employees can vary their work time to fit their personal schedules, if they need not "report" to a central location, and if they are accountable only in terms of results, then the concept of "absenteeism" may not have meaning. Many teleworkers fit this category.

On the other hand, workers who come to work sick, when they should stay home instead, cost their employers an average of $255 per year in reduced productivity due to "presenteeism." Presenteeism refers to slack productivity from ailing workers (Goetzel et al. 2004). It often results from employees showing up but working at sub-par levels due to chronic ailments (Rubinstein 2005). For example, the estimated productivity loss associated with depression is 6.4 percent. It is 4.9 percent for arthritis, and 3.2 percent for obesity. In the aggregate, economists estimate that presenteeism costs U.S. businesses $180 billion annually. The next section examines the broader issue of the relationship between lifestyle choices and healthcare costs.

### Linking Unhealthy Lifestyles to Healthcare Costs

A four-year study of 15,000 Ceridian Corporation employees showed dramatic relationships between employees' health habits and their insurance-claim costs. For example, people whose weekly exercise was equivalent to climbing fewer than five flights of stairs or walking less than half a mile spent 114 percent more on health claims than those who climbed at least 15 flights of stairs or walked 1.5 miles weekly.

Healthcare costs for obese workers were 11 percent higher than those for thin ones, and workers who routinely failed to use seat belts spent 54 percent more days in the hospital than those who usually buckled up.

Finally, people who smoked an average of one or more packs of cigarettes a day had 118 percent higher medical expenses than nonsmokers (Jose, Anderson, and Haight 1987). Rockford Products Corp., which makes metal parts used in items from Caterpillar earthmovers to yo-yos, combed through 15 years of records and found that 31 out of 32 workers who had heart attacks or required major heart surgery—including two who keeled over in the factory—were smokers (Aeppel 2003). Results like these may form the basis for incentive programs to both improve workers' health habits and reduce employees' contributions to health insurance costs or increase their benefits.

A recent analysis revealed that for an individual employee a healthier lifestyle could mean a personal saving of as much as $7,868 *per year* (Andrews 2004). Here is how.

1. *Stop smoking.* A pack-a-day smoker could save $1,460 per year in cigarette costs, plus $1,623 per year in excess medical costs relative to nonsmokers, according to the Centers for Disease Control and Prevention.
2. *Lose weight.* On average, an obese person spends $900 more per year in medical expenses than a person of normal weight. In addition, regular-size clothing is 10 to15 percent cheaper than "plus-size" or "big and tall" clothes. This accounts for an estimated additional savings of $200 per year.
3. *Drink no-fat, no-frills coffee.* A five-cup-a-week drinker will save $520 per year (and more than 300 calories per serving) by drinking basic black, brewed coffee instead of caramel Frappuccino blended coffee with whipped cream served at a coffee shop.
4. *Requalify for life insurance.* Healthy people pay lower premiums. For example, a 45-year old with healthy levels of blood pressure, weight, and cholesterol will pay $770 per year for a $500,000, 20-year term life insurance policy through The Hartford. A less healthy, nonsmoking counterpart will pay $1,385. Smokers who quit will see their $3,735 annual premiums drop by 63 percent.
5. *Use employer incentives.* For example, Blue Shield of California pays $200 to members who successfully complete a 35-week online program that includes exercise, nutrition, stress-management, and smoking-cessation support.

Of course, savings for individual employees also translate into savings for companies (Epstein 1989; Terborg 1998; Wellness plans 2000). Yet there is much that companies themselves can do to encourage healthier lifestyles among employees, from educating employees about health- risk factors, to serving healthier food in company cafeterias and vending machines, to instituting work/life programs to reduce stress levels among employees (Halpern and Murphy 2005; Kahn and Byosiere 1992). How much can employers expect to gain from these efforts? Johnson & Johnson Health Management, Inc., which sells wellness programs to companies, estimates that fully 15 to 25 percent of corporate healthcare costs stem from employees' unhealthy lifestyles (Hirschman 2003).

In light of these potential savings, some companies preempt excess healthcare costs by imposing additional charges or by not hiring those with unhealthy lifestyles in the first place. For example, Rockford Products imposes a $50 per month fee on employees who smoke, are obese, or suffer from hypertension (Aeppel 2003). Turner Broadcasting will not hire smokers. Multi-Developers will not hire anyone who engages in what the company views as high-risk activities: skydiving, piloting a private aircraft, mountain climbing, or motorcycling.

Federal civil rights laws generally do not protect individuals against "lifestyle discrimination" because smokers and skydivers are not named as protected classes. However, more than half of all states prohibit termination for various types of off-duty conduct (e.g., use of tobacco products). There is no right or wrong answer here. Perhaps the best advice is for each company to develop its own policy in a manner that is consistent with its values.

Why should employers worry about what their employees do? To put that issue into perspective, consider that from 1999–2004 the average increase in health insurance premiums among U.S. employers was 32 percent. In 2004, employers paid an average of 79 percent of those healthcare premiums (Fuhrmans 2004). Over time, costs like these make companies less competitive in global markets, as the U.S. auto industry illustrates. Until it modified its plans in late 2005, General Motors spent about $1,784 per vehicle just for retiree pension and healthcare costs, compared with less than $200 per vehicle for Toyota. Together, GM, Chrysler, and Ford have 524,000 hourly worker retirees. Toyota has 49 (Colvin 2003). (Toyota has not had U.S. facilities long enough to build a sizable number of retirees.) Without those costs the American companies could cut prices or offer better cars, either of which would make them far more competitive with Toyota.

## The Financial Impact of Employee Attitudes

Employee turnover or employee retention are by no means the only areas where enlightened human resource management policies can pay off. As just one example, consider an in-depth study conducted by the Gallup Organization, the Princeton, New Jersey–based polling and research firm (Micco 1998). Gallup identified 12 worker beliefs (measures of employee satisfaction/engagement) that play the biggest role in triggering a profitable, productive workplace. Its multiyear study was based on an analysis of data from more than 100,000 employees in 12 industries. A subsequent meta-analysis (quantitative cumulation of research results across studies) included data from almost 8,000 business units in 36 companies (Harter, Schmidt, and Hayes 2002).

Analysis showed a consistent, reliable relationship between the 12 beliefs and outcomes, such as profits, productivity, employee retention, and customer loyalty. For example, work groups that have these positive attitudes are 50 percent more likely to achieve customer loyalty and 44 percent more likely to produce above-average profitability.

At the level of the business unit, those in the top quartile on employee engagement had, on average, $80,000 to $120,000 higher monthly revenues or sales than those in the bottom quartile. Even an $80,000 difference per month per business unit translates into $960,000 per year per business unit. Harter et al. (2002) concluded that the causal order runs from employee attitudes to organizational performance, although they recognized that the relationship might also be reciprocal in nature.

Gallup analyzed employee data to determine how well the respondents' organizations support the 12 employee statements. Organizations whose support of the statements ranked in the top 25 percent averaged 24 percent higher profitability, 29 percent higher revenue, and 10 percent lower employee turnover than those that scored lowest on the statements. Here are the 12 basic belief statements that underlie the most important worker attitudes:

1. I know what is expected of me at work.
2. I have the materials and equipment I need to do my work right.
3. At work I have the opportunity to do what I do best every day.
4. In the last seven days I have received recognition or praise for doing good work.
5. My supervisor, or someone at work, seems to care about me as a person.
6. There is someone at work who encourages my development.
7. In the last six months someone at work has talked to me about my progress.
8. At work, my opinions seem to count.
9. The mission/purpose of my company makes me feel my job is important.
10. My fellow employees are committed to doing quality work.
11. I have a best friend at work.
12. This last year I have had opportunities at work to learn and grow.

The good news about these beliefs is that all 12 of them can be coaxed forth with sound management techniques, and both managers and team members can really do something about them. Unlike pay issues, which most managers and workers have no control over, every individual team member can do something to help create these beliefs.

For instance, consider belief number four ("In the last seven days I have received recognition or praise for doing good work"). Although it requires long-term commitment, managers can deliver on this, at very little cost. Belief number seven ("In the last six months someone at work has talked to me about my progress") is even less time-consuming.

Interestingly, researchers found significant variances among work groups or operating units within the same company. This implies, paradoxically, that while we tend to celebrate great companies, in reality there are only great managers, for it is on the front line that the hard work of building a stronger workplace gets done.

Thus far we have been examining the costs associated with employee behavior. In the next two sections we change focus and examine the financial benefits associated with the wise management of people. Our first topic is training and development.

## The Benefits Associated with Wise Management of People

### Economic Benefits of Training and Development Programs

We use the terms training and development interchangeably. Training consists of planned programs designed to improve performance at the individual, group, and/or organizational levels. Improved performance, in turn, implies that there have been measurable changes in knowledge, skills, attitudes, and/or social behavior. Such changes may be evaluated at the level of the individual (e.g., reactions to the training, demonstrated new knowledge or skills, changes in behavior), at the level of a team (e.g., improved ability to function effectively in a collective effort), or at the level of the organization, in terms of the overall return on investment of a training and development program. For purposes of this chapter, we shall focus on the latter. To illustrate such returns, let us consider the approach taken by one company.

A large, U.S.-based multinational firm conducted a four-year investigation of the economic benefits of its corporate/managerial and sales/technical-training functions (Morrow, Jarrett, and Rupinsky 1997). The study is noteworthy, for it adopted a strategic focus by comparing the payoffs from different types of training in order to assist decision makers in allocating training budgets and specifying the types of employees to be trained.

*Project History*
The CEO, a former research scientist, requested a report on the economic impact of training. He indicated that training should be evaluated experimentally, and it should be aligned strategically with the business goals of the organization to determine whether or not it is a worthwhile investment for the company. Thus the impetus for this large-scale study came from the top of the organization.

*Methodological Issues*
For the training to have value, skills must be generalized to the job (that is, exhibited on the job), and such transfer must be maintained for some period of time. To address the issue of transfer, the measure of effectiveness of all training programs was the change in behavioral performance on the job. Performance was assessed by means of a survey completed by each trainee's supervisor (for most courses), peers (for Hazardous Energy Control), or subordinates (for Team Building) before and after training.

Because in this study it was not possible to measure the duration of the effects of the training, decision makers assumed that the effects (and economic utility) were maintained without reduction or growth for precisely one year. In addition, the researchers calculated *break-even values*, which indicate the length of time the observed effect would need to be maintained in order to recover the cost of the training program.

*Training Programs Evaluated*
A sample of 18 high-use or high-cost courses was selected based on the recommendation of the training departments throughout the organization. Managerial training courses were defined as courses developed for individuals with managerial or supervisory duties. Sales training courses were defined as programs designed to enhance the performance of sales representatives. Technical training courses (e.g., Hazardous Energy Control, In-House Time Management) were defined as courses not specifically designed for sales or supervisory personnel.

Of the 18 programs, eight evaluation studies used a control-group design in which training was provided to one group and not provided to a second group that was similar to the trained group in terms of relevant characteristics. In the remaining ten training programs, the performance of the trained group alone was evaluated before and after the training program.

*Results*
Overall all 18 programs, assuming a normal or bell-shaped distribution of performance on the job, the average improvement in performance was about 17 percent.

However, for technical/sales training it was higher (about 22 percent), and for managerial training it was lower (about 11 percent). Thus training in general was effective.

The average return on investment (ROI) was 45 percent for the managerial training programs, and 418 percent for the sales/technical training programs. However, one inexpensive time management program developed in-house had an ROI of nearly 2,000 percent! When the economic benefits of that program are removed, the overall average ROI of the remaining training programs was 84 percent, and the ROI of sales/technical training was 156 percent.

### Time to Break-Even Values
There was considerable variability in these values. Break-even periods ranged from a few weeks (e.g., time management, written communications) to several years (e.g., supervisory skills, leadership skills). Several programs were found to have little positive or even slightly negative effects and thus would never yield a financial gain.

### A Note of Caution
Despite the overall positive effects and economic benefits of the training, there were some exceptions. The important lesson to be learned is that it is necessary to evaluate each training program separately before drawing conclusions about the overall impact of training. It would be simplistic to claim either that "training is a good investment" or that "training is a waste of time and money."

### Make or Buy?
A key issue in any company's decision making with respect to human capital is whether to "make" competent employees through training or to "buy" the skill sets the organization needs (paying a premium to do so, thereby increasing compensation costs) by selecting individuals who can be productive almost immediately. Given a choice between selection and training, the best strategy is to choose selection. Selection of high-caliber employees will enable these individuals to learn more and to learn faster from subsequent training programs than will the selection of lower-caliber employees. Of course, labor market conditions can eliminate such choices. If the supply of labor is tight, then organizations have only one option: to select the highest-caliber employees they can, and then to train them in skills that they specifically require.

### General Estimates of Training Effectiveness

Meta-analytic methods (quantitative cumulations of research results across studies) have also been used to reach more general conclusions on the effectiveness of different kinds of training, both management and nonmanagement training. Results show that the particular training method used, the skill or task trained, and the choice of training evaluation criteria (e.g., trainee reactions, measures of learning, on-the-job changes in behavior, or bottom-line results) all relate to the observed effectiveness of training programs.

However, consider some overall results for an individual whose pre-training performance is right at the mean (fiftieth percentile). The results of one large-scale meta-analysis of training's effects (397 independent studies from 162 sources and thousands of subjects) revealed an improvement in performance of about 20 percent for that individual regardless of the training-evaluation criterion used (Arthur, Bennett, Edens, and Bell 2003).

Such studies are valuable, because they allow managers to rely on cumulative knowledge of the expected payoffs of proposed training programs. Indeed, a "menu" of such expected payoffs will allow managers and HR professionals to estimate expected economic benefits to their organizations *before* the decision is made to allocate resources to such programs. Now let us consider the gains associated with valid hiring and promotion programs.

### Economic Benefits of Valid Employee Staffing Programs

The most important characteristic of any procedure used as a basis for an employment decision, such as hiring or promotion, is validity. Validity refers to the job-relatedness of a measure—shown, for example, by assessing the strength of the relationship between scores from the measure (such as a written test or an interview) and some indicator or rating of actual job performance (such as supervisory ratings, dollar volume of sales). A correlation coefficient, whose value may vary between $-1$ and $+1$, typically provides a statistical index of the strength of that overall relationship. In employment contexts, the validities of staffing procedures typically vary between about .20 and .50. Such validities yield high economic payoffs to firms when the firms can be selective in choosing whom to hire or promote, when the percentage of successful hires is not extremely high already, and when the cost of a mistake—selecting or promoting the wrong person—is high.

A large body of research has shown that the economic gains in productivity that are associated with the use of valid staffing procedures far outweigh the cost of those procedures (Schmidt and Hunter, 1998; Schmidt, Hunter, and Pearlman 1982). This means that people who score high (low) on such procedures also tend to do well (poorly) on their jobs. High scores suggest a close "fit" between individual capabilities and organizational needs, while low scores suggest a poor fit. By hiring or promoting those who score high on valid measures of performance (and rejecting those who score poorly) productivity, quality of work life, and the bottom line all stand to gain. Thus a study of firms in the service and financial industries reported correlations ranging from .71 to .86 between the use of progressive staffing practices (e.g., validation studies, use of structured interviews, biographical data, and mental ability tests) and measures of organizational performance over a five-year period (annual profit, profit growth, sales growth, and overall performance) (Terpstra and Rozell 1993).

At a broader level, many firms have adopted so-called high-performance work practices that include the use of valid staffing procedures, as well as practices such as the following:

- organizational cultures that emphasize team orientation and respect for people,
- employee involvement in decision making,
- compensation linked to firm or worker performance, and
- substantial investments in training and development.

Numerous studies have found that such practices can have an economically significant effect on the market value of the firm (Welbourne and Andrews 1996). For example, a large-scale study of 702 publicly traded firms analyzed the financial impact of HR systems that incorporate such high-performance work practices. Each firm received a score based on its use of these practices. Results indicated that an improvement of one standard deviation in the HR system (movement from the fiftieth percentile to the eighty-fourth percentile of scores) was associated with an increase in shareholder wealth of $41,000 per employee—about a 14 percent market-value premium (Becker, Huselid, and Ulrich 2001).

## Policy Implications for Employers

Thus far we have examined several areas where the behavior of employees has significant economic implications for employers. They are: the impact on employee turnover and productivity of high- versus low-wage employment strategies; the costs of absenteeism, presenteeism, and unhealthy lifestyles; and the financial payoffs associated with improving employee retention, developing positive employee attitudes, implementing well-designed training and development programs, and using valid staffing procedures. As we have seen, the implementation of progressive management practices has the potential to reduce operating costs and to increase considerably organizational performance and productivity. Such practices also have positive economic and psychological benefits for employees, families, and communities.

What should employers do to begin to reap these benefits for their organizations and for those who work in them? At the outset it is important to recognize that in 2005, fewer than 20 percent of U.S. workers were employed in manufacturing, the lowest level since 1850. We live in the information economy, and in it, as noted at the beginning of this chapter, the most important assets are not buildings and equipment; they are human assets—the kind that walk out the door every night at five o'clock (or later). Shareholders do not own those assets. To attract and retain them, the challenge is to create a culture that makes the best among them want to stay. In our final section we offer some specific steps that employers can take to reduce costs and increase employee productivity (in the areas of retention, absenteeism, and presenteeism) and look for means of reducing healthcare costs through healthier lifestyles. We conclude by showing some of the positive payoffs associated with avoiding employment downsizing.

### Enhancing Employee Retention

In general, what drives retention? What do workers want? A 2005 study by Gantz Wiley Research found that across all generations, the top five drivers are opportunities for career development, a sense of confidence about the future of their current employers, feelings of accomplishment, the amount of joy at work, and employment security (Wiley 2005). Table 14.1 lists some specific actions that employers can take to address these concerns.

In terms of best practices, firms that excel in employee retention seem to do three other things well (Cascio and Fogli 2004):

1. Each is a company that people want to work for. Management inspires commitment to a clear vision and definite objectives, or as Bill Gates recently noted, "It's important to work at a place where you are connected to a dream."

2. They get new employees off to a great start, beginning with proactive management of the first 90 days (orientation and socialization). They recognize that most employee turnover occurs early in the employment relationship, and so they provide the kind of information, support, and tools that employees need to do their jobs well. They never stop communicating how each employee's work is vital to the organization's success, and they ensure that each new employee has a performance agreement. That agreement clearly identifies expectations, time frames for performance, and the standards that will be used to measure performance.

3. They provide regular coaching and rewards to sustain commitment. To do that, they proactively manage the performance agreement, they recognize results regularly, and they give employees the tools they need to take charge of their own careers.

### Controlling Absenteeism and Presenteeism

What can organizations do to control or reduce absenteeism? A comprehensive review of research findings in this area revealed that absence-control systems can neutralize some forms of absence behavior, but at the same time they may catalyze others (Harrison and Martocchio 1998). For example, research shows that punishments, or stricter enforcement of penalties for one type of absence, tend to instigate other forms of missing work. This is not to suggest, however, that absence-control policies should be lenient. Lenient policies convey a relaxed norm about absenteeism, and research evidence clearly indicates that those norms can promote absence-taking.

A first step is to assess the problem correctly so that the organization knows where to apply control mechanisms. Organization-wide absenteeism-control methods (such as rewards for good attendance, progressive discipline for absenteeism, daily attendance records) may be somewhat successful, but they may not be effective in dealing with specific individuals or work groups that have excessively high absenteeism rates. Special methods (such as flexible work schedules, job redesign, and improved safety

**Table 14.1**   Some Steps Employers Can Take to Enhance Employee Retention

| | |
|---|---|
| 1. Career-Development Opportunity | • Provide mentoring, access to information, informal and formal learning programs, up-to-date training<br>• Provide career-advancement opportunities |
| 2. Confidence in Future | • Communicate the business condition (quarterly or semi-annually) |
| 3. Feeling of Accomplishment | • Listen to employee ideas (e.g., through one-on-ones)<br>• Provide recognition |
| 4. Amount of Joy | • Use humor to retain employees<br>• Make work fun |
| 5. Employment Security | • Provide a challenging but supportive environment<br>• Involve employees in decisions that affect them<br>• Recognize that pay is important, but not more so than other practices |

measures) may be necessary for them. It is the careful analysis of detailed absenteeism research data that can facilitate the identification of these problems and suggest possible remedies (Miners, Moore, Champoux, and Martocchio 1995).

With regard to presenteeism, companies such as Comerica Bank, Dow Chemical, and J. P. Morgan Chase are among those that have put programs in place to help employees avoid or treat seasonal or chronic health conditions, or at least to stay productive in spite of them (Rubinstein 2005). To ensure employee privacy, for example, Comerica Bank used a third party to survey its employees and found that about 40 percent of them said they suffered from irritable bowel syndrome (IBS), which can involve abdominal discomfort, bloating, or diarrhea. Extrapolating from that, the company estimated its annual cost of lost productivity to be at least $8 million a year. Comerica now provides written materials for its employees about IBS and has sponsored physician seminars to educate workers about how to recognize and deal with it through their living habits, diet, and possible medications.

### Changing Unhealthy Lifestyles

At first glance, it might appear that changing employees' unhealthy lifestyles is a win-win for employers and employees. Perhaps, but beware of violating the Americans with Disabilities Act (ADA)! Employers violate the ADA if they *require* employees to submit to wellness initiatives, such as health-risk appraisals (questionnaires about one's health history and current lifestyle) and assessments (physical and biomedical tests that screen for specific health conditions). This is so because the ADA forbids employers from conducting mandatory medical exams once an employee is hired, unless the inquiry is "job-related and consistent with business necessity."

Employers also must be careful when tying financial incentives or disincentives (such as cash bonuses or reduced health insurance contributions) to test results. The employer can offer an incentive only upon verification that the employee went for the test. The incentive cannot be tied to the test results (Matthes 1992).

Educational wellness programs that encourage people to sign up for tests and instruct them on how to improve their lifestyles do not violate the ADA. Here are four steps that employers might take to promote healthier lifestyles among employees:

1. Educate employees about health-risk factors—life habits or body characteristics that may increase the chances of developing a serious illness. For heart disease (the leading cause of death), some of these risk factors are high blood pressure, cigarette smoking, high cholesterol levels, diabetes, a sedentary lifestyle, and obesity. Some factors, such as smoking, physical inactivity, stress, and poor nutrition, are associated with many diseases.
2. Identify the health-risk factors that each employee faces.
3. Help employees eliminate or reduce these risks through healthier lifestyles and habits.
4. Help employees maintain their new, healthier lifestyles through self-monitoring and evaluation, work/life programs, and healthy food alternatives in vending machines and cafeterias at the workplace.

Unfortunately, evidence indicates that employees who are most at risk are often the most difficult to induce to change their lifestyles, though monetary incentives often make it attractive and in their best interest. Here is an example.

At Johnson & Johnson, employees get $500 discounts on their insurance premiums if they agree to have their blood pressure, cholesterol, and body fat checked and fill out detailed health-risk questionnaires. Among the more than 150 questions, there are questions such as "Do you drive within the speed limit?" "How often do you eat fried foods?" "Do you exercise regularly, and if not, why not?"

Workers found to be at high risk of having health problems receive letters urging them to join a diet and exercise program. Those who refuse lose the $500 discount. Before the discount was offered, only 40 percent of the company's 35,000 U.S. employees completed the health assessments. After the discount was offered, more than 96 percent did (Jeffrey 1996).

## Conclusions

As we have seen, the behavior of individual workers has important financial consequences for organizational performance and productivity, as well as for employees themselves. In this chapter we have examined just a few of the many possible areas where the control of costs associated with employee behaviors (e.g., turnover, absenteeism, presenteeism, unhealthy lifestyles) and the benefits associated with wise management of employees (promotion of positive employee attitudes, training and development programs targeted to strategic challenges, use of valid staffing practices for hiring and promotion) can increase productivity and decrease operating expenses. These are things employers can do now. Comprehensive audits of human resource policies at all levels of employees and managers may well reveal opportunities for even greater gains.

Some employers may choose to accept high employee turnover, by externalizing some of their healthcare costs and offering little or no healthcare or pension coverage to their employees, and to downsize their employee populations indiscriminately. There are, however, alternative approaches. Xilinx, Inc., is an example of one of them (Cascio and Wynn 2004).

Based in San Jose, California, Xilinx is a semiconductor company known as the world's leading supplier of programmable logic solutions. With approximately 2,600 employees, Xilinx's annual revenues exceeded one billion dollars for the last several years. When the semiconductor and other high-technology sectors experienced a significant downturn in 2001, a downturn that was global in its reach and effects, Xilinx's revenues plummeted 50 percent in six months. How quickly things change! Just the year before, the company had hired over 1,000 people to keep pace with the better than 50 percent per year growth rate from the previous two years.

During this difficult time, teams at Xilinx convened regularly. There were two recurring themes during those meetings: one was that the teams did not want to continue to lose money, and the other, that Xilinx should not mortgage its future with short-term actions. The company's strategy was to reduce expenses, maintain productivity, and emerge as a stronger organization. The seasoned semiconductor executives at Xilinx were well aware of the cyclical nature of the industry, and they were confident that it would eventually rebound as it had done in past cycles. They believed strongly that the intellectual capital at Xilinx would enable it to maintain its innovation edge, and they were not about to undercut that source of competitive advantage. Xilinx president and CEO Wim Roelandts was fond of saying, "De-motivated engineers do not create breakthrough products."

The company implemented a complete shutdown for two weeks. In addition, focus groups of employees developed a menu of options for taking multitiered pay cuts, from 20 percent for senior executives all the way down to zero percent for the lowest-level employees. Managers agreed to hold mid-term performance reviews of all employees, to provide stock options to 85 percent of the employee population, and to send very clear messages regarding the need for performance improvement to the bottom 15 percent of the employee population. The company also offered voluntary resignation and retirement programs, as well as sabbatical leaves to employees. All of this was in marked contrast to what competitors were doing—massive layoffs of their employees.

The following quarter, which was the first quarter of 2002, the company's business improved significantly. Xilinx restored employees' pay halfway through the quarter, and although it could not pay its typical profit-sharing bonus to all employees, it did award each employee a one-time "recognition bonus" for weathering the storm with the company.

Two years later, results at the company clearly justified its management approach during the economic downturn. Prior to the downturn in its core business, Xilinx's worldwide market share was 30 percent. By the second quarter of 2003 it was 51 percent. At the same time, the company's revenues exceeded that of all three of its major competitors combined! Xilinx brought more products to market on time than at any other period in its corporate history.

Looking to the future, the Xilinx management team is more financially savvy regarding the management of company expenses, and it is also more disciplined in its management of poor performers within the organization. Shareholders understand the value of maintaining committed people after the 21 percent market-share boost. Employees are proud to tell others that they work for Xilinx, one of the few companies to have emerged from the economic downturn without a layoff. Finally, the downturn focused the company on its driving principles: First, put a programmable logic device in every piece of electronic equipment, and second, set a new standard for how to manage a high-technology company.

# 15

# Global Sourcing of Talent: Implications for the U.S. Workforce

*Fred K. Foulkes, Sushil Vachani, and Jennifer Zaslow*

The global sourcing of talent—commonly called "offshoring"—has become an issue of substantial public and political interest in the last few years. Although the 1973 landmark publication *Work in America* made no mention of outsourcing to third-party providers or the movement of jobs abroad, these trends have been shaping employment dynamics in the manufacturing sector for more than three decades. Historically, American employees in the service sector have gained from global trade, because companies around the world sought expertise from U.S. providers, particularly in high-end technology and research and development.[1] However, it is the more recent phenomenon of global talent sourcing—in which white-collar service jobs move from high-wage to low-wage countries—that has captured new attention. With services making up 67 percent of the U.S. economy and the substantial increase in global trade in services over the last 20 years (Karoly and Panis 2004, 133–134), it is no surprise that Americans express alarm when service jobs start moving offshore.

The reality is, however, that the offshoring of services from high-wage to low-wage countries puts us in uncharted territory. Theoretical frameworks, consultant forecasts of companies' offshore activities, and our past experience with globalization in the manufacturing sector give us only partial insights. The many stakeholders affected by the global sourcing trend, including companies, individual employees, unions, trade and professional associations, governments, and educational institutions, have to wade through a multitude of different forecasts and analyses to make sense of what is happening—and could happen—to the U.S. workforce (see Boston Consulting Group 2004; Deloitte Research 2003; Foote Partners 2005; Forrester Research 2004; Information Technology Association of America 2004; Kirby and Shinai 2004; Mann 2003; McDougall 2005; McKinsey Global Institute 2005; Uchitelle 2003). In this chapter, we summarize the major literature to date on offshoring services in order to present a comprehensive perspective on the key issues for individuals, policymakers, and business leaders who are looking to make decisions and investments regarding their careers, constituents, and companies in an increasingly global context.

## Defining Offshoring

For clarity, we define "offshoring" as the movement of work from high-cost locations (such as the United States, Western Europe, and Japan) to low-cost foreign locations (such as India, China, the Philippines, Russia, and Eastern Europe). The McKinsey Global Institute (MGI) (2005) suggests that work eligible for offshoring includes "any task that requires no physical or complex interaction between an employee and customers or colleagues, and little or no local knowledge" (10). In fact, even if local knowledge is required, offshoring is feasible if the knowledge is codifiable. Estimates of the number of jobs that could be moved from high-wage countries to low-wage countries have ranged widely: 3.4 million U.S. service jobs by 2015 (Forrester Research 2004), 4.1 million service jobs worldwide by 2008 (MGI 2005), and, theoretically, the total could ultimately be as many as 14 million U.S. jobs (representing 11 percent of jobs in all occupations) (Bardhan and Kroll 2003).

A company might pursue offshoring as part of a broader "global sourcing" strategy to grow capabilities and pools of talent around the world. Companies differ in how they execute global sourcing strategies—for instance by building internally managed operations, outsourcing to third-party vendors, or forming joint ventures that involve some hybrid of in-house management and partnerships. Companies have also differed in how their U.S.-based employees have been impacted by the offshoring decisions.

## Today's Global Sourcing is Different

We believe that global sourcing today is different from that of earlier years and that the potential impact on the U.S. workforce in the coming decades will be vast. While much can be learned from companies' past globalization efforts, four factors distinguish contemporary global talent sourcing in services from past experiences:

- more industries and occupations are being affected;
- services make seamless human interactions more critical;
- talent sourcing is now simultaneously both global and local; and
- global sourcing arrangements for services are being decided upon and implemented faster.

### Impact on Diverse Industries and Occupations

In contrast to earlier phases of globalization in the manufacturing sector, today's global sourcing applies to many different kinds of activities (e.g., call centers, accounts receivable, software development, business process outsourcing, scientific research) and cuts across a variety of industries (e.g., high tech, financial services, pharmaceutical, telecommunications, consulting, consumer products). Small companies, including early stage venture-based ones, are involved in offshoring services today, just as they participated in foreign sourcing of manufacturing components before.[2]

The diversity of occupations and industries affected by global sourcing increases the perceived impact of offshoring on the economy and on the potential for individual employees to be at risk. The Progressive Policy Institute analyzed data classified by Forrester Research to determine the extent to which high- and low-wage service jobs were at risk (Atkinson 2004a). While more than half (54 percent) of the jobs Forrester forecasted to be offshored paid less than the U.S. median wage of $25,580, almost one-third of the jobs paid in the top quintile (11). The variety of educational and professional backgrounds of occupations affected—ranging from high school diplomas to advanced graduate degrees—also creates a more complex environment for designing public policies and educational programs to retrain people affected by the movement of work offshore. Existing federal legislation, such as the Trade Adjustment Assistance (TAA) program and the Trade Promotional Authority Act, targets manufacturing employees. Only recently (2006) did the US Department of Labor allow "intangible articles," such as software to meet the regulators requirement of the Act (Shew 2006).

Although offshoring is occurring in many industries and occupations, some sectors and job roles will be affected more than others. According to MGI (2005), the global packaged software and IT services industries could each source nearly half of their total employment anywhere in the world because much of the work is not location-specific. Worldwide, these two sectors could impact up to 300,000 and 2.8 million employees respectively (MGI, 2005, 22). MGI also states that one-quarter of banking employment and almost one-fifth of insurance employment could theoretically be sourced globally as well.

Engineers, finance and accounting professionals, and generalists (those with a college degree but no specialized training) are those most likely to be affected by the movement of work offshore (MGI 2005, 24). Employment in the Indian call center and business process outsourcing sectors is forecasted to increase tenfold, from approximately 100,000 to 1.1 million employees by 2008 (Karoly and Panis 2004, 142). The full impact of such substantial job growth in India on the employment prospects for U.S. workers in these sectors is not clear.

### Services Highlight Importance of Human Interactions

Services have traditionally been considered nontradable because buyers and sellers were required to be in the same place at the same time. However, advances in information and communication technologies have allowed information to be digitized and transported quickly and cost effectively around the world. Traditional barriers of geography and time no longer hinder information flow, service delivery, or competition.

The use of such technologies allows knowledge to be codified, standardized, and digitized. In turn, this enables services to be split up, or "fragmented," into smaller components that can be located elsewhere to take advantage of cost, quality, economies of scale, or other factors (UNCTAD 2004, 148–149). This makes it possible for services to be produced in one location and consumed in another. Services provided in a different location might be consumed in real time, for instance, through customer-facing call centers, or asynchronously, such as with software programming or back-office work (also see Karoly and Panis 2004, 180; Jensen and Kletzer 2005).

In contrast to globalization in the manufacturing sector, the globalization of service delivery requires, by the very nature of the work being performed, more awareness and active involvement in people management issues. Manufacturers outsourcing the production of shoes or toys from a global supplier can use tangible metrics of product quality or timeliness as measures of vendor effectiveness. By contrast, services expand the scope of personal interactions between staff and customers, whether internal or external. While innovative new metrics have been developed to monitor service quality levels, the process of delivering services from a foreign location requires greater care in managing the human relations across multiple boundaries: distance, organization, culture, and time zone.

### Talent Sourcing Is Both Global and Local

Globalization in the service sector allows companies to deliver on the often-touted objective of "recruiting the best talent, wherever it resides." Research and development (R&D) investments provide an example of this trend. While high-wage countries continue to dominate R&D spending, the percentage of R&D work performed in emerging markets is growing. GE, GM, Intel, and Microsoft are just some of the companies that have established global R&D networks with locations in both high-wage and low-wage countries.

Two-thirds of the R&D performed overseas by U.S.-owned companies in 2000 ($13.2 billion out of $19.8 billion) took place in six countries: United Kingdom, Germany, Canada, Japan, France, and Sweden (National Science Board 2004, 4–68). By contrast, the ten locations shown in table 15.1 hosted $3.5 billion in R&D expenditures (18 percent of worldwide spending) by majority-owned foreign affiliates of U.S. parent companies in 2000, up from $1.3 billion (11 percent) in 1994. U.S.-owned R&D expenditures in these ten emerging markets increased by 15.9 percent annually (real average annual growth) from 1994 to 2000, compared with 6.9 percent annual growth for the aggregate of all host countries. As examples, in 2000, Singapore, Israel, Ireland, and China each hosted U.S.-owned R&D expenditures of $500 million or more, levels considerably higher than those in 1994 (National Science Board 2004, 4–65).

**Table 15.1** R&D Performed Overseas by Majority-Owned Foreign Affiliates of U.S. Companies in Selected Economies: 1994 and 2000 (Millions of Current U.S. Dollars)

| Location | 1994 | | 2000 | |
| --- | --- | --- | --- | --- |
| | Rank | R&D | | R&D |
| Singapore | 14 | 167 | 8 | 548 |
| Israel | 16 | 96 | 9 | 527 |
| Ireland | 8 | 396 | 10 | 518 |
| China | 30 | 7 | 11 | 506 |
| Hong Kong | 19 | 51 | 14 | 341 |
| Mexico | 13 | 183 | 16 | 305 |
| Brazil | 10 | 238 | 17 | 250 |
| Malaysia | 20 | 27 | 19 | 214 |
| Taiwan | 15 | 110 | 21 | 143 |
| South Korea | 26 | 17 | 22 | 131 |

*Note:* Rank refers to the relative position of the host country in terms of the amount of U.S.-owned R&D expenditures.

*Sources:* U.S. Bureau of Economic Analysis, U.S. Department of Commerce, Survey of U.S. Direct Investment Abroad, annual series, http://www.bea.gov/bea/di/diluse-dop.htm.
National Science Board. *Science & Engineering Indicators*-2004, 4–69.

To maximize the return on these global operations, U.S.-based companies must simultaneously balance plans for expansion to low-cost regions with initiatives to develop capabilities of their existing U.S. workforce. This involves analyzing the current and future condition of a local geographic market's labor pool, the competitive environment for talent, as well as the region's infrastructure, education, and other factors.

### Speed of Change Heightens Anxiety for Affected Employees

Certain segments of the business, professional, and technical service sector have experienced offshoring faster and on a larger scale than others. The United Nations Conference on Trade and Development, using growth in imports by the United States as a proxy for offshore expenditures by U.S. companies, estimated that computer and data processing services grew at an average annual growth rate of 31 percent between 1992 and 2002, reaching a value of over one billion dollars (UNCTAD, 2004, p. 151). Imports of accounting, auditing, and bookkeeping services also experienced rapid expansion, growing an average of 21 percent annually between 1992 and 2002. Such fast growth has been achievable, in part, because to offshore services is structurally simpler in terms of space and equipment requirements when compared with the resources required to establish manufacturing operations (UNCTAD, 2004, p. 152). A 2004 study of primarily U.S. companies found that while only 25 percent had offshored some services to date, more than three-quarters (79 percent) said they planned to offshore within two years (Bajpai, Sachs, Arora, and Khurana, 2004).

The macro-level growth rates mask the speed of change occurring at the micro level of individual companies. In some cases, companies have chosen to use offshoring to augment existing staff, with no U.S.-based reductions in workforce occurring. However, when existing workloads are moved offshore, companies have chosen from three approaches to transition the U.S. workforce. Affected employees could be "reassigned," where the company actively manages the transition, matching the employee with other opportunities in the organization appropriate for the individual's skill set and experience. Employees could be "redeployed," which places the responsibility for finding a new position in the company squarely on the employee. Companies, sometimes those in difficult financial circumstances, have also chosen a third course of action—laying off the employees whose work was being moved offshore. In an example of good practice, one financial services company we interviewed had approximately 90 days from the CIO's announcement that the company would outsource 30 percent of its IT work offshore to the sign-off by the CIO of a contract with an Indian IT services vendor. The company held frequent "town-hall style" meetings with employees whose work was being outsourced offshore. The IT, HR, and product management leaders responsible for the implementation facilitated the sessions with open, ongoing communication about the strategic reasons for the decision as well as about how projects and jobs would be affected. The company facilitated employees' transitions to new areas of the organization, even allowing them to start new jobs before the transition to the outsourcing vendor had been completed.

Convergys, a leading U.S.-based contract service company with locations in 25 U.S. states, provides another example of the speed and scale of job growth occurring outside the United States. The company established its first offshore center in India in 2000. By 2003, the company had centers in Argentina, Brazil, Indonesia, Mexico, the

Philippines, the Republic of Korea, Singapore, Sri Lanka, Taiwan, and Thailand as well (UNCTAD 2004, 158). In early 2005, Convergys employed more than 10,000 people in India, nearly 17 percent of the company's workforce, and it announced plans to grow its India-based BPO headcount to 20,000 within two years (Business Line 2005).

## Drivers of Global Sourcing Activities

Several factors, shown in table 15.2, are driving interest in and implementation of global sourcing strategies. The most commonly reported driver is the opportunity to achieve cost savings by leveraging lower-cost workforces. In a survey of 90 *Fortune* 500 companies conducted by Duke University and Archstone Consulting (2004), 93 percent of companies cited cost reduction as the primary driver for pursuing an off-shoring strategy. MGI (Farrell 2004) estimated that companies could save as much as 70 percent of their total production costs through a combination of offshoring (reducing cost by 50 percent), task redesign and training (reducing cost a further 5 percent), and process improvements (cutting an additional 15 percent). In the Duke/Archstone survey, 72 percent of companies' offshore implementations met or exceeded expected cost savings.

But cost reduction alone does not drive the tremendous interest we have seen in global talent sourcing. As companies that we visited, both here and in India, said of their Indian initiatives, "We went for cost; we stay for quality." In our interviews, companies also cited the desire for enhanced organizational flexibility, the ability to react more quickly to competitive pressures, and greater business continuity across time zones as important factors in their offshoring decisions.

As an example, India, which has received the majority of offshored work to date, offers an attractive combination of educated, English-speaking, high-quality technical and professional talent at a substantially lower labor cost than the United States. Approximately 1.3 million people graduate from universities in India each year, of which 350,000 are engineering graduates (Dange 2005, 3). In business process outsourcing or call center work, companies have been able to recruit college graduates for jobs in India that are typically difficult to fill even with high school graduates in the United States. Several companies we interviewed reported process improvements that translated into error reduction and value enhancement for customers, suppliers, and managers at various locations in the multinational network, which provided new ways to enhance the competitive advantage of these U.S.-based companies in the face of global competition.

While cost reduction remains the number one objective of companies today, the goals for global sourcing will likely change over time, as the rapidly rising wages and the more widespread use of offshoring reduces the cost advantages achieved by early

**Table 15.2** Drivers of Global Sourcing Decisions

- Cost Reduction
- Quality
- Capacity and Flexibility
- Customer / Investor Pressures
- Competitive Pressures

entrants. A 2004 survey of large U.S. companies indicated that over the next three years more companies would expand global sourcing initiatives in order to focus on their core competencies and improve flexibility (Hewitt Associates 2004). Similarly, Bain & Company predicted that the primary drivers of global sourcing would evolve over the next several years from cost reduction to quality and, ultimately, to a focus on efficiency through achieving world-class capabilities at the least cost possible (Bain & Company 2004).

### Configuration of Global Sourcing Operations

In establishing offshore operations, companies have generally embraced one of three business models, based on the strategic drivers they are trying to achieve. The three models are: "captive," where the operation is staffed by internal employees; outsourced, where staffing is contracted with a third-party provider; and a hybrid model involving both internal employees and vendor partnerships. Companies have focused on several factors when evaluating potential offshore business models. These include the amount of initial investment, the time required to get the operation up and running, the degree of control and risk associated with the business model, the type of work being performed, and the intellectual capital being used. A company may change its business model over time, as the company's leadership gains experience in managing offshore projects or as the business objectives or type of work changes.

For instance, as fully owned entities, captive organizations enable companies to maintain closer control and management over high-value projects and higher-risk processes. The people doing the work are employees of the company, and their rewards are often tied to company performance. The captive model can reduce internal resistance to offshoring and the geographic decentralization of proprietary information or sensitive data by retaining the knowledge within the company.

Outsourcing contracts place responsibility for managing people and meeting quality standards squarely on the vendor. Companies pursuing an outsourced offshore model reduce their direct control over the work, but also reduce the extent to which managers have to spend time managing the day-to-day operations and finances of the offshore unit. Some companies outsource to multiple vendors in order to foster competition between the vendors around cost and quality. Outsourcing is considered appropriate for intellectual capital that is commoditized or common across industries (Bain and Company 2004).

Whether a company sets up its own operations or outsources to the foreign location depends on the nature of the activities to be located there and the magnitude of the operations. If the company plans to do simple data processing, it could outsource the work entirely and deal with vendors' representatives in the United States. An advantage of using suppliers for software development or call-center operations is that costs can be kept low. However, as a company expands into more specialized, company-specific, or proprietary activities, there are greater advantages to in-house operations.

Table 15.3 presents some of the companies, identified through authors' interviews and secondary research, that have adopted various offshore business models. In some cases, the leadership at companies pursuing the captive model (column I) felt that work could be done more cheaply and "the company way" (i.e., the "right" way) by hiring internal employees. Some companies pursuing the captive business model

**Table 15.3** Companies Adopting Major Offshore Business Models

| I. Captive | II. Outsourced | III. Hybrid of Captive & Outsourced |
| --- | --- | --- |
| • Accenture | • Analog Devices | • AIG |
| • American Express | • AT&T | • British Telecom |
| • Bank of America | • Bear Stearns | • Dell |
| • Convergys | • Boeing | • General Electric |
| • Ford | • Cisco Systems | • Microsoft |
| • HBSC | • Honeywell | |
| • Hewitt Associates | • Lehman | |
| • IBM | Brothers | |
| • Sapient | • Lucent | |
| • Sun Microsystems | Technologies | |
| • Texas Instruments | • Morgan Stanley | |
| • Unilever | • Prudential | |
| | Insurance U.S. | |
| | • State Street Bank | |

have chosen to acquire Indian companies in order to grow their employee base quickly. For example, in 2004 IBM acquired Daksh, a leading Indian BPO service provider. The acquisition added 6,000 employees and contributed to IBM's growth in India from 9,000 employees in 2003 to 23,000 by the end of 2004 (India Business Insight 2005a). Also in 2004, Citibank acquired majority ownership in e-Serve International Limited, a provider of IT-enabled services.

The companies listed in the outsourced column (column II) contracted work directly to India-based outsourcing companies, rather than to U.S.-based outsourcing service providers, many of which also employ thousands of people in India through captive business models. For example, Accenture employed 15,000 people in India, or 10 percent of its total workforce, according to a February 2005 report, while Sapient, a Cambridge, Massachusetts-based IT consulting firm, located more than 50 percent of its employees in India (India Business Insight 2005b).

## Outlook for the Future

The global sourcing trend is likely to continue in the coming years, and, in so doing, will become a significant factor shaping the American workplace. The global sourcing of talent in the service sector represents a paradigm shift in how business leaders think about how work can be organized and delivered. In the current competitive environment, companies ranging from large multinationals to small, venture-funded start-ups cannot neglect to consider global sourcing as a possible means of cost reduction, flexibility, and/or competitive differentiation. While the exact scale and scope of the trend will not be known for some time, it is clear that global sourcing is an important issue with potentially serious impact for individuals, companies, educational institutions at all levels, and governments around the world.

We anticipate the following global sourcing developments:

1. Global sourcing is likely to continue and extend beyond today's major talent supply hubs (such as Bangalore, India) to other countries and to secondary and

tertiary cities within major talent markets. Within the United States, demand for talent in rural areas may increase as an alternative for companies looking to enhance their flexibility and cost position without sourcing exclusively overseas.

2. Companies will expand the types of jobs performed offshore, performing both core and noncore work. Focus will shift from cost reduction to also achieving competitive differentiation and greater operational flexibility.

3. Start-ups will launch businesses by leveraging low-cost offshore talent to develop prototype products and services faster in order to maximize the return on private funding sources with low labor expenses. While Silicon Valley will likely remain a central location for technology companies, production-style programming talent can now be obtained at a much lower cost in other locations.

4. Unions will make offshoring a focus of union-organizing campaigns in the service sector. WashTech and Alliance@IBM are two examples of unions that have galvanized prospective members around concerns about offshoring.

5. Mainstream press coverage will appear less critical of offshoring when the economy is strong. In an economic downturn, however, offshoring will likely become a hot political issue, as it did during the 2004 presidential election campaign.

6. New high-skill jobs will emerge, as companies seek expertise in starting and managing offshore operations, cross-cultural relations, and vendor selection and management.

Despite these anticipated developments, several drivers and inhibitors will shape the way global sourcing trends actually evolve. Three important factors support increased global sourcing. First, pressure from customers, competitors, and investors creates an environment in which global sourcing needs to be at least considered, if not implemented. Second, companies that have experimented with offshore or outsourced operations, after working through common operational and cross-cultural pitfalls, have begun to learn lessons that will make future initiatives even more effective. Once business leaders have seen how work can be parsed and distributed around the world, their thinking about how to run their businesses is likely to change, making global sourcing a more common practice across industries and occupations. Third, technology innovations could further reduce the cost of geographically distributing work.

In addition, several factors could inhibit global talent sourcing practices. First, high-wage countries could enact legislation that restricts the options companies have for using offshore talent or laws that change tax policy, resulting in smaller cost savings expected from operating in low-wage countries. Second, a security scandal in an offshore location, particularly around data privacy, would raise awareness of the processing of personal information in foreign locations. This could lead to a consumer backlash against offshore services. Third, the tightening labor market in key areas, such as Bangalore, India, has already caused wages there to rise significantly. The preferred sources of talent may be saturated, thus making the growth of operations in those cities less tenable. Fourth, cultural differences have challenged companies establishing offshore operations, and this is likely to remain an important issue for companies even in the future. Finally, the management philosophies within individual companies make organizations more or less inclined to engage in some form of global talent sourcing. As competitive pressures continue to cause businesses to look offshore for some advantage, this inhibitor will likely decrease as more leaders are forced to think differently about how and where work can be done.

## Implications of Global Sourcing
## for Individuals

The good news: The United States almost certainly isn't going to run out of jobs, even though history shows that it's impossible to predict what new jobs will replace those that are destroyed. The bad news: Outsourcing overseas and technology could widen the gap between the wages of well-paying brainpower jobs and poorly paid hands-on jobs. (Wessel 2004, A1)

Many of the concerns Americans have about global sourcing are because it is not clear what opportunities will come next. The offshoring trend spurs anxiety about potential job loss, concern about downward wage pressure, and questions about whether to pursue further education or retraining. When manufacturing jobs began moving overseas in the 1980s, policymakers, corporate leaders, and educators touted services and the IT sector as providing career opportunities for the future. The shift toward globalization of service work has raised questions about the viability of pursuing employment in information-intensive service jobs.

Brainard and Litan (2004) described global sourcing as a structural change that influences where the jobs are, not the total number of jobs (3). Total employment remains related to the size of the labor force, but the types of jobs change. They went on to describe offshoring, similar to trade and technology, as a "process of creative destruction" in which people in affected industries could lose not only their jobs, but all their benefits, including healthcare insurance. People, naturally, are uncertain about how to proceed with their careers and education.

A major concern is about the downward pressure on wages due to the cheaper labor available abroad. The "skills premium" that educated professionals benefited from could be eroded in the future due to the larger, global talent pool. An analysis of data from the 2004 Displaced Worker Survey indicated that about three-quarters of nonmanufacturing employees had found new employment, of which 72 percent to 78 percent had been reemployed full-time. Workers whom the service sector displaced experienced less erosion of earnings (30 percent decrease for tradable services and 14 percent decrease for nontradable services) compared with those in the manufacturing sector who experienced earnings decreases averaging 32 percent (Jensen and Kletzer 2005, 50). It is not known how redistributive services offshoring might be. Globalization theories and evidence from the manufacturing sector provide only partial insights for individuals seeking guidance on how to orient their lives and work in a global economy.

Workers concerned about the impact of offshoring should understand, first, which types of jobs are likely to be offshored, and, second, how they as individuals can develop skills and capabilities that make them more employable. As previously noted, jobs that, do not require physical interaction between employee and customer involve codifiable local knowledge and are at greater risk of being offshored. More specifically, Bardhan and Kroll (2003) identified six attributes of jobs that increase their likelihood of being offshored. These attributes include

- no face-to-face customer service requirement;
- high information content;
- work process is telecommutable and Internet enabled;
- high wage differential with similar occupations in destination country;
- low setup barriers; and
- low social networking requirement.

At an individual level, in an environment of global talent sourcing, Friedman (2005) wrote that individuals should strive to be "untouchables"—those whose jobs cannot be outsourced (238–239). Friedman described four broad categories of untouchables. The first category is that of the "specials," the global elite of entertainers, athletes, and intellectuals whose talents are sought worldwide. Of course, this is a very limited group. If one cannot be "special," the second category may be available, according to Friedman. Here, one can become "specialized," with unique, distinguishing skills. Third, one can choose to be "anchored" by providing services rooted in face-to-face contact or local knowledge. Some doctors, lawyers, and teachers are examples of professional-level anchored roles; other anchored jobs include chefs, plumbers, nurses, hairdressers, and other roles involving personal contact with a customer, patient, or client. To maintain a competitive edge as someone "special," "specialized," or "anchored" requires continuous learning and skill development. Friedman's fourth recommendation for ensuring future job security is to be "really adaptable."

Higher-level jobs, particularly among consultants and managers, may experience a boost from offshoring. Leading Indian outsourcing companies have established offices in the United States to gain expertise and get closer to the U.S. market. For example, Infosys, the Indian IT firm with nearly US$1.6 billion in revenue, announced plans in April 2004 to invest US$20 million in a business consulting subsidiary in the United States to "match rivals and counter a possible political backlash against outsourcing" (UNCTAD 2004, 158). Senior consultants and rainmakers who can win business and manage stateside relationships for the foreign outsourcers will be in demand. In addition, as U.S. companies begin to offshore higher-value-added activities, such as R&D for new drugs, there will likely be higher demand for professionals able to direct and coordinate such activities across countries.

## Implications for Companies

Companies face considerable public scrutiny of their efforts to source talent globally, and it is likely that criticism will continue, particularly in an economic downturn. Despite the criticism, companies are not likely to curb efforts to lower their labor costs or stem efforts to find qualified talent across the globe. A *New York Times* article on IBM's job cuts in the United States and Europe, even as the company plans to expand in India, reflects the trend: "Cutting Here, But Hiring Over There" (Lohr 2005). Indeed, HR executives we interviewed at several multinational corporations captured the sentiment as follows: "We are growing, just not in the U.S."

Figure 15.1 illustrates this trend on a macro level, showing the changing location of employment in U.S.-based multinational companies (MNCs) between 1988 and 2003. The percentage of total employment in U.S.-based MNCs in the United States declined from 79 percent in 1988 to 72 percent in 2003, while employment in the

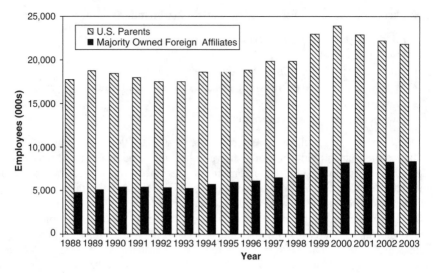

**Figure 15.1** U.S. and Foreign Employment by Non-Bank U.S. Multinational Companies, 1988–2003

*Source*: Adapted from Bureau of Economic Affairs, "Summary Estimates for Multinational Companies: Employment, Sales, and Capital Expenditures for 2003" Press Release, April 19, 2005, http://www.bea.gov/bea/newsrelarchive/2005/mnc2003.xls (Table 1).

MNCs' majority-owned foreign affiliates grew from 21 percent to 28 percent in the same period (Bureau of Economic Affairs 2005). This trend reflects broader globalization. The data, however, are aggregate and do not show the breakdown of foreign employment either by country or by occupation.

For companies planning to increase their global sourcing of talent, the early entrants provide good examples to follow. While the focus of offshoring to date has been largely on cost savings, some companies have expanded beyond cost considerations to achieve broader transformation of their businesses. Companies need to keep the strategic drivers in mind and the business models flexible to meet the changing global context.

General Electric was an early mover in the global sourcing of talent, and the company's experience provides an example of how the drivers and offshore business models have evolved in response to the Indian market's maturation. In 1993, GE Capital pursued a cost-saving strategy by hiring employees in India to provide operations support. GE Capital International Services (GECIS) was formed in 1997 to formalize the operations support services organization. GECIS began by operating call centers, then added basic data processing, moved to higher value-addition within data processing, and then phased into other higher-level activities such as product development. Over time, GE gradually sought to exploit the driver of differentiation by expanding the strategic value and complexity of services GECIS performed in India. In November 2004, GE sold a 60 percent stake in GECIS to two private-equity firms for $500 million (*The Economist* 2004).[3] The sale enabled GECIS to provide outsourced BPO services to a broader range of customers than might have been possible if the service provider had remained wholly owned by GE.

In the late 1990s, while GECIS's business process operations were proving the viability of offshore operations, GE further leveraged the differentiation driver by focusing on opportunities in India to add value in other activities of the value chain, especially engineering design and development. The Bangalore-based John F. Welch Technology Centre was launched in 2000. The multidisciplinary research and product development center employs 1,600 scientists, researchers, and engineers and serves multiple GE divisions. It was GE's first R&D center outside the United States and is part of GE's global research network with locations in the United States, China, Germany, and India.

Two other examples to highlight are IBM and British Telecommunications plc (BT). Both companies have been criticized for cutting jobs in their home countries (the United States and the United Kingdom, respectively), while growing overseas. Yet the companies' actions show awareness of the impact of offshoring decisions on their employees and communities. In March 2004, IBM created a $25 million fund called the Human Capital Alliance to support retraining for IBM employees whose jobs were affected by the movement of work outside the United States. Once retrained, the alliance would help find jobs for the former IBM employees with IBM's business partners (Zarley 2004).

Also early in 2004, BT contracted with SustainAbility, an independent, third-party observer, to assess the corporate social responsibility (CSR) impact of the company's migration of call-center jobs to outsourced operators overseas (Kuszewski, Prakash-Mani, and Beloe 2004). BT made the commitment that none of its employees would suffer involuntary redundancy and that any interested employees would be given assistance with retraining and finding a new position within BT or even elsewhere. Based on its analysis of BT's experience, SustainAbility identified twelve steps, shown

**Table 15.4**    Steps for Socially Responsible Offshoring

1. Consult with affected stakeholders before making a decision to offshore.
2. Clearly articulate policy and be honest and transparent about company decisions.
3. Limit or avoid involuntary redundancy.
4. Invest in retraining and skill development for affected employees.
5. Work with communities to help find ways to fill the gaps created by offshoring.
6. Work with suppliers in the recipient country to develop best practice and CSR awareness.
7. Set standards for suppliers and monitor their implementation.
8. Train and develop new employees and provide growth opportunities.
9. Help employees deal with psychological and cultural issues that may be involved.
10. Listen to local stakeholders to understand their needs and perspectives.
11. Invest in community, to secure the company's long-term social license to operate.
12. Share technologies and skills to enable local people and companies to advance.

*Source*: Judy Kuszewski, Kavita Prakash-Mani and Seb Beloe, *Good Migrations? BT, corporate social responsibility and the geography of jobs*, February 2004, London: SustainAbility, p. 4. Available at http://www.btplc.com/Societyandenvironment/ Hottopics/Geographyofjobs/Geographyofjobs.htm

in table 15.4, that companies might adopt to manage the community and social implications of offshoring, both in the home country and the recipient country.

One long-term implication of global sourcing for companies is the potential impact that the movement of work offshore will have on the development of future leaders and the cohesion of corporate cultures. The storehouses of a company's business processes, management styles, and corporate culture norms frequently are the same individuals who feel they are losing ground because of globalization. In addition, the rapid timeframes many companies experience between the offshoring decision and the start of implementation concentrates the time available to transmit knowledge to the new service provider. Effectively transferring knowledge across locations and organizational boundaries, while maintaining the dignity of affected home country staff, is a delicate issue, and one that many companies new to global sourcing have not handled well.

## Implications for Educational Institutions

Because it takes fifteen years to create a scientist or advanced engineer, starting from when that young man or woman first gets hooked on science and math in elementary school, we should be embarking on an all-hands-on-deck, no-holds-barred, no-budget-too-large crash program for science and engineering education immediately. The fact that we are not doing so is our quiet crisis. Scientists and engineers don't grow on trees. They have to be educated through a long process, because, ladies and gentlemen, this really is rocket science. (Friedman 2005, 275)

As Americans have become aware of the global competition for skilled service jobs and the substantial numbers of engineering graduates in other, low-wage countries, more attention has been paid to the challenges of educating U.S.-based students in the areas of science and engineering. While there have been some calls to reduce engineering education in the United States and let low-wage countries take up the engineering jobs, organizations such as the National Science Board (2003), National Academy of Engineering (2005), and the McKinsey Global Institute (2005) have argued in favor of increased investment in science and engineering education and curricular reform to make such fields more attractive to U.S. students. MGI argued against calls to shut down engineering education in high-wage countries. Their analysis indicated that although the population of engineering graduates is smaller in the United States than in either China or India, a greater proportion of the U.S.-trained engineers would be qualified for employment with multinational corporations than those graduating in other countries.

Two long-term trends have challenged future growth of the U.S. science and engineering (S&E) workforce. The first is the intensifying global competition for S&E talent. The United States has relied upon foreign-born S&E professionals, and, according to the National Science Board (NSB) (2003), the growing U.S. dependence on international S&E talent, particularly on foreign nationals, has become problematic. The increased availability of good jobs for international S&E professionals in their countries of origin reduces opportunities for U.S. employers to fill unmet skill needs using the international S&E labor market. The second challenge cited by the NSB was the anticipated decline in the number of U.S. native-born S&E graduates entering the workforce. The NSB recommended an active intervention by policy, community, and education stakeholders to improve success in educating S&E students from all demo-graphic groups, especially those underrepresented in S&E careers (9–10).

Recommendations have called for more funding for science education, curricu-lum reform, and raising the public profile of math, science, and engineering fields (Atkinson 2004b; National Academy of Engineering 2005). Specifically, the NSB called for more funding for science and technology education, particularly federal support via scholarships to reduce the cost of undergraduate education; funding for advanced science and engineering research; and encouraging S&E education in com-munity colleges. The National Academy of Engineering (NAE) proposed reforming undergraduate engineering curricula to create a broader array of engineering degrees, including a bachelor of arts degree positioned as a "liberal arts" degree that prepares students for a wide range of careers in the twenty-first century. The NAE also recommended curriculum redesign to engage students in design and real-world problem solving early in their undergraduate programs "so that the social relevance of engineering is apparent" (33), rather than have students spend the first years focused only on mathematical calculations.

## Implications for Governments and Policymakers

Global talent sourcing by U.S. companies raises several challenging issues for policy-makers and political leaders at local, state, and national levels. First and foremost is how government policies can support constituents, communities, and companies in the midst of the struggle between the benefits of global trade and the redistribution of employment that local communities will likely experience. Initial reactions exhib-ited protectionist tones, proposing to prevent state funds from going to companies that performed work overseas (Atkinson 2004b, 1). Policies and legislation regarding immigration, the social safety net for individuals made redundant by offshoring, and corporate taxes could significantly impact the way the U.S. economy and population experience the transition to a world where services are delivered globally. Without appropriate policies, the United States might experience a backlash against interna-tional integration similar to the opposition to trade and immigration that occurred in the interwar period of the last century (Karoly and Panis 2004, 158).

According to globalization theory, offshoring and global talent sourcing provide three main benefits to developed countries (UNCTAD 2004, 176). First, such prac-tices enable companies to reduce costs and/or improve quality, making them more competitive in the global marketplace. Managers of U.S. and European multination-als that we interviewed were convinced of the impact offshoring can have on enhanc-ing their competitiveness. Second, they enable the home country to shift to more productive and higher-value activities, assuming the labor markets are dynamic and people can adapt to take advantage of emerging employment opportunities. The U.S. labor markets are in the process of adjusting to services globalization, so the benefits of this aspect of globalization are not yet being felt. Third, countries doing the off-shore work might increase their imports of goods from the developed countries. Countries such as India, which used to severely restrict imports, have continued to liberalize trade and are importing larger quantities of products from developed coun-tries. Yet, despite these anticipated benefits, job losses in developed countries also lead to reduced tax revenue for governments and greater expenditures for unemployment and retraining support (Bottino 2004).

*Immigration*

As stated previously, foreign-born individuals make up an important labor source for science and technology jobs. U.S. census data show that for all degree levels, the share of U.S. science and engineering occupations filled by scientists or engineers who were born abroad increased from 14 to 22 percent between 1990 and 2000. During the same period, the share increased from 11 to 17 percent at the bachelor's degree level; at the master's level, from 19 to 29 percent; and at the doctorate level, from 24 to 38 percent (NSB 2003, 9).

In 2001, more than 330,000 temporary work visas were issued for specialty occupations, mostly computer-related jobs (Karoly and Panis 2004, 146). However, increased concerns about security and the loss of U.S. jobs reduced the number of visas authorized in subsequent years. Such policies pose short-term challenges for companies seeking labor. Reducing immigration to the United States encourages companies to seek talented labor sources abroad; if no visas are available to bring the person to work, the work can now theoretically move to the person, wherever he or she may live. Immigration restrictions could also negatively impact U.S. innovation and entrepreneurship in the long run. In *The 21st Century at Work* (2004, 146–147), Karoly and Panis wrote:

> In high-tech centers such as California's Silicon Valley, immigrants make up substantial portions of the scientific and engineering workforce (about one-third in the case of Silicon Valley as of 1990) (Saxenian 1999). Their contributions extend to entrepreneurship as well: as of 1998, Chinese and Indian immigrant engineers led one in four high-technology Silicon Valley firms . . . .Current estimates suggest 70 percent of foreign-born U.S. Ph.D. recipients do not return to their country of origin (Bhagwati 2003).

*Social Safety Net*

A key ingredient to enhance the employability of U.S. workers is the creation of a legal and institutional framework for the portability of pensions and healthcare.[4] The current framework, which ties health insurance almost exclusively to one's employer, hinders people's willingness to voluntarily change employers and increases anxiety over the financial impact of losing a job. Brainard and Litan (2004) recommended addressing the problem of employee dislocation through a combination of wage insurance, adjustment assistance, and training (7). As previously noted, existing federal legislation does not adequately address the diversity of U.S. employees being affected by global sourcing of services. The Trade Adjustment Assistance (TAA) Program, which was amended in 2002 to add a healthcare benefit, was authorized initially only for manufacturing workers (Atkinson 2004b, 10). However, in early 2006, the US Department of Labor, in response to remarks from the U.S. Court of International Trade, changed its policy to allow an expansion of the term "article" under TAA to include products that do not exist on a physical medium. "Intangible articles," such as software, now satisfy its regulatory requirement (Shew 2006). The Trade Promotional Authority Act was amended in 2002 to provide wage insurance also to workers aged 50 or older who can prove that trade is a "major cause" of their displacement. Kletzer and Litan (2001) proposed expanding wage insurance policies to cover all displaced workers, regardless of age.

A second important factor in helping people find work sooner is providing employees longer notice of their termination. The Progressive Policy Institute supported legislation to bring more companies under the Worker Adjustment and Retraining Notification (WARN) Act so as to include companies with 50 or more employees (versus 100 or more employees currently), layoffs of 15 or more workers (as opposed to 50 or more workers), and to provide three months (versus 60 days) of notice about the layoffs (Atkinson 2004b, 11).

*Corporate Tax Policy*

Tax policies may artificially encourage offshoring. The current corporate tax system permits companies to defer taxation on foreign earnings but not on domestic earnings (Brainard and Litan 2004, 6). The Progressive Policy Institute (Atkinson 2004b) advocates expanding and updating the tax credit for R&D expenditures to increase the credit level and introduce a tax credit in order to encourage collaborative research at universities, federal laboratories, and research consortia.

## Conclusion

American workers have experienced considerable change in their employment environments since *Work in America* was published in 1973. More than two-thirds of the economy is now in the service sector. Globalization has opened new markets for U.S. goods and services, as well as for foreign labor. And technology has facilitated the transformation and segmentation of business processes to allow for outsourcing and movement of work to locations near and far. Despite the many forecasts about future global sourcing activity, it is only over time that we will know the long-term economic, political, and social impacts of the global sourcing trend.

Individuals, companies, governments, professional and trade associations, and educational institutions will need to adapt to meet the changing demands of the global labor market. The calls to invest heavily in science, math, and engineering education and to enact government policies that provide a cushion for individuals affected by the redistributive effects of offshoring are a starting point for the construction of a framework within which to position the U.S. economy and American workers for the remainder of the twenty-first century.

# Shared Capitalism at Work: Impacts and Policy Options

*Joseph Blasi, Douglas Kruse, and Richard B. Freeman*

For the last several decades, various companies have shared the benefit of corporate results with employees of the firm, using profit-sharing, gain sharing, bonuses, employee stock ownership, or stock options. All of these approaches have one thing in common: offering the worker a share in profits or stock appreciation when the company makes a profit on the capital that investors have provided. For the first time, a comprehensive picture of shared capitalism in the United States has become available as a result of a national random sample of all employed adults in the U.S. government-supported 2002 General Social Survey (GSS).[1] This survey provides new information about the impact of shared capitalism on the experiences of workers and their companies. Since these results are statistically representative of the country at large, they are especially salient for policy discussions of these issues. Furthermore, they do not have the disadvantages of the biases introduced by nonrepresentative or small samples, surveys of companies or managers, case studies, or conceptual discussions of these issues.

Before discussing the results of this study, we give a brief historical overview of shared capitalism, describe how it works, and discuss why we should care about it. Then we turn to who works under shared capitalism and what we can now say about its impact on the worker and the corporation. Finally, we will discuss how the study can inform policy toward shared capitalist enterprises. Our goal is to understand whether various shared capitalist approaches play a role in how work can be made meaningful and rewarding for employees, and how workplaces can be made more productive.

## Historical Highlights

Throughout U.S. history, businesses have developed a variety of mechanisms to allow employees to directly participate in the financial performance of the firm. Albert Gallatin, a signatory to the Declaration of Independence and Secretary of the Treasury under Thomas Jefferson, said, "the democratic principle upon which this

Nation was founded should not be restricted to the political processes but should be applied to the industrial operation." True to his word, he set up a profit-sharing plan at the Pennsylvania Glass Works in 1795. In the late 1790s, small groups of craftspeople set up cooperative firms, owned among themselves.

Profit-sharing and employee ownership were used in companies and by various trade unions in a wide variety of industries throughout the 1800s. Charles Pillsbury used profit-sharing with half of his mill workers in 1882. In 1886, mapmaker Rand McNally did the same with his employees, as did William Procter, who set up a profit-sharing plan for Procter & Gamble (P&G) that went on to encourage broad-based employee ownership. More than a hundred years later, P&G is 15 to 20 percent owned by its worldwide employees, has profit-sharing, and also shares stock options broadly.

The phenomenon was seen as being so important that John Bates Clark, a key founder of the American Economics Association, wrote a book in the 1880s calling for the combination of profit-sharing and employee ownership in companies to improve business performance by motivating worker involvement (Clark 1886). With his encouragement, the first volume of the journal of the American Economics Association included an article surveying shared capitalism in companies in the Northeast (Bemis 1886) and in a Midwestern city, Minneapolis (Shaw 1886).

Employee ownership, employee involvement in corporate decision-making, and profit-sharing were also encouraged by the Special Conference Committee set up by John D. Rockefeller in 1919 with other corporate leaders, which helped spread the ideas and practices of "welfare capitalism" in the 1920s and beyond (Jacoby 1997). Princeton University's Industrial Relations Section published a special study on this phenomenon at the time. In 1919, George Eastman became one of the first "high-technology moguls" of his day to embrace employee ownership by offering 8 percent of his own Eastman Kodak stock to employees who would remain for a certain period of time with the company (for an overview in American history, see Blasi, Kruse, and Bernstein 2003, 158–170).

The enormous losses that employee stock owners suffered during the stock market crash—and the knowledge from Congressional investigations that insiders profited while workers lost—tempered interest in employee ownership. Profit-sharing became more popular and was advanced in Congressional hearings by Republican Senator Arthur Vandenberg. Employees at many firms such as Hewlett-Packard, Sears, Procter & Gamble, Harris Bank, and Safeway Stores also became major shareholders in these corporations as a result of profit-sharing checks that were invested in company stock.

Meanwhile, in 1958, California investment banker Louis Kelso, along with former University of Chicago philosopher, Encyclopedia Britannica chairman, and Aspen Institute leader Mortimer Adler, published a book called *The Capitalist Manifesto*, in which they called for loans to workers to buy stock in order to give them a greater stake in capitalism. Kelso and Adler digested the experience of the crash and determined that workers should not use their salaries or savings to buy company stock. In the 1970s and 1980s, using the ideas of Kelso and Adler, Senator Russell Long, a Louisiana Democrat, pushed bipartisan federal legislation creating an Employee Stock Ownership Plan (ESOP) that was specifically not funded by worker savings. ESOPs have now spread to millions of workers and created thousands of companies with broadly-held ownership (for information see www.beysterinstitute.org, http://www.esopassociation.org or http://www.nceo.org).

Also in the 1950s, venture capitalist Arthur Rock and scientists Robert Noyce and Gordon Moore put together an exodus from Shockley Semiconductor Laboratories to form Fairchild Semiconductor. They were partly motivated by a lack of willingness of Nobel Prize–winner William Shockley to share power and profits with knowledge workers through broad-based stock options and more participatory management approaches. In 1968, they also left Fairchild Semiconductor to start Intel, which was built around these ideas. J. Robert Beyster mined a similar vein with the founding of an engineering consulting firm, SAIC, in 1969. Meanwhile, an explosion of software and hardware and engineering consulting start-ups in Silicon Valley and beyond was inspired by the Intel and SAIC models (for a detailed high-tech history see Blasi, Kruse, Bernstein 2003, 3–30).

Finally, since the 1970s, larger corporations have made 401k plans a major vehicle for employee ownership by matching employee contributions to such plans in company stock and encouraging workers to buy stock with their own savings. This violated the views of both scholars and experts on investing and Kelso's advice by introducing substantial risk to many workers' portfolios, and that risk came home to roost in the stock market decline of 2000, followed by the notable failures of Enron and WorldCom and other corporate governance disasters. On the high-tech front, the broad-based stock option and profit sharing have now spread to biotech and new health-tech companies.

### How Does Shared Capitalism Work?

Thus, by 1973, when the first *Work in America* report was published, a quiet evolution of shared capitalism institutions was only just beginning in the United States. Profit-sharing continued to be used by some corporations, but ESOPs were not established in federal law until 1974, 401k plans were not introduced until 1981, and some well-known tech companies that popularized broad-based stock options such as Microsoft (started in 1975) and Apple (started in 1977) and Compaq (started in 1982) were not founded yet. Now, in 2006, we can examine all forms of shared capitalism side by side and in combination to see what workers actually have and what their experience with them has been.

Profit-sharing offers workers a payment based on increases in the profit of the company, which may be paid in cash or put in a retirement plan (called "deferred profit-sharing"). Sometimes profit-sharing is paid to workers in company stock, so what is received as a profit share may end up as employee ownership. Gain sharing offers workers regular payments based on the performance of their work units.

Employee ownership refers to ownership of company stock through any number of plans. The most popular is the ESOP, which is distinguished by the fact that workers do not have to use their own money to buy the stock (although there are a few cases in which employees take wage concessions in exchange for an ESOP or roll over 401k assets into an ESOP). Federal legislation allows companies to borrow money from a bank to fund the worker stock and pay for it in installments from company revenues. Employees can also purchase stock through their company 401k plan, a retirement plan in which they make pre-tax contributions from their paychecks. Sometimes corporations will match employee contributions to 401k plans with company stock, so that the type of employee ownership resulting specifically from the company matching contribution is closer to an ESOP, because workers do not buy it.

Employee Stock Purchase Plans (ESPPs) that allow workers to buy stock with deductions from their paychecks with a discount from the market price have also become common. Some corporations provide employees direct grants of stock as part of a stock bonus plan as well. (For the number of employees and assets in such plans and an estimate of their losses in the 2000 crash, see Blasi, Kruse, and Bernstein 2003, 249.)

Stock options represent a kind of hybrid between profit-sharing and employee ownership. A stock option is the right to buy the stock at a set price anytime during a specified period following the option grants. The worker is granted the option and does not have to purchase it. So, for example, 100 stock options to purchase Biotech Inc. stocks at $10 per share give the worker the right to exercise this option anytime over ten years if the stock price goes above $10 a share. During the ten years, the worker could buy the stock for $10 per share when it is trading at $15 per share, then sell the stock, and pocket the $5 profit (after taxes). Though stock option excesses among higher executives have maligned this instrument of profit sharing, for other managers and workers a stock option has less risk than using one's savings to buy the stock, because it in fact offers the right to the upside gain without the downside risk of losing one's capital.

## Why Should We Care about Shared Capitalism?

The principal reason for caring about shared capitalism is that the core idea of capitalism is about giving organizations incentives to produce efficiently what society wants through distributing profits to capital based on performance. Economists have expected capitalist systems to be more efficient than systems based on feudalism or socialism, specifically because of the role of the individual's personal economic self-interest in making both individual work and enterprises function better. Capitalism emerged as a rebellion against feudalism, where one class of persons had ownership and control of economic assets and another class simply worked these assets without a clear incentive to improve their value. In feudalism, income is based on custom, tradition, and class rather than individual performance and team performance. Power, prestige, and rewards principally accrue to the ruling class in feudal economic systems, no matter what the individual achievements of the "serfs" are.

Entrepreneurial drive is a basic element of capitalism because it gives the investor of capital an incentive to make available capital to others. This drive then provides motivation for those who work with the capital in companies to shepherd its growth responsibly and turn a profit. Those who revolted against feudalism wanted individuals to have more personal control over their income and investments. This obviously led to the expectation and the widely held view that capitalism would have better organizational performance than feudalism.

Shared capitalism is about extending the entrepreneurial drive to groups of workers within company settings. It is not about "socialist equality" inside companies, where everyone gets a share no matter what. It is about giving people a stake in their better performance and managing this performance through responsible involvement. But this is not as simple as it sounds, since workers are not like rats responding to sugar cubes. Most scholars have concluded that profit-sharing, employee ownership, and broad stock options need to be combined with a culture of fairness, empowerment, and high performance work practices to affect company performance (see Rosen, Case, and Staubus 2005). When workers in a corporation have the proper incentives and cooperative work arrangements, shared capitalism may align the interests of the shareholders or investors with those who "work" their capital inside corporations, the workers (for a theoretical discussion, see Freeman, Kruse, and Blasi 2004).

A final reason for caring about shared capitalism is that it strengthens democratic practices. Imagine if the United States evolved toward a model where a small number of citizens owned most of the assets and pocketed most of the profits of industrial and service enterprises, while paying minimum wages to everyone else. Such a system would likely produce a government that was heavily under the influence of the controlling minority, with a majority that had little incentive to participate and exercise their voting rights, save possibly to seek huge tax redistributions. From this point of view, shared capitalism can be seen as a component to a strong democratic state, in that it encourages and defends widespread citizen involvement in protecting basic liberties and freedoms. For these reasons, shared capitalism has had a rare bipartisan appeal. Republicans like President Ronald Reagan praised the emphasis on broadened property ownership. Democrats have liked the potential expansion of worker income and participation in corporate performance.

Insight from recent empirical research gives meaning to this perspective. Median inflation-adjusted wage growth has been slower in the past three decades than in the three decades after World War II. Those American families who have experienced meaningful inflation-adjusted income growth obtained this added income from income on capital—that is, stocks, bonds, real property, and interests in businesses (for the study, see Mishel, Bernstein, and Allegretto 2005). Greater worker participation in capital income through shared capitalism is a promising way of improving the incomes of more Americans and strengthening the middle class.

Moreover, research indicates that the intangible assets of companies, such as the intellectual capital of workers and the corporate culture and human resource systems, now account for a large share of the market value of publicly traded corporations, even more than the book value of fixed assets of these companies. Indeed, "Over the last twenty years the ratio of market price to book value for the S&P 500 has increased nearly sixfold" (Huselid, Becker, and Beatty 2005, 17). By helping change the way companies work, shared capitalism can enhance these intangible assets. That is why the idea is so central in high-tech entrepreneurial firms. For these reasons, an examination of the impact of different systems of shared capitalism and different workplace cultures can have enormous policy value.

## Who Works under Shared Capitalism?

While separate estimates about the incidence of the different approaches to shared capitalism have been available over the last quarter century, the U.S. General Social Survey (GSS) provides a single picture with one comprehensive random sample of the entire working population, based on 90-minute personal interviews with 2765, adults conducted in the spring of 2002. The biennial GSS, which has been conducted since 1972, is one of the largest survey projects funded by the U.S. government and is second only to the U.S. census in its use by sociologists to study the population. Its major core funding is from the National Science Foundation.

The 2002 GSS had a response rate of 70 percent and included a special shared capitalism segment along with extensive questions on the quality of working life sponsored by another federal agency. The results presented here are based on interviews with the approximately 1200 adults who were working in the private sector.

While we cannot look into every key question that has interested observers of shared capitalism with this survey, we can begin to sketch some of the principal trends. The GSS will repeat and expand the shared capitalism survey in 2006 with more questions. We plan to continue this study every four years in order to monitor this important phenomenon.

Table 16.1 provides a picture of shared capitalism in the United States from the GSS. Thirty six percent of the private sector working population reported that they participated in some kind of shared capitalism in the United States, and 64 percent of the U.S. population was not involved in shared capitalism practices (Part A).[2] The percent of the population receiving each type of shared capitalism is distributed as follows: 25 percent of the private sector working population reported receiving profit-sharing or gain sharing bonuses (henceforth called performance sharing) along with their regular wages, 21 percent of them owned stocks in the company where they work, and 13 percent were holding stock options on their company's stock (Part B). But this does not reflect the types of shared capitalism workers actually have. Within the 36 percent of workers receiving shared capitalism, 15 percent have only performance sharing, 5 percent have only employee ownership, 1 percent have only stock options, while the rest of them were receiving various combinations of the three. The most prevalent combinations are all three received by 6 percent of workers, and employee ownership and stock options received by about 6 percent of workers, and employee ownership and performance sharing received by 4 percent of workers (Part B).

The table also indicates that shared capitalism has highly disparate effects on worker incomes (Part C). Dividing those receiving performance payments into thirds, the third obtaining the least amount received an annual payment constituting less than 3 percent of their annual income, for the middle third, the performance share equaled three to 7 percent of annual income, and the highest third got payments of more than 7 percent of their annual income. Similarly, a third of those with employee ownership had a company stock portfolio worth less than 12 percent of their annual income, for the middle third it equaled 12 to 46 percent of their annual income, and for the upper third it equaled more than 46 percent of their annual income. As we examine the impacts on workers and corporations, we will keep a close eye on how much the relative size of low, medium, and high shared capitalism matters. Information on stock option profits and potential profits is not available, so the results on options are much less fine-tuned.

Appendix I provides a demographic breakdown of shared capitalism by age, sex, marital status, class, income, and supervisory role compared to the U.S. working population. Workers with shared capitalism are fairly evenly distributed along these dimensions, with the exception that they are under-represented in the less than $15,000 per year income range and over-represented in the more than $50,000 per year income range. In absolute numbers, more than half are in the $15,000 to $50,000 per year income range. While about half the workers participating in shared capitalism practices are regular workers who are not supervisors, participation in shared capitalism is somewhat over-represented among low-level supervisors and very over-represented among mid- and high-level supervisors. This last group makes up 8 percent of all workers, but 16 percent on average of the workers for the most common shared capitalism practices.

**Table 16.1**  Percent of Workers with Shared Capitalism and Size of Stakes

*A. Overall Picture*

| | |
|---|---|
| Performance Sharing or Employee Ownership or Stock Options | 36% |
| No Shared Capitalism | 64% |
| | 100% |

*B. What Workers Actually Have*

| | |
|---|---|
| Only Performance Sharing | 15% |
| Only Employee Ownership | 5% |
| Only Stock Options | 1% |
| Employee Ownership and Stock Options | 6% |
| Performance Sharing and Stock Options | <1% |
| Employee Ownership and Performance Sharing | 4% |
| All Three (PS, EO, SO) | 6% |
| No Shared Capitalism | 64% |
| | 100% |

| | Percent of Population Receiving | Percent of Annual Income for | | |
|---|---|---|---|---|
| | | Lowest Third | Middle Third | Highest Third |
| *C. Percent of Annual Income* | | | | |
| Performance Sharing | 25% | <3% | 3–7% | >7% |
| Employee Ownership | 21% | <12% | 12–46% | >46% |
| Stock Options | 13% | Not available | – | – |

*Source*: General Social Survey, National Opinion Research Center, University of Chicago. Numbers are rounded. In Part C, the performance sharing row presents bonuses as a percent of annual income, while the employee ownership row presents value of employer stock held as a percent of annual income (since total wealth data are not available).

## What Is the Impact of Shared Capitalism on the Worker?

Overall relations between management and workers represent the most fundamental evaluation by workers of their workplace. Eight percent of workers overall reported quite bad or very bad relations with management. When this is examined through the prism of shared capitalism practices, 4 percent of workers with shared capitalist arrangements report quite or very bad relations with shared capitalism, compared to 9 percent of workers who report quite or very bad relations without shared capitalism.

There are more subtle differences, depending on the type of shared capitalism. Two percent of workers overall reported very bad relations with their employers, but workers with performance sharing reported this only a third as much (1 percent) as those without performance sharing (3 percent). At the other end of the spectrum, while 68 percent of workers without performance sharing reported very good or quite good relations, 78 percent of those with performance sharing had positive views of labor-management relations. Workers with performance sharing have less very bad relations but only slightly better good relations. As the percent of workers' annual income represented by the performance payments goes up, they have better relations with their employer, but the really large differences happen when annual performance sharing exceeds 7 percent of annual income. These workers were the least likely to report quite or very bad relations. Almost 90 percent of them reported very good or quite good relations with their employers, versus 68 percent of workers without performance sharing.

Do we observe the same differences with employee stock ownership? Unfortunately, the GSS could not measure the difference between employee ownership that workers buy with their own wages or savings (such as 401k plans or ESPPs) versus employee ownership received on top of wages (such as most ESOPs) or whether workers felt they were being paid below market wages. Employee ownership in ESOPs, which represents an added incentive above wages where workers do not buy the stock with their savings, appears to be associated with a positive influence on labor management relations (Freeman, Kruse, and Blasi 2004). If we lump all the employee ownership in the country together as the 2002 GSS did, there is no meaningful difference in employer relations, whether or not one looks at simply having employee ownership or the levels of employee ownership as a percent of income.

But do you remember Kelso's and Adler's prescient warning in the 1950s against employee ownership that workers have to buy, which opens them to too much risk? This is the Rosetta Stone that unlocks the distinction. From federal records on retirement plans, we have estimated that almost three out of every four dollars of employee stock ownership is stock that workers bought with their savings and paychecks in their 401k plans (see Blasi, Kruse, and Bernstein 2003, 249). These workers are likely to feel very differently about management and their firm than those who feel they are paid equal to the market wage and receive a meaningful amount of stock in a plan on top of it. The GSS thus provides some evidence of two worlds of employee ownership in the country, one most commonly represented by ESOPs and similar arrangements that provide workers stock on top of their wages, and the other typified by company stock in 401k plans where workers have to buy their employee ownership with their own savings. The size of the shared capitalism stake and the way workers acquire it seems to be a key variable to which employers must pay attention.

The original *Work in America* report focused heavily on the quality of working life, so it makes sense to compare workers with and without shared capitalism practices in terms of the quality of work life characteristics measured by the 2002 GSS. These results can be examined in table 16.2. Workers under shared capitalism report that they have greater job satisfaction; better relations with the employer, supervisors, and coworkers; more pride in their employer; more employee participation in decisions; and more acceptable pay, benefits, and incentives. However, they do not report significantly more smoothly running workplaces, trust in management, help from supervisors, or job security. These results suggest a mostly better quality of working life in general for workers under shared capitalism, with some bumps.

One skeptical view about the value of shared capitalism to workers is that when workers are tied in any of these ways to the performance of the firm, the firm may use this to give them less desirable workplace relations. Another part of the skepticism is the claim that workers under shared capitalism are less unionized than the general population. The argument goes that because of the pecuniary incentives under

**Table 16.2**   Shared Capitalism versus No Shared Capitalism: Some Quality of Working Life Differences

| | Job Satisfaction | Any Shared Capitalism | No Shared Capitalism |
|---|---|---|---|
| Overall Job Satisfaction | Very or somewhat satisfied | 91% | 83%** |
| *Overall Evaluations of the Employer* | | | |
| Am proud to be working for my employer | Agree or strongly agree | 91% | 86%** |
| Relations between mgt. and employees | Good or very good | 73% | 69%* |
| Trust management at work | Agree or strongly agree | 76% | 76% |
| Workplace is run in a smooth and effective manner | Agree or strongly agree | 74% | 73% |
| *Supervisory Relations* | | | |
| Supervisor cares about welfare of those under him or her | Very or somewhat true | 88% | 82%** |
| Supervisor is helpful to me | Very or somewhat true | 86% | 83% |
| Am treated with respect at work | Agree or strongly agree | 94% | 90%** |
| When do job well, likely to be praised by supervisor or employer | | 58% | 51%** |
| *Relations with Coworkers* | | | |
| Coworkers take personal interest in me | Very or somewhat true | 88% | 84%* |
| Coworkers can be relied on | Very or somewhat true | 92% | 89%* |
| *Employee Participation* | | | |
| Have lot of say about what happens on my job | Agree or strongly agree | 76% | 64%** |
| Take part with others in making decisions that affect you | Often or sometimes | 84% | 74%** |
| Participate with others in setting way things are done on the job | Often or sometimes | 84% | 79%** |
| Given a lot of freedom to decide how to do work | Very or somewhat true | 89% | 85%** |
| *Pay and Incentives* | | | |
| How fair is pay | As much or more than what you deserve | 61% | 55%** |
| Fringe benefits are good | Very or somewhat true | 85% | 61%** |
| When do job well, likely to get bonus or raise | | 39% | 18%** |
| *Job Security and Promotions* | | | |
| Job security is good | Very or somewhat true | 85% | 82% |
| Chances for promotion are good | Very or somewhat true | 68% | 50%** |
| Promotions are handled fairly | Very or somewhat true | 74% | 65%** |

\* Difference is significant at 90% level ** Significant at 95% level

*Source*: Analysis of the 2002 General Social Sirvey by the authors.

shared capitalism, workers will put up with more unfairness and less representation in the workplace, and will injure themselves more often out of a desire to improve performance than under other forms of compensation. Even worse, some are suspicious that shared capitalism is a manipulative front for stingy low wage employers.

The GSS results do not support such claims. Workers in all three forms of shared capitalism structures report significantly more positive attitudes about the ability of their income to cover their bills than those without shared capitalism (in results not reported but available). They do not report more cases of discrimination or harassment of any kind, more injuries, or more work/family conflict. They do not report that they feel more exhausted/burned out at the end of the day or have insufficient time to get their jobs done than workers without these shared capitalism practices. Finally, the workers in the low-, medium-, or high-income categories of performance sharing or employee ownership were not more or less unionized than the economy as a whole. "Bad" employers are not the ones using shared capitalism and the various mechanisms are not leading to some kind of unreasonable speedup or toleration of unfortunate circumstances in these companies.

Regarding the quality of working life, workers under shared capitalism report that they are on average faring better. Indeed, one historical debate over shared capitalism companies is resolved with evidence that they tend to have more employee participation. At the same time, there is also variation within shared capitalism companies, variations that the single label does not help us understand. And the data do not allow us to determine whether better employers offer shared capitalism or whether shared capitalism encourages them to change their workplaces for the better. This is not a controlled "before and after" experiment for shared capitalism. Still, some light can be shed on the dynamics of shared capitalism by exploring the role of empowerment in these companies more closely.

## What Is the Impact of Shared Capitalism on the Employer?

Whenever employers adopted shared capitalism practices, they typically argued that these practices were good for both the worker and the business; namely, that they did in fact align the interests of investors of capital with those of the workers in shareholder-owned corporations. Studies based on production function data provide such evidence for firms or establishments (see Kruse 1993a, 1993b; Kruse and Blasi 1995, 1997; Blasi, Kruse, and Bernstein 2003, 153–184), but do not illuminate what it is that workers do to improve productivity, and in particular, how shared capitalist firms and their employees are able to overcome the "free rider" problem inherent in any group incentive scheme. By this we mean the incentive that any given worker has to take it easy since their contribution to the total profit or revenue is small.

While the GSS did not collect information on the financial performance of the companies, it asked workers questions that may reflect their contribution to company operations (Freeman and Dube 2000, report similar evidence based on questions asked workers in the mid 1990s; see also Freeman and Rogers 1999) and which can cast light on free riding. Our hypothesis is that shared capitalist firms maintain incentives and limit free riding behavior because shared capitalist workers are more willing to intervene when they see someone "shirking" than are workers in other firms.

*Intervening with a Shirker*

If shared capitalism does affect firm performance, economic theory suggests that a critical mechanism should be the willingness of workers in such arrangements to intervene with a fellow worker when he or she is not doing the job properly. When we designed the shared capitalism segment of the GSS, we included an entire series of questions on this issue in order to measure whether or not greater worker monitoring and intervention with shirkers took place under shared capitalism (Freeman, Kruse, and Blasi 2004). One of the questions was, "If you were to see a fellow employee not working as hard or well as he or she should, how likely would you be to do nothing?" The answers were not at all likely, not very likely, somewhat likely, or very likely. Twenty-four percent of workers in the economy in general say they are very likely to do nothing when they observe a fellow worker not doing a job properly, and an additional 17 percent say they are somewhat likely to do nothing.

But the situation looks different in firms with shared capitalism practices. Eighteen percent of workers who receive performance shares report they will do nothing, compared to 27 percent of workers who do not get such payments. Furthermore, the percent who say they will do nothing goes down as performance shares represent a higher percent of a workers' annual income. The same is true with employee ownership, where 14 percent of workers whose employee stock ownership represents a high percent of their annual income say they will do nothing, versus 26 percent of workers without any employee ownership. In this case, we surmise that both workers with stock they got from the company (such as in ESOPs) and those with stock they that bought with their savings (such as worker purchases in a 401k plan or an ESPP) appear to feel a greater identification with the company, although, obviously, the incentive value of each may vary. Workers with stock options are also less likely to say they will do nothing about a shirker, but the difference is not statistically significant (in part due to the small sample size and the problem that we did not have low, medium, and high categories for stock option profits if workers exercised their options on the day of the survey).

So far, we have been looking at shared capitalism practices in isolation. Now let us look more closely at the role of corporate culture by examining empowerment. To measure the extent to which workers are empowered to work in their firm, we created an Empowerment Score from a set of nine questions in the GSS. These questions asked such things as: the amount of say workers had on their job, their freedom to decide how to do their work; the information they had to get the job done; their participation in decisions; and so on.[3] To make a readily interpretable measure, we formed a scalar "summated rating" of the responses to the questions—that is we measured the answers to each question on a scale from 1 (least empowerment) to 3 or 4 (greatest empowerment) and simply summed up these answers. Thus, the Empowerment Score has its highest value when respondents gave high empowerment answers to most or all of the questions and the least value when they gave low empowerment answers to most or all of the questions.

For decades, observers of shared capitalism have argued about whether these firms tend to be more participatory. The GSS begins to answer that debate. Significantly more workers with performance shares and employee ownership have High Empowerment Scores, although this is not true of workers with stock options. However, for the purposes of looking at intervention with a shirker, what we want to examine is evidence on the combination of empowerment and shared capitalism.

**Table 16.3**    Empowerment, Shared Capitalism, and Unwillingness to Intervene with a Shirker

| Low Empowerment<br>No Shared Capitalism<br>32% | High Empowerment<br>No Shared Capitalism<br>20% |
|---|---|
| Low Empowerment<br>Any Amt. of Shared Capitalism<br>25% | High Empowerment<br>Any Amt. of Shared Capitalism<br>17% |

*Note*: The percent describes the workers who say they are very likely to do nothing.

*Source*: General Social Survey, National Opinion Research Center, University of Chicago.

Table 16.3 provides a general overview of the findings indicating the percent of workers who report that they will do nothing to intervene with a shirker. Those workers with Low Empowerment and No Shared Capitalism are most likely to do nothing, while those with High Empowerment and Any Amount of Shared Capitalism are least likely to do nothing. High Empowerment is better than Low Empowerment, yet adding Any Amount of Shared Capitalism is also better. Those workers *most* willing to intervene with a shirker have both empowerment and shared capitalism.

Going beyond this general picture the evidence in Appendix II shows that workers are more likely to intervene with a shirker when they have performance shares and employee ownership representing medium and high levels of their annual income; and that using shared capitalism approaches in combination with Low Empowerment does not significantly improve workplace outcomes for employers. This is consistent with research on employee ownership that shows that positive effects are realizable only with a participatory company culture.[4]

Managers who say they do not have time to worry about empowerment often speak of an "independent incentive effect" of shared capitalism. Indeed, workers with *any* level of performance sharing, stock options, or high performance sharing with Low Empowerment do appear to experience an independent incentive effect by saying that they are somewhat less likely to do nothing. These results shed light on an additional debate. Is High Empowerment without shared capitalism likely to have as much as an impact on company operations? From this vantage point, the answer is no. While High Empowerment employees without shared capitalism are more likely to intervene with a shirker than virtually any Low Empowerment group of workers, adding significant shared capitalism is associated with the most intervention. The lack of data on stock option profits or expected profits limits this analysis regarding options.

A persistent theme of this chapter gets underlined once again by these results: A shared capitalism approach that adds significant incentives to worker income and wealth will have the greatest effect. With employee ownership, the 2002 GSS questions did not distinguish between the ESOP form of employee ownership that gives workers incentives on top of their pay versus the 401k or ESPP type of employee ownership that generally has workers buying their stock with their salary. We would expect that measuring this distinction (as the 2006 GSS will do) will introduce more texture into the employee ownership results.

*Searching for a Job with Another Employer*

Another important measure of the impact of shared capitalism on the company is whether workers want to leave the company. Workers were asked, "How likely is it that you would make a genuine effort to find a new job with another employer within the next year?" The answers were very likely, somewhat likely, and not at all likely. We will report only on the "very likely" category. Among workers in general, 21 percent say they are very likely to make an effort to change employers in the next year. Again, more workers without performance sharing say they plan to leave (24 percent) than with performance sharing (12 percent), and the number goes down as performance sharing as a percent of annual income goes up. Workers with performance sharing that is a low percent of their annual income say they plan to leave as much as workers in the general population (21 percent). Further, more workers without employee ownership say they plan to leave (23 percent) than with employee ownership (13 percent), and the number also goes down as the size of the employee ownership stake goes up. As with performance sharing, workers with the lowest employee ownership stakes say they plan to leave as much as workers in the general population (21 percent). Finally, more workers without stock options say they are planning to leave (21 percent) than with stock options (16 percent).

Table 16.4 below provides a general overview of the findings, indicating the percent of workers who report that they are very likely to make an effort to leave their company in the next year. Those workers with Low Empowerment and No Shared Capitalism are the most likely to leave, while those with High Empowerment and Any Amount of Shared Capitalism are the least likely to leave. High Empowerment always produces better outcomes than Low Empowerment. The group that has High Empowerment and No Shared Capitalism say they plan to leave as much as the group that has Low Empowerment and Any Amount of Shared Capitalism. Yet, adding Any Amount of Shared Capitalism is also better. Those workers most planning to stay with their firms have both High Empowerment and some shared capitalism.

As was the case with doing nothing with a shirker, this general picture does not tell the entire story. Appendix III shows that workers have fewer plans to leave when they have performance shares and employee ownership representing medium and high levels of their annual income, although there is still evidence of an independent incentive effect: workers with large amounts of shared capitalism say they have fewer plans to leave even if they have Low Empowerment. What is most interesting is that

**Table 16.4**  Empowerment, Shared Capitalism, and Workers who Say They Are Very Likely to Leave their Company in the Next Year

| | |
|---|---|
| Low Empowerment | High Empowerment |
| No Shared Capitalism | No Shared Capitalism |
| 29% | 18% |
| Low Empowerment | High Empowerment |
| Any Amt. of Shared | Any Amt. of Shared Capitalism |
| Capitalism 18% | 9% |

*Note*: The percent describes the workers who say they are very likely to leave their company in the next year.

*Source*: General Social Survey, National Opinion Research Center, University of Chicago.

workers with Low Empowerment combined with no shared capitalism practices or employee ownership representing a low percent of annual income are most likely to be planning to leave. Clearly, low levels of shared capitalism—for the purposes of ensuring attachment to the company—are somewhat wasted under a Low Empowerment culture.

Finally, the results suggest that involvement in company operations without sharing the fruits of that involvement is not attractive to workers. High Empowerment workers with little or no shared capitalism or with shared capitalism at low levels of annual income are about half as likely to want to leave the company as Low Empowerment workers without shared capitalism. But, High Empowerment workers with greater amounts of shared capitalism as a percent of their income say they want to leave the company much less. It also appears that companies that rely mostly on High Empowerment are not achieving the full potential of empowerment as a work system. Adding shared capitalism makes quite a meaningful difference. Finally, workers with stock options and High Empowerment are less likely to be planning to leave than workers with High Empowerment without stock options or workers with Low Empowerment with or without stock options.

Our examination of how High and Low Empowerment and various shared capitalism practices relate to workers' willingness to intervene with a shirker and their desire to leave their company leads to similar conclusions. Low Empowerment cultures generally discourage workers from seeking to reduce shirking behavior or to stay with their firm no matter what shared capitalism they have. High Empowerment alone is not associated with the most engaged worker behaviors; it must be combined with shared capitalism practices. Workers will not fully engage in firms that say, "Act empowered, but top executives and shareholders keep all the gains!"

In general, the greater the proportion that annual performance shares and total employee ownership are of a worker's annual income, the greater the likelihood that empowerment and shared capitalism will be associated with responsible worker behaviors. And some evidence suggests that employee ownership and stock options are more likely to drive responsible worker behaviors when they are structured like "pure profit-sharing," namely, that they represent an additional incentive on top of a fair wage rather than some kind of wage substitution. Wage substitution is where workers are being asked or required to "buy" employee ownership or stock options with their own wages or their savings or wage sacrifices, and where they get shared capitalism but feel they are paid below market wages anyway.

We find similar results when looking at other measures of workplace performance (not reported here due to space limitations): Workers in High Empowerment and Any Shared Capitalism systems are the most likely to report that their coworkers work hard, and the most likely to report that they themselves work extra time each month that is not mandatory.

## How Will Shared Capitalism Determine the Future of Work?

Students of the workplace often do not pause to take the long view and realize that in the last hundred years, work has undergone an almost complete transformation from manufacturing, manual labor, strict hierarchies, and diffuse individual ownership to a workplace where services, intellectual labor, flattened hierarchies, and corporate ownership are dominant and expanding. Far-reaching changes in ownership, control, and the structure of work have already come to pass. The importance of intellectual capital, teamwork, high performance work systems, and problem-solving skills in the newly emerging workforce cannot be overestimated. In a way, we are returning to the craft period of work, where the individual's mind and contribution are paramount.

Given the evidence of the GSS that a work system that bundles empowerment and shared capitalism is associated with more responsible worker behaviors, one can use this sector of the workforce to envision the future of work. Think of it as something like predicting the future of the economic system in the 1930s by looking at railroad workers in the 1880s. They were a minority in the workforce, a remnant, even an oddity, yet they presaged what was to come. Only 36 percent of the U.S. population is currently involved in shared capitalism. Most of this shared capitalism provides workers levels of performance shares, employee ownership, and historical and potential stock option profits that are not meaningful, but some shares really add up to something that has an economic impact on individual pay and wealth.

Imagine a workplace future where virtually all menial tasks are performed by machines, computers, software, biological/chemical devices, robots, cyborgs, and combinations of all these.[5] With work becoming mainly the reworking of intellectual problems and capital by individuals and teams, industrial supervision as we know it will largely disappear. As one Silicon Valley software executive told us, "I cannot supervise the minds of my workers. I can only provide a corporate culture where they will be committed enough and not so upset that they will really mess up the software they are designing and tank the company when we roll out the product in six months!"

We suggest that the combination of shared capitalism and empowerment is that future corporate culture. It will make sense for several other reasons.

*First, workers are increasingly the capital from which value emerges.* As each decade progresses and computing and robotic power becomes cheaper, shareholder assets will largely be used to pay for intellectual capital. As we have noted, the stock market value of companies will be less determined by the book value of their assets than by the creativity, innovation, and problem solving this intellectual capital can create from these assets.

*Second, shared capitalism and empowerment are reasonable choices to solve the heightened principal/agent problem when supervision of physical behavior can no longer control what workers produce.* A work system that uses shared capitalism incentives and that empowers workers to make decisions can create the kind of monitoring that principals can have greater confidence will encourage responsible behavior by agents. Such a work system is built not on physical capital, but on social capital. The evidence of the 2002 GSS suggests that shared capitalism and empowerment constitute essential elements of the social capital that can resolve the principal/agent problem in the twenty-first and twenty-second century workforce.

*Third, it is difficult to see how workers can significantly improve living standards through negotiated or administered wage increases at substantial rates above inflation —as they did after World War II.* In a globally competitive economy with countries where wages are far below those in the US the only "labor income" that will provide steady inflation-adjusted increases will be one that includes a share of capital income tied to corporate performance.

*Fourth and finally, if workers are going to create, run, and problem-solve the machines, computers, software, biological/chemical devices, robots, cyborgs, and cross-combinations of these productive elements, then they should share ownership in these "technologies" with shareholders and become shareholders themselves.* As problem-solving and team collaboration regimes represent an increasing part of the value of these technologies, the argument that they are merely owned by the investors who put up the finance capital becomes less and less tenable. Workers could "charge" investors for creating capital that is more than the sum of the physical and finance capital which investors contributed. Indeed, in this futuristic economy, the entire idea of the investor *exclusively* being someone other than the worker might be seen as unreasonable.

We suggest that these four elements could conceivably represent a very promising model of futuristic work—that has the potential under certain conditions to be much better for workers, companies, and the capitalist economic system than the alternative, where productive intellectual and social capital is divorced from economic rewards, and average worker incomes continue to stagnate.

### Policy Implications: Government, Employers, Workers

#### Government

The government has a role to play here. A democratic government in a capitalist country has a role to play in whether broad elements of the population actually participate in the capitalist system. Shared capitalism policies in the United States have properly been born in the private sector and designed by entrepreneurial persons throughout its history. But tax, regulatory, and legislative regimes do provide incentives for different kinds of corporate behaviors. It would be useful for a National Commission to consider ways the government could encourage shared capitalism through incentives in its tax, regulatory, and legislative regimes. Such an assessment should range widely, from re-examining the tax incentives for ESOPs in public companies that were gutted in the nineties by Congress; to taking a second look at the new rule of the Financial Accounting Standards Board on the expensing of stock options, which has resulted in many corporations cutting mid- and lower-level workers from their stock option plans in order to lessen the expense. To the extent that hard evidence is forthcoming that this resulted in mid- and lower-level employees being cut from stock option plans and the narrowing of participation in these plans where it did not make business sense, the unintended consequences of stock option expensing need to be considered within a broad policy discussion. For example, there might be ways to address these unintended consequences. This commission could review tax incentives that encourage 401k employee ownership that creates risk for workers as opposed to broad-based ESOPs and stock options that reduce risk for workers. Another issue is that the role of profit sharing and performance sharing in U.S. economic policy has not really been reexamined and thoughtfully considered since the nineteen fifties.

Indeed, one can make the case that the evolution of laws, regulations, and incentives in this area has been uncoordinated and piecemeal with the addition of new policies without evaluating the overall effect and consistency of all the thematically related policies. Thus, the surprising emergence and dominance of 401k plans as a retirement vehicle in this century has played a role in encouraging the reduced use of deferred profit sharing that was thought to be a useful tool for corporations in the last century. Without going into too much technical detail, the decline of profit sharing has largely been an unintended consequence of how Congress structures corporate tax deductions for pension plans. A comprehensive policy examination of shared capitalism would look at policy objectives and evaluate intended and unintended consequences in the context of intentional policy rather than let our policy be the result of successive uncoordinated legislation and regulation.

## Employers

Employers busy running corporations tell us that they have limited time to innovate in the management of people. Those employers in the country using shared capitalism can function as a laboratory for all other employers. The principal lesson learned for employers from the 2002 GSS is that meaningful empowerment must be combined with performance sharing, employee ownership, and stock options for these practices to make a maximum difference for company operations. Employers who claim they have "profit-sharing" or "employee ownership" or "broad-based stock options" and have only low levels are really fooling themselves and their workers. Our results show that employers and their shareholders have a lot to gain from doing this right. While we present some evidence that all forms of employee ownership create greater identification with the firm, company stock that workers merely substitute for wages does not meet the test of a meaningful new real incentive on top of wages.

The biggest failure of majority employee ownership in the United States, United Airlines, is a case in point for the analysis of this paper. It did virtually everything wrong in its efforts to harness shared capitalism to improve company performance. The company built employee ownership on wage and benefit sacrifices. They constructed their employee ownership program so that when the stock went up and investors saw immediate profits, the workers got no performance sharing and the workers were prevented from cashing out their stock unless they retired. Moreover, United never embraced a High Empowerment work system for the airline. Our findings indicate that unions have little to fear from shared capitalism. Since it represents a way to increase worker incomes and encourage empowerment, it has a place. Unfortunately, unions—as in the United Airlines case—have sometimes turned to employee ownership in situations where it has been structured in the worst way.

## Workers

The need of workers for appropriate inflation-adjusted increases to their incomes when corporate performance warrants it may provide a compelling reason that shared capitalism be a priority for workers. If increases in capital incomes represent the main way in which family incomes are increasing, then a shared capitalism policy that encourages wider worker participation in capital incomes should be a priority for most workers. From a broader perspective, citizens need to be educated so that they know enough about shared capitalism to care about which way capitalism works in the United States. Young workers need to be educated about how to progress in an economy where empowerment and shared capitalism play a joint role in how and whether they will experience gains in their family wealth. Unfortunately, this is part and parcel of the wider lack of economics and business education in our schools.

## Conclusion

For the first time, the GSS has allowed a comprehensive review of all shared capitalism in the United States. Our analysis of the GSS points towards some answers, but it also raises many questions. As we have been doing this analysis, we have been completing an extensive survey in 14 corporations of about 50,000 workers as part of the Shared Capitalism Project at the National Bureau for Economic Research (NBER). These surveys provide more detailed data to help us study the issues highlighted in this study more carefully. In the NBER study, we are able to attach economic values to every type of shared capitalism for each worker. We make the critical distinction between employee ownership that is an added incentive above wages and employee ownership that is the result of workers simply replacing their wages/savings with stock. We have more sophisticated measurements of many behaviors, including high performance work practices and empowerment. These results will be available in late 2007. A serious discussion about shared capitalism in the United States requires both careful policy discussions and better research. In 2006, the GSS included its second segment on shared capitalism. We hope that successive General Social Surveys every four years will provide a regular way to assess how shared capitalism is developing.

**Appendix I**    Demographic Characteristics of Shared Capitalism Workers vs. All Workers

| | All workers | Workers with any performance shares | Workers with any employee ownership | Workers with any stock options | Workers with performance shares & employee ownership and stock options | Workers with employee ownership and stock options | Workers with employee ownership and performance shares |
|---|---|---|---|---|---|---|---|
| *Age* | | | | | | | |
| 18–34 | 41 | 38 | 32 | 29 | 33 | 30 | 31 |
| 35–44 | 24 | 29 | 36 | 38 | 42 | 38 | 35 |
| 45–54 | 22 | 23 | 21 | 23 | 15 | 17 | 24 |
| 55–64 | 9 | 8 | 10 | 8 | 7 | 13 | 10 |
| 65–99 | 4 | 1 | 1 | 2 | 2 | 2 | 0 |
| Total | 100 | 100 | 100 | 100 | 100 | 100 | 100 |
| *Sex* | | | | | | | |
| Male | 49 | 53 | 60 | 55 | 60 | 62 | 42 |
| Female | 51 | 47 | 40 | 45 | 40 | 38 | 48 |
| Total | 100 | 100 | 100 | 100 | 100 | 100 | 100 |
| *Marital Status* | | | | | | | |
| Married | 45 | 49 | 52 | 49 | 51 | 51 | 45 |
| Widowed | 3 | 2 | 3 | 2 | 2 | 4 | 7 |
| Divorced | 16 | 15 | 14 | 19 | 11 | 15 | 21 |
| Separated | 4 | 3 | 3 | 5 | 5 | 6 | 0 |
| Never married | 32 | 31 | 28 | 25 | 31 | 24 | 27 |
| Total | 100 | 100 | 100 | 100 | 100 | 100 | 100 |
| *Class* | | | | | | | |
| Lower | 3 | 0 | 1 | 2 | 0 | 2 | 0 |
| Working | 55 | 47 | 39 | 45 | 35 | 43 | 45 |

Continued

**Appendix I**   Continued

| | All workers | Workers with any performance shares | Workers with any employee ownership | Workers with any stock options | Workers with performance shares & employee ownership and stock options | Workers with employee ownership and stock options | Workers with employee ownership and performance shares |
|---|---|---|---|---|---|---|---|
| Middle | 39 | 49 | 55 | 47 | 58 | 51 | 45 |
| Upper | 2 | 4 | 5 | 6 | 7 | 4 | 10 |
| Total | 100 | 100 | 100 | 100 | 100 | 100 | 100 |
| *Income/Year* | | | | | | | |
| <$15,000 | 22 | 7 | 5 | 6 | 2 | 4 | 7 |
| $15–<30,000 | 29 | 26 | 23 | 20 | 16 | 24 | 21 |
| $30–<50,000 | 26 | 31 | 29 | 28 | 27 | 21 | 34 |
| >$50,000 | 23 | 36 | 43 | 46 | 55 | 51 | 38 |
| Total | 100 | 100 | 100 | 100 | 100 | 100 | 100 |
| *Worker or Supervisor* | | | | | | | |
| Worker | 63 | 48 | 47 | 51 | 49 | 44 | 45 |
| Lower sup* | 29 | 36 | 35 | 35 | 36 | 40 | 22 |
| Mid/high sup* | 8 | 16 | 18 | 14 | 15 | 16 | 33 |

*A lower supervisor has no others supervisors below him or her while a mid or high level supervisor has other supervisors below.

**Appendix II**   Detailed Picture: Shared Capitalism/Empowerment and Unwillingness to Intervene with a Shirker

| Workplace System | Percent of Workers Who Report That They Will Very Likely Do Nothing to Intervene With a Shirker |
|---|---|
| Workers in the United States in General | 24% |
| *Combinations of Low Empowerment and Shared Capitalism:* | |
| Low Empowerment/Low Employee Ownership | 39% |
| Low Empowerment/No Shared Capitalism of Any Kind | 32% |
| Low Empowerment/Medium Employee Ownership | 32% |
| Low Empowerment/ All Types of Shared Capitalism (Any Size) | 31% |
| Low Empowerment/No Stock Options | 31% |
| Low Empowerment/Medium Performance Sharing | 29% |
| Low Empowerment/Any Employee Ownership | 28% |
| Low Empowerment/Any Amount of Shared Capitalism | 24% |
| Low Empowerment /Any Performance Sharing | 22% |
| Low Empowerment /Any Stock Options | 22% |
| Low Empowerment/High Performance Sharing | 20% |
| *Combinations of High Empowerment and Shared Capitalism:* | |
| High Empowerment/Low Employee Ownership | 23% |

Continued

**Appendix II**   Continued

| Workplace System | Percent of Workers Who Report That They Will Very Likely Do Nothing to Intervene With a Shirker |
|---|---|
| High Empowerment/Low Performance Sharing | 21% |
| High Empowerment/Stock Options | 21% |
| High Empowerment/No Shared Capitalism of Any Kind | 20% |
| High Empowerment/ All Types of Shared Capitalism (Any Size) | 19% |
| High Empowerment/No Stock Options | 18% |
| High Empowerment/Any Employee Ownership | 18% |
| High Empowerment/Any Amount of Shared Capitalism | 17% |
| High Empowerment/Medium and High Employee Ownership | 16% |
| High Empowerment/Medium Performance Sharing | 15% |
| High Empowerment/Any Performance Sharing | 15% |
| High Empowerment/Medium and High Performance Sharing | 12% |
| High Empowerment/ High Performance Sharing | 10% |

*Note*: Some categories that have few workers are not presented.

*Source*: General Social Survey, National Opinion Research Center, University of Chicago. Analysis by Douglas Kruse and Joseph Blasi of Rutgers University and Richard Freeman of Harvard University

**Appendix III**   Detailed Picture: Shared Capitalism/Empowerment and Looking for a Job with another Employer

| Workplace System | Percent of Workers Very Likely to Try to Find a Job With Another Employer Next Year |
|---|---|
| All Workers in General | 21% |
| *Combinations of Low Empowerment and Shared Capitalism:* | |
| Low Empowerment Alone/No Shared Capitalism of Any Kind | 30% |
| Low Empowerment/Low Performance Sharing | 28% |
| Low Empowerment/No Employee Ownership | 27% |
| Low Empowerment/No Performance Sharing | 27% |
| Low Empowerment/Low Employee Ownership | 26% |
| Low Empowerment/No Stock Options | 26% |
| Low Empowerment/Any Stock Options | 19% |
| Low Empowerment/Any Amount of Shared Capitalism | 18% |
| Low Empowerment /Any Performance Sharing | 17% |
| Low Empowerment/Any Employee Ownership | 16% |
| Low Empowerment/Medium Employee Ownership | 14% |
| Low Empowerment/ All Types of Shared Capitalism (Any Size) | 13% |
| Low Empowerment/Medium Performance Sharing | 11% |
| Low Empowerment/High Performance Sharing | 10% |
| Low Empowerment/High Performance Sharing | 10% |
| *Combinations of High Empowerment and Shared Capitalism:* | |
| High Empowerment/No Shared Capitalism of Any Kind | 18% |

Continued

**Appendix III** Continued

| Workplace System | Percent of Workers Very Likely to Try to Find a Job With Another Employer Next Year |
|---|---|
| High Empowerment/No Performance Sharing | 17% |
| High Empowerment/No Employee Ownership | 16% |
| High Empowerment/Low Employee Ownership | 14% |
| High Empowerment/No Stock Options | 15% |
| High Empowerment/All Types of Shared Capitalism of Any Size | 14% |
| High Empowerment/Any Stock Options | 13% |
| High Empowerment/Medium Employee Ownership | 10% |
| High Empowerment/Low Performance Sharing | 14% |
| High Empowerment/Any Employee Ownership | 11% |
| High Empowerment/Any Performance Sharing | 8% |
| High Empowerment/ All Types of Shared Capitalism of Any Size | 8% |
| High Empowerment/Medium and High Employee Ownership | 8% |
| High Empowerment/ High Performance Sharing | 7% |
| High Empowerment/High Employee Ownership | 7% |
| High Empowerment/Medium and High Performance Sharing | 6% |
| High Empowerment/Medium Performance Sharing | 4% |

*Note*: Some categories that have few workers are not presented.

*Sources*: General Social Survey, National Opinion Research Center, University of Chicago. Analysis by Douglas Kruse and Joseph Blasi of Rutgers University and Richard Freeman of Harvard University.

# About the Contributors

**Edward E. Lawler III** is Distinguished Professor of Business in the Management and Organization department of the Marshall School of Business at the University of Southern California. He is also Director of the School's Center for Effective Organizations.

After receiving his Ph.D. from the University of California at Berkeley in 1964, Ed Lawler joined the faculty of Yale University as Assistant Professor of Industrial Administration and Psychology. Three years later he was promoted to Associate Professor.

Ed Lawler moved to the University of Michigan in 1972, as Professor of Psychology, and also became a Program Director in the Survey Research Center at the Institute for Social Research. He held a Fulbright Fellowship at the London Graduate School of Business. In 1978, he became a professor in the Marshall School of Business at the University of Southern California. During 1979, he founded and became the Director of the University's Center for Effective Organizations. In 1982, he was named Professor of Research at the University of Southern California. In 1999, he was named Distinguished Professor of Business.

Ed Lawler has been honored as a major contributor to theory, research, and practice in the fields of human resources management, compensation, organizational development, and organizational effectiveness. He is the author and coauthor of over 300 articles and 41 books. His most recent books include *Rewarding Excellence* (Jossey-Bass, 2000), *Corporate Boards: New Strategies for Adding Value at the Top* (Jossey-Bass, 2001), *Organizing for High Performance* (Jossey-Bass, 2001), *Treat People Right* (Jossey-Bass, 2003), *Human Resources Business Process Outsourcing* (Jossey-Bass, 2004), *Achieving Strategic Excellence: An Assessment of Human Resource Organizations* (Stanford Press, 2006), *Built to Change* (Jossey-Bass, 2006), and *The New American Workplace* (Palgrave-Macmillan, 2006). For more information, go to http://www.edwardlawler.com

**James O'Toole** is Research Professor in the Center for Effective Organizations at the University of Southern California (USC). He is also Mortimer J. Adler Senior Fellow of the Aspen Institute.

At USC he has held the University Associates' Chair of Management and served as Executive Director of the Leadership Institute. He has been editor of *New Management* magazine and Director of the Twenty-Year Forecast Project (where he interpreted social, political, and economic change for the top management of thirty of the largest US corporations).

O'Toole's research and writings have been in the areas of leadership, political/economic philosophy, and corporate culture. He has addressed dozens of major corporations and professional organizations, and has published over seventy articles. Among his fourteen books, *Vanguard Management* was named "One of the best business and economics books of 1985" by the editors of *Business Week* and *Leadership A to Z*, received an enthusiastic review in *Fortune* (December 6, 1999). His latest books are *Creating the Good Life: Applying Aristotle's Wisdom to Find Meaning and Happiness* (Rodale, 2005) and the *New American Workplace* (Palgrave-Macmillan, 2006).

O'Toole received his Doctorate in Social Anthropology from Oxford University, where he was a Rhodes Scholar. He served as a Special Assistant to Secretary of Health, Education and Welfare, Elliot Richardson, as Chairman of the Secretary's Task Force on Work in America, and as Director of Field Investigations for President Nixon's Commission on Campus Unrest. He won a Mitchell Prize for a paper on economic growth policy, has served on the prestigious Board of Editors of the *Encyclopaedia Britannica*, and was editor of *The American Oxonian* magazine.

From 1994–1997 O'Toole was Executive Vice President of the Aspen Institute. He also has served recently as Managing Director of the Booz ïAllen & Hamilton Strategic Leadership Center, and Chair of the Center's academic Board of Advisors. For more information go to http://www.jamesotoole.com

## Contributors

**Stephen R. Barley** is the Charles M. Pigott Professor of Management Science and Engineering, the codirector of the Center for Work, Technology and Organization at Stanford's School of Engineering and the codirector of the Stanford/General Motors Collaborative Research Laboratory. He holds a Ph.D. in Organization Studies from the Massachusetts Institute of Technology. He was editor of the *Administrative Science Quarterly* from 1993 to 1997 and the founding editor of the *Stanford Social Innovation Review* from 2002 to 2004. Barley has written extensively on the impact of new technologies on work, the organization of technical work, and organizational culture. He edited a volume on technical work entitled *Between Craft and Science: Technical Work in the United States* published in 1997 by the Cornell University Press. In collaboration with Gideon Kunda of Tel Aviv University, Barley has also published a book on contingent work among engineers and software developers, entitled *Gurus, Hired Guns and Warm Bodies: Itinerant Experts in the Knowledge Economy*, with the Princeton University Press.

**Joseph Blasi** is a professor in the School of Management and Labor Relations at Rutgers University. He is a sociologist who received his Ed.D. from Harvard University. His research has focused on employee participation in stock, stock options, and profit sharing in American industry over the last 30 years. His books on the subject include *Employee Ownership* (HarperCollins, 1988), *The New Owners with Douglas Kruse* (HarperCollins, 1991), and *In the Company of Owners* (Basic Books, 2003) with Douglas Kruse and Aaron Bernstein. His published articles appear in scholarly journals such as *Industrial Relations and Industrial and Labor Relations Review*. He worked as a legislative assistant in the U.S. House of Representatives in the late 1970s and early 1980s on these issues.

**Peter Cappelli** is the George W. Taylor Professor of Management at The Wharton School and director of Wharton's Center for Human Resources. He is also a research associate at the National Bureau of Economic Research in Cambridge, Massachusetts and currently serves as senior advisor to the Government of Bahrain for Employment Policy. He has degrees in industrial relations from Cornell University and in labor economics from Oxford where he was a Fulbright Scholar. Professor Cappelli's research examines changes in employment relations in the United States. His publications include *The New Deal at Work: Managing the Market-Driven Workforce* (Harvard Business School Press, 1999), which examines the challenges associated with the decline in lifetime employment relationships. Much of his recent work is based on his National Employer Survey project with the Bureau of the Census, which provides detailed information on employment practices across the U.S. economy. His recent work on managing retention, electronic recruiting, and changing career paths appears in the *Harvard Business Review*. His work in progress includes a study of talent management practices in the United States.

**Wayne F. Cascio** holds a B.A. from Holy Cross College, an M.A. from Emory University, and a Ph.D. in industrial/organizational psychology from the University of Rochester. Currently he is US Bank Term Professor of Management at the University of Colorado at Denver and Health Sciences Center. He has written 21 books and more than 125 journal articles and book chapters on human resource management issues, including downsizing, restructuring, and the economic impact of behavior in organizations. An elected Fellow of the Academy of Management, the American Psychological Association, and the National Academy of Human Resources, he received the Distinguished Career award from the Academy of Management's HR Division in 2000, and an honorary doctorate from the University of Geneva (Switzerland) in 2004. He serves on the boards of CPP, Inc., the Society for Human Resource Management Foundation, and the Academy of Management.

**Elizabeth F. Craig** is an assistant professor of Organizational Behavior at Boston University's School of Management. She earned a Ph.D. in Management from The Wharton School at University of Pennsylvania, as well as a Masters degree in Human Resource Management from the School of Management and Labor Relations at Rutgers University, and a Bachelor of Arts degree in Economics also from Rutgers. She conducts research on work careers and career processes, the changing nature of employment relationships, and organizational commitment and mobility. Her current research addresses the organization and meaning of work careers in contemporary society and the effects of career complexity on career construction and career management processes.

**David Finegold** is a professor of Strategy and Organization at the Keck Graduate Institute of Applied Life Sciences in Claremont, CA. He has conducted two decades of research comparing different countries' education and training systems and their relationship with work organization and economic performance. His books on this topic include *Are Skills the Answer?* (Oxford University Press, 1999), *The German Skills Machine* (Berghahn Books, 1999), and *Something Borrowed, Something Blue* (The Brookings Institution, 1990). Professor Finegold has provided policy advice on skills issues to the OECD and the governments of United Kingdom, United States, Australia, and South Korea. He is also is an award-winning teacher who provides executive education and consulting to public and private sector organizations on issues about designing effective organizations.

**Fred K. Foulkes** received the A.B. degree from Princeton University, magna cum laude and Phi Beta Kappa, and the M.B.A. and D.B.A. degrees from Harvard Business

School. He has been a professor of Organizational Behavior and the director of the Human Resources Policy Institute for Boston University School of Management since 1981 and has taught courses in human resource management and strategic management at Boston University since 1980. From 1968 to 1980, Professor Foulkes was a member of the Harvard Business School faculty. His principal publications include *Creating More Meaningful Work* (American Management Association, 1969), *Personnel Policies in Large Nonunion Companies* (Prentice-Hall, 1980) and *Executive Compensation: A Strategic Guide for the 1990s* (Harvard Business School Press, 1991). Professor Foulkes is a recipient of the Employment Management Association Award and the Fellow Award, the National Academy of Human Resources award of distinction for outstanding achievement in the human resource profession. Professor Foulkes is a member of the boards of Bright Horizons Family Solutions, Deploy Solutions, Panera Bread, and the Society for Human Resource Management Foundation.

**Richard B. Freeman** holds the Herbert Ascherman Chair in Economics at Harvard University. He is also director of the Labor Studies Program at the National Bureau of Economic Research, senior research fellow in Labor Markets at the Centre for Economic Performance, London School of Economics, and visiting professor at the London School of Economics. He has published over 300 articles dealing with a wide range of research interests including the job market for scientists and engineers; the growth and decline of unions; the effects of immigration and trade on inequality; restructuring European welfare states; Chinese labor markets; transitional economies; youth labor market problems; crime; self-organizing non-unions in the labor market; employee involvement programs; and income distribution and equity in the marketplace. In addition, he has written or edited over 25 books. Some of his books include *What Workers Want*, with Joel Rogers. (New York: Cornell University Press, 1999, 2006 updated edition, forthcoming), and *What Do Unions Do?* with James Medoff (New York: Basic Books, currently Perseus Book Group, 1984).

**Douglas T. Hall** is the Morton H. and Charlotte Friedman Professor of Management in the School of Management at Boston University. He is the faculty director of the MBA program. He is also the director of the Executive Development Roundtable and a core faculty member of the Human Resources Policy Institute. He has held faculty positions at Yale University, York University, Michigan State University, and Northwestern University. He is the author of *Careers in Organizations* and *Careers In and Outside of Organizations* and a coauthor of *The Career Is Dead—Long Live the Career, The Handbook of Career Theory*, and several other books on career and management. His research and consulting activities have dealt with strategic human resource development, women's careers, work/life balance, leadership development, and executive succession planning.

**Michael J. Handel** is associate professor of Sociology at Northeastern University. He studies the impacts of information technology and employee involvement practices on employee skills and wages. He recently published *Worker Skills and Job Requirements: Is There a Mismatch?* (Economic Policy Institute, www.epinet.org). He is currently conducting a two-wave national survey of employees on the specific skills and technologies they use at work and the employee involvement practices in which they participate.

**Thomas A. Kochan** is the George M. Bunker Professor of Work and Employment Relations at MIT's Sloan School of Management and codirector of the MIT

Workplace Center and of the Institute for Work and Employment Research. His most recent book is *Restoring the American Dream: A Working Families' Agenda for America* (MIT Press, 2005).

**Ellen Ernst Kossek**, a Ph.D. from Yale University, is professor of HRM and Organizational Behavior at Michigan State University's School of Labor and Industrial Relations with a courtesy appointment in Management. She is elected to the board of governors of the National Academy of Management (2003–2006) and was the 2002 division chair of the Gender and Diversity in Organizations Division. She is an elected fellow of the American Psychological Association (2002) and the Society of Industrial Organizational Psychology (2001) in recognition of her research on employer support of work and family. Her new research includes serving as coprincipal investigator of the Center for Work, Family Health and Stress at Portland State University as part of the workplace, Family Health and well-being Network, funded by the National Institute of Occupational Safety and Health Supported by the Alfred P. Sloan Foundation, she is also starting a new study on flexibility in work groups in unionized contexts and has just finished another Sloan study on managing professionals in new work forms, a study that examines the careers of professionals who chose to reduce their work hours.

**Douglas Kruse** is a Professor in the School of Management and Labor Relations at Rutgers University, and a Research Associate at the National Bureau of Economic Research in Cambridge, Massachusetts. He received an M.A. in Economics from the University of Nebraska-Lincoln and a Ph.D. in Economics from Harvard University. His research has focused on the employment and earnings effects of disability, and the causes, consequences, and implications of employee ownership and profit sharing. His publications include *Profit Sharing: Does It Make a Difference?*, which won Princeton's Richard A. Lester prize as the year's Outstanding Book in Labor Economics and Industrial Relations, and *In the Company of Owners*, which was coauthored with Joseph Blasi and Aaron Bernstein. In addition, his published articles have appeared in scholarly journals such as *Economic Journal, Industrial Relations* and *Industrial and Labor Relations Review*. He has testified four times before Congress on his economic research and authored or coauthored three U.S. Department of Labor studies. He worked with the U.S. Bureau of Labor Statistics to design new questions to measure disability on the monthly employment survey. He was appointed by the governor to New Jersey's State Rehabilitation Council and served on the President's Committee on Employment of People with Disabilities. He is also on the Board of Reviewers of Industrial Relations, and the Board of the Profit Sharing Research Foundation in Chicago, IL.

**Gideon Kunda** is associate professor in the Department of Labor Studies at Tel Aviv University, Israel. He holds a B.A. in Economics and an M.A. in Social Psychology from the Hebrew University of Jerusalem and he received his Ph.D. in Management and Organization Studies from the Sloan School of Management at the Massachusetts Institute of Technology in 1987. Kunda's research has focused on the cultural aspects of work and organization. His book *Engineering Culture: Control and Commitment in a High-Tech Corporation* was chosen as Book of the Year by the American Sociological Association's Culture Section in 1994 and has been translated into Italian, Japanese, and Hebrew. His recent book (with Stephen Barley), *Gurus, Hired Guns and Warm Bodies: Itinerant Experts in a Knowledge Economy* (Princeton University Press, 2004), examines the social organization of temporary work among engineers in Silicon Valley.

**Alec Levenson** is a research scientist at the Center for Effective Organizations, University of Southern California. His research focuses on the economics of human resources and organization design; HR and human capital metrics, analytics, and return on investment; and strategy. His topics include estimating the business impact of HR and human capital; identifying attraction, retention, motivation, and productivity drivers for key talent pools; aligning competency systems with strategic and bottom-line objectives; measuring and maximizing the economic value of leadership development, including executive coaching; measuring the return on investment to globally distributed software development; how companies manage for success in times of adversity; and contingent work. His research has been published in numerous academic outlets and has been funded by the Sloan Foundation, Russell Sage Foundation, Rockefeller Foundation, National Science Foundation, and National Institute for Literacy. Dr. Levenson received his Ph.D. and M.A. in Economics from Princeton University.

**David I. Levine** is a professor at the Haas School Business at the University of California, Berkeley. Levine is also research director of the Center for Responsible Business and Chair of the Center for Health Research. Levine was an undergraduate at University of California, Berkeley, and has taught at the Haas School since receiving his Ph.D. in economics from Harvard University in 1987. He has also visited the Sloan School of Management at MIT, the U.S. Department of Labor, and the Council of Economic Advisers.

**Paul Osterman** received his Ph.D. in Economics from MIT and is the Nanyang Professor of Human Resources at the MIT Sloan School of Management. He is also deputy dean of the MIT Sloan School. His most recent book is *Gathering Power: The Future of Progressive Politics in America* (Beacon Press, 2003). Osterman is also the author of *Securing Prosperity: How the American Labor Market Has Changed and What to Do about It* (Princeton University Press, 1999); *Employment Futures: Reorganization, Dislocation, and Public Policy* and *Getting Started: The Youth Labor Market*; the coauthor of *Working In America; A Blueprint for the New Labor Market; The Mutual Gains Enterprise; Forging a Winning Partnership among Labor, Management, and Government*, and *Change at Work*, and the editor of two books, *Internal Labor Markets*, and *Broken Ladders; Managerial Careers in the New Economy*. In addition, he has written numerous academic journal articles and policy issue papers on topics such as the organization of work within firms, labor market policy, and economic development.

**Jeffrey Pfeffer** is the Thomas D. Dee II Professor of Organizational Behavior at the Graduate School of Business Stanford University, where he has taught since 1979. Prior to joining the Stanford faculty, Pfeffer taught at the University of Illinois and the University of California, Berkeley, and he has been a visiting professor at the Harvard Business School. Pfeffer is the author or coauthor of eleven books including *The Human Equation: Building Profits by Putting People First, Managing with Power*, and *The Knowing-Doing Gap: How Smart Companies Turn Knowledge Into Action*. In March 2006 he and Bob Sutton published their latest book, *Hard Facts, Dangerous Half-Truths, and Total Nonsense: Profiting from Evidence-Based Management*. Pfeffer writes a monthly column, "The Human Factor," for the business magazine *Business 2.0* and has presented seminars in 27 countries throughout the world as well as for numerous organizations in the United States.

**Richard H. Price** is Barger Family Professor and Director of the Interdisciplinary Program on Organizational Studies at the University of Michigan. He is also professor of Psychology and research professor at the Institute for Social Research. He is cofounder of the University of Michigan Rackham Interdisciplinary Committee on Organizational Studies. Professor Price's research is focused on the links between the organization of work and health. His books include *Person-Environment Psychology, Fourteen Ounces of Prevention, and Evaluation* and *Action in the Social Environment*. His articles have appeared in *American Psychologist, Journal of Personality and Social Psychology, Journal of Health and Social Behavior*, and *Psychological Bulletin*. Dr. Price has served as an advisor on prevention research in health to Institute of Medicine and the National Institutes of Health. He has also been as an advisor to government agencies on work and health policies in a number of countries.

**Denise M. Rousseau** is H.J. Heinz II Professor of Organizational Behavior and Public Policy at Carnegie Mellon University, jointly in the Heinz School of Public Policy and Management and in the Tepper School of Business; and faculty director of the Institute for Social Entrepreneurship and Innovation. Her research focuses on the employment relationship, the processes that underlie its mutuality, reciprocity, and change. She is editor-in-chief of the *Journal of Organizational Behavior* and was president of the Academy of Management from 2004 to 2005. Her award-winning book *Psychological Contracts in Organizations: Understanding Written and Unwritten Agreements* (Sage, 1995) demonstrated how organizations, social forces, and workers themselves affect their beliefs regarding the employment relationship. Her most recent book *I-deals: Idiosyncratic Deals Employees Bargain with their Employers* (M.E. Sharpe, 2005) examines how individual workers shape the nature and conditions of their relationships with employers. An advisor to the Institute of Medicine and the British civil service, Rousseau has presented seminars in 22 countries and numerous American organizations. She has been elected Fellow in the Academy of Management, the American Psychological Association, the British Academy of Management, and the Society for Industrial/Organizational Psychology.

**Kathryn Shaw** is Ernest C. Arbuckle Professor of Economics at the Graduate School of Business, Stanford University. Shaw was previously the Ford Distinguished Research Chair and Professor of Economics at Carnegie Mellon University, after completing her Ph.D. in Economics at Harvard University in 1981. Professor Shaw served as a Senate-confirmed Member of President Clinton's Council of Economic Advisers, 1999–2001. Her most recent research focuses on managing talent in high performance organizations. More broadly, Professor Shaw studies how the firm's choice of their human resource management practices can produce measurable performance gains for the company. She is a leading developer of the new field of "insider econometrics" that uses production-level data to model the effects of alternative management strategies.

**Sushil Vachani** has a doctorate in International Business from Harvard Business School and is associate professor and faculty director of the doctoral program at Boston University's School of Management. He previously served as chair of the Strategy and Policy Department and director of the International Management Program in Japan. He has worked with Boston Consulting Group, the Tata group, and Philips. His research, which includes topics focusing on globalization, governance, and multinational enterprises, has been published in the *Journal of International*

*Business Studies, Harvard Business Review, California Management Review* and elsewhere. He is editor of *Transformations in Global Governance: Implications for Multinationals and other Stakeholders* (Edward Elgar Publishing, forthcoming), coeditor of *Multinationals and Global Poverty Reduction* (Edward Elgar Publishing, 2006), and author of *Multinationals in India* (Oxford & IBH Publishers, 1991).

**Jennifer Zaslow** is Assistant Director of the Human Resources Policy Institute at Boston University's School of Management, and an MBA, High Honors, from Boston's University's Graduate School of Management. She holds a B.A., magna cum laude from Smith College. Ms. Zaslow has conducted research on human resources and management trends with the Corporate Leadership Council, BNA, Inc., Kennedy Information, *Inc.* magazine, as well as consulting and career services firms.

# Notes

## Foreword

1. A complete bibliography for this project is available at http://www.america-at-work.com.

## Chapter 3   Restoring Voice at Work and in Society

1. A complete bibliography for this project is available at http://www.america.at. work.com. Portions of this essay are drawn from Thomas A. Kochan, *Restoring the American Dream: A Working Families' Agenda for America*. Support for this work was provided by the Alfred P. Sloan Foundation. The views expressed are solely those of the author.

## Chapter 5   The Effects of New Work Practices on Workers

1. We appreciate comments from the editors and Paul Adler, David Fairris, Mark Gilkey, Sue Helper, Jon Jellema, Ed Lawler, Daniel Levine, and George Strauss.
2. This section draws on Helper, Levine, and Bendoly (2002).
3. For business press accounts of wage concessions in firms that adopted high performance practices, see The New World of Work. 1994. *Business Week*, Special Report, October 17: 86; The Factory Worker. 1996. *Business Week*, September 30: 66; The New Deal—What Companies and Employees Owe one another. 1994. *Fortune*, June 13: 50. For a contrary view, see "Breaking the Chains of Command." 1994. *Business Week*, special issue on "The Information Revolution": 113.

## Chapter 8   Bringing Careers Back in . . . The Changing Landscape of Careers in American Corporations Today

1. Our thanks to Dr. Paul Yost for providing information about the Boeing Waypoint project.
2. The authors are grateful to Carol Yamartino, senior Director of Learning and Development at Millennium Pharmaceuticals, for providing this information.

## Chapter 10   Itinerant Professionals: Technical Contractors in a Knowledge Economy

1. This chapter draws on data and arguments elaborated more fully in our book *Gurus, Hired Guns and Warm Bodies* (Barley and Kunda 2004).
2. Under its most liberal, restricted definition the BLS defines the contingent workforce as the sum of (a) all wage and salary workers who "do not expect their employment to last," except for those who planned to leave their jobs for personal reasons, (b) all "self

employed (both the incorporated and the unincorporated) and independent contractors who expect to be and had been in their present assignment for less than one year,"
and (c) temporary help and contract workers who "expected to work for the customers
to whom they were assigned for one year or less" (Cohany et al. 1998, 43–44).

3. The staffing industry recovered from the recession more quickly than many other
industries. By 2004 the number of people placed daily by staffing agencies had
returned to the level it had achieved at the height of the dot-com bubble in 2000
(Berchon 2005).

4. For a more detailed account of the study, see Barley and Kunda (2004), Kunda, Barley
and Evans (2002).

5. The blurring of the distinction between newcomers and old-timers may reflect the fact
that so many of the contractors we encountered worked in software development and IT
related occupations. These areas of practice change so quickly that newly minted graduates are likely to have more cutting edge skills than practitioners with years of experience.

6. Working Today is a nonprofit affinity and advocacy group founded by Sara Horowitz
in 1993. Working Today serves contractors and other contingent workers in New York
City. It offers contractors health insurance, portable pensions, and other benefits. More
information on Working Today can be found at http://www.workingtoday.org. PACE
was organized by James R. Ziegler, who also publishes the extremely useful online book
*The Contractor Employees Handbook*. Information on PACE and the Handbook can be
found at http://www.cehandbook.com.

### Chapter 11    The Changing Employment Circumstances of Managers

1. These data are from the November 2003 Bureau of Labor Statistics Occupational
Employment Survey. See http://www.bls.gov/oes. The Current Population Survey,
which is a survey of individuals, reports a substantially higher number of managers,
14,535,000 in 2004. See U.S. Bureau of Labor Statistics. 2005. Employment and
earnings. January: 210.

2. The source for the dislocation figures is U.S. Bureau of Labor Statistics' news release,
Worker displacement, 2001–2003, dated July 30, 2004. The source for total
employment by occupation is the Bureau of Labor Statistics, National Employment
and Wage Estimates, found at http://www. bls.gov.

3. Economic    Policy    Institute,    http://www.epinet.org/content.cfm/webfeatures_
snapshots_archive_2002_0724_snap07242002.

### Chapter 12    Changing Career Paths and Their Implications

1. In European work systems, the individual employee might have a designation or rank
that traveled with them across jobs. DiPrete (1989, 14) notes this distinction.

2. A smaller survey of corporate Presidents from the American Management Association
in the late 1970s found that 38 percent had been outside hires, as opposed to only 20
percent in the Newcomer study conducted a generation before. (An outside hire in this
context meant that the executive had not begun their career at their current company,
not necessarily that they had been hired into their current job from outside.) The
authors concluded that "One can argue that there is a trend toward selecting the professional manager from the outside as opposed to encouraging the internal succession
route to the top." Brady, Gene F., Robert M. Fulmer, and Donald L. Helmich. 1982.

Planning executive succession: The effect of recruitment source and organizational problems on anticipated tenure. *SMJ* 3: 269–275.

3. Among the more influential arguments that the U.S. economy had undergone fundamental and painful change in this period was Dertouzos, Michael L. et al. 1989. *Made in America: Regaining the Productive Edge.* Cambridge, MA: MIT Press; and Cappelli, Peter et al. 1997. *Change at Work.* New York: Oxford University Press, suggests that the economic restructuring of the 1980s had a range of negative consequences for employees.

4. Given an average age in 1980 of 56, the 1980 executives would have been 22—a typical graduation age—in 1946, and many of these executives would have served in World War II, beginning their careers later. A much smaller percentage of the 2001 executives, who on average were 22 in 1972, would have served in the military during the Vietnam War. Differences in the incidence of military experience may account for some of the age difference in the two cohorts.

5. In the 1950s, when the 1980 executives would have been hired, four-year graduates from public institutions were equal to 34 percent of the graduates from private institutions. That figure rose only to 35 percent by 1970, when the 2001 executives would have been hired. See Table 243, Degree Granting Institutions by Control and Type of Institution. 2002. In *Digest of Educational Statistics.* National Center for Educational Statistics: Washington, DC.

6. Princeton and Brown have neither a law school nor a business school. Dartmouth has a business school but no law school.

7. When executives are grouped into five broad job titles, the same pattern of results applies with the exception of CFO/CTO positions:

| | Gender | N | Mean | Standard Deviation | Sign |
|---|---|---|---|---|---|
| C-Suite | Female | 10 | 22.80 | 9.47 | 0.061 |
| | Male | 216 | 27.43 | 7.51 | |
| CF/T/O/O | Female | 7 | 20.14 | 5.40 | 0.318 |
| | Male | 24 | 22.50 | 5.41 | |
| EVP | Female | 34 | 21.32 | 4.82 | 0.019 |
| | Male | 195 | 24.31 | 7.11 | |
| Group Head | Female | 15 | 21.27 | 2.05 | 0.003 |
| | Male | 147 | 26.50 | 6.55 | |
| SVP | Female | 28 | 20.93 | 5.84 | 0.065 |
| | Male | 206 | 23.62 | 7.37 | |

## Chapter 13    The Value of Innovative Human Resource Management Practices by Kathryn Shaw

I would like to acknowledge the excellent support by the Alfred P. Sloan Foundation, the Russell Sage Foundation, and the Rockefeller Foundation for my ongoing research. Also, my coauthors have contributed very significantly to the research that I refer to herein and to my understanding of these issues, though they are in no way responsible for the views I express below. I thank Brent Boning, Casey Ichniowski, and Giovanna Prennushi.

1. Levy and Murnane (1995) make a strong case for the investment in basic skills that emphasize problem solving. Other researchers making this point include: Autor, Levy, and Murnane (1999, 2001, 2001); Bartel, Ichniowski, and Shaw (2005); Black and

Lynch (2001); Dunlop and Weil (1996); Hunter and Lafkas (1998); and Milgrom and Roberts (1990).

2. For reviews of the training practices of firms, see Leuven and Oosterbeek (1999); Finegold and Mason (1999); Lowenstein and Spletzer (1999); Barron, Berger, and Black (1999); and Bishop (1997). Overall, firms are unlikely to teach basic cognitive skills, such as math and reading, but they do provide some training that is of a general nature. They do provide training in specific problem-solving methods (such as "6-sigma") and communications skills. But such training is only effective if the workforce already has the basics skills, in math, reading, and noncognitive motivational factors.

## Chapter 15   Global Sourcing of Talent: Implications for the U.S. Workforce

1. Employment in U.S. subsidiaries of foreign companies more than doubled between 1987 and 2002, providing jobs to 5.42 million people (Slaughter 2004b, 3).

2. IBM, GE, Unilever, American Express, and Accenture are among the "global majors" sourcing talent in India. Deploy Solutions, Sierra Atlantic, and RealMetrix are among the many small, venture-funded companies reported to have adopted a global sourcing strategy to scale their operations quickly.

3. At the time of the sale, GECIS employed 17,000 people—12,000 employees in India and 5,000 employees in Hungary, Mexico, and China—and was expected to grow to 23,000 employees in 2005. The division generated $420 million in annual revenue, 95% of which was from serving internal GE business units.

4. Retirement savings in many industries have become more portable as employers have moved away from traditional defined benefit pension plans in favor of defined contribution 401(k) retirement mechanisms. However, for the industries that have defined benefit pensions, the lack of portability remains a constraint to labor mobility.

The authors wish to thank Dawn Chandler, Doctor of Business Administration, Boston University School of Management, for her assistance with this research .We also thank Som Mittal, former chairman, NASSCOM, and President, HP Global Soft, for his valuable onsights.

## Research Methodology

This chapter is based on a review of many academic, consultant, and analyst reports chronicling the growth of offshore operations. The authors also conducted personal interviews in the United States and India between July 2003 and spring 2005 with 16 senior human resources executives and general managers from a dozen companies that are sourcing talent in India. Ten of the interviewed companies are headquartered in the United States, one in Europe, and one in India. Almost half of the interviews were conducted in India.

## Chapter 16    Shared Capitalism at Work: Impacts and Policy Options

1. The authors wish to express their gratitude to the Rockefeller Foundation and the Russell Sage Foundation for supporting the research of the Shared Capitalism Project at the National Bureau for Economic Research (NBER) in Cambridge, Massachusetts, which included sponsoring a segment of the 2002 General Social Survey (GSS). We are grateful to Dr. Tom Smith of the National Opinion Research Center at the University of Chicago for his assistance with the GSS. We also thank the other nonprofit organizations who are members of the Shared Capitalism Research Consortium that supported the General Social Survey's work in this area: the Employee Ownership Foundation and the ESOP Association, of Washington, DC, the Beyster Institute at the Rady School of Business of the University of California at San Diego, California, the National Center for Employee Ownership in Oakland, California, and the Profit Sharing Council of America in Chicago, Illinois. The other principal nonprofit organizations studying this issue are the Center for Economic and Social Justice in Washington, DC, the Global Equity Organization of the United States and the United Kingdom, the Kelso Institute in San Francisco, California, the National Association of Stock Plan Professionals, the Northeast Ohio Employee Ownership Center at Kent State University in Kent, Ohio, and the Vermont Employee Ownership Center in Burlington, Vermont.

2. The 36 percent figure is conservative, since it excludes those who say they are eligible for performance sharing but did not receive a bonus in the past year.

3. The Empowerment Score was created with the following GSS questions, which had 1 to 3 or 4 scales:

   - I have a lot of say what happens on my job.
   - I am given a lot of freedom to decide how to do my own work; I have enough information to get the job done.
   - How often do you participate with others in helping set the way things are done on your job?
   - In your job, how often do you take part with others in making decisions that affect you?
   - Conditions on my job allow me to be about as productive as I could be.
   - At the place where I work, I am treated with respect
   - My supervisor is concerned about the welfare of those under him or her.
   - My supervisor is helpful to me in getting the job done.
   - When you do your job well, are you likely to be praised by your supervisor or employer?

4. These results confirm the findings of several key studies using a previous national survey (Freeman and Dube 2000; see also Freeman and Rogers 1999), nonrandom samples (Rosen, Klein, and Young 1986; Quarry and Rosen 1986; Blasi, Conte, and Kruse 1992; Sesil, Kroumova, Blasi, and Kruse 2002), and case studies (Rosen, Case, and Staubus 2005).

5. We are indebted to our sociologist colleague, Professor Maurie Cohen of the New Jersey Institute of Technology for raising these issues and shaping this discussion for us.

# Combined References

AAC&U. 2004. Surveys Show Declining Foreign Enrollment at U.S. Colleges and Universities. http://www.Aacuedu.Org/Aacu_News/AACUNews04/November04/Facts_Figures.Cfm.

Aaronson, Daniel, and Eric French. 2004. The Effect of Part-Time Work on Wages: Evidence from the Social Security Rules. Journal of Labor Economics 22 (2): 329–353.

Abowd, John, John Haltiwanger, Julia Lane, and Dristin Sandusky. 2001. Within and between Firm Changes in Human Capital, Technology, and Productivity. Working Paper.

Abraham, Katharine G. 1988. Flexible Staffing Arrangements and Employers' Short-Term Adjustment Strategies. In *Employment, Unemployment and Labour Utilization*, ed. Robert A. Hart, 288–311. London: Unwin Hyman.

Abraham, Katharine G., and Susan K. Taylor. 1996. Firms' Use of Outside Contractors: Theory and Evidence. *Journal of Labor Economics* 14 (3): 394–424.

Abrahamson, Eric. 1996. Management Fashion. *Academy of Management Review* 21: 254–285.

Abrahamson, Eric, and Gregory Fairchild. 1999. Management Fashion: Lifecycles, Triggers, and Collective Learning Processes. *Administrative Science Quarterly* 44: 708–740.

*ACA News.* 1999. More Companies Give Stock Options to Broad Number of Employees. September 9: 12.

Adelman, C. 1997. *Leading, Concurrent, or Lagging?: The Knowledge Content of Computer Science in Higher Education and the Labor Market.* Washington, DC: United States Department of Education; Madison, WI: National Institute for Science Education.

Adler, Paul S. 1993. The New "Learning Bureaucracy": New United Motors Manufacturing, Inc. In *Research in Organizational Behavior*, ed. Barry Staw and Larry Cummings, 111–194. Greenwich CT: JAI Press.

Adler, Paul S., Barbara Goldoftas, and David I. Levine. 1997. Ergonomics, Employee Involvement, and the Toyota Production System: A Case Study of NUMMI's 1993 Model Introduction. *Industrial and Labor Relations Review* 50(3): 416–437.

Aeppel, T. 2003. Ill Will: Skyrocketing Health Costs Start to Pit Worker vs. Worker. *The Wall Street Journal*, June 17.

Akerlof, George A. 1982. Labor Contracts as Partial Gift Exchange. *Quarterly Journal of Economics* 97: 543–569.

Akron Beacon Journal. 2005. Officer Granted Partial Clemency for Scavenging Parts. June 2. http://www.Ohio.Com/Mld/Beaconjournal/News/State/11793125.Html.

Allen, T. D., D. E. Herst, C. S. Bruck, and M. Sutton. 2000. Consequences Associated with Work to Family Conflict: A Review and Agenda for Future Research. *Journal of Occupational Health Psychology* 5: 278–308.

Andersson, Fredrick, Harry J. Holzer, and Julia I. Lane. 2005. *Moving up or Moving on: Who Advances in the Low-Wage Labor Market?* New York: Russell Sage Foundation.

Andrews, M. 2004. Get Healthy, Get Wealthy. *Money*, December: 57.

Aoki, Masahiko. 1988. *Information, Incentives, and Bargaining in the Japanese Economy*. Cambridge, U.K.: Cambridge University Press.

Appelbaum, Eileen. 2004. No Jobs, Bad Jobs, Trying Times for America's Working Families: What Democrats Can Do about It. Paper Prepared for the Democratic Policy Committee Issues Conference. April.

Appelbaum, Eileen, Thomas Bailey, Peter Berg, and Arne L. Kalleberg. 2000. *Manufacturing Advantage: Why High Performance Work Systems Pay Off*. Ithaca, NY: Cornell/ILR Press.

Appelbaum, Eileen, and Rosemary Batt. 1994. *The New American Workplace*. Ithaca, NY: ILR Press.

Ariss, Sonny S. 2002. Employee Involvement as a Prerequisite to Reduce Workers' Compensation Costs: A Case Study. Review of Business 23(2): 12–17.

Arthur, Jeffrey B. 1992. The Link between Business Strategy and Industrial Relations Systems in American Steel Minimills. *Industrial and Labor Relations Review* 45: 488–506.

Arthur, M. B., and D. M. Rousseau. 1996. *The Boundaryless Career: A New Employment Principle for a New Organizational Era*. New York: Oxford University Press.

Arthur, W. Jr., W. Bennett Jr., P. S. Edens, and S. T. Bell. 2003. Effectiveness of Training in Organizations: A Meta-Analysis of Design and Evaluation Features. *Journal of Applied Psychology* 88: 234–245.

Ashmos, D. P., and D. Duchon. 2000. Spirituality at Work: A Conceptualization and Measure. *Journal of Management Inquiry* 9: 134–145.

Aspen Institute. 2001. *Where Will They Lead? MBA Students Attitudes about Business and Society*. New York: Aspen Institute for Social Innovation Through Business.

Atkinson, R. D. 2004. *Meeting the Offshoring Challenge*. Washington, DC: Progressive Policy Institute.

———. 2004. *Understanding the Offshoring Challenge*. Washington, DC: Progressive Policy Institute.

———. 2001. Wiring the Labor Market. *Journal of Economic Perspectives* 15 (1): 25–40.

———. 2004. Labor Market Intermediaries: What It Is, Why It Is Growing, and Where It Is Going. *NBER Reporter*, Fall.

Autor, David. 2001. Why Do Temporary Help Firms Provide Free General Skills Training? *Quarterly Journal of Economics* 116 (4): 1409–1448.

———. 2003. Outsourcing at Will: Unjust Dismissal Doctrine and the Growth of Temporary Help Employment. *Journal of Labor Economics* 21 (1): 1–42.

Autor, David, and Lawrence Katz. 1998. Computing Inequality: Have Computers Changed the Labor Market. *Quarterly Journal of Economics* 113 (4): 1169–1214.

Autor, David, Frank Levy, and Richard Murname. 2001. The Skill Content of Recent Technological Change: An Empirical Investigation.

Autor, David, Frank Levy, and Richard Murname. 2001. Upstairs Downstairs: Computers and Skills in Two Floors of a Large Bank.

Azfar, Omar, and Stephan Danninger. 2001. Profit-Sharing, Employment Stability, and Wage Growth. *Industrial and Labor Relations Review* 54: 619–630.

Bailey, T., M. Alfonso, M. Scott, and T. Leinbach. 2005. *Educational Outcomes of Occupational Postsecondary Students*. Washington, DC: Report for the U.S. Department of Education, National Assessment of Vocational Education.

Bailey, T., G. Kienzl, and D. Marcotte D. 2004. The *Return to a Sub-Baccalaureate Education: The Effects of Schooling, Credentials and Program of Study on Economic Outcomes*. Washington, DC: Report for the U.S. Department of Education, National Assessment of Vocational Education.

Bailey, Thomas R., and Annette D. Bernhardt. 1997. In Search of the High Road in a Low-Wage Industry. *Politics and Society* 25: 179–201.

Bailyn, Lotte. 2003. Academic Careers and Gender Equity: Lessons from MIT. *Gender, Work, and Organization* 10 (2): 137–153.

Bain & Company. 2004. Capability Sourcing. Presentation by Steve Berez, Partner, at the Spring Meeting of the Human Resources Policy Institute, School of Management, Boston University.
———. 2005. Management Tools: The Tools. http://www.Bain.Com/Management_Tools/Tools_Activity.Asp?Groupcode= 2.

Bajpai, N., J. D. Sachs, R. Arora, R., and H. Khurana. 2004. Global Services Sourcing: Issues of Cost and Quality. Center on Globalization and Sustainable Development Working Paper No. 16, Columbia University, New York, NY.

Baker, G., M. Gibbs, and B. Homstrom. 1994. The Internal Economics of the Firm: Evidence from Personnel Data. *Quarterly Journal of Economics*, November: 881–919.

Baker, T., and Aldrich, H. E. 1996. Prometheus Stretches: Building Identity and Cumulative Knowledge in Multiemployer Careers. In *The Boundaryless Career: A New Employment Principle for a New Organizational Era*, ed. M. B. Arthur and D. M. Rousseau, 132–149. New York: Oxford University Press.

Bakker, Arnold B., and Sabine A. E. Geurts. 2004. Toward a Dual-Process Model of Work-Home Interference. *Work and Occupations* 31: 345–366.

Ballot, G., F. Fakhfakh, and E. Taymaz. 2002. Who Benefits from Training and R&D: The Firm or the Workers? A Study on Panels of French and Swedish Firms. Working Paper.

Bardhan, A. D., and C. Kroll. 2003. *The New Wave of Outsourcing*. Berkeley, CA: Fisher Center for Real Estate and Urban Economics.

Barker, James R. 1993. Tightening the Iron Cage: Concertive Control in Self-Managing Teams. *Administrative Science Quarterly* 38: 408–437.

Barker, Kathleen, and Kathleen Christensen. 1998. Controversy and Challenges Raised by Contingent Work Arrangements. In *Contingent Work: American Employment in Transition*, ed. Kathleen Barker and Kathleen Christensen, 1–20. Ithaca, NY: ILR Press.

Barley, S. R. 1989. Careers, Identities, and Institutions: The Legacy of the Chicago School of Sociology. In *Handbook of Career Theory*, ed. M. B. Arthur, D. T. Hall, and B. S. Lawrence, 41–65. New York: Cambridge University Press.

Barley, S. R., and P. S. Tolbert. 1997. Institutionalization and Structuration: Studying the Links between Action and Institution. *Organization Studies* 18: 93–117.

Barley, Stephen R. 2005. What We Know (and mostly Don't Know) about Technical Work. In *The Oxford Handbook of Work and Organization*, ed. Stephen Ackroyd, Rosemary Batt, Paul Thompson, and Pamela Tolbert, 376–403. Oxford: Oxford University Press.

Barley, Stephen R., and Gideon Kunda. 1992. Design and Devotion: Surges of Rational and Normative Ideologies of Control in Managerial Discourse. *Administrative Science Quarterly* 37: 363–399.

Barley, Stephen R., and Gideon Kunda. 2004. *Gurus, Hired Guns and Warm Bodies: Itinerant Experts in a Knowledge Economy*. Princeton, NJ: Princeton University Press.

Barley, Stephen R., Gideon Kunda, and James Evans. 2002. Why Do Contractors Contract? The Experience of Highly Skilled Technical Professionals in a Contingent Labor Market. *Industrial and Labor Relations Review* 55: 234–261.

Barnett, R. C. 1994. Home-to-Work Spillover Revisited: A Study of Full-Time Employed Women in Dual-Earner Couples. *Journal of Marriage and the Family* 56: 647–656.

Barron, John, Mark Berger, and Dan Black. 1999. Replacing General With Specific Training. *Research in Labor Economics* 18: 281–302.

Barstow, D., and D. B. Henriques. 2001. Families of Victims Fault Benefits Plan of Insurance Giant. *New York Times*, December 26.

Bartel, Ann. 1995. Training, Wage Growth, and Job Performance: Evidence from a Company Database. *Journal of Labor Economics* 13 (3): 401–425.

Bartel, Ann, Casey Ichniowski, and Kathryn Shaw. 2005. How Does Information Technology Really Affect Productivity? Plant-Level Comparisons of Product Innovation, Process Improvement and Worker Skills, National Bureau of Economic Research Working Paper No. 11773.

Bartel, Ann, Casey Ichniowski, and Kathryn Shaw. 2002. New Technology, Human Resource Practices and Skill Requirements: Evidence from Plant Visits in Three Industries.

Bartlett, C. A., and S. Ghoshal. 2002. Building Competitive Advantage through People. *MIT Sloan Management Review* 43 (2): 34–41.

Bartunek, J. M., and M. K. Moch. 1987. First-Order, Second-Order, and Third-Order Change and Organization Development Interventions: A Cognitive Approach. *Journal of Applied Behavioral Science* 23 (4): 483–500.

Bassi, Laurie, Baruch Lev, Jonathan Low, Daniel McMurrer, and G. Anthony Siesfeld. 2000. Measuring Corporate Investments in Human Capital. In *The New Relationship: Human Capital in the American Corporation*, ed. M. M. Blair and T. A. Kochan, 334–369. Washington, DC: Brookings Institution Press.

Batt, Rosemary. 1999. Work Organization, Technology, and Performance in Customer Services and Sales. *Industrial and Labor Relations Review* 52: 539–564.

———. 2001a. Explaining Wage Inequality in Telecommunications Services: Customer Segmentation, Human Resource Practices, and Union Decline. *Industrial and Labor Relations Review* 54: 425–449.

———. 2001b. The Economics of Teams Among Technicians. *British Journal of Industrial Relations* 39: 1–24.

———. 2004. Who Benefits from Teams? Comparing Workers, Supervisors, and Managers. *Industrial Relations* 43: 183–212.

Bauer, T. 2002. Incidence and Labor Market Effects of High-Performance Work Practices in Germany. Working Paper.

Bauer, Thomas K., and Stefan Bender. 2001. Flexible Work Systems and the Structure of Wages: Evidence from Matched Employer-Employee Data. IZA Discussion Paper No. 353. Bonn, Germany.

Baumol, W. J., A. S. Blinder, and E. N. Wolff. 2003. *Downsizing in America: Reality, Causes and Consequences*. New York: Russell Sage Foundation.

Baura, Anitesh, and Tridas Mukhopadhyay. 2000. Information Technology and Business Performance: Past, Present and Future. In *Framing the Domains of IT Management*, ed. Robert W. Zmud, 65–84. Cincinnati: Pinnaflex Educational Resources, Inc.

Becker, B. E., and M. A. Huselid. 1998. High Performance Work Systems and Firm Performance: A Synthesis of Research and Managerial Implications. *Research in Personal and Human Resources Management* 16: 53–101.

Becker, B. E., M. E. Huselid, and D. Ulrich. 2001. *The HR Scorecard: Linking People, Strategy, and Performance*. Boston: Harvard Business School Press.

Becker, Gary. 1964. *Human Capital*. Chicago: Chicago University Press.

———. 1975. *Human Capital*. 2nd ed. Chicago: University of Chicago Press.

Beckman, Sara. 1996. Evolution of Management Roles in a Networked Organization: An Insider's View of the Hewlett-Packard Company. In *Broken Ladders: Managerial Careers in the New Economy*, ed. Paul Osterman, 155–184. New York: Oxford University Press.

Beehr, T. A. 1995. *Psychological Stress in the Workplace*. London: Routledge.

Belkin, L. 2003. Q: Why Don't More Women Get to the Top? A: They Choose not to. *New York Times Magazine*. October 26.

Bell, Linda A., and David Neumark. 1993. Lump-Sum Payments and Profit-Sharing Plans in the Union Sector of the United States Economy. *Economic Journal* 103: 602–619.

Belous, R. S. 1989. The *Contingent Economy: The Growth of the Temporary, Part-Time, and Subcontracted Workforce*. Washington, DC: National Planning Association.

Bemis, Edward W. 1886. Cooperation in the Northeast. *Publications of the American Economic Association* 1 (5): 7–136.

Benson, G., D. Finegold, and S. Mohrman. 2004. You Paid for the Skills, Now Keep Them: Tuition Reimbursement and Voluntary Turnover. *Academy of Management Journal* 47 (3): 315–331.

Benson, K. 1983. A Dialectical Method for the Study of Organizations. In *Beyond Method*, ed. G. Morgan, 331–346. Beverly Hills: Sage.

Berchem, Steven P. 2005. *Rebound: ASA's Annual Economic Analysis of the Staffing Industry.* Washington, DC: American Staffing Association.

Berg, P. 2004. Work-Life Balance Tensions and Solutions in the United States. Paper Presented at the Economic and Social Research Council (ESRC) Conference, Second International Colloquium on the Future of Work, Leeds, England. September.

Berg, P., E. Appelbaum, and A. Kalleberg. 2003. Balancing Work and Family: The Role Of High Commitment Environments. *Industrial Relations* 42 (2): 168–188.

Berg, Peter, Eileen Appelbaum, Thomas Bailey, and Arne Kalleberg. 1996. The Performance Effects of Modular Production in the Apparel Industry. *Industrial Relations* 35: 356–373.

———. 2004. Contesting Time: International Comparisons of Employee Control of Working Time. *Industrial and Labor Relations Review* 57: 331–349.

Berger, J. 1972. *Ways of Seeing.* Harmondsworth: Penguin.

Berman, Eli, John Bound, and Zvi Griliches. 1994. Changes in the Demand of Skilled Labor Within U.S. Manufacturing Industries: Evidence from the Annual Survey of Manufacturers, *Quarterly Journal of Economics* 109 (2): 367–397.

Bernhardt, Annette, Martina Morris, Mark S. Handcock, and Marc A. Scott. 2001. *Divergent Paths: Economic Mobility in the New American Labor Market.* New York: Russell Sage Foundation.

Bernstein, Aaron. 2005. A Major Swipe at Sweatshops. *Business Week*, May 23: 98–100.

Bhagwati, Jagdish, Arvind Panagariya, and T. N. Srinivasan. 2004. The Muddles over Outsourcing. *Journal of Economics Perspectives* 18(4).

Bishop, John. 1997. What We Know about Employer Provided Training. *Research in Labor Economics* 16: 19–87.

Black, Sandra E., and Lisa M. Lynch. 1996. Human Capital Investments and Productivity. *American Economic Review Papers and Proceedings* 86 (May): 263–267.

———. 1997. How to Compete: The Impact of Workplace Practices and IT on Productivity. NBER Working Paper No. 6120.

———. 2000. What's Driving the New Economy: The Benefits of Workplace Innovation. NBER Working Paper No. 7479.

———. 2001. How to Compete: The Impact of Workplace Practices and IT on Productivity. *Review of Economics and Statistics* , 83: 434–445.

———. 2000. What's Driving the New Economy: The Benefits of Workplace Innovation. National Bureau of Economic Research Working Paper No. 7479, Cambridge, MA.

———. 2001. How to Compete: The Impact of Workplace Practices and Information Technology on Productivity. *Review of Economics and Statistics*, 83: 434–445.

Black, Sandra E., Lisa M. Lynch, and Anya Krivelyova. 2004. How Workers Fare when Employers Innovate. *Industrial Relations* 43: 44–66.

Blair, M. M., and T. A. Kochan. 2000. The *New Relationship: Human Capital in the American Corporation.* Washington, DC: Brookings Institution Press.

Blair, Margaret. 1995. *Ownership and Control.* Washington, DC: The Brookings Institution.

Blair, Margaret, and Lynn A. Stout. 1999. A Team Production Theory of Corporate Law. *Virginia Law Review* 85: 247–328.

Blank, Rebecca M. 1990. Are Part-Time Jobs Bad Jobs? In *A Future of Lousy Jobs? the Changing Structure of U.S. Wages*, ed. Gary Burtless. Washington, DC: The Brookings Institution.

Blasi, J., D. Kruse, and A. Bernstein. 2003. In *The Company of Owners: The Truth about Stock Options (and why every Employee Should Have Them)*. New York: Perseus Books.

Blasi, Joseph. 2006. High Performance Work Practices at Century's End: Incidence, Diffusion, Industry Group Differences, and the Economic Environment. *Industrial Relations*.

Blasi, Joseph, Michael Conte, and Douglas Kruse. 1996. Employee Stock Ownership and Corporate Performance Among Public Companies. *Industrial & Labor Relations Review* 50: 60–79.

Blasi, Joseph, Douglas Kruse, and Aaron Bernstein. 2003. *In the Company of Owners*. New York: Basic Books.

Blau, Francine D., Marianne A. Ferber, and Anne E. Winkler. 2002. *The Economics of Women, Men and Work*. 4th ed. Englewood Cliffs, NJ: Prentice-Hall.

Blau, Francine D., and Lawrence M. Kahn. 1997. Swimming Upstream: Trends in the Gender Wage Differential in the 1980s. *Journal of Labor Economics* 15(1), Part 1: 1–42.

———. 2000. Gender Differences in Pay. *The Journal of Economic Perspectives* 14 (4): 75–99.

———. 2001. Do Cognitive Test Scores Explain Higher U.S. Wage Inequality? National Bureau of Economic Research Working Paper 8210. http://www.NBER.Org/Papers/W8210.

———. 2002 *At Home and Abroad: U.S. Labor Market Performance in International Perspective*. New York: Russell Sage Foundation.

Block, R., M. Malin, E. Kossek, and A. Holt. 2006. The Legal and Administrative Context of Work and Family Policies in the United States, Canada, and the European Union. In *Managing the Work-Home Interface*, ed. F. Jones, R. Burke, and M. Westman, 39–68, Oxford: Routledge Press.

Block, Richard N., P. Berg, and D. Belman. 2004. The Economic Dimension of the Employment Relationship. In *The Employment Relationship: Examining Psychological and Contextual Perspectives*, ed. J. A-M Coyle-Shapiro, L. M. Shore, M. S. Taylor, and L. E. Tetrick, 94–118. Oxford, UK: Oxford University Press.

Bluestone, Barry, and Irving Bluestone. 1992. *Negotiating the Future: A Labor Perspective on American Business*. New York: Basic Books.

Bohen, H., and A. Viveros-Long. 1981. *Balancing Jobs and Family Life: Do Flexible Work Schedules Help?* Philadelphia: Temple.

Bolger, N., A. Delongis, and R. C. Kessler. 1989. The Contagion of Stress Across Multiple Roles. *Journal of Marriage and the Family* 51: 175–183.

Bolles, R. N. 2005. *What Color Is Your Parachute? 2005: A Practical Manual for Job-Hunters and Career-Changers*. Berkeley, CA: Ten Speed Press.

Bond, J. 2003. *The Impact of Job and Workplace Conditions on Low-Wage and -Income Employees and their Employers*. New York: Families and Work Institute.

Bond, J., C. Thompson, E. Galinsky, and D. Prottas. 2002. *Highlights of the National Study of the Changing Workforce*. New York: Families and Work Institute.

Bond, T., E. Galinsky, and J. E. Swanberg. 1998. *The 1997 National Study of the Changing Workforce*. New York (NK): Families and Work Institute.

Boning, Brent, Casey Ichniowski, and Kathryn Shaw. 2001. Opportunity Counts: Teams and the Effectiveness of Production Incentives. NBER Working Paper #8306, May.

Borghans, Lex, and Bas Ter Weel. 2001. Computers, Skills and Wages. Maastricht University Working Paper. May.

Boris, E., and C. Lewis. 2006. Caregiving and Wage-Earning: A Historical Perspective on Work and Family. In *The Work and Family Handbook: Multi-Disciplinary Perspectives, Methods and Approaches*, ed. M. Pitt-Catsouphes, E. Kossek, and S. Sweet. Mahwah, NJ: Lawrence Erlbaum Associates.

The Boston Consulting Group. 2004. *Capturing Global Advantage: How Leading Industrial Companies Are Transforming Their Industries by Sourcing and Selling in China, India, and*

*Other Low-Cost Countries.* http://www.Bcg.Com/Publications/Files/Capturing_Global_ Advantage_Apr04_Rpt.Pdf.

Bottino. S. J. 2004. Perspectives on Offshoring and New Jersey. New Jersey Policy Perspective. http://www.NJPP.Org/Rpt_Offshoring.Html.

Brainard, L., and R. E. Litan. 2004. "Offshoring" Service Jobs: Bane or Boon—and What to Do? *The Brookings Institution Policy Brief* 132.

Brenner, Mark D., David Fairris, and John Ruser. 2004. "Flexible" Work Practices and Occupational Safety and Health: Exploring the Relationship between Cumulative Trauma Disorders and Workplace Transformation. Industrial Relations 43: 242–267.

Bresnahan, Timothy F., E. Brynjolfsson, and L. M. Hitt. 2002. Information Technology, Workplace Organization, and the Demand for Skilled Labor: Firm-Level Evidence. *Quarterly Journal of Economics* 117: 339–376.

Bresnahan, Timothy F., and Shane Greenstein. 1996. Technical Progress in Computing and in the Uses of Computers. In *Brookings Papers on Economic Activity, Microeconomics*, 1–83.

Britt, J. 2004. Expert: Disease Management Programs Cut Health Care Costs. http:// www.Shrm.Org.

Brofenbrenner, Kate, and Thomas Juravich. 1995. The Impact of Employer Opposition on Union Certification Win Rates: A Private/Public Comparison. Economic Policy Institute Working Paper No. 113, Washington, DC.

Brown, Charles. 1980. Equalizing Differences in the Labor Market. *Quarterly Journal of Economics* 94: 113–134.

Brown, Clair, Yoshi Nakata, Michael Reich, and Lloyd Ulman. 1997. *Work and Pay in the United States and Japan.* New York: Oxford University Press.

Brown, J. D. 1986. Evaluation of Self and Others: Self-Enhancement Biases in Social Judgments. *Social Cognition* 4: 353–376.

Brown, S., F. Fakhfakh, and J. G. Sessions, J. G. 1999. Absenteeism and Employee Sharing: An Empirical Analysis Based on French Panel Data, 1981–1991. *Industrial and Labor Relations Review* 52: 234–251.

Brynjolfsson, Eric. 1993. The Productivity Paradox of Information Technology. *Communications of the Acm* 35, December: 66–77.

Brynjolfsson, Erik, and Loren Hitt. 2000. Beyond Computation: Information Technology, Organizational Transformation, and Business Performance. *Journal of Economic Perspectives.*

Buchmann, M. 1989. *The Script of Life in Modern Society: Entry into Adulthood in a Changing World.* Chicago: University of Chicago Press.

Budros, Art. 1997. The New Capitalism and Organizational Rationality: The Adoption of Downsizing Programs, 1979–1994. *Social Forces* 76: 229–250.

Bureau of Economic Affairs, United States Department of Commerce. 2005. Summary Estimates for Multinational Companies: Employment, Sales, and Capital Expenditures for 2003. April 19. http://www.Bea.Gov/Bea/Newsrelarchive/2005/Mnc2003.Htm.

Bureau of Labor Statistics. 1996a. BLS Reports on the Amount of Employer-Provided Formal Training. Washington, DC: U.S. Department of Labor Press Release, Usdl96–268, July 10.

Bureau of Labor Statistics. 1996b. 1995 Survey of Employer Provided Training—Employee Results. Washington, DC: U.S. Department of Labor Press Release, Usdl96–515, December 19.

———. 1997. Contingent and Alternative Employment Arrangements, February 1997. http://Ftp.BLS.Gov/Pub/News.Release/Conemp.Txt.

———. 1998. Employee Tenure in 1998. http://Stats.BLS.Gov/News.Release/Tenure.Toc.Htm.

———. 2000. National Compensation Survey, Survey of Employee Benefits. 2000. http://www.BLS.Org.

———. 2001. Contingent and Alternative Employment Arrangements, February 2001. http://www.BLS.Gov/News.Release/Conemp.Nr0.Htm.

Bureau of Labor Statistics. 2003. Tables 5 & 6. Percent of Workers With Access to Selected Benefits, by Selected Characteristics, Private Industry. National Compensation Survey, Survey of Employee Benefits 2003. http://www.BLS.Org.

———. 2004. The Effect of Outsourcing and Offshoring on BLS Productivity Measures. March 26.

———. 2005. Contingent and Alternative Employment Arrangements, February 2005. United States Department of Labor Press Release 05–1433, July 27.

Burgess, S., and P. Metcalfe. 1999. The Use of Incentive Schemes in the Public and Private Sectors: Evidence from British Establishments. CMPO Working Paper Series No. 00/15.

Burton, M. Diane, and Christine Beckman. 2005. Leaving a Legacy: Role Imprints and Succor Turnover in Young Firms. MIT Sloan School Working Paper, March.

Business Line. 2005. Convergys Plans to Double BPO Headcount. February 9. http://Web.Lexis-Nexis.Com/Universe/Document?_M = 5a27ec04115e809086c441c5765246b9&_Docnum = 1&Wchp = Dglbvtb-Zskva&_Md5 = Bb3d378d703f0b90496d289fc810e8fd.

Business: Out of Captivity: GE in India. 2004. The Economist 373 (8401): 82. http://Proquest.Umi.Com/Pqdweb?Did = 735262341&Sid = 2&Fmt = 3&Clientid = 4676&Rqt = 309&Vname = Pqd

Byrne, John A. 1999. Chainsaw: The Notorious Career of Al Dunlap in the Era of Profit-At-Any-Price. New York: Harper Business.

California, State Of. 2004. California Unemployment Insurance Code, Part 2, Disability Benefits, Chapter 7, Paid Family Leave, §§ 3300—3306. http://www.Leginfo.Ca.Gov/Cgi-Bin/Displaycode?Section = Uic&Group = 03001–04000&File = 3300–3306.

Campion, M. A., and P. W. Thayer. 1985. Development and Field Evaluation of an Interdisciplinary Measure of Job Design. Journal of Applied Psychology 70: 29–43.

Cantor, D., Waldfogel, J., Kerwin, J., Wright, M., Levin, K., Rauch, J., Hagerty, T., Kudela, M. 2000. Balancing the Needs of Families and Employers: The Family and Medical Leave Surveys, 2000 Update, 2.2.2, Table 2.3., Washington, DC: U.S. Deptartment of Labor.

Caplan, R. D., A. D. Vinokur, R. H. Price, and M. Van Ryn. 1989. Job Seeking, Reemployment, and Mental Health: A Randomized Field Experiment in Coping With Job Loss. Journal of Applied Psychology 74(5): 759–769.

Caplow, Theodore. 1954. The Sociology of Work. Minneapolis: University of Minnesota Press.

Cappelli, P., L. Bassi, H. Katz, D. Knoke, P. Osterman, and M. Useem. 1997. Change at Work. New York: Oxford University Press.

Cappelli, P., and M. Hamori. 2005. The New Road to the Top. Harvard Business Review 83 (1): 25.

Cappelli, Peter. 1996. Technology and Skill Requirements: Implications for Establishment Wage Structures. New England Economic Review, May/June: 138–154.

———. 1999. Career Jobs Are Dead. California Management Review 42 (1): 146–167

———. 1999. The New Deal at Work: Managing the Market-Driven Workforce. Boston: Harvard Business School Press.

Cappelli, Peter, and William Carter. 2000. Computers, Work Organization, and Wage Outcomes. NBER Working Paper 7987, October.

Cappelli, Peter, and Anne Crocker-Hefter. 1996. Distinctive Human Resources Are Firms' Core Competencies. Organizational Dynamics 24 (Winter): 7–22.

Cappelli, Peter, and Monika Hamori. 2005a. The Institutions of Outside Hiring. In The Handbook of Career Studies.

———. 2005b. The New Road to the Top. Harvard Business Review 83 (1): 24–32.

Cappelli, Peter, and David Neumark. 2001. Do "High Performance" Work Practices Improve Establishment-Level Outcomes? Industrial and Labor Relations Review 54: 737–775.

———. 2004. External Churning and Internal Flexibility: Evidence on the Functional Flexibility and Core-Periphery Hypotheses. Industrial Relations 43: 148–182.

Carberry, Ed. 2000. Employee Involvement in Companies With Broad-Based Stock Option Programs. In *Stock Options, Corporate Performance, and Organizational Change*, ed. Scott S. Rodrick, 38–51. Oakland, CA: National Center for Employee Ownership.

Card, David, and John E. Dinardo. 2002. Skill Biased Technological Change and Rising Wage Inequality: Some Problems and Puzzles. *Journal of Labor Economics* 20 (4): 733–783.

Carneiro, P., and J. J. Heckman. 2002. Human Capital Policy. Working Paper, University of Chicago.

Caroli, Eve, and John Van Reenen. 1998. Human Capital and Organizational Change: Evidence from British and French Establishments in the 1980s and 1990s. *Journal of Economic Literature*.

Caroli, Eve, and John Van Reenen. 2001. Organization, Skills and Technology: Evidence from a Panel of British and French Establishments. *Quarterly Journal of Economics* 116: 1449–1492.

Carrig, K. 2004. As Described in *HR in Alignment: The Link to Business Results*. Dvd Produced by the Shrm Foundation, Alexandria, VA.

Cascio, W. F. 2000. *Costing Human Resources: The Financial Impact of Behavior in Organizations*. 4th ed. Cincinnati: South-Western.

Cascio, W. F. and L. Fogli. 2004. Talent Acquisition: New Realities of Attraction, Selection, and Retention. Workshop Presented at the Annual Conference of the Society for Industrial and Organizational Psychology, Chicago, April.

Cascio, W. F. and P. Wynn. 2004. Managing a Downsizing Process. *Human Resource Management Journal* 43 (4): 425–436.

Cascio, W. F., C. E. Young, and J. R. Morris. 1997. Financial Consequences of Employment Change Decisions in Major U.S. Corporations. *Academy of Management Journal* 40: 1175–1189.

Case, J. 1995. *Open Book Management*. New York: Harpercollins.

Catalano, R., D. Dooley, R. Novaco, G. Wilson, and R. Hough. 1993a. Using Eca Survey Data to Examine the Effect of Job Layoffs on Violent Behavior. Hospital and Community Psychiatry 44 (9): 874–879.

Catalano, R., D. Dooley, G. Wilson, and R. Hough. 1993b. Job Loss and Alcohol Abuse: A Test Using Data from the Epidemiologic Catchment Area Project. *Journal of Health and Social Behavior* 34 (3): 215–225.

Caulkin, S. 2003. "Who's in Charge Here? No one. But It's not a Recipe for Failure—just the Opposite." *The Observer*, Sunday April 27.

Celner, A., C. Gentrl, P. Lowes, and P. Nikolic. 2003. The Offshore Imperative: Managing the Forces and the Issues in the New Mandatory World of Offshoring. *Waters*, June: 1.

Chakrabarti, Monamii. 2004. Labor and Corporate Governance: Testing the Theory of Social Embeddedness. *Working USA*.

Chen, Jennjou. 2004. Essays on Part-Time Labor Markets for Older Workers. Ph.D. Dissertation, Cornell University.

Chinoy, Eli. 1955. *Automobile Workers and the American Dream*. Garden City, NY: Doubleday.

Cho, Cindy. 2003. Workers' Center Fights for Immigrant Worker Rights. *Labor Notes* 10: 3–4.

Clark, John Bates. 1886. *The Philosophy of Wealth*. Boston: Ginn & Company.

Cobble, D. S. 2004. *The Other Women's Movement: Workplace Justice and Social Rights in Modern America*. Princeton: Princeton University Press.

Coff, Russell W., and Denise M. Rousseau. 2000. Sustainable Competitive Advantage from Relational Wealth. In *Relational Wealth: The Advantages of Stability in a Changing Economy*, ed. Carrie R. Leana and Denise M. Rousseau, 27–48. New York: Oxford University Press.

Cohany, Sharon R. 1996. Workers in Alternative Employment Arrangements. *Monthly Labor Review* 119 (10): 31–45.

Cohany, Sharon R., Steven F. Hipple, Thomas J. Nardone, Anne E. Polivka, and Jay C. Stewart. 1998. Counting the Workers: Results of a First Survey. In *Contingent Work: American*

*Employment Relations in Transition*, ed. Kathleen Barker and Kathleen Christensen, 41–68. Ithaca, NY: ILR Press.

Cohen, P. N. 2002. Cohabitation and the Declining Marriage Premium for Men. *Work and Occupations* 29 (3): 346–363.

Cole, Robert E. 2000. Market Pressures and Institutional Forces: The Early Years of the Quality Movement. In *The Quality Movement and Organization Theory*, ed. Robert E. Cole and W. Richard Scott, 67–88. Thousand Oaks, CA: Sage Publications, Inc.

Coleman, Mary T., and John Pencavel. 1993a. Changes in Work Hours of Male Employees, 1940–1988. *Industrial and Labor Relations Review* 46 (2): 262–283.

———. 1993b. Trends in Market Work Behavior of Women Since 1940. *Industrial and Labor Relations Review* 46 (4): 653–676.

Collins, J. 2001. *Good to Great: Why Some Companies Make the Leap—And Others Don't*. New York: Harperbusiness.

Collison, J. 2005. *2005 Future of the U. S. Labor Pool: Survey Report*. Alexandria, VA: Society for Human Resource Management.

Colvin, Alexander J.S., Rosemary Batt, and Harry C. Katz. 2001. How High Performance Work Human Resource Practices and Workforce Unionization Affect Managerial Pay. *Personnel Psychology* 54: 903–934.

Colvin, G. 2003. Detroit's Health-Care Crisis—And Ours. *Fortune*, September 29: 50.

———. 2005. America Isn't Ready: Here's What to Do about It? *Fortune*, July 25: 70–85.

———. 2005. Can America Compete? *Fortune*, July: 70–80.

Commission on the Future of Worker Management Relations. 1994. *Fact Finding Report*. Washington, DC: U.S. Departments of Labor and Commerce.

———. 1995. *Final Report and Recommendations*. Washington, DC: U.S. Departments of Labor and Commerce.

Committee on the Consequences of Uninsurance, Institute of Medicine. 2001. *Coverage Matters: Insurance and Health Care*, September: 1–8.

Conference Board. 2005. U.S. Job Satisfaction Keeps Falling, the Conference Board Reports Today. News Release, February 28.

Cooper, C. 1998. The Changing Psychological Contract at Work. In *Work and Stress*, Vol. 12, #2, 97–100.

Cooper, C. L., and S. Clarke. 2004. The "Black Hole" of Work Organization Interventions. *Soz Preventive Med* 49: 87–88.

Cooper, C. L., P. Dewe, and M. O'Driscoll. 2003. Employee Assistance Programs. In *Handbook of Occupational Health Psychology*, Edited by J. C. Quick and L. E. Tetrick, 289–304. Washington, DC: American Psychological Association.

Corporate University Xchange. 2001. *Corporate University Xchange: 5th Annual Benchmarking Report*. New York: Cux.

Costa, Dora. 1999. Has the Trend toward Early Retirement Reversed? Presentation at the First Annual Joint Conference for the Retirement Research Consortium, May 20–21.

Cotton, John L. 1993. *Employee Involvement*. Newbury Park, CA: Sage.

Council of Economic Advisers. 2001. *The Economic Report of the President, 2001*. Washington, DC: Government Printing Office.

Cowherd, D. M., and D. I. Levine. 1992, Product Quality and Pay Equity between Lower Level Employees and Top Management: An Investigation of Distributive Justice Theory. *Administrative Science Quarterly* 37: 302–320.

Cox, W. Michael, and Richard Alm. 2005. Scientists Are Made, not Born. *New York Times*, Op-Ed Column, February 28.

Coy, P. and D. Brady. 2005. Old, Smart, Productive. *Business Week*, June 27: 78–86.

Craig, E. F. 2002. Confronting the Possibilities: The Dynamic Interplay of Action and Structure in Institutional and Individual Careers. Unpublished Doctoral Dissertation, University of Pennsylvania.

Craig, E., J. Kimberly, and H. Bouchikhi. 2002. Can Loyalty Be Leased? *Harvard Business Review* 80(9): 24.

Crouch, C. D. Finegold, and M. Sako 1999. *Are Skills the Answer?* Oxford: Oxford University Press.

Cullen, M. R. 1999. Personal Reflections on Occupational Health in the Twentieth Century. *Annual Review of Public Health* 20: 1–13.

Cutcher-Gershenfeld, Joel, and Thomas A. Kochan. 2004. Taking Stock: Collective Bargaining at the Turn of the Century. *Industrial and Labor Relations Review* 58 (1): 3–27.

Dabos, G. E., and D. M. Rousseau. 2004. Mutuality and Reciprocity in the Psychological Contracts of Employee and Employer. *Journal of Applied Psychology* 89: 52–72.

———. 2004. Social Interaction Patterns Shaping Employee Psychological Contracts: Network-Wide and Local Effects. *Proceedings of the Academy of Management Meetings, 2004.* New Orleans.

Dalton, D., and D. Mesch. 1990. The Impact of Flexible Scheduling on Employee Attendance and Turnover. *Administrative Science Quarterly* 35: 370–387.

Dange, A. 2005. Analyzing Attrition. *CLSA Asia-Pacific Markets India IT Services*, February: 3.

Davey, M. 2004. Former Soldiers Ordered to Go to War Fight not to Go. *New York Times*, November 16.

Davis, Steven J., John C. Haltiwanger, and Scott Schuh. 1998. *Job Creation and Destruction.* Cambridge, MA: The MIT Press.

Davis-Blake, Allison, and Brian Uzzi. 1993. Determinants of Employment Externalization: A Study of Temporary Workers and Independent Contractors. *Administrative Science Quarterly* 38: 195–223.

Deal, Terrence E., and Allan A. Kennedy, *Corporate Cultures: The Rites and Rituals of Corporate Life.* Reading, MA: Addison-Wesley.

Dearden, L., H. Reed, and J.Van Reenen. 2000. Who Gains when Workers Train? Training and Corporate Productivity in a Panel of British Industries. Working Paper.

Deloitte Research. 2003. *The Cusp of a Revolution: How Offshoring Will Transform the Financial Services Industry.* New York: Deloitte Research.

Deloitte Research. 2004. *It's 2008: Do You Know Where Your Talent Is?* New York: Deloitte Research.

Demby, E. R. 2004. Do Your Family-Friendly Programs Make Cents? *HRMagazine*, January: 75–78.

Deparle, Jason. Goals Reached, Donor on Right Closes up Shop. *New York Times*, May 29.

Department of Health and Human Services (DHHS). 2004. Rrfa-Hd-04–017. Call for Proposals Developing Study Designs to Evaluate the Health Benefits of Workplace Policies and Practices. September 24.

Department of Professional Employees. 2005. Professionals' Views of Work and Representation. Washington, DC: Professional Employees' Department, Afl-Cio.

Dertouzos, Michael L., Richard K. Lester, and Robert M. Solow. 1989. *Made in America.* Cambridge, MA: MIT Press.

Deutsch, C. H. 2005. Behind the Exodus of Executive Women: Boredom. *New York Times*, May 1. http://www.NYtimes.Com/2005/05/01/Business.

Devine, Teresa J. 1994. Characteristics of Self-Employed Women in the United States. *Monthly Labor Review* 117 (3): 20–34.

Dillon, Rodger L. 1987. *The Changing Labor Market: Contingent Workers and the Self-Employed in California.* Sacramento, CA: Senate Office of Research.

Dillon, S. 2004. Sharp Drop in Foreign Applications for U.S. Grad Schools. *New York Times*, December 21.

Dinardo, John E., and Jörn-Steffen Pischke. 1997. The Returns to Computer Use Revisited: Have Pencils Changed the Wage Structure Too? *Quarterly Journal of Economics* 112 (1): 291–303.

Diprete, Thomas A. 1989. *The Bureaucratic Labor Market: The Case of the Federal Civil Service.* New York: Plenum Press.

Dolezelak, H. 2004. *Training Magazine's* 23rd-Annual Comprehensive Analysis of Employer-Sponsored Training in the U.S. *Training* 41 (10): 20.

Drago, Robert. 1996. Workplace Transformation and the Disposable Workplace: Employee Involvement in Australia. *Industrial Relations* 35: 526–543.

Dunlop, John, and David Weil. 1996. Diffusion and Performance of Modular Production in the U.S. Apparel Industry. *Industrial Relations* 35: 334–354.

Eaton, Adrienne E. 1994. The Survival of Employee Participation Programs in Unionized Settings. *Industrial and Labor Relations Review* 47 (3): 371–389.

Eaton, Adrienne, Saul Rubistein, and Thomas Kochan. Forthcoming. *The Union Coalition at Kaiser Permanente.* http://www/MIT/Sloan/Iwer.

Eckhom, E. 2005. Whistle-Blower Suit May Set Course on Iraq Fraud Cases. *New York Times*, May 22.

Economic Policy Institute. 2004. Issue Guide: Offshoring. http://www.Epinet.Org/ Content. Cfm/Issueguide_Offshoring.

Edwards, Richard. 1979. *Contested Terrain: The Transformation of the Workplace in the Twentieth Century.* New York: Basic Books.

Ehrenreich, Barbara. 2002. *Nickel and Dimed.* New York: Holt.

Employment Policy Foundation. 2005. Employee Turnover Rises, Increasing Costs. http://www.epf.org. March 22.

Engardio, P., A. Bernstein, and M. Kripalani. 2003. The New Global Job Shift. Business Week Online.

Epperson, S. 2001. Don't Bet It All on Your Employer. *Time*, December: 79.

Epstein, S. S. 1989. *A Note on Health Promotion in the Workplace.* Boston: Harvard Business School.

Erfurt, J. C., A. Foote, and M. A. Heirich. 1991. The Cost Effectiveness of Work Site Wellness Programs for Hypertension Control, Weight Loss and Smoking Cessation. *Journal of Occupational Medicine* 33: 962–970.

Eriksson, T. 2003. The Effects of New York Practices—Evidence from Employer-Employee Data. *Elsevier Science* 7: 3–30.

Evans, Davis S., and Linda S. Leighton. 1989. Some Empirical Aspects of Entrepreneurship. *American Economic Review* 79 (3): 519–535.

Evans, James, Gideon Kunda, and Stephen R. Barley. 2004. Beach Time, Bridge Time and Billable Hours: The Temporal Structure of Technical Contracting. *Administrative Science Quarterly* 49: 1–38.

Ezzy, D. 1997. "Subjectivity and the Labour Process: Conceptualising 'Good Work.' " *Sociology* 31: 427–444.

Farber, Henry S. 1997. Trends in Long Term Employment in the United States, 1979–1996. Working Paper #384, Industrial Relations Section, Princeton University, July 17.

———. 1998. Mobility and Stability: The Dynamics of Job Change in Labor Markets. Working Paper #400. Industrial Relations Section, Princeton University, June.

———. 2000. Alternative Employment Arrangements as a Response to Job Loss. In *On the Job: Is Long-Term Employment a Thing of the Past?*, ed. D. Neumark. New York: Russell Sage Foundation.

———. 2005. What Do We Know about Job Loss in the United States? Evidence from the Displaced Workers Survey, 1984–2004. Princeton University Industrial Relations Section Working Paper 498.

Farrell, D. 2004. Beyond Offshoring: Assess Your Company's Global Potential. *Harvard Business Review*, December.

———. 2004. Farewell, *The wall street Journal.* 2004. Farewell, organization Man. December 31.

Favennec-Hery, F. 1996. Work and Training: A Blurring of the Edges. *International Labour Review* 135: 665–674.

Feeney, Sheila Anne. 2004. Love Hurts. *Workforce Management*, February: 36–40.

Feinberg, Phyllis. 2004. Defined Benefit Pension Plans Falling out of Favor. *Business Insurance* 38 (20): 46.

Fernie, S., and D. Metcalf. 1995. Participation, Contingent Pay, Representation and Workplace Performance: Evidence from Great Britain. *British Journal of Industrial Relations* 33 (3): 378–415.

Ferrante, C. J., and D. M. Rousseau. 2001. Bringing Open Book Management into the Academic Line of Sight. In *Employee versus Owner Issues*, ed. C. L. Cooper and D. M. Rousseau, 97–116. Vol. 8 of *Trends in Organizational Behavior*. Chichester: Wiley.

Ferraro, Fabrizio, Jeffrey Pfeffer, and Robert I. Sutton. 2005. Economics Language and Assumptions: How Theories Can Become Self-Fulfilling. *Academy of Management Review* 30: 8–24.

Fine, Janice. 2003. Non-Union, Low-Wage Workers Are Finding a Voice as Immigrant Workers' Centers Grow. *Labor Notes* 8: 2–4.

Finegold, D. 1998. The New Learning Contract: Developing Competencies in a Turbulent Environment. In *Tomorrow's Organization*, ed. S. Mohrman et al. San Francisco; Jossey-Bass.

———. 2006. The Role of Education and Training Systems in Innovation. In *Innovation, Learning and Institutional Change*, ed. G. Hage and M. Meus. Oxford: Oup.

Finegold, D., P. K. Kam, and T. C. Cheah. 2004. Adapting a Foreign Direct Investment Strategy to the Knowledge Economy: The Case of Singapore's Emerging Biotech Cluster. *European Planning Studies* 12(7): 921–941.

Finegold, D., A. Levenson, and M. Van Buren. 2003. A Temporary Route to Advancement? the Career Opportunities for Low-Skilled Workers in Temporary Employment. In *Low-Wage America: How Employers Are Reshaping Opportunity in the Workplace*, ed. E. Appelbaum, A. Bernhardt, and R. Murnane. New York: Russell Sage Foundation.

Finegold, D., A. Levenson, and M. Van Buren. 2005. Training Without 'Jobs': Skill Development for Temporary Workers. *Human Resource Management Journal* 15(2).

———. 2005. A New Model of Biotech Development: A Case Study of India's Biotech Industry. Paper Presented at Egos Annual Conference, Berlin, June 30–July 2.

Fleming, S. H. 2001. Osha at 30: Three Decades of Progress in Occupational Safety and Health. *Journal of Occupational Safety and Health* 12(3), Spring.

Flyer, Frederick, And Sherwin Rosen. 1994. The New Economics of Teachers and Education. National Bureau of Economic Research Working Paper 4828.

Foote Partners. 2005. New It Pay Research Refutes Claims of Offshore Outsourcing U.S. Wage Deflation. News Release. July 18. http://www.Footepartners.Com/Fpnewsrelease_2q2005skills.Pdf.

Ford, J. D., and L. W. Ford. 1994. Logics of Identity, Contradiction, and Attraction in Change. *Academy of Management Review* 19: 756–785.

Forrester Research. 2004. Forrester Finds Near-Term Growth of Offshore Outsourcing Accelerating. Press Release, May 17. http://www.Forrester.Com/Er/Press/Release/0,1769,922,00.Html.

Forth, John and Neil Millward. 2004. High-Involvement Management and Pay in Britain." *Industrial Relations* 43: 98–119.

Fortune 500. 2005. Fortune 500: How the Companies Stack up. *Fortune*, April 18: F30–F33.

Frankenhaeuser, M. 1991. The Psychophysiology of Workload Stress, and Health: Comparison between the Sexes. *Annals of Behavioral Medicine* 13: 197–204.

Frazis, Harley J., Maury Gittleman, Michael W. Horrigan, and Mary Joyce. 1998. Results from the 1995 Survey of Employer-Provided Training. *Monthly Labor Review*, June: 3–13.

Freeman, C. E. 2004. *Trends in Educational Equity of Girls & Women: 2004*. NCES 2005–2016. U.S. Department of Education, NCES. Washington, DC: GPO.

Freeman, Richard B. 1976. *The Overeducated American*. New York: Academic Press.

————. 2002. The Labour Market in the New Information Economy. NBER Working Paper Number 9254.

————. 2003. Searching Outside the Box: The Road to Union Renascence and Worker Well-Being in the United States in the *Future of Labor Unions*, ed. Julius G. Getman and Ray Marshall, 75–92. Austin, TX: Lyndon B. Johnson School of Public Affairs, University of Texas.

Freeman, Richard, and Arin Dube. 2000. Shared Compensation Systems and Decision Making in the U.S. Job Market. Draft Paper, Harvard University Department of Economics.

Freeman, Richard, Douglas Kruse, and Joseph Blasi. 2004. Monitoring Colleagues at Work: Profit Sharing, Employee Ownership, Broad-Based Stock Options and Workplace Performance in the U.S. Paper Presented at Industrial Relations Research Association Annual Conference, January 2–5, 2004, San Diego.

Freeman, Richard B., and James L. Medoff. 1984. *What Do Unions Do?* New York: Basic Books.

Freeman, Richard B., and Joel Rogers. 1999. *What Workers Want.* New York and Ithaca: Cornell University Press and Russell Sage Foundation.

————. 2002. Open Source Unionism. *Working USA.*

French, J. R. P., and B. Raven. 1962. The Bases of Social Power. In *Group Dynamics: Research and Theory*, ed. D. Cartwright. Evanston, IL: Row, Peterson.

Frese, M., and D. Zapf. 1986. Shiftwork, Stress and Psychosomatic Complaints: A Comparison between Workers in Different Shift Work Schedules. *Ergonomics* 29: 99–114.

Friede, A., E. Kossek, M. Lee, and S. MacDermid. 2004. The Role of Human Resource Policies and Systems in the Initiation and Institutionalization of Reduced Workload Initiatives. Paper Presented at Academy of Management 2004 Meetings, New Orleans.

Friedland, D. and R. H. Price. 2003. Underemployment: Consequences for the Health and Well-Being of Workers. *American Journal of Community Psychology* 32 (1 and 2): 33–45.

Friedman, Raymond, and Donna Carter. 1993. *African American Network Groups: Their Impact and Effectiveness.* New York: Executive Leadership Council.

Friedman, T. L. 2005. *The World Is Flat.* New York: Farrar, Straus & Giroux.

Frone, M. R., M. Russell, and M. L. Cooper. 1992. Antecedents and Outcomes of Work-Family Conflict: Testing a Model of the Work-Family Interface. *Journal of Applied Psychology* 77: 65–78.

Frontline. 2005. *Is Wal-Mart Good for America?* http://www.Pbs.Org/ Wgbh/Pages/Frontline/ Shows/Walmart/.

Fugate, M., A. J. Kinicki, and B. E. Ashforth. 2004. Employability: A Psycho-Social Construct, Its Dimensions, and Applications. *Journal of Vocational Behavior* 65 (1): 14–38.

Fuhrmans, V. 2004. Attacking Rise in Health Costs, Big Company Meets Resistance. *The Wall Street Journal*, July 13.

The Fuqua School of Business, Duke University. 2004. Fortune 500 Reap Early Cost Benefits from Offshoring Initiatives. Press Release. December 14. http://www.Fuqua.Duke.Edu/ Admin/Extaff/News/Fortune_Offshore_Dec_2004.Htm.

Furstenberg, F. 1974. Work Experience and Family Life. In *Work and Quality of Life*, ed. J. O'Toole, 341–360. Cambridge, MA: MIT Press.

Galbraith, J. 1998. The Global Organization. In *Tomorrow's Organization*, ed. S. Mohrman et al. San Francisco: Jossey-Bass.

Galbraith, John Kenneth. 1967. *The New Industrial State.* Boston: Houghton Mifflin.

Galinsky, E., J. Bond, and D. E. Friedman. 1993. *The Changing Workforce: Highlights of the National Study.* New York: Families and Work Institute

Galinsky, E., J. Bond, and E. J. Hill. 2004. *When Work Works: A Status Report on Workplace Flexibility.* New York: Families and Work Institute. http://www. Harrisinteractive.Com/ Harris_Poll.

Ganster, D. C., M. L. Fox, and D. J. Dwyer. 2001. Explaining Employees' Health Care Costs: A Prospective Examination of Stressful Job Demands, Personal Control, and Physiological Reactivity. *Journal of Applied Psychology* 86: 954–964.

Gant, Jon, Casey Ichniowski, and Kathryn Shaw. 2002. Social Capital and Organizational Change in High-Involvement and Traditional Work Organizations. *Journal of Economics and Management Science.*

Gardyn, R. 2000. Retirement Redefined. *American Demographics.*

Gareis, K. C., and R. C. Barnett. 2002. Under What Conditions Do Long Work Hours Affect Psychological Distress: A Study of Full-Time and Reduced-Hours Female Doctors. *Work and Occupations* 29: 483–497.

Garud, R., and Z. Shapira. 1997. Aligning the Residuals: Risk, Return, Responsibility, and Authority. In *Organizational Decision Making*, ed. Z. Shapira, 238–256. Cambridge: Cambridge University Press.

Geisel, Jerry. 2002. Retirees to Face Higher Costs for Employer Health Plans. *Business Insurance* 36 (37): 3.

George, M. L., J. Works, and K Watson-Hemphill. 2005. *Fast Innovation: Achieving Superior Differentiation, Speed to Market, and Increased Profitability.* New York: McGraw-Hill.

Gereffi, G., and V. Wadhwa, V. 2005. Framing the Engineering Outsourcing Debate: Placing the U.S. on a Level Playing Field With China and India. Report of the Duke Master of Engineering Management Program.

Gerson, K., and J. Jacobs. 2004. *The Time Divide: Work, Family, and Gender Inequality.* Cambridge, MA: Harvard University Press.

Geurts, S. A. E., and E. Demerouti. 2003. Work/Nonwork Interface: A Review of Theories and Findings. In *The Handbook of Work and Health Psychology*, Edited by M. J. Schabracq, J. A. M. Winnebust, and C. L. Cooper, 279–312. New York: John Wiley and Sons.

Ghoshal, Sumantra. 2005. Bad Management Theories Are Destroying Good Management Practices. *Academy of Management Learning and Education* 4: 75–91.

Gibson, Cristina B., and Susan G. Cohen. 2003. *Virtual Teams That Work: Creating Conditions for Virtual Team Effectiveness.* San Francisco: Jossey-Bass.

Giddens, A. 1991. *Modernity and Self-Identity: Self and Society in the Late Modern Age.* Stanford, CA: Stanford University Press.

Giele, J. Z. 1998. Innovation in the Typical Life Course. In *Methods of Life Course Research: Qualitative and Quantitative Approaches*, ed. J. Z. Giele and G. H. Elder, 231–263. Thousand Oaks, CA: Sage Publications.

———. 2003. Women and Men as Agents of Change in Their Own Lives. In *Advances in Life Course Research: Changing Life Patterns in Western Industrial Societies*, ed. J. Z. Giele and E. Hoist, 8: 299–317. London, Elsevier.

Giles, William F., and William H. Holley, Jr. 1978. Job Enrichment Versus Traditional Issues at the Bargaining Table: What Union Members Want. *Academy of Management Journal* 21: 725–730.

Gittell, Jody Hoffer. 2003. *The Southwest Airlines Way: Using the Power of Relationships to Achieve High Performance.* New York: McGraw-Hill.

Gittleman, Maury, Michael Horrigan, and Mary Joyce. 1998. "Flexible" Workplace Practices: Evidence from a Nationally Representative Survey. *Industrial and Labor Relations Review* 52 (1): 99–115.

Gladwell, M. 2002. *The Tipping Point: How Little Things Can Make a Big Difference.* New York: Little, Brown.

Glass, J., and L. Riley. 1998. Family Responsive Policies and Employee Retention Following Child Birth. *Social Forces* 76: 1401–1435.

Glennan, T. S. Bodilly, J. Galegher, and K. Kerr. 2004. Expanding the Reach of Education Reforms. Santa Monica: RAND.

Goetzel, R. Z., S. R. Long, R. J. Ozminkowski, K. Hawkins, S. Wang, S., and W. Lynch. 2004. Health, Absence, Disability, and Presenteeism Cost Estimates of Certain Physical and Mental Health Conditions Affecting U.S. Employers. *Journal of Occupational and Environmental Medicine* 46 (4): 398–412.

Goldberg, Albert I. 1976. The Relevance of Cosmopolitan/Local Orientations to Professional Values and Behavior. *Sociology of Work and Occupations* 3: 331–354.

Goldner, Fred H., and Richard. R. Ritti. 1967. Professionalization as Career Immobility. *American Journal of Sociology* 72: 489–501.

Goldscheider, F. K., and J. DaVanzo. 1985. Living Arrangements and the Transition to Adulthood. *Demography* 22: 545–563.

Gordon, David. 1996. *Fat and Mean: The Corporate Squeeze of Working Americans and the Myth of Managerial Downsizing.* New York: Martin Kessler Books.

Gouldner, Alvin W. 1957–1958. Cosmopolitans and Locals: Toward an Analysis of Latent Social Roles Ii. *Administrative Science Quarterly* 2: 444–477.

Graham, Laurie. 1993. Inside a Japanese Transplant: A Critical View. *Work and Occupations* 20: 147–173.

Grant, A. M., M. K. Christianson, and R. H. Price. Forthcoming. *Tradeoffs in Well Being at Work: Toward an Integrated Understanding.*

Greenan, Nathalie, and Dominique Guellec. 1997. Firm Organization, Technology and Performance: An Empirical Study. *Economic Innovation New Technology* 6: 313–347.

Gregory, Frances W., and Irene D. Neu. 1952. The American Industrial Elite in the 1870s. In *Men in Business*, ed. William Miller. Cambridge, MA: Harvard University Press.

Griffin, Larry J., Michael E. Wallace, and Beth A. Rubin. 1986. Capitalist Resistance to the Organization of Labor Before the New Deal: Why? How? Success? *American Sociological Review* 51: 147–167.

Grimes, A. 2005. Even Tech Execs Can't Get Kids to Be Engineers. *The Wall Street Journal*, 29 March: B1.

Groshen, Erica, and David I. Levine. 1998. The Rise and Decline (?) of U.S. Internal Labor Markets. NY Federal Reserve Working Paper.

Groshen, Erica, and Simon Potter. 2003. Has Structural Change Contributed to a Jobless Recovery? *Federal Reserve Bank of New York Current Issues in Economics and Finance* 9 (8).

Grote, D. 1999. Staff Performance Advice for Cpas. *Journal of Accountancy* 188: 51–54.

Groysberg, B., A. Nanda, and N. Nohria. 2004. The Risky Business of Hiring Stars. *Harvard Business Review* 82 (5): 92–101.

Guillen, Mauro. 1994. *Models of Management: Work, Authority, and Organization in a Comparative Perspective.* Chicago: University of Chicago Press.

Guptara, P. 2005. Rising Elephant: The Growing Clash With India over White-Collar Jobs and Its Challenge to America and the World. *Far Eastern Economic Review* 168 (5): 75.

Gustman, A., and T. Steinmeier. 1984. Partial Retirement and the Analysis of Retirement Behavior. *Industrial and Labor Relations Review* 37: 403–415.

Hackman, J. Richard, and Greg R. Oldham. 1980. *Work Redesign.* Reading MA: Addison Wesley.

Hackman, J. Richard, and Ruth Wageman. 1995. Total Quality Management: Empirical, Conceptual, and Practical Issues. *Administrative Science Quarterly* 40: 309–342.

Hall, D. T. 1976. *Careers in Organizations.* Glenview: Scott, Foresman.

———. 1993. The "New Career Contract": Alternative Career Paths. In *Die Ressource Mensch Im Mittelpunkt Innovativer Unternehmensfuehrung*, ed. OFW (Hrsg.), 229–243. Gabler.

———. 2002. *Careers in and out of Organizations.* Thousand Oaks, CA: Sage Publications.

———. 2004. The Protean Career: A Quarter-Century Journey. *Journal of Vocational Behavior* 65 (1): 1.

Hall, D. T., and L. A. Isabella. 1985. Downward Movement and Career Development. *Organizational Dynamics* 14: 5–23.

Hall, D. T., and J. E. Moss. 1998. The New Protean Career Contract: Helping Organizations and Employees Adapt. *Organizational Dynamics* 26 (3): 22–37.

Hall, D. T., and S. Rabinowitz. 1988. Maintaining Employee Involvement in a Plateaued Career. In *Career Growth and Human Resource Strategies: The Role of the Human Resource Professional in Employee Development*, ed. Manuel London and Edward M. Mone, 67–80. Westport, CT.

Hall, D. T., and B. Schneider. 1973. *Organizational Climates and Careers: The Work Lives of Priests*. New York: Seminar Press.

Hall, D. T., G. Zhu, and A. Yan. 2001. Developing Global Leaders: To Hold on to them, Let them Go! In *Advances in Global Leadership*, Vol. 2, ed. W. H. Mobley and M. W. McCall, 327–349.

Halpern, D. F., and S. E. Murphy, eds. 2005. from *Work-Family Balance to Work-Family Interaction: Changing the Metaphor*. Mahwah, NJ: Lawrence Erlbaum Associates.

Hamilton, Barton H., Jack A. Nickerson, and Hideo Owan. 2003. Team Incentives and Worker Heterogeneity: An Empirical Analysis of the Impact of Teams on Productivity and Participation. *Journal of Political Economy* 111: 465–497.

Hammer, L., and E. Kossek. Under-Emphasized Constructs for Evaluating the Health Benefits of Workplace Interventions: Identifying and Fostering Supportive Supervisor Behaviors and Considering Family Cross-Over Effects. RFA-Hd-04–017. National Institute of Child and Health Development.

Hammer, M., and J. Champy. 1993. *Reengineering the Corporation*. New York: Harberbusiness.

Handel, Michael J. 2000. Models of Economic Organization and the New Inequality in the United States. Ph.d. Diss., Harvard University.

———. 2003a. Implications of Information Technology for Employment, Skills, and Wages: A Review of Recent Research. *SRI International*. http://www.Sri.Com/Policy/Csted/Reports/Sandt/It/.

———. 2003b. Skills Mismatch in the Labor Market. *Annual Review of Sociology* 29: 135–165.

Handel, Michael J., and Maury Gittleman. 2004. Is There a Wage Payoff to Innovative Work Practices? *Industrial Relations* 43: 67–97.

Handy, Charles. 1989. *The Age of Unreason*. Boston: Harvard University Press.

Hansen, B. E. 2001. The New Economics of Structural Change: Dating Breaks in U.S. Labor Productivity. *Journal of Economic Perspectives* 15: 117–128.

Hansen, D. G. 1997. Worker Performance and Group Incentives: A Case Study. *Industrial and Labor Relations Journal* 51: 37–39.

Hareven, T. K. 1994. Aging and Generational Relations: A Historical and Life Course Perspective. *Annual Review of Sociology* 20: 437–461.

Harris, R. 2004. Making It Work. *CFO*, June: 47–58.

Harrison, Bennett, and Mary E. Kelley. 1993. Outsourcing and the Search for 'Flexibility'. *Work, Employment and Society* 7: 213–235.

Harrison, D. A., and J. J. Martocchio. 1998. Time for Absenteeism: A 20-Year Review of Origins, Offshoots, and Outcomes. *Journal of Management* 24 (3): 305–350.

Hart, Peter, and Associates. 2002. Americans' Views on the Economy, Corporate Behavior and Union Representation. Washington, DC: Peter Hart and Associates.

Harter, J. K., F. L. Schmidt, and T. L. Hayes. 2002. Business-Unit-Level Relationship between Employee Satisfaction, Employee Engagement, and Business Outcomes: A Meta-Analysis. *Journal of Applied Psychology* 87: 268–279.

Hayes, C., et al. 1984. *Competence and Competition*. London: NEDO/MSC.

Haynes, G., T.Dunnagan, and V. Smith. 1999. Do Employees Participating in Voluntary Health Promotion Programs Incur Lower Health Care Costs? *Health Promotion International* 14 (1): 43–51.

Heaney, C. A., R. H. Price, and J. Rafferty. 1995a. The Caregiver Support Program: An Intervention to Increase Employee Coping Resources and Enhance Mental Health. In *Job Stress*

*Interventions*, ed. L. R. Murphy, J. J. Hurrell, S. L. Sauter and G. P. Keita, 93–108. Washington, DC: American Psychological Association.

Heaney, C. A., R. H. Price, and J. Rafferty. 1995b. Increasing Coping Resources at Work: A Field Experiment to Increase Social Support, Improve Work Team Functioning, and Enhance Employee Mental Health. *Journal of Organizational Behavior*, 16: 335–352.

Heckscher, Charles. 1995. *White Collar Blues*. New York: Basic Books.

Helfand, D. 2005. Nearly Half of Blacks, Latinos Drop Out, School Study Shows. *Los Angeles Times*, March 24.

Helper, Susan, David I. Levine, and Elliot Bendoly. 2002. Employee Involvement and Pay at American Auto Suppliers. *Journal of Economic Management and Strategy* 11 (2): 329–377.

Helyar, John. 1991. Playing Ball: How Peter Ueberroth Led the Major League in the "Collusion Era." *The Wall Street Journal*, May 20.

Henretta, J. C. 1994. Social Structure and Age-Based Careers. In *Age and Structural Lag: Society's Failure to Provide Meaningful Opportunities in Work, Family, and Leisure*, ed. M. W. Riley, R. L. Kahn, and A. Foner, 57–79. New York: John Wiley & Sons, Inc.

Henson, Kevin D. 1996. *Just a Temp*. Philadelphia: Temple University Press.

Hewitt Associates. 2004. Employer Perspectives on Global Sourcing: Key Human Capital Issues and Lessons. Presented by Richard Kantor, Senior Consultant, at the Spring Meeting of the Human Resources Policy Institute, School of Management, Boston University.

Hill, L. A. 1998. Developing the Star Performer. *Leader to Leader*, Spring.

Hilsenrath, J. E. 2004. Forrester Revises Loss Estimates to Overseas Jobs. *The Wall Street Journal*, May 17.

Hiltzik, M. 2005. Shipping out U.S. Jobs—to a Ship. *L.A. Times*, May 1.

Hipple, Steven. 2004. Self-Employment in the United States: An Update. *Monthly Labor Review* 127 (7): 13–23.

Hira, R. 2004. White Collar Jobs Move Overseas: Implications for States. *Spectrum: The Journal of State Government*, Winter: 12–18.

Hirschman, C. 2003. Off Duty, out of Work. *HRMagazine* 48 (2): 50–56.

Hochschild, A. R. 1997. *Time-Bind: When Work Becomes Home and Home Becomes Work*. New York: Metropolitan.

Hodson, Randy. 2001. *Dignity at Work*. New York: Cambridge University Press.

Hoerr, John. 1997. *We Can't Eat Prestige: The Women Who Organized Harvard*. Philadelphia: Temple University Press.

Hofmann, Mark A. 2003. Employers Attempt to Keep Health Care Costs under Control. *Business Insurance* 37 (37): 4.

Hofstede, Geert. 1980. *Culture's Consequences: International Differences in Work-Related Values*. Beverly Hills: Sage.

Holmes, S., and W. Zellner. 2004. The Costco Way. *Business Week*, April 12: 76–77.

Holstein, W. J. 2005. Cutting the Losses from Outsourcing. *New York Times*, July 3: 8.

Honold, L. 1991. The Power of Learning at Johnsonville Foods. *Training* 28 (4): 54–58.

Hood, J. 1995. OSHA's Trivial Pursuit: In Workplace Safety, Business Outperforms Regulations. *Policy Review*, Summer: 3.

House, J. S. 1981. *Work Stress and Social Support*. Reading: MA: Addison-Wesley.

House, J. S., and R. L. Kahn. 1985. Measures and Concepts of Social Support. In *Social Support and Health*, ed. S. Cohen and S. L. Syme. Orlando, Fl: Academic Press.

House, J. S., and D. A. Smith. 1985. Evaluating the Health Effects of Demanding Work on and Off the Job. In *Assessing Physical Fitness and Physical Activity in Population Base Surveys*, ed. T. F. Drury, 481–508. Hyattsville, Md: National Center for Health Statistics.

Houseman, Susan N. 2001. Why Employers Use Flexible Staffing Arrangements: Evidence from an Establishment Survey. *Industrial and Labor Relations Review* 55 (1): 149–170.

Hughes, E. C. 1937. Institutional Office and the Person. *American Journal of Sociology* 43: 404–413.

Hunter, Larry W., and John J. Lafkas. 2003. Opening the Box: Information Technology, Work Practices, and Wages. *Industrial & Labor Relations Review* 56: 224–243.

Hunter, Larry W., John Paul MacDuffie, and Lorna Doucet. 2002. What Makes Teams Take? Employee Reactions to Work Reforms. *Industrial and Labor Relations Review* 55: 448–472.

Huselid, M. A., and J. E. Barnes. 2002. Human Capital Measurement Systems as a Source of Competitive Advantage. Working Paper.

Huselid, Mark. 1995. The Impact of Human Resource Management Practices on Turnover, Productivity, and Corporate Financial Performance. *Academy of Management Journal* 38: 635–672.

Huselid, Mark, Brian Becker, and Richard Beatty. 2005. *The Workforce Scorecard*. Boston, MA: Harvard Business School Press.

Ichniowski, Casey, Thomas Kochan, David I. Levine, Craig Olson, and George Strauss. 1996. What Works at Work: A Critical Review. *Industrial Relations* 35 (3): 299–333.

Ichniowski, Casey, Kathryn Shaw, and Giovanna Prennushi. 1997. The Effects of Human Resource Management Practices on Productivity. *American Economic Review* 86: 291–313.

Ichniowski, Casey, and Kathryn Shaw. 1995. Old Dogs and New Tricks: Determinants of the Adoption of Productivity-Enhancing Work Practices. *Brookings Papers: Microeconomics* 1–65.

Imada, Sachiko. 1997. Work and Family Life. http://www.Jil.Go.Jp/Bulletin/Year/1997/Vol36–08/O6.Htm.

*India Business Insight.* 2005. IBM Headcount Close to 25,000 Here: Acquisition of Daksh Brought in 6,000 Employees. May 19.

*India Business Insight.* 2005. MNCs Rely on India for Delivery, Growth: Accenture Employs Close to 15,000 People in India. February 19.

Information Technology Association of America. 2004. *Executive Summary: The Impact of Offshore IT Software and Services Outsourcing on the U.S. Economy and the IT Industry.* Lexington, MA: Global Insight.

Ingersoll-Dayton, B., M. B. Neal, and L. B. Hammer. 2001. Aging Parents Helping Adult Children: The Experience of the Sandwiched Generation. *Family Relations* 50 (3): 262–271.

Iyengar, S. S., and M. Lepper. 1999. Rethinking the Value of Choice: A Cultural Perspective on Intrinsic Motivation. *Journal of Personality and Social Psychology* 76: 349–366.

———. 2000. When Choice Is Demotivating: Can One Desire too Much of a Good Thing? *Journal of Personality and Social Psychology* 76: 995–1006.

———. 2000. When Choice Is too Much of a Good Thing. *Journal of Personality and Social Psychology* 79: 995–1006.

Jackall, Robert. 1988. *Moral Mazes: The World of Corporate Managers*. New York: Oxford University Press.

Jacobs, Jerry A., and Kathleen Gerson. 2004. Understanding Changes in American Working Time: A Synthesis. In *Fighting for Time: Shifting Boundaries of Work and Social Life*, ed. Cynthia Fuchs Epstein and Arne L. Kalleberg. New York: Russell Sage Foundation.

Jacobs, Michael T. 1991. *Short-Term America: The Causes and Cures of Our Business Myopia.* Boston: Harvard Business School Press.

Jacoby, Sanford. 1985. *Employing Bureaucracy: Managers, Unions, and the Transformation of Work in the 20th Century.* New York: Columbia University Press.

Jacoby, Sanford M. 1997. *Modern Manors: Welfare Capitalism Since the New Deal.* Princeton, NJ: Princeton University Press.

———. 1998. *Modern Manors: Welfare Capitalism Since the New Deal.* Princeton: Princeton University Press.

———. 1999. Are Career Jobs Headed for Extinction? *California Management Review* 42 (Fall): 123–145.

Jacoby, Sanford, and Peter Cappelli. 1999. *California Management Review* 42 (1).

Jaeger, David A., and Ann Huff Stevens. 1999. Is Job Stability in the United States Falling? Reconciling Trends in the Current Population Survey and the Panel Study of Income Dynamics. *Journal of Labor Economics* 17 (4), Part 2, S1-S28.

Jalland, R. M., and Gunz, H. P. 1993. Strategies, Organizational Learning and Careers: The Fallout from Restructuring. In *Advances in Strategic Management*, ed. P. Shrivistava, A. S. Huff, and J. Dutton, 193–216. Greenwich, CT: JAI Press.

Jeffrey, N. A. 1996. "Wellness Plans" Try to Target the Not-So-Well. *The Wall Street Journal*, June 21, pp. B1, B6.

Jensen, Michael C., and William H. Mechling. 1992. Specific and General Knowledge and Organizational Structure. In *Contract Economics*, ed. Lars Werin and Hans Wijkander, 251–274. Blackwell: Oxford.

Jenson, J. B., and L. G. Kletzer. 2005. *Tradable Services: Understanding the Scope and Impact of Services Offshoring*. Washington, DC: Institute for International Economics.

Johnson, George. 1997. Changes in Earnings Inequality: The Role of Demand Shifts. *Journal of Economic Perspectives* 11: 41–54.

Jones, Arthur F., Jr., and Daniel H. Weinberg. 2000. The Changing Shape of the Nation's Income Distribution. U.S. Census Bureau. Current Population Report #P60-204, June.

Jorgenson, D. W., M. S. Ho, and K. J. Stiroh. 2002. Information Technology, Education, and Sources of Economic Growth Across U.S. Industries. NBER Working Paper Series.

———. 2002. Lessons from the U.S. Growth Resurgence. *Federal Reserve Bank of Atlanta Economic Review* Third Quarter: 1–14.

Jose, W. S., D. R. Anderson, and S. A. Haight. 1987. The Staywell Strategy for Health Care Cost Containment. In *Health Promotion Evaluation: Measuring the Organizational Impact*, ed. J. P. Opatz, 15–34. Stevens Point, WI: National Wellness Institute.

Joslyn, Carl S., and Frank W. Taussig. 1932. *American Business Leaders*. New York: MacMillian.

Juhn, Chinhui, Kevin M. Murphy, and Brooks Pierce. 1993. Wage Inequality and the Rise in Return to Skill. *Journal of Political Economy* 101: 410–442.

Juhn, Chinhui, Kevin M. Murphy, and Robert H. Topel. 1991. Why Has the Natural Rate of Unemployment Increased over Time? In *Brookings Papers on Economic Activity 1991:92, Macroeconomics*, ed. William C. Brainard and George L. Perry. Washington, DC: Brookings Institution Press, 75–142.

Jurik, Nancy J. 1998. Getting Away and Getting by: The Experiences of Self-Employed Homeworkers. *Work and Occupations* 25: 7–35.

Kahn, R. L., and P. Byosiere. 1992. Stress in Organizations. In *Handbook of Industrial and Organizational Psychology*, 2nd ed., Vol. 3, ed. M. D. Dunnette and L. M. Hough, 571–650. Palo Alto, CA: Consulting Psychologists Press.

Kahn, R. L., D. Wolfe, R. Quinn, J. Snoek, and R. Rosenthal. 1964. *Organizational Stress: Studies in Role Conflict and Ambiguity*. New York: John Wiley and Sons.

Kahn, Robert L. 1981. *Work and Health*. New York: Wiley.

Kahn, Robert L. and Robert P. Quinn. 1970. Role Stress: A Framework for Analysis. In *Occupational Mental Health*, ed. A. McLean, 50–115. New York: Rand McNally.

Kalleberg, Arne L., Edith Rasell, Ken Hudsin, David Webster, Barbara F. Reskin, Cassirer Naoi, and Eileen and Appelbaum. 1997. *Non Standard Work, Substandard Jobs: Flexible Work Arrangements in the U.S.* Washington, DC: Economic Policy Institute.

Kaminsky, M. 2004. If Only Guilt Would Take a Holiday. *The Wall Street Journal*, June 4.

Kanter, R. M. 1977. *Work and Family in the United States: A Critical Review and Agenda for Research and Policy*. New York: Russell Sage Foundation.

———. 1991. The Future of Bureaucracy and Hierarchy in Organizational Theory: A Report from the Field. In *Social Theory for a Changing Society*, ed. Bourdieu and J. Coleman, 67–87. Boulder: Westview.

————. 2006. Foreword. Beyond the Myth of Separate Worlds. In *The Work and Family Handbook: Multi-Disciplinary Perspectives, Methods and Approaches*, ed. M. Pitt-Catsouphes, E. Kossek, and S. Sweet. Mahwah, NJ: Lawrence Erlbaum Associates.

Kanter, Rosabeth Moss. 1977. *Men and Women of the Corporation*, 130–140. Boston: Basic Books.

————. 1989. When Giants Learn to Dance. New York: Simon & Schuster.

Kaplan, Robert. 1992. *The Balanced Scorecard*. Cambridge: Harvard University Press.

Karaevli, A. 2003. Antecedents and Consequences of New CEO's Origins and Degrees of Insiderness/Outsiderness: A Longitudinal Study of the United States Airline and Chemical Industries, 1972–2002. Unpublished Doctoral Dissertation, Boston University.

Karaevli, A., and D. T. Hall. 2002. Growing Leaders for Turbulent Times: Is Succession Planning up to the Challenge? *Organizational Dynamics* 32: 62–79.

————. 2004. Career Variety and Executive Adaptability in Turbulent Environments. In *Leading in Turbulent Times: Managing in the New World of Work*, ed. R. J. Burke and C. L. Cooper, 54–74. Malden, MA: Blackwell Publishing, Ltd.

Karasek, R., and T. Theorell. 1990. *Healthy Work*. New York: Basic Books.

Karmarkar, U. 2004. Will You Survive the Service Revolution? *Harvard Business Review*, June: 101–107.

Karoly, L. and J. Bigelow. 2005. *The Economics of Investing in Universal Pre- School Education in California*, Santa Monica: RAND.

Karoly, L. A., and C. W. A. Panis. 2004. The *21st Century at Work: Forces Shaping the Future Workforce and Workplace in the United States*. Santa Monica, CA: Rand Labor and Population.

Karrh, B. W. 1983. The Critical Balance: The Influence of Government Regulation, Past and Present. *Journal of Occupational Medicine* 25: 21–25.

Katcher, Bruce. 2004. How to Improve Employee Trust in Management. http://www.Hr.Com/Hrcom/Index/Cfm/83/13178977–963b-11d5–9aca009027e0248f.

Katz, Lawrence. 1987. Efficiency Wage Theories: A Partial Evaluation. In *NBER Macroeconomics Annual*, ed. S. Fischer. Cambridge, MA: MIT Press.

Katz, Lawrence F., and Alan B. Krueger. 1999. New Trend in Unemployment? The High-Pressure U.S. Labor Market of the 1990s. *The Brookings Review* 17(4): 4–8.

Katz, Lawrence, and Kevin M. Murphy. 1992. Changes in Relative Wages, 1963–1987: Supply and Demand Factors. *Quarterly Journal of Economics* 107: 35–78.

Kelley, Maryellen R. 1996. Participative Bureaucracy and Productivity in the Machined Products Sector. *Industrial Relations* 35: 374–399.

Kelly, E. 2006. Work-Family Policies: The U.S in International Perspective. In *The Work and Family Handbook: Multi-Disciplinary Perspectives, Methods and Approaches*, ed. M. Pitt-Catsouphes, E. Kossek, and S. Sweet, 99–124. Mahwah, NJ: Lawrence Erlbaum Associates.

Kelso, Louis, and Mortimer Adler. 1958. *the Capitalist Manifesto*. New York: Random House.

Kessler, R., J. Turner, and J. House. 1987. Intervening Processes in the Relationship between Unemployment and Health. *Psychological Medicine* 17: 949–961.

Khurana, Rakesh. 2002. *Searching for a Corporate Savior: The Irrational Quest for Charismatic CEOs*. Princeton: Princeton University Press.

Kimberly, J. R., H. Bouchikhi, and E. F. Craig. 2001. The Customized Workplace: Copernician Revolution or Romantic Fantasy? *European Business Forum* 6: 7–10.

Kirby, C., and J. Shinai. 2004. Offshoring's Giant Target: The Bay Area Silicon Valley Could Face Export of 1 in 6 Jobs-Worst in Nation. *San Francisco Gate Online*. http://www.Sfgate.Com/Cgi-Bin/Article.Cgi?F=/C/A/2004/03/07/Mngrt5g2c11. Dtl&Hw=Offshoring&Sn=001&Sc=1000.

Kirkegaard, J. F. 2004. *Outsourcing: Stains on the White Collar?* Washington DC: Institute for International Economics.

Kletzer, L. G. 2001. Globalization and Job Loss, from Manufacturing to Services. Federal Reserve Bank of Chicago. http://www.Chicagofed.Org/ Publications/Economicperspectives/ Ep_2qtr2005_Part4_Kletzer.Pdf.

Kletzer, L. G., and R. E. Litan. 2001. A Prescription to Relieve Worker Anxiety. Policy Brief 01–2. Institute for International Economics, Washington DC. http://www.Iie.Com/Publications/Pb/Pb.Cfm?Researchid=70.

Kletzer, L. G., and H. Rosen. 2005. Easing the Adjustment Burden on U.S. Workers. In *The United States and the World Economy*, ed. C. Fred Bergsten and the Institute for International Economics, 313–340. Washington, DC: Institute for International Economics.

Knight, F. H. 1921. *Risk, Uncertainty, and Profit*. Boston: Hougton Mifflin.

Kochan, Thomas A. 1979. How American Workers View Unions. *Monthly Labor Review* 102: 15–22.

———. 1995. Using the Dunlop Report for Mutual Gains. *Industrial Relations* 34: 350–366.

Kochan, Thomas A. 2005. *Restoring the American Dream: A Working Families' Agenda for America*. Cambridge, MA: MIT Press.

Kochan, Thomas A., Harry C. Katz, and Robert B. McKersie. 1986. *The Transformation of American Industrial Relations*. New York: Basic Books.

Kochan, Thomas A., Harry C. Katz, and Nancy Mower. 1984. *Worker Participation and Labor Unions: Threat or Opportunity?* Kalamazoo, MI: W. E. Upjohn Institute.

Kochan, Thomas A., and Paul Osterman. 1994. *The Mutual Gains Enterprise*. Boston: Harvard Business School Press.

Kohli, M. 1986. Social Organization and Subjective Construction of the Life Course. In *Human Development and the Life Course: Multidisciplinary Perspectives*, ed. A. B. Sorensen, F. E. Weinert, and L. R. Sherrod, 271–292. Hillsdale, NJ: Lawrence Erlbaum Associates.

Kompier, M. 2002. Job Design and Well-Being. In *Handbook Of Work and Health Psychology*, ed. M. Schabracq, J. Winnubst, and C. Cooper, 429–454. Chichester: Wiley.

Kompier, M., C. Cooper, and S. A. E. Geurts. 2000. A Multiple Case Study Approach to Work Stress Prevention in Europe. *European Journal of Work and Organizational Psychology* 9: 371–400.

Kompier, M. A. J., S. A. E. Geurts, R. W. M. Gründemann, P. Vink, and P. G. W. Smulders. 1998. Cases in Stress Prevention: The Success of a Participative and Stepwise Approach. *Stress Medicine* 14: 144–168.

Kompier, M. A. J., and T. S. Kristensen. 2000. Organizational Work Stress Interventions in a Theoretical, Methodological and Practical Context. In *Stress in the Workplace: Past, Present, and Future*, ed. Jack Dunham. London and Philadelphia: Whurr Publishers.

Konrad, A., and R. Mangel. 2000. The Impact of Work-Life Programs on Firm Productivity. *Strategic Management Journal* 21: 1225–1237.

Korczyk, Sophie M. 2004. Is Early Retirement Ending? Aarp Public Policy Institute Working Paper, October 10, 2004.

Korn/Ferry International. 2003. 62% of Global Executives Dissatisfied With Current Positions. Press Release, September 30. http://www.Kornferry.Com/Library/Process.Asp?P=Pr_Detail&Cid=491&Lid=1.

Kossek, E. 2005. Workplace Policies and Practices to Support Work and Families. In *Work, Family, Health and Well-Being*, ed. S. Bianchi, L. Casper, and R. King, 97–115. Mahwah, NJ: Lawrence Erlbaum Associates.

Kossek, E., and P. Berg. 2005. *The* Role of Unions in Fostering Flexibility: Changing Dialogue and Negotiating Change. Michigan State University. Research Proposal to the Alfred P. Sloan Foundation.

Kossek, E., B. Lautsch, and S. Eaton. 2005a. Flexibility Enactment Theory: Relationships between Type, Boundaries, Control and Work-Family Effectiveness. In *Work and Life*

*Integration: Organizational, Cultural and Individual Perspectives*, ed. E. Kossek and S. Lambert, 243–262. Mahwah, NJ: Lawrence Erlbaum Associates.

Kossek, E., B. Lautsch, and S. Eaton. 2005b. Telecommuting, Control, and Boundary Management: Correlates of Policy Use and Practice, Job Control, and Work-Family Effectiveness. *Journal of Vocational Behavior.*

Kossek E., and M. Lee. 2005a. Making Flexibility Work: What Managers Have Learned about Implementing Reduced Load Work. Michigan State and McGill University Technical Report. Alfred P. Sloan Foundation Grant 2002–6-11. http://Flex-Work.Lir.Msu.Edu/.

———. 2005b. Benchmarking Survey: A Snapshot Of Human Resource Managers Perspectives on Implementing Reduced Load Work. Michigan State and McGill University Technical Report. Alfred P. Sloan Foundation Grant 2002–6-11. http://Flex-Work.Lir.Msu.Edu/.

Kossek E., and V. Nichols. 1992. The Effects of Employer-Sponsored Child Care on Employee Attitudes and Performance. *Personnel Psychology* 45: 485–509.

Kossek, E. E, J. Colquitt, and R. Noe. 2001. Caregiving Decisions, Well-Being and Performance: The Effects of Place and Provider as a Function of Dependent Type and Work-Family Climates. *Academy of Management Journal* 44: 29–44.

Kossek, E. E., and S. J. Lambert. 2005. Work-Family Scholarship: Voice and Context. In *Work and Life Integration: Organizational, Cultural and Individual Perspectives*, ed. E. Kossek and S. Lambert, 3–18. Mahwah, NJ: Lawrence Erlbaum Associates.

Kossek. E. E., and C. Ozeki. 1998. Work-Family Conflict, Policies, and the Job-Life Satisfaction Relationship: A Review and Directions for Organizational Behavior/Human Resources Research. *Journal of Applied Psychology* 83: 139–149.

Kossek, E. E., and C. Ozeki. 1999. Bridging the Work-Family Policy and Productivity Gap: A Literature Review. *Community, Work, and Family* 2: 7–32.

Kossek, E. E., S. Sweet, and S. J. Pitt-Catsouphes. In Press. Part Ii: Introduction: The Insights Gained from Integrating Disciplines. In *The Work and Family Handbook: Multi-Disciplinary Perspectives, Methods and Approaches*, ed. M. Pitt-Catsouphes, E. Kossek, and S. Sweet. Mahwah, NJ: Lawrence Erlbaum Associates.

Kotter, John P., and James L. Heskett. 1992. *Corporate Culture and Performance.* New York: Free Press.

Kram, K. E., and D. T. Hall. 1991. Mentoring as an Antidote to Stress During Corporate Trauma. *Human Resource Management* 28: 493–510.

Kreiner, G. E., and B. E. Ashforth. 2003. Evidence toward an Expanded Model of Organizational Identification. *Journal of Organizational Behavior* 25: 1–27.

Kronus, Carol L. 1976. Occupational Versus Organizational Influences on Reference Group Identification. *Sociology of Work and Occupations* 3: 303–330.

Krueger, Alan B. 1993. How Computers Have Changed the Wage Structure: Evidence from Microdata 1984–1989. *Quarterly Journal of Economics* 108 (1): 33–60.

Kruse, D., R. Freeman, J. Blasi, R. Buchele, A. Scharf, L. Rodgers, and C. Mackin. 2003. Motivating Employee-Owners in ESOP Firms: Human Resource Policies and Company Performance. Working Paper Series, National Bureau of Economic Research, Cambridge, MA.

Kruse, D. L. 1996. Why Do Firms Adopt Profit-Sharing and Employee Ownership Plans? *British Journal of Labor Relations* 43: 515–538.

Kruse, Douglas. 1993a. *Profit Sharing: Does It Make a Difference?* Kalamazoo, Michigan: W.E. Upjohn Institute for Employment Research.

Kruse, Douglas. 1993b. Does Profit Sharing Affect Productivity? Working Paper No. 4542, National Bureau of Economic Research, Cambridge, MA.

Kruse, Douglas, and Joseph Blasi. 1995. Employee Ownership, Employee Attitudes, and Firm Performance. Working Paper No. W5277, National Bureau of Economic Research, Cambridge, MA.

———. 1997. Employee Ownership, Employee Attitudes, and Firm Performance: A Review of the Evidence. In *The Human Resource Management Handbook, Part I*, ed. David Lewin, Daniel J. B. Mitchell, and Mahmood A. Zaidi, 113–152. Greenwich, CT, and London, England: Jai Press.

Kulik, C. 2004. *Human Resources for the Non-Hr Manager*. Mahwah, NJ: Lawrence Erlbaum Associates.

Kunda, Gideon, and Galit Ailon-Souday. 2005. Managers, Markets, and Ideologies: Design and Devotion Revisited. In *The Oxford Handbook of Work and Organization*, ed. Stephen Ackroyd, Rosemary Batt, Paul Thompson, and Pamela Tolbert, 200–219. New York: Oxford University Press.

Kuszewski, J., K. Prakash-Mani, and S. Beloe. 2004. *Good Migrations? BT, Corporate Social Responsibility and the Geography of Jobs*. London: Sustainability.

Kuttner, Robert. 1996. *Everything for Sale: The Virtues and Limits of Markets*. Chicago: University of Chicago Press.

Lacey, Robert. 1986. *Ford: The Men and the Machine*. New York: Little, Brown and Company.

Lambert, S., and E. Kossek. 2005. Future Frontiers: Enduring Challenges and Established Assumptions in the Work-Life Field. In *Work and Life Integration: Organizational, Cultural and Psychological Perspectives*, ed. E. E. Kossek and S. Lambert, 513–532. Mahwah, NJ: Lawrence Erlbaum Associates (Lea) Press.

Lambert, S. J. 2000. Added Benefits: The Link between Work-Life Benefits and Organizational Citizenship Behavior. *Academy of Management Journal* 43: 801–815.

Lambert, S. J., and E. Waxman. 2005. Organizational Stratification: Distributing Opportunities for Balancing Work and Life. In *Work and Life Integration: Organizational, Cultural and Individual Perspectives*, ed. E. E. Kossek and S. J. Lambert, 103–126. Mahwah, NJ: Erlbaum.

Landers, R, J. Rebitzer, and L. Taylor. 1996. Rat Race Redux: Adverse Selection in the Determination of Work Hours in Law Firms. *American Economic Review* 86: 329–348.

Langer, B. 1996. *The Consuming Self*. Melbourne: Oxford University Press.

Langfred, C. W. 2000. The Paradox of Self-Management: Individual and Group Autonomy in Work Groups. *Journal of Organizational Behavior* 21: 563–585.

Lawler, Edward E.. 2003. *Treat People Right!* San Francisco: Jossey-Bass.

Lawler, Edward E., and M. McDermott. 2003. Current Performance Management Practices: Examining the Varying Impacts. *World at Work Journal* 12 (2): 49–60.

Lawler, Edward E., Susan Albers Mohrman, and George Benson. 2001. *Organizing for High Performance: Employee Involvement, TQM, Reengineering, and Knowledge Management in the Fortune 1000*. San Francisco: Jossey-Bass.

Lawler, Edward E., Susan A. Mohrman, and Gerald E. Ledford Jr. 1995. *Creating High Performance Organizations: Practices and Results of Employee Involvement and Total Quality Management in Fortune 1000 Companies* San Francisco: Jossey-Bass.

Lawler, Edward E., Susan A. Mohrman, and Gerald E. Ledford Jr. 1998. *Strategies for High Performance Organizations: The CEO Report*. San Fransisco: Jossey-Bass.

Lawler, Edward E., Alec Levenson, and John Boudreau. 2004. HR Metrics and Analytics: Use and Impact. *Human Resource Planning* 27 (4).

Lazear, E. P. 1981. Agency Earnings Profiles, Productivity, and Hours Restrictions. *American Economic Review* 71: 606–620.

Lazear, Edward. 1995. *Personnel Economics*. Cambridge, MA: MIT Press.

———. 2000. Performance Pay and Productivity. *American Economic Review* 90 (5): 1346–1361.

Leana, C. R., and D. C. Feldman. 1992. *Coping With Job Loss: How Individuals, Organizations, and Communities Respond to Layoffs*. New York: Lexington Books.

Leana, C. R., and D. M. Rousseau. 2000. *Relational Wealth: The Advantages of Stability in a Changing Economy*. New York: Oxford.

Leana, Carrie R., and Denise M. Rousseau. 2000. Relational Wealth. In *Relational Wealth: The Advantages of Stability in a Changing Economy*, ed. Carrie R. Leana and Denise M. Rousseau, 3–24. New York: Oxford University Press.

Lee, M., and E. E. Kossek. 2004. Crafting Lives That Work. Feedback Report from Alfred P. Sloan Foundation Study. http://www.Polisci.Msu.Edu/Kossek/Final.Pdf.

Lee, Y., and L. Waite. 2005. Husbands' and Wives' Time Spent on Housework. *Journal of Marriage and the Family* 67(2) 328–336.

Leitch Review of Skills. 2005. Skills in the UK: The long-term challenge, Interim Report. London: HM Treasury, December.

Lemieux, Thomas, Daniel Parent, and Bentley MacLeod. 2005. Performance Pay and Wage Inequality. Working Paper.

Leuven, Edwin, and Hessel Oosterbeek. 1999. The Demand and Supply of Work-Related Training: Evidence from Four Countries. *Research in Labor Economics* 18: 303–333.

Lev, B. 2001. *Intangibles: Management, Measurement and Reporting*. UK: The Brookings Institution, Press.

Lev B., and S. Radhakrishnan. 2002. Structural Capital. NBER Working Paper Series.

Levenson, Alec. 2000. Long-Run Trends in Part-Time and Temporary Employment: Toward an Understanding. In *On the Job: Is Long-Term Employment a Thing of the Past?*, ed. David Neumark. New York: Russell Sage Foundation.

Levine, David I. 1993. What Do Wages Buy? *Administrative Science Quarterly* 38 (3): 462–483.

———. 1995. *Reinventing the Workplace: How Business and Employees Can Both Win*. Washington DC: Brookings Institution.

Levine, David I., Dale Belman, Gary Charness, Erica Groshen, and K.C. O'Shaughnessy. 2002. *How New Is the "New Employment Contract"?* Kalamazoo, MI: W.E. Upjohn Institute for Employment Research.

Levine, David I., and Richard Parkin. 1994. Work Organization, Employment Security, and Macroeconomic Stability. *Journal of Economic Behavior and Organization* 24 (3): 251–271.

Levy, Frank, and Richard J. Murnane. 1992. U.S. Earnings and Earnings Inequality: A Review of Recent Trends and Proposed Explanations. *Journal of Economic Literature* 30: 1333–1381.

———. 1996. *Teaching the New Basic Skills*. New York: Free Press.

———. 2004. *The New Division of Labor: How Computers Are Creating the Next Job Market*. New York: Russell Sage Foundation.

Lewis, S., and L. Haas. 2005. Work-Life Integration and Social Policy: A Social Justice Approach to Work and Family. In *Work-Life Integration: Organizational, Cultural and Individual Perspectives*, ed. E. Kossek and S. Lambert, 349–374. New Jersey: Lea Press.

Lifton, R. J. 1993. *The Protean Self: Human Resilience in an Age of Fragmentation*. New York: Basic Books.

Lipset, Seymour Martin, and Noah M. Meltz. 2004. *The Paradox of American Unionism*. Ithaca, NY: Cornell/ILR Press.

Lobel, S. 1991. Allocation of Investment in Work and Family Roles: Alternative Theories and Implications for Research. *Academy of Management Review* 16: 501–521,

Locke, Richard. 2003. The Promise and Perils of Globalization: The Case of Nike. In *Management: Inventing and Delivering the Future*, ed. Richard Schmalensee and Thomas Kochan. Cambridge, MA: MIT Press.

Lohr, J. 2005. Cutting Here, but Hiring over There. *New York Times*, June 24.

Lovell, Malcolm, Susan Goldberg, Larry W. Hunter, Thomas A. Kochan, John Paul MacDuffie, Andrew Martin, and Robert McKersie. 1992. Making It Together: The Chrysler-Uaw Modern Operating Agreement. Washington, DC: Department of Labor.

Lucier, C., E. Spiegel, and R. Schuyt. 2002. Why CEOs Fall. Booz Allen Hamilton Report. http://Extfile.Bah.Com/Livelink/Livelink/110173/?Func=Doc.Fetch&Nodeid=110173.

Lynch, Lisa M., and Sandra E. Black. 1998. Beyond the Incidence of Employer Provided Training. *Industrial and Labor Relations Review*, October.

MacDuffie, John Paul. 1995. Human Resource Bundles and Manufacturing Performance: Organizational Logic and Flexible Production Systems in the World Auto Industry. *Industrial and Labor Relations Review* 48 (2): 197–221.

MacDuffie, John-Paul. 1996. Automotive White-Collar: The Changing Status and Roles of Salaried Employees in the North American Automobile Industry. In *Broken Ladders: Managerial Careers in the New Economy*, ed. Paul Osterman, 81–125. New York: Oxford University Press.

Maher, K. 2004. Next on the Outsourcing List. *The Wall Street Journal*, March 23.

Maier, Matthew. 2005. How to Beat Wal-Mart. *Business 2.0* May: 108–114.

Mairesse, Jacques, and Nathalie Greenan. 1999. Organizational Change and Productivity in French Manufacturing: What Do We Learn from Firm Representative and Their Employees? NBER Conference on Organizational Change and Performance Improvement.

Mandel, M. 2004. *Rational Exuberance*.

Mangum, Garth, Donald Mayall, and Kristin Nelson. 1985. The Temporary Help Industry: A Response to the Dual Internal Labor Market. *Industrial and Labor Relations Review* 88: 599–611.

Mann, C. L. 2003. International Economics Policy Brief. Washington, DC: Institute for International Economics.

Marcotte, Dave E. 1999. Has Job Stability Declined? Evidence from the Panel Study of Income Dynamics. *American Journal of Economics and Sociology* 58 (2): 197–216.

Markoff, J., and M. Richtel. 2005. Profit, not Jobs, in Silicon Valley. *New York Times*, July 3.

Marscke, G. 2002. Performance Incentives and Organizational Behavior: Evidence from a Federal Bureaucracy, October. http://www.Albany.Edu/~Marschke/Papers/Perfinc1.Pdf.

Matthes, K. 1992. Ada Checkup: Assess Your Wellness Program. *HR Focus* 69 (12): 15.

Matusik, Sharon F., and Charles W. L. Hill. 1998. The Utilization of Contingent Work: Knowledge Creation and Competitive Advantage. *Academy of Management Review* 23: 680–697.

McAllister, Jean. 1998. Sisyphus at Work in the Warehouse: Temporary Employment in Greenville, South Carolina. In *Contingent Work: American Employment in Transition*, ed. Kathleen Barker and Kathleen Christensen, 221–242. Ithaca, NY: ILR Press.

McCabe, D. L., and L. K. Trevino. 1995. Cheating Among Business Students: A Challenge for Business Leaders and Educators. *Journal of Management Education* 19: 205–218.

McCall, Jr., M. W. 1998. *High Flyers: Developing the Next Generation of Leaders*. Boston: Harvard Business School Press.

McCall, Jr., M. W., M. M. Lombardo, and A. M. Morrison, A. M. 1989. Great Leaps in Career Development. *Across the Board* 26 (3): 54–61.

McDonald, Steven, and Glen H. Elder, Jr. 2005. When Does Social Capital Matter? Non-Searching and the Life Course. Paper Presented at 2004 American Sociological Association Annual Meeting.

McDougall, P. 2005. 30% of Tech Jobs at Risk from Offshoring, Gartner Says. *Informationweek*, April: 16.

McFeatters, A. 2005. When Pensions Go Poof. *Pittsburgh Post Gazette*, May 7.

McKinsey Global Institute. 2005. The Emerging Global Market: Parts I-III. San Francisco: McKinsey & Company. http://www.McKinsey.Com/Mgi/Publications/Emerginggloballabormarket/Index.Asp.

McLean, Bethany, and Peter Elkind. 2003. *The Smartest Guys in the Room: The Amazing Rise and Scandalous Fall of Enron*. New York: Penguin.

Meredith, R. 2003. Giant Sucking Sound. *Forbes*, September 29: 58–60.

Meyerson, S., Weick, K. E. and Kramer, R. M. 1996. Swift Trust and Temporary Groups. In *Trust in Organizations: Frontiers of Theory and Research*, ed. R. M. Kramer and T. R. Tyler, 166–195. CA: Sage Publications, Thousand Oaks.

Micco, L. 1998. Gallup Study Links Worker Beliefs, Increased Productivity. *HR News*, September: 16.

Milgrom, Paul, and John Roberts. 1990. The Economics of Modern Manufacturing. *American Economic Review* 80 (30): 511–528.

Milgrom, Paul, and John Roberts. 1995. Complementarities and Fit: Strategy, Structure, and Organizational Change in Manufacturing. *Journal of Accounting and Economics* 19: 179–208.

Milkman, R., and E. Appelbaum. Forthcoming. Paid Leave in California: New Research Findings. The *State of California Labor*. Berkeley: The University of California Press.

Miller, Dale T. 1999. The Norm of Self-Interest. *American Psychologist* 54: 1053–1060.

Miller, J., and M. Miller. 2005. Get a Life! Ditching the 24/7 Culture. *Fortune*, November 11.

Miller, William. 1949. American Historians and the Business Elite. *Journal of Economic History* 9(2).

Mills, C. Wright. 1951. *White Collar*. New York: Oxford University Press.

Mills, D. Quinn. 1979. Flawed Victory in Labor Law Reform. *Harvard Business Review* 53 (May-June): 99–102.

Miners, I. A., M. L. Moore, J. E. Champoux, and J. J. Martocchio. 1995. Time-Serial Substitution Effects of Absence Control on Employee Time Use. *Human Relations* 48 (3): 307–326.

Mirvis, P. H., D. T. Hall. 1996. Psychological Success and the Boundaryless Career. In *The Boundaryless Career: A New Employment Principle for a New Organizational Era*, ed. M. B. Arthur and D. M. Rousseau, 237–255. New York: Oxford University Press.

Mishel, L., J. Bernstein, and S. Allegretto. 2005. *The State of Working America 2004/2005*. Ithaca, NY: ILR Press.

Mishel, Lawrence, Jared Bernstein, and Heather Boushey. 2003. *The State of Working America 2002/2003*. Ithaca: Cornell University Press.

Mitroff, Ian I., and Elizabeth A. Denton. 1999. A Study of Spirituality in the Workplace. *Sloan Management Review* 40 (Summer): 83–92.

Morgan Stanley. 2004. http://www.Morganstanley.Com/About/Pressroom/News251.Html.

Morris, Charles J. 2005. *The Blue Eagle at Work: Restoring the Right of Association to the American Workplace*. Ithaca, NY: Cornell University ILR Press.

Morris, Michael W., and K. Peng. 1994. Culture and Cause: American and Chinese Attributions for Social and Physical Events. *Journal of Personality and Social Psychology* 67: 949–971.

Morrow, C. C., M. Q. Jarrett, and M. T. Rupinski. 1997. An Investigation of the Effect and Economic Utility of Corporate-Wide Training. *Personnel Psychology* 50: 91–119.

Muhl, Charles J. 2002. What Is an Employee? the Answer Depends on the Federal Law. *Monthly Labor Review*, January: 3–11.

Murnane, R. J., and F. Levy. 1996. *Teaching the New Basic Skills: Principles for Educating Children to Thrive in a Changing Economy*. New York: The Free Press.

Murphy, Kevin J., and Jan Zabojnik 2004. CEO Pay and Appointments: A Market-Based Explanation for Recent Trends. *The American Economic Review* 94 (2): 192–196.

———. 2003. Managerial Capital and the Market for CEOs. Marshall School of Business, University of Southern California, December.

Murphy, L., S. Sauter, M. Tausig, and R. Fenwick. In Press. Changes in the Quality of Work Life: 1972–2002. *Journal of Occupational and Environmental Medicine*.

Murphy, L. R. In Press. Job Stress Among Healthcare Workers. In *Handbook of Human Factors and Ergonomics in Healthcare and Patient Safety*, ed. P. Carayon. Lawrence Erlbaum, Inc.

Murphy, L. R., and S. L. Sauter. 2004. Work Organization Interventions: State of Knowledge and Future Directions. *Soz Preventive Med* 49: 79–86.

Musich, S. A., L. Adams, and D. W. Edington. 2000. Effectiveness of Health Promotion Programs in Moderating Medical Costs in the USA. *Health Promotion International* 15 (1): 5–15.

Nadler, R. 1998. Stocks Populi: As Workers Join the Investing Class, America May Undergo a Political Realignment. *National Review*, March 9: 36–39.

National Academy of Engineering. 2005. *Educating the Engineer of 2020: Adapting Engineering Education to the New Century*. Washington, DC: The National Academies Press.

National Center on Education and the Economy. 1990. *America's Choice: High Skills or Low Wages!* Rochester, NY.

National Commission on Excellence in Education (NCEE). 1983. *A Nation at Risk*. Washington, DC: GPO.

National Labor Relations Board. 2004. *Annual Report*. Washington, DC, Government Printing Office. http://www.Nlrb.Gov.

National Science Board. 2003. *The Science and Engineering Workforce: Realizing America's Potential*. Arlington, VA: National Science Foundation.

———. 2004. *Science and Engineering Indicators 2004*. 2 Vols. Arlington, VA: National Science Foundation.

Nayar, N., and G. L. Willinger. 2001. Financial Implications of the Decision to Increase Reliance on Contingent Labor. *Decision Sciences* 32 (4): 661–681.

Nelson, Daniel. 1975. *Managers and Workers: Origins of the New Factory System in the United States, 1880–1920*. Madison, WI: University of Wisconsin Press.

Nelson, G. 1999. Science Literacy for All in the 21st Century. *Educational Leadership* 57(2).

Neumark, David. 2000. on *The Job: Is Long-Term Employment a Thing of the Past?* New York: Russell Sage.

Neumark, David, Daniel Polsky, and Daniel Hansen. 1999. Has Job Stability Declined Yet? New Evidence for the 1990s. *Journal of Labor Economics* Part 2 17(4): S29–S64.

Newcomer, Mabel. 1955. *The Big Business Executive: The Factors That Made Him, 1900–1950*. New York: Columbia University Press.

Newman, Katherine. 1999. *Falling from Grace*. Berkeley: University of California Press.

Nichols, L. S., and V. W. Junk. 1997. The Sandwich Generation: Dependency, Proximity, and Task Assistance Needs of Parents. *Journal of Family and Economic Issues* 18: 299–326.

Nickell, Steve, Daphne Nicolitsas, and Malcolm Patterson. 2001. Does Doing Badly Encourage Management Innovation? *Oxford Institute for Economics and Statistics* 63 (1): 5–28.

North, D. 1995. *Soothing the Establishment*. University Press of America.

O'Driscoll, M. P., S. Poelmans, P. E. Spector, T. Kalliath, T. D. Allen, C. L. Cooper, and J. I. Sanchez. 2003. Family-Responsive Interventions, Perceived Organizational and Supervisor Support, Work-Family Conflict, and Psychological Strain. *International Journal of Stress Management* 10: 326–344.

O'Neill, June, and Solomon Polachek. 1993. Why the Gender Gap in Wages Narrowed in the 1980s. *Journal of Labor Economics* 11 (1), Part 1: 205–228.

O'Reilly, Charles A. 1989. Corporations, Culture, and Commitment: Motivation and Social Control in Organizations. *California Management Review* 31: 9–25.

O'Reilly, Charles A., III, and Jeffrey Pfeffer. 2000. *Hidden Value: How Great Companies Achieve Extraordinary Results With Ordinary People*. Boston: Harvard Business School Press.

O'Shaughnessy, K. C., David Levine, and Peter Cappelli. 2001. Changes in Managerial Pay Structures 1986–1992 and Rising Returns to Skill. *Oxford Economics Papers*, 3: 482–507.

O'Toole, J. 1974. *Work and Quality of Life*. Cambridge, MA: MIT Press.

O'Toole, James, Elisabeth Hansot, William Herman, Neal Herrick, Elliot Liebow, Bruce Lusignan, Harold Richman, Harold Sheppard, Ben Stephansky, and James Wright. 1973. Work in America: Report of a Special Task Force to the Secretary of Health, Education, and Welfare. Cambridge, MA: MIT Press.

Ocasio, W. 1999. Institutionalized Action and Corporate Governance: The Reliance on Rules of CEO Succession. *Administrative Science Quarterly* 44 (2): 384–417.

OECD. 2001. Balancing Work and Family Life: Helping Parents into Paid Employment. In *OECD Employment Outlook 2001*, 129–166. Paris: OECD.

———. 2004. *Learning for Tomorrow's World: First Results from Pisa 2003*. Paris: OECD.

Oliner, Stephen, and Daniel Sichel. Information Technology and Productivity: Where Are We Now and Where Are We Going? *Federal Reserve Bank of Atlanta Economic Review*. Third Quarter: 15–44.

Onsite childcare can reduce absenteeism, turnover. 2003. September 9. http://www.shm.org.

Opdyke, J. D., and K. Greene. 2005. Is Your Retirement Money Safe? *The Wall Street Journal*, May 12.

O'Reilly, C. A., III, and J. Pfeffer. 2000. *Hidden Value: How Great Companies Achieve Extraordinary Results With Ordinary People*. Boston: Harvard Business School Press.

Orr, Julian E. 1997. *Talking about Machines: An Ethnography of a Modern Job*. Ithaca, NY: ILR Press.

Orrange, R. M. 2003. The Emerging Mutable Self: Gender Dynamics and Creative Adaptations in Defining Work, Family, and the Future. *Social Forces* 82 (1): 1–34.

Osha. 1998 Workplace Injury and Illness Statistics. http://www.Osha.Gov/Oshstats/ Work.Html.

Osterman, Paul. 1994. How Common Is Workplace Transformation and Who Adopts It? *Industrial and Labor Relations Review* 47 (2): 175–188.

———. 1996. *Broken Ladders: Managerial Careers in the New Economy*. New York: Oxford University Press.

———. 2000. Work Reorganization in an Era of Restructuring: Trends in Diffusion and Effects on Employee Welfare. *Industrial and Labor Relations Review* 53 (2): 179–196.

———. 2003. *Gathering Power*. Boston: Beacon Press.

———.2006. The Wage Effects of High Performance Work Organization. *Industrial and Labor Relations Review* 59 (2): 187–204.

Ouchi, William G. 1981. *Theory Z: How American Business Can Meet the Japanese Challenge*. Reading, MA: Addison-Wesley.

Ouchi, William G., and Alfred M. Jaeger. 1978. Type Z Organizations: Stability in the Midst of Mobility. *Academy of Management Review* 3: 305–314.

Overby, S. 2003. The Future of Jobs and Innovation. *CIO Magazine Online* December. http://www.Cio.Com/Archive/121503/Jobfuture.Html.

Panel on Musculoskeletal Disorders and the Workplace. 2001. *Musculoskeletal Disorders and the Workplace*. Washington, DC: National Academy of Science, Institute of Medicine, National Academies Press.

Parker, Mike, and Jane Slaughter. 1988. *Choosing Sides: Unions and the Team Concept*. Detroit: Labor Notes Book.

Parker, Robert E. 1994. *Flesh Peddlers and Warm Bodies: The Temporary Help Industry and Its Workers*. New Brunswick, NJ: Rutgers University Press.

Parker, S., and T. Wall. 1998. *Job and Work Design*. Thousand Oaks, CA: Sage.

Parkes, K. R. 1987. Relative Weight, Smoking, and Mental Health as Predictors of Sickness and Absence from Work. *Journal of Applied Psychology* 72: 275–286.

Pear, Robert. 2005. Health Leaders Seek Consensus over Uninsured. *New York Times*, May 29. http://www.NYtimes.Com/2005/05/29/National/29insure.Html.

———. 2005. Health Leaders Seek Consensus over Uninsured. *New York Times*, May 29.

Pearce, J. L., and A. E. Randal. 2004. Expectations of Organizational Mobility, Workplace Social Inclusion, and Employee Job Performance. *Journal of Organizational Behavior* 25: 81–98.

Pearson, Christine M., and Christine L. Porath. 2005. on the Nature, Consequences and Remedies of Workplace Incivility: No Time for "Nice"? Think Again. *Academy of Management Executive* 19: 7–18.

Pelletier, K. R. 1996. A Review and Analysis of the Health and Cost-Effective Outcome Studies of Comprehensive Health Promotion and Disease Prevention Programs at the Work Site: 1993–1995 Update. *American Journal of Health Promotion* 10: 380–388.

Perrucci, Robert, and Joel E. Gerstl. 1969. *Profession Without Community*. New York: Random House.

Peter, K., L. Horn, and C. D. Carroll. 2005. *Gender Differences in Participation and Completion of Undergraduate Education and How They Have Changed over Time*. NCES Pedar Report, Washington, DC, U.S. Department of Education, Institute of Education Sciences, NCES 2005–169, February.

Peters, T. 1999. *The Brand You 50*. New York: Alfred A. Knopf.

———. 1999. *The Professional Service Firm 50 (Reinventing Work): Fifty Ways to Transform Your "Department" into a Professional Service Firm whose Trademarks Are Passion and Innovation*. New York: Knopf.

Pfeffer, Jeffrey. 1994. *Competitive Advantage through People: Unleashing the Power of the Work Force*. Boston: Harvard Business School Press.

Pfeffer, Jeffrey. 1998. *The Human Equation: Building Profits by Putting People First*. Boston: Harvard Business School Press.

———. 1998. Seven Myths about Employee Pay. *Harvard Business Review* 76 (May-June): 108–119.

———. 2005. The Myth of the Disposable Worker. *Business 2.0*, October, 78.

Pfeffer, Jeffrey, and James N. Baron. 1988. Taking the Workers Back Out: Recent Trends in the Structuring of Employment. In *Research in Organizational Behavior*, ed. Barry Staw and Lawrence Cummings 10: 257–303. Greenwich, CT: JAI Press.

Pierce, J. L., and C. A. Furo. 1990. Employee Ownership: Implications for Management. *Organizational Dynamics* 18: 32–43.

Pink, D. H. 2001. *Free Agent Nation: The Future of Working for Yourself*. New York: Warner.

Piore, Michael J., and Charles Sabel. 1984. *The Second Industrial Divide*. New York: Basic Books.

Pitt-Catsouphes, M., E. Kossek, and S. Sweet. 2006. Charting New Territory: Advancing Multi-Disciplinary Perspectives, Methods and Approaches in the Study of Work and Family. In *The Work and Family Handbook: Multi-Disciplinary Perspectives, Methods and Approaches*, ed. M. Pitt-Catsouphes, E. Kossek, and S. Sweet, 1–16. Mahwah, NJ: Lawrence Erlbaum Associates.

Polivka, Anne E. 1996. A Profile of Contingent Workers. *Monthly Labor Review* 119: 10–21.

———. 1996. Are Temporary Help Agency Workers Substitutes for Direct Hire Temps? Searching for an Alternative Explanation of Growth in the Temporary Help Industry. Bureau of Labor Statistics Working Paper, Presented at the Society for Labor Economists Conference, Chicago, May 3–4.

———. 1996. Contingent and Alternative Work Arrangements, Defined. *Monthly Labor Review* 119: 3–9.

Price, R. H. 1992. Psychosocial Impact of Job Loss on Individuals and Families. *Current Directions in Psychological Science* 1 (1): 9–11.

Price, R. H., J. N. Choi, and A. Vinokur. 2002. Links in the Chain of Adversity Following Job Loss: How Economic Hardship and Loss of Personal Control Lead to Depression, Impaired Functioning and Poor Health. *Journal of Occupational Health Psychology* 7 (4): 302–312.

Price, R. H., D. S. Friedland, J. Choi, and R. D. Caplan. 1998. Job Loss and Work Transitions in a Time of Global Economic Change. In *Addressing Community Problems*, ed. X. Arriaga and S. Oskamp , 195–222. Thousand Oaks, CA: Sage Publications.

Price, R. H., and M. Kompier. In Press. Work Stress and Unemployment: Risks, Mechanisms, and Prevention. In *Prevention of Mental Disorders: Evidence Based Programs and Policies*, ed. C. M. Hosman, E. Jane-Llopis, and S. Saxena. Oxford: Oxford University Press.

Princeton Survey Research Associates. 1994. *Worker Representation and Participation Survey: Report on the Findings*. Princeton, NJ: Princeton Survey Research Associates.

Putnam, Robert D. 2000. *Bowling Alone: The Collapse and Revival of American Community*. New York: Simon and Schuster.

Quarrey, Michael, and Corey Rosen. 1986. *Employee Ownership and Corporate Performance.* Oakland, California: National Center for Employee Ownership.

Quinn, J., R. Burkhauser, and D. Myers. 1990. *Passing the Torch: The Influence of Economic Incentives on Work and Retirement.* Kalamazoo: W. E. Upjohn Institute for Employment Research.

Quinn, Robert P., Thomas W. Mangione, et al. 1973. *The 1969–1970 Survey of Working Conditions: Chronicles of an Unfinished Enterprise.* Ann Arbor, MI: Institute for Social Research, University of Michigan.

Quinn, Robert P., Stanley E. Seashore, and Thomas W. Mangione. 1975. *Survey of Working Conditions, 1969–1970.* Icpsr Computer File. Ann Arbor, MI: Institute for Social Research, Social Science Archive.

Quinn, Robert P., and Graham L. Staines. 1979. *The 1977 Quality of Employment Survey: Descriptive Statistics With Comparison Data from the 1969–1970 Survey of Working Conditions and the 1972–1973 Quality of Employment Survey.* Ann Arbor, MI: Institute for Social Research, the University of Michigan.

Radcliffe Public Policy Center With Harris Interactive. 2000. *Life's Work: Generational Attitudes toward Work and Life Integration.* Cambridge, MA: Radcliffe Public Policy Center.

Rainwater, L. 1974. Work, Well-Being, and Family Life. In *Work and Quality of Life*, ed. J. O'Toole, 361–378. Cambridge, MA: MIT Press.

Rajan, R. G., and Julie Wulf. 2003. The Flattening Firm: Evidence from Panel Data on the Changing Nature of Corporate Hierarchies. National Bureau of Economic Research Working Paper 9633. http://www.NBER.Org/Papers/W9633.

Rajan, R. G., and L. Zingales. 2003. *Saving Capitalism from the Capitalists.* Random House Business Books.

Rambo, W. W., A. M.. Chomiak, and J. M. Price. Consistency of Performance Under Stable Conditions of Work. *Journal of Applied Psychology* 68: 78–87.

Rapoport, R., L. Bailyn, J. Fletcher, and B. Pruitt. 2002. *Beyond Work-Family Balance: Advancing Gender Equity and Workplace Performance.* San Francisco: Jossey-Bass.

Reich, C. 1970. *The Greening of America.* New York: Random House.

Reichheld, F. F., and T. Teal. 2001. *The Loyalty Effect: The Hidden Force Behind Growth, Profits, and Lasting Value.* Boston: Harvard Business School Press.

Rénaud, Stephane, Sylvie St-Onge, and Michel Magnan. 2004. The Impact of Stock Purchase Plan Participation on Workers' Individual Cash Compensation. *Industrial Relations* 43: 120–147.

Riche, M. 2006. Demographic Implications for Work-Family Research. In *The Work and Family Handbook: Multi-Disciplinary Perspectives, Methods and Approaches*, ed. M. Pitt-Catsouphes, E. Kossek, and S. Sweet, 121–140. Mahwah, NJ: Lawrence Erlbaum Associates.

Rifkin, J. 1995. *The End of Work: The Decline of the Global Labor Force at the Dawn of the Post Market Era.* New York: G. P. Putnam.

Riley, M. W. 1988. Overview and Highlights of a Sociological Perspective. In *Social Change and the Life Course*, ed. M.W. Riley, B.J. Huber, & B.B Hess. Newbury Park, CA: Sage Publications.

Ritter, J. A., and L. J. Taylor. 2000. Are Employees Stakeholders? Corporate Finance Meets the Agency Problem. In *Relational Wealth: The Advantages of Stability in a Changing Economy*, ed. C. R. Leana and D. M. Rousseau, 49–61. New York: Oxford.

Roehling, P., M. Roehling, and R. Moen. 2001. The Relationship between Work-Family Policies and Practices and Employee Loyalty: A Life Course Perspective. *Journal Of Family and Economic Issues* 22: 141–170.

Rogers, Jackie K. 1995. Just a Temp: Experience and Structure of Alienation in Temporary Clerical Employment. *Work and Occupation* 22: 137–166.

Rose, N. 1989. *Governing the Soul: The Shaping of the Private Self.* London: Routledge.

Rosen, C. 2005. Personal Communication Via E-Mail, May.

Rosen, C., and E. Carberry. 2002. Ownership Matters! A Culture of "Doing" Is Better than a Culture of "Being." *Workspan*, October: 28–32.

Rosen, Corey, John Case, and Martin Staubus. 2005. *Equity: Why Employee Ownership Is Good for Business*. Boston, MA: Harvard Business School Press.

Rosen, Corey, Katherine Klein, and Karen M. Young. 1986. *Employee Ownership in America: The Equity Solution*. Lexington, MA: D.C. Heath, Lexington Books.

Rothausen, T. 2004. Job Satisfaction and the Parent Worker: The Role of Flexibility And Rewards. *Journal of Vocational Behavior* 44: 31–336.

Rousseau, D. M. 1995. *Psychological Contracts in Organizations: Understanding Written and Unwritten Agreements*. Newbury Park, CA: Sage.

Rousseau, D. M. 1997. Changing the Deal While Keeping the People. *Academy of Management Executive* 10(1): 50–60.

———. 2000. Psychological Contracts in the United States: Diversity, Individualism, and Associability in the Market Place. In *Psychological Contracts in Employment: Cross-National Perspectives*, ed. D. M. Rousseau and R. Schalk, 250–282. Newbury Park, CA: Sage.

———. 2001. The Idiosyncratic Deal: Flexibility Versus Fairness? *Organizational Dynamics* 29: 260.

———. 2003. New Meaning for Old Concepts in Human Resource Management and Industrial Relations. In *Negotiations and Change: From the Workplace to Society*, ed. T. Kochan and D. B. Lipsky. ILR/Cornell University Press.

———. 2004. Under the Table Deals: Idiosyncratic, Preferential or Unauthorized? in *Darkside of Organizational Behavior*, ed. R. Griffin and A. O'Leary-Kelly, 262–290. San Francisco: Jossey-Bass.

———. 2005. *I-Deals: Idiosyncratic Deals Employees Negotiate for Themselves*. Armonk, NY: M. E. Sharpe.

Rousseau, D. M., and M. B. Arthur. 1999. Building Agency and Community in the New Economic Era. *Organizational Dynamics*, Spring: 7–18.

Rousseau, D. M., and V. Ho. 2000. Psychological Contract Issues in Compensation. In *Compensation*, ed. S. Rynes and B. Gephart. Frontiers of Industrial/Organizational Psychology Series. San Francisco: Jossey-Bass.

Rousseau, D. M., V. T. Ho, and G. Greenberg. 2006, 31. Idiosyncratic Deals: Theoretical Implications of Workers Bargaining as Individuals. *Academy of Management Review*.

Rousseau, D. M., V. T. Ho, and T. G. Kim. Idiosyncratic Deals and the Psychological Contract. Manuscript Under Review.

Rousseau, D. M., and Z. Shperling. 2003. Pieces of the Action: Ownership and the Changing Employment Relationship. *Academy of Management Review* 28: 115–134.

Rousseau, D. M., and Z. Shperling. 2004. Ownership and the Changing Employment Relationship: Why Stylized Notions of Labor No Longer Generally Apply. Reply to Zarkhoodi and Paetzgold. *Academy of Management Review* 29: 562–569.

Rubinstein, S. 2005. Nursing Employees Back to Health. *The Wall Street Journal*, p. D5. January 18.

Sampson, A. 1995. *Company Man*. NY: Crown Business Books.

Sawhill, I. V. 1974. Perspectives on Women and Work in America. In *Work and Quality of Life*, ed. J. O'Toole, 88–106. Cambridge, MA: MIT Press.

Saxenian, A. 1994. *Regional Advantage: Culture and Competition in Silicon Valley and Route 128*. Cambridge: Harvard University Press.

———. 1999. Silicon Valley's New Immigrant Entrepreneurs. San Francisco, CA: Public Policy Institute of California.

Schein, E. H. 1978. *Career Dynamics: Matching Individual and Organizational Needs*. Reading, MA: Addison-Wesley.

Schiffries, C. M. Shockley and L. Pidot. 2005. NSF Budget cut by 1.9% in Omnibus Appropriations Bill. Washington, DC: National Council for Science and the Environment.

Schmidt, F. L., J. E. Hunter, and K. Pearlman. 1982. Assessing the Economic Impact of Personnel Programs on Productivity. *Personnel Psychology* 35: 333–347.

Schmidt, F. L., and J. E. Hunter. 1998. The Validity and Utility of Selection Methods in Personnel Psychology: Practical and Theoretical Implications of 85 Years of Research Findings. *Psychological Bulletin* 124: 262–274.

Schor, Juliet B. 1991. *The Overworked American: The Unexpected Decline of Leisure*. New York: Basic Books.

Schwartz, B. 2000. Self-Determination: The Tyranny of Freedom. *American Psychologist* 55: 79–88.

———. 2004. *The Paradox of Choice: Why More Is Less*. New York: Ecco.

Scoeff, Jr., M. 2005. U.S. Manufacturers Face Skills Shortage. *Workforce Management* September 6. http://www.Workforce.Com/Section/00/Article/24/15/37.Html.

Scott, Elizabeth, K. C. O'Shaughnessy, and Peter Cappelli. 1996. Management Jobs in the Insurance Industry: Organizational Deskilling and Rising Pay Inequality. In *Broken Ladders: Managerial Careers in the New Economy*, ed. Paul Osterman, 126–154. New York: Oxford University Press.

Scott, W. R. 1965. Reactions to Supervision in a Heteronomous Professional Organization. *Administrative Science Quarterly* 10: 65–81.

———. 1981. *Organizations: Rational, Natural, and Open Systems*. Englewood Cliffs, NJ: Prentice Hall.

Scully, Maureen, and Amy Segal. 2003. Passion With an Umbrella. *Research on Organizational Sociology* 19: 125–168.

Segal, Lewis M., and Daniel G. Sullivan. 1997. The Growth of Temporary Services Work. *Journal of Economic Perspectives* 11 (2): 117–136.

Semler, Ricardo. 2000. How We Went Digital Without a Strategy. *Harvard Business Review*, September-October.

Semmer, N. K. 2003. Job Stress Interventions and Organization of Work. In *Handbook of Occupational Health Psychology*, ed. C. Quick and L. E. Tetrick, 325–354. Washington, DC: American Psychological Association.

———. 2004. Health Related Interventions in Organizations: Stages, Levels, Criteria, and Methodology. *Soz Preventive Med* 49: 89–91.

Sesil, James, Maya Kroumova, Joseph Blasi, and Douglas Kruse. 2002. Broad-Based Employee Stock Options in U.S. New Economy Firms. *British Journal of Industrial Relations* 4 (2): 273–294.

Sethi, V, R. King, and J. C. Quick. 2004.What Causes Stress in Information System Professionals. *Communication of the Acm* 47: 3, 99–102.

Shahi, G. 2004. *Bio Business in Asia*. Singapore: Pearson Prentice Hall.

Shannon, H. S. and D. C. Cole. 2004. Making Workplaces Healthier: Generating Better Evidence on Work Organization Intervention Research. *Soz Preventive Med* 49: 92–94.

Shaw, Albert. 1886. Cooperation in a Western City. *Publications of the American Economic Association* 1 (4): 7–106.

Shaw, J. D., N. Gupta, and J. E. Delery. 2002. Pay Dispersion and Workforce Performance: Moderating Effects of Incentives and Interdependence. *Strategic Management Journal* 23: 491–512.

Shew, Robert. 2006. Job openings and Hires Held steady in February. Career Journal.com, April 28. http://www.career journal.com/hrcenter/briefs/20060428-bna.htm/

Sheahan, Maureen, Et. Al. 1996. *A Union Guide to Qs9000*. Detroit: Labor-Management Council for Economic Renewal.

Shellenbarger, S. 2002. The Incredible Shrinking Family Leave: Pressed Bosses Are Cutting into Time Off. *The Wall Street Journal*, October 17.

Shinn, Sharon. 2003. Luv, Colleen. *Bized*, March/April: 18–23.

Shir, R. A., and F. Li. Outsourcing Employees. *Proceedings of the Eastern Academy of Management Meetings*. Springfield, MA, May.

Shore, L. M., L. E. Tetrick, S. Taylor, J. A-M. Coyle Shapiro, R. Liden, J. McLean Parks, E. Wolfe Morrison, L. W. Porter, S. L. Robinson, M. Roehling, D. M. Rousseau, R. Schalk, A. Tsui, and L. Van Dyne. 2004. The Employee-Organization Relationship: A Timely Concept in a Period of Transition. In *Research in Personnel and Human Resource Management*, ed. J. Martucchio, 291–370. Volume 23. Elsevier.

Shperling, Z., and D. M. Rousseau. 2001. Why Employers Share Ownership With Workers. In *Trends in Organizational Behavior*, ed. C. L. Cooper and D. M. Rousseau, 19–44. Volume 8. Chichester: Wiley.

Shperling, Z., D. M. Rousseau, and C. J. Ferrante. 2002. Ownership and Control in High Technology Start-Up Firms. Technical Report, Heinz School of Public Policy and Management, Carnegie Mellon University, Pittsburgh, PA.

SHRM Survey Program. 2003. 2003 Elder Care Survey. Alexandria, Virginia: Society for Human Resource Management.

Shuit, Douglas P. 2004. People Problems on Every Aisle. *Workforce Management*, February: 26–34.

Simkins, C. 2005. Number of Foreign Students Declining at U.S. Universities. Voice of America News, April 15. http://www.Voanews.Com/English/2005–04–15–Voa61.Cfm.

Slaughter, M. J. 2004. Globalization and Employment by U.S. Multinationals: A Framework and Facts. Tuck School of Business, Dartmouth College, Hanover NH. http://MBA.Tuck.Dartmouth.Edu/Pages/Faculty/Matthew.Slaughter/Mne%20outsourcing%200304.Pdf.

———. 2004. Insourcing Jobs: Making the Global Economy Work for America. Organization for International Investment Study. http://www.Ofii.Org/Insourcing/Insourcing_Study.Pdf

Smith, M. L., J. Pfeffer, and D. M. Rousseau. 2000. Patient Capital: How Investors Contribute to (and Undermine) Relational Wealth. In *Relational Wealth: Advantages of Stability in a Changing Economy*, ed. C. R. Leana and D. M. Rousseau, 261–246. New York: Oxford.

Smith, Vicki. 1996. Employee Involvement, Involved Employees: Participative Work Arrangements in a White-Collar Service Occupation. *Social Problems* 43: 166–179.

———. 1998. The Fractured World of the Temporary Worker: Power, Participation, and Fragmentation in the Contemporary Workplace. *Social Problems* 45: 1–20.

———. 1990. *Managing in the Corporate Interest: Control and Resistance in an American Bank.* Berkeley: University of California Press.

Society for Human Resource Management. 2003. Onsite Childcare Can Reduce Absenteeism, Turnover. September 9. http://www.Shrm.Org.

Solomon, C. M. 1999. Moving Jobs to Offshore Markets: Why It's Done, and How It Works. Workforce Management Online. http://www.Workforce.Com/Archive/Feature/22/26/42.

Solomon, D. 2005. Investor Education Spurs Looming Duel between U.S., States. *The Wall Street Journal*, May 26.

Sorokin, Pitirum. 1925. American Millionaires and Multi-Millionaires: A Comparative Statistical Study. *Journal of Social Forces* 3 (4): 627–640.

Spalter-Roth, Roberta M., Arne L. Kalleberg, Edith Rasell, Naomi Cassirer, Barbara F. Reskin, Ken Hudson, David Webster, Eileen Appelbaum, and Betty F. Dooley. 1997. *Managing Work and Family: Nonstandard Work Arrangements Among Managers and Professionals.* Washington, DC: Economic Policy Institute.

Spencer, L. M., Jr., and Spencer, S. M. 1993. *Competence at Work: Models for Superior Performance.* New York: John Wiley & Sons, Inc.

St. Paul, G. 1997. *Dual Labor Markets: A Macro-Economic Perspective.* Cambridge, MA: MIT Press.

Stack, J., and B. Burlingham. 2003. *A Stake in the Outcome: Building a Culture of Ownership That Will Enable You to Outperform the Competition.* New York.

Staffing Industry Report. 1977. *Staffing Industry Report* 8: 6 (Los Altos, CA).

Stayer, R. 1990. How I Learned to Let My Workers Lead. *Harvard Business Review*, November–December: 2–11.

Stebbins, L. F. 2001. *Work and Family in America: A Reference Handbook*. Santa Barbara, CA: Abc-Clio, Inc.

Stellman, J. M., ed. 1997. *Encyclopedia of Occupational Health and Safety*. 4th ed. Geneva: International Labor Office.

Stephan, P. 2002. Consequences for U.S. Science of an International Scientific Workforce. Presentation to Sigma Xi Forum, Atlanta, Georgia State University.

Stern, R. J., and T. H. Hammer. 1978. Buying Your Job: Factors Affecting the Success or Failure of Employee Acquisition Attempts. *Human Relations* 31: 1101–1117.

Story, L. 2005. Many Women at Elite Colleges Set Career Path to Motherhood. *New York Times*, September 20.

Stratton, Leslie S. 1996. Are 'Involuntary' Part-Time Workers Indeed Involuntary? *Industrial and Labor Relations Review* 49 (3): 522–536.

Super, D. E. 1957. *The Psychology of Careers*. New York: Harper & Row.

Talk Left. 2002. Dramatic Rise in Number of Black Males in Prison. http://Talkleft.Com/New_Archives/000316.Html.

Tausig, M.., R. Fenwick, S. L. Sauter, L. R. Murphy, and C. Graif. 2004. The Changing Nature of Job Stress: Risk and Resources. In *Research in Occupational Stress and Well Being*, ed. P. L. Perrewe and D. Ganster, 4: 93–126. New York: JAI Press.

Taylor, S. E., and R. L. Repetti. 1997. Health Psychology: What Is an Unhealthy Environment and How Does It Get Under the Skin? *Annual Review of Psychology* 48: 411–447.

Teitelbaum, M. 2002. The U.S. Science and Engineering Workforce: An Unconventional Portrait. *Guirr Summit* Nov. 12. http://www.Phds.Org/Reading/Guirr2002/ Teitelbaum.Php.

Terborg, J. 1998. Health Psychology in the United States: A Critique and Selected Review. *Applied Psychology: An International Review* 47 (2): 199–217.

Terpstra, D. E., and E. J. Rozell. 1993. The Relationship of Staffing Practices to Organizational-Level Measures of Performance. *Personnel Psychology* 46: 27–48.

Terry, K. 2005. "Pay for Performance": A Double-Edged Sword. *Medical Economics* 82: 64–72.

The Stat. 2005. *Business Week*, March 28: 14.

Thompson, C. A., L. L. Beauvais, and K. S. Lyness. 1999. When Work-Family Benefits Are not Enough: The Influence of Work-Family Culture on Benefit Utilization, Organizational Attachment, and Work-Family Conflict. *Journal of Vocational Behavior* 54: 392–415.

Thompson, James D. 1967. *Organizations in Action*. New York: McGraw-Hill.

Tolbert, P. S. 1996. Occupations, Organizations, and Boundaryless Careers. In *The Boundaryless Career: A New Employment Principle for a New Organizational Era*, ed. M. B. Arthur and D. M. Rousseau, 331–149. New York: Oxford University Press.

Tomsho, R. 2005. Diploma Bar Is Getting Higher at Many U.S. High Schools. *The Wall Street Journal*, March 29.

Tsui, A., and J. Wu. 2005. The New Employment Relationship Versus the Mutual Investment Approach: Implications for Human Resource Management. *Human Resource Management* 44: 115–120.

Tullar, Willam L. 1998. Compensation Consequences Of Reengineering. *Journal of Applied Psychology* 83: 975–980.

U.S. Army War College Department of Command, Leadership, and Management. 2005. *How the Army Runs: A Senior Leader Reference Handbook, 2005–2006*. Carlisle Barracks, PA: Defense Dept., Army War College.

U.S. Bureau of Labor Statistics. 2003. http://www.BLS.Gov/Cps

U.S. Census Bureau. 2001. Number of Firms, Number of Establishments, United States, All Industries 2001. Washington, DC: Government Printing Office.

U.S. Census Bureau. 2002. Statistical Abstract of the United States 2002. The National Data Book, Section 12, 2002: Labor Force Employment and Earnings, Table 578, Persons Doing Job Related Work at Home, 2001. Washington, DC: Government Printing Office.

U.S. Census Bureau. Undated. Family and Medical Leave Act, 1993. http://www.Dol.Gov.

U.S. Department of Labor. 2004. *We the People: Asians in the United States*. Washington DC: GPO.

———. 2004. Women in the Labor Force: A Databook. Report 973, Table 6. http://www.BLS.Gov/Cps/Wlf-Databook.Pdf.

Uchitelle, L. 2003. A Statistic That's Missing: Jobs That Moved Overseas. *New York Times*, October 5.

United Nations Conference on Trade and Development. 2004. World Investment Report 2004: The Shift towards Services. New York and Geneva: United Nations. http://www.Unctad.Org/Wir.

United States Department of Commerce, Bureau O. T. C. 1997. *Statistical Abstract of the United States: 1996*. Washington, DC: U.S. Government Printing Office.

United States Department of Health, Education, and Welfare. 1973. *Work in America: Report of a Special Task Force to the Secretary of Health, Education, and Welfare*. Cambridge, MA: MIT Press.

Useem, J. 2005. 1914: Ford Offers $5 a Day. *Fortune*, June 27: 65.

Useem, Michael. 1996. Corporate Restructuring and the Restructured World of Senior Management. In *Broken Ladders: Managerial Careers in the New Economy*, ed. P. Osterman, 23–54. New York: Oxford University Press.

———. 1996. *Investor Capitalism*. New York: Basic Books.

Useem, Michael, and Jerome Karabel. 1986. Pathways to Top Corporate Management. *American Sociological Review* 51 (2): 184–200.

Vallas, Steven P. 2003. Why Teamwork Fails: Obstacles to Workplace Change in Four Manufacturing Plants. *American Sociological Review* 68: 223–250.

Van Maanen, J. 1977. *Organizational Careers: Some New Perspectives*. New York: Wiley.

Van Maanen, John, and Stephen R. Barley. 1984. Occupational Communities: Culture and Control in Organizations. In *Research in Organizational Behavior*, ed. Barry M. Staw and Larry L. Cummings, 6: 287–365. Greenwich, CT: JAI Press.

Vinokur, A. D. 1997. Job Security: Unemployment. In *Encyclopedia of Occupational Health and Safety*, ed. J. M. Stellman, 34.31–34.32. 4th ed. Geneva: International Labor Office.

Vinokur, A. D., R. H. Price, and R. D. Caplan. 1996. Hard Times and Hurtful Partners: How Financial Strain Affects Depression and Relationship Satisfaction of Unemployed Persons and Their Spouses. *Journal of Personality and Social Psychology* 71 (1): 166–179.

Vinokur, A. D., R. H. Price, and Y. Schul. 1995. Impact of the Jobs Intervention on Unemployed Workers Varying in Risk for Depression. *American Journal of Community Psychology* 23 (1): 39–74.

Vinokur, A. D., Y. Schul, J. Vuori, and R. H. Price. 2000. Two Years After a Job Loss: Long-Term Impact of the Jobs Program on Reemployment and Mental Health. *Journal of Occupational Health Psychology* 5 (1): 32–47.

Vinokur, A. D., M. Van Ryn, E. M. Gramlich, and R. H. Price. 1991. Long-Term Follow-Up and Benefit-Cost Analysis of the Jobs Program: A Preventive Intervention for the Unemployed. *Journal of Applied Psychology* 76 (2): 213–219.

Wahlgren, E. 2004. Going Global: The Outsourcing Dilemma. *Inc. Magazine*, April: 41–42.

Walsh, M. W. 2004. A Hard-to-Swallow Lesson on Pensions. Halliburton Uses Loophole to Reduce Payouts at an Upstate New York Unit. *New York Times*, October 14.

Walton, Richard. 1985. from Control to Commitment in the Workplace. *Harvard Business Review* 63 (2): 77–84.

Warner, W. Lloyd, and James C. Abbeglen. 1995. *Occupational Mobility in American Business and Industry*. Minneapolis: University of Minnesota Press.

Weick, K. E. 1996. Enactment and the Boundaryless Career: Organizing as We Work. In *The Boundaryless Career: A New Employment Principle for a New Organizational Era*, ed. M. B. Arthur and D. M. Rousseau, 40–57. New York: Oxford University Press.

Weick, K. E., and Berliner, L. R. 1989. Career Improvisation in Self-Designing Organizations. In *Handbook of Career Theory*, ed. M. B. Arthur, D. T. Hall, and B. S. Lawrence, 313–328. New York: Cambridge University Press.

Weinberg, Bruce. 2000. Computer Use and the Demand for Female Workers. *Industrial and Labor Relations Review* 53 (2): 290–308.

Welbourne, T. M., and A. O. Andrews, A. O. 1996. Predicting the Performance of Initial Public Offerings: Should Human Resource Management Be in the Equation? *Academy of Management Journal* 39: 891–919.

Wellness Plans Cut U. S. Firms' Health Cost. 2000. *Manpower Argus* 381: 8.

Wessel, D. 2004. Barbell Effect—The Future of Jobs: New Ones Arise, Wage Gap Widens; Outsourcing, Technology Cut Need for Rote Workers; Brainpower Is in Demand; Hot Area: Massage Therapy. *The Wall Street Journal*, April 2: A1.

Westman , M. and C. S. Piotrkowski. 1999. Introduction to the Special Issue: Work-Family Research in Occupational Health Psychology. *Journal of Occupational Health Psychology* 4 (4): 301–306.

Whalley, Peter. 1986. *The Social Production of Technical Work*. Albany, NY: State University of New York Press.

Whalley, Peter, and Stephen R. Barley. 1997. Stalking the Wily Anomaly: Technical Work in the Division of Labor. In between *Technology and Society: Technical Workers in Modern Settings*, ed. Stephen R. Barley and Julian E. Orr. Ithaca, NY: ILR Press.

Wheeler, Hoyt N. 1985. *Industrial Conflict: An Integrative Approach*. Columbia, SC: University of South Carolina Press.

Whyte, William Foote, and Burleigh Gardner. 1945. The Man in the Middle. *Applied Anthropology* 4: 1–28.

Whyte, William H., Jr. 1956. *The Organization Man*. New York: Simon and Schuster.

Wiggenhorn, W. 1990. When Training Becomes an Education. *Harvard Business Review*, July.

Wiley, J. 2005. Gantz-Wiley Research: Work Trends 2005. Presentation to the Human Resource Planning Society Global Conference, Miami, April.

Williams, J. 2000. *Unbending Gender: Why Work and Family Conflict and What to Do about It*. New York: Oxford University Press.

Williamson, Oliver E. 1975. *Markets and Hierarchies*. New York: Free Press.

Williamson, Oliver E. 1985. *The Economic Institutions of Capitalism*. New York: Free Press.

Work and Health. 1973. In *Work in America: Report of a Special Task Force to the Secretary of Health, Education and Welfare*, 76–92. MIT Press: Cambridge, MA.

World Trade Organization. 2005. Average Number of Vacation Days Around the World. http://www.Infoplease.Com/Ipa/A0922052.Html.

Wright, Patrick M., Timothy M. Gardner, Lisa M. Moynihan, Hyeon Jeong Park, Barry Gerhart, and John E. Delery. 2001. Measurement Error in Research on Human Resources and Firm Performance: Additional Data and Suggestions for Future Research. *Personnel Psychology* 54: 875–901.

Yeung, A. K., and B. Berman. 1997. Adding Value Through Human Resources: Reorienting Human Resource Measurement to Drive Business Performance. *Human Resource Management* 36: 321–335.

Yost, P. R., and M. M. Plunkett. 2002. Turn Business Strategy into Leadership Development. T + D 56 (3): 48–51.

Yu, Kyoung-Hee. 2005. Hybrid Institutions in the Labor Market: New Immigrants and Forms of Representation. Working Paper, MIT Workplace Center.

Zabusky, S. E., and S.R. Barley. 1996. Redefining Success: Ethnographic Observations on the Careers of Technicians. In *Broken Ladders: Managerial Careers in the New Economy*, ed. P. Osterman, 23–54. New York: Oxford University Press.

Zardkoohi, A., and R. L. Paetzold. 2004. Ownership and the Changing Employment Relationship: A Comment on Rousseau and Shperling. *Academy of Management Review* 29: 556–562.

Zarley, Craig. 2004. IBM Invests in Retraining. CRN. June 11. http://www.Crn.Com/Sections/Whitebox/Whitebox.Jhtml?Articleid=21700435.

Zuboff, Shoshana. 1988. *In the Age of the Smart Machine: The Future of Work and Power*. New York: Basic Books.

Zysman, J. 2004. Outsourcing, Offshoring, and Service Automation: Are Capacities for Innovation at Risk? Notes toward a BRIE/CITRIS Research Project. Berkeley, CA: Berkeley Roundtable on the International Economy.

# Index